Photographs by Thomas Yellowley, Paul Jones and Peter Beacock unless otherwise stated.

Newcastle & Gateshead: Architecture and Heritage is a revised and updated edition of *Newcastle & Gateshead: Architecture and Heritage* (ISBN 978-1-904438-29-8) published by Bluecoat Press in 2006.

Published by
City of Newcastle upon Tyne
Newcastle Libraries
Tyne Bridge Publishing, 2014

www.tynebridgepublishing.co.uk
www.newcastle.gov.uk/libraries

ISBN: 978-1-85795-219-3

Design and artwork by Paul Robertson

Printed by HPM&ADDO, Newton Aycliffe

Front cover: Newcastle and Gateshead Quaysides.

Back cover: A view across the Newcastle rooftops towards *Sage Gateshead.*

Endpapers: *A View of Newcastle upon Tyne in the Reign of Queen Victoria, 1862* by John Storey. (Newcastle Libraries)

Left: No. 35 The Close, Quayside. Photograph Bethany Jane Robertson.

NEWCASTLE & GATESHEAD
ARCHITECTURE AND HERITAGE

Thomas Faulkner, Peter Beacock and Paul Jones

Principal photographer Tom Yellowley

In memory of Thomas Faulkner 1943-2014

CONTENTS

PREFACE

Few areas in the United Kingdom can boast such an ancient and diverse architectural heritage as that comprising the urban areas of Newcastle and Gateshead. The first edition of this book appeared in 2006, under the imprint of the Bluecoat Press, in response to the perceived need for a substantial yet accessible account of this heritage. Now, we are delighted to be publishing a new and revised edition of *Newcastle & Gateshead: Architecture and Heritage* which brings the book up to date.

The aim, format and remit of the book remain essentially the same. We have again respected the boundaries of Newcastle and Gateshead, except for the inclusion of a few closely adjacent buildings of particular interest. Chapters are arranged chronologically and each has its own illustrated introduction giving important background information and discussing both the historical evolution and the wider context of the particular period under review. Buildings are arranged as nearly as possible in chronological order, and each is illustrated with at least one colour photograph.

The text of this new edition has been thoroughly revised and updated, following changes to buildings originally described and in the light of recent research. Also, a significant number of new entries have been added, relating either to historic buildings that perhaps should have been included in the first edition or to new structures that have been built since that date. A few of the more minor entries in the original edition have been omitted. Similarly, in line with our policy of including only examples that exist, original entries have been deleted where the buildings described – many from the period immediately following the Second World War – have now been demolished. Our final chapter deals with work from c.1980. Some new photographs have been provided, not only for the new entries but also in the case of existing entries where changed circumstances or the need for improvement have necessitated them. Colour photographs in this edition are by Tom Yellowley, Paul Jones and Peter Beacock unless otherwise indicated.

Our aim is still to provide an overall architectural history while focusing on significant individual buildings. *Newcastle & Gateshead: Architecture and Heritage* can thus be read as a narrative, or, if preferred, as a catalogue of important individual works from which one can gain a very good idea of what was being built on both sides of the Tyne at any given time. Intended as a work of reference covering the wide range of architecture, and its development, found in the locality, this remains a book directed at the general reader – although naturally it is hoped that the student and academic specialist will find much of interest within its pages.

A number of books have appeared since 2006 that have been very useful in the production of this new edition of *Newcastle & Gateshead: Architecture and Heritage*. Particularly noteworthy are *Newcastle and Gateshead* (Pevsner Architectural Guide) by Grace McCombie (who has kindly also given us personal help) and A.W. Purdue's *Newcastle: The Biography*, published in 2009 and 2011 respectively. *The Arts and Crafts Movement in the North East of England: A Handbook*, by Barrie and Wendy Armstrong (2013), contains a great deal of relevant information, as do, for the post-Second World War period, Rutter Carroll's 2009 monograph on Ryder and Yates and Chris Foote Wood's 2010 biography of T. Dan Smith, subtitled *Downfall of a Visionary*.

At the same time, three important PhD theses on aspects of Newcastle and Gateshead architecture have been completed since 2006. These are, in chronological order of submission: "Architectural Taste and Patronage in Newcastle upon Tyne, 1870-1914" by Michael Johnson (University of Northumbria at Newcastle, 2008), "A Theatre for the Soul: St George's Church, Jesmond: The Building and Cultural Reception of a Late-Victorian Church" by Neil Moat (University of Newcastle, 2011) and "William Newton (1730-1798), and the Development of the Architectural Profession in North-East England" by Richard Pears (University of Newcastle, 2012). These three works have been of enormous value to the present authors, to whom their writers have also given much additional, personal help. Indeed, Dr Johnson has gone even further by assisting with the formulation of some of the new entries on historic buildings and in checking the entire text. Thanks are due to all these scholars.

Others whose assistance we would like to recognise in the production of this second edition include Doreen Chilvers, Lavinia Down, Neil Elborn, Dr Martin Harrop, Michael March, Sarah Mulligan and Arthur Nelson. We are also extremely grateful to our designer, Paul Robertson, and to Ian Chilvers, who once again suggested numerous improvements to the text, as well as contributing the glossary and index. Nor must we omit to thank our generous sponsors Ryder Architecture, and of course our publishers, not least for their enthusiasm and encouragement.

View across the Newcastle rooftops towards Gateshead Millennium Bridge, Baltic Centre for Contemporary Art and Sage Gateshead.

CHAPTER 1

MEDIEVAL TO THE SEVENTEENTH CENTURY

St Nicholas's Cathedral, Newcastle upon Tyne, mainly fourteenth- and fifteenth-century: detail of lantern tower.

INTRODUCTION

Newcastle originated around a Roman fort and river bridge, situated at the most eastward convenient crossing point along the Tyne and therefore an important junction of land and water traffic. This location was also near the eastern end of Hadrian's Wall. There is abundant archaeological evidence of Roman occupation throughout the area. Later, a Saxon village known as Monkchester developed here. However, it was after centuries of obscurity that the strategic importance of this settlement, particularly as a potential bastion against the Scots, was recognised by the Normans with the building, in 1080, of the 'New Castle'. From this, as the Elizabethan antiquarian and cartographer John Speed correctly stated, the town "did afterwards take both her beginning and name".

The site chosen by the Normans was much the same as that which the Romans had used and was virtually impregnable. It occupied a small area enclosed by walls, with its flanks further protected by the deep ravines of small tributaries flowing into the Tyne, now mostly filled in. The topographical importance of these watercourses (especially, the Skinner Burn, the Lort Burn and the Pandon Burn), as well as that of the still-existing and much larger Ouseburn, to the east, is implicit in the following description of Newcastle by the early nineteenth-century historian Eneas Mackenzie: "the situation of Newcastle, however well chosen it may have been for the purposes of security, is but ill adapted to answer those of neatness and convenience … the higher parts [of the town] stand upon three steep and lofty eminences. The western ridge terminates exactly in front of the bridge, on which the Romans, Saxons, and Normans, have successively erected their chief fortress … this mount was separated by a deep ravine ... from the middle ridge, which, stretching northward, is bounded by another deep ravine formed by a brook, or burn."

The western of the three "eminences" to which Mackenzie refers was bounded to the west by the Skinner Burn, and to the east by the Lort Burn. The central one – dominated by the castle and St Nicholas's Church (now Cathedral) – was demarcated by the Lort Burn to the west and, to the east, by the larger Pandon Burn. The eastern "eminence" lay in turn between the Pandon Burn and the Ouseburn. On it stood the Pandon Gate (demolished in 1795) and the Wall Knoll (Sallyport) Tower of the town wall, each probably incorporating much earlier masonry, of Saxon and even Roman origin.

By the later Middle Ages Newcastle's basic character had been established. The town had grown up "embanked from the river", as Mackenzie put it, and it was this precipitousness that had given it the defensive potential that was so crucial to its development. Even so, Newcastle was never a planned medieval town, although it had been 'planted' and was now walled. Instead it presented an irregular, horseshoe-like layout on the north bank of the Tyne (see p.10). The river was crossed by one bridge only, probably seen as an adjunct to the castle and sited on the alignment of original Roman bridge. It was rebuilt in 1248. Like most medieval urban bridges it had houses, shops and inns built upon it, and also boasted a bridge-end chapel (St Thomas's) as well as a hermit's chapel on the bridge itself. Outside the town wall, to the north and west, was the Town Moor, a very large area of inalienable grazing land owned by the Freemen of Newcastle and still present today. On all sides was already the visible evidence of coal mining.

Newcastle's centre of population and commercial activity was near the quayside. From this, narrow alleys, or chares, ran northwards, while the town's (still-existing) principal streets, Pilgrim, Newgate and Westgate Streets, ran north, north-west and west respectively. Along Pilgrim Street, described by the seventeenth-century topographer William Gray as "the longest and fairest street in the town", came numerous pilgrims travelling to worship at shrines in the village of Jesmond, to the north. However, the entrance into Newcastle from the river bridge was steep and difficult, a situation that began to be remedied only very much later, and then only partially, in the 1780s (see Chapter Two).

During the Middle Ages and subsequently, Newcastle possessed at least 30 religious foundations (of which only six survive in any sort of recognisable form). Two of the largest of these, the Nunnery of St Bartholomew and the adjacent Franciscan Friary to the east, occupied nearly the whole of the area between Newgate and Pilgrim Streets.

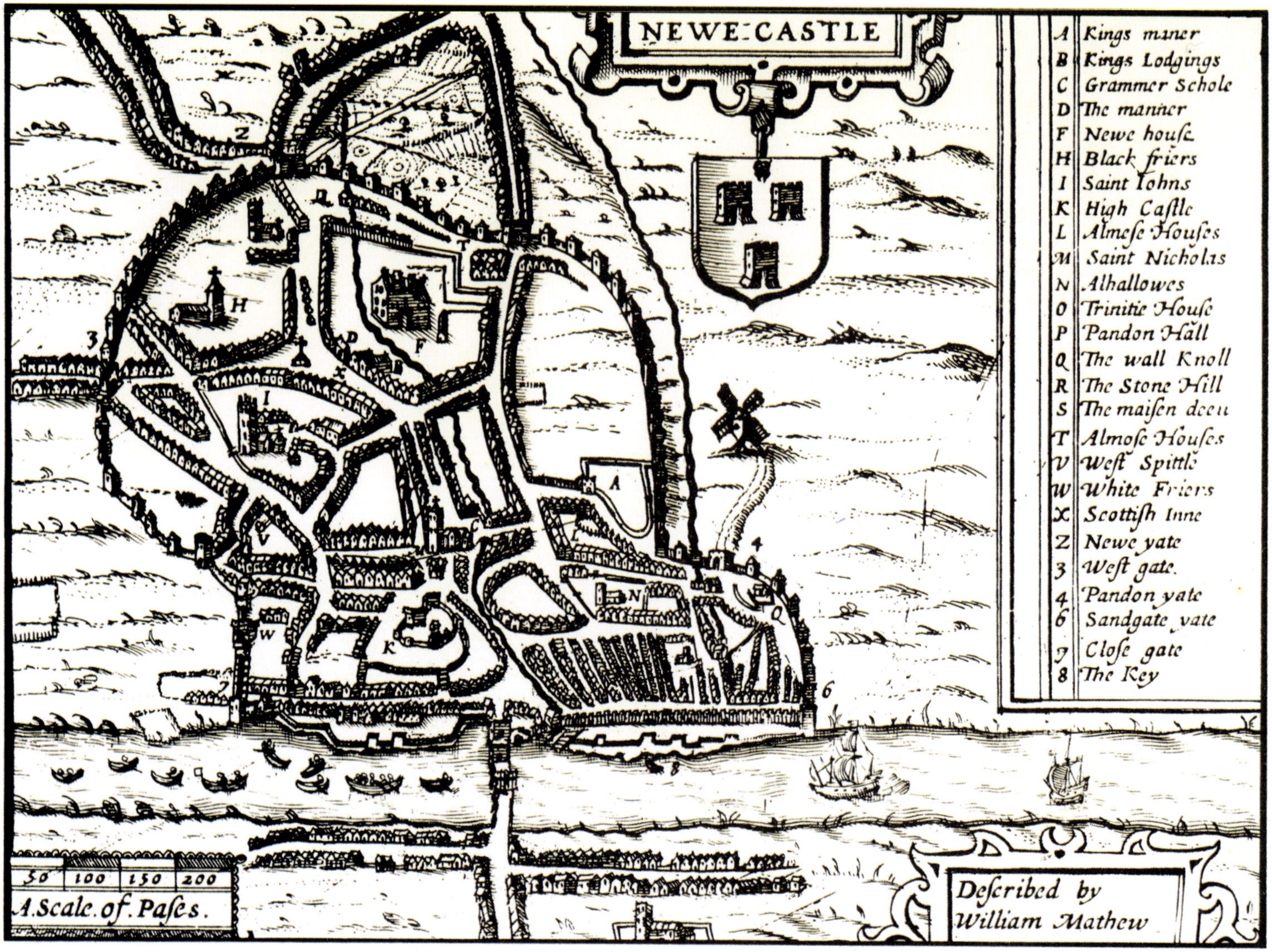

After the Dissolution of the Monasteries this substantial combined site – so important for the later development of the town – was sold. On part of it the merchant Robert Anderson built in about 1580 the 'Newe House', a large mansion later known as Anderson Place (see p.11). Outside London, this was said to be the largest house in the country which lay within a walled town. The fact that it was built within the town, rather than in the countryside beyond, reminds us that even at this comparatively late date, the inhabitants of North East England still lived in constant and very real fear of attack from the Scots. Indeed, during the Civil War, the Scots actually occupied Newcastle (see below).

Meanwhile, on the south bank of the river was Gateshead, always a much less substantial settlement, that was evolving, ribbon-like, on each side of the Great North Road, and to a lesser extent along the river-bank. There was coal-mining here as well, promoted and encouraged by the bishops of Durham, but there was little housing apart from that concentrated close to the river. Even by the time of Elizabeth I, the town's population was probably no more than 3,000 (Newcastle's being at this time about 10,000). Gateshead remained a comparatively workaday place. There are few surviving buildings of great antiquity in the town.

By the fourteenth century Newcastle's wealth, founded largely on the coal and – to a lesser extent – wool trades, was ranked third among English towns (after London and Bristol). In 1400 Newcastle was given separate county status by Henry IV, while another, later charter granted by Elizabeth I reinforced its position by giving it a monopoly of local trading in

Left John Speed's Map of Newcastle upon Tyne, from his *Theatre of the Empire of Great Britain* (1611).

Right Anderson Place, off Pilgrim Street (seen in the foreground of this illustration), Newcastle upon Tyne; engraving by J. Kip and L. Knyff, c.1715.

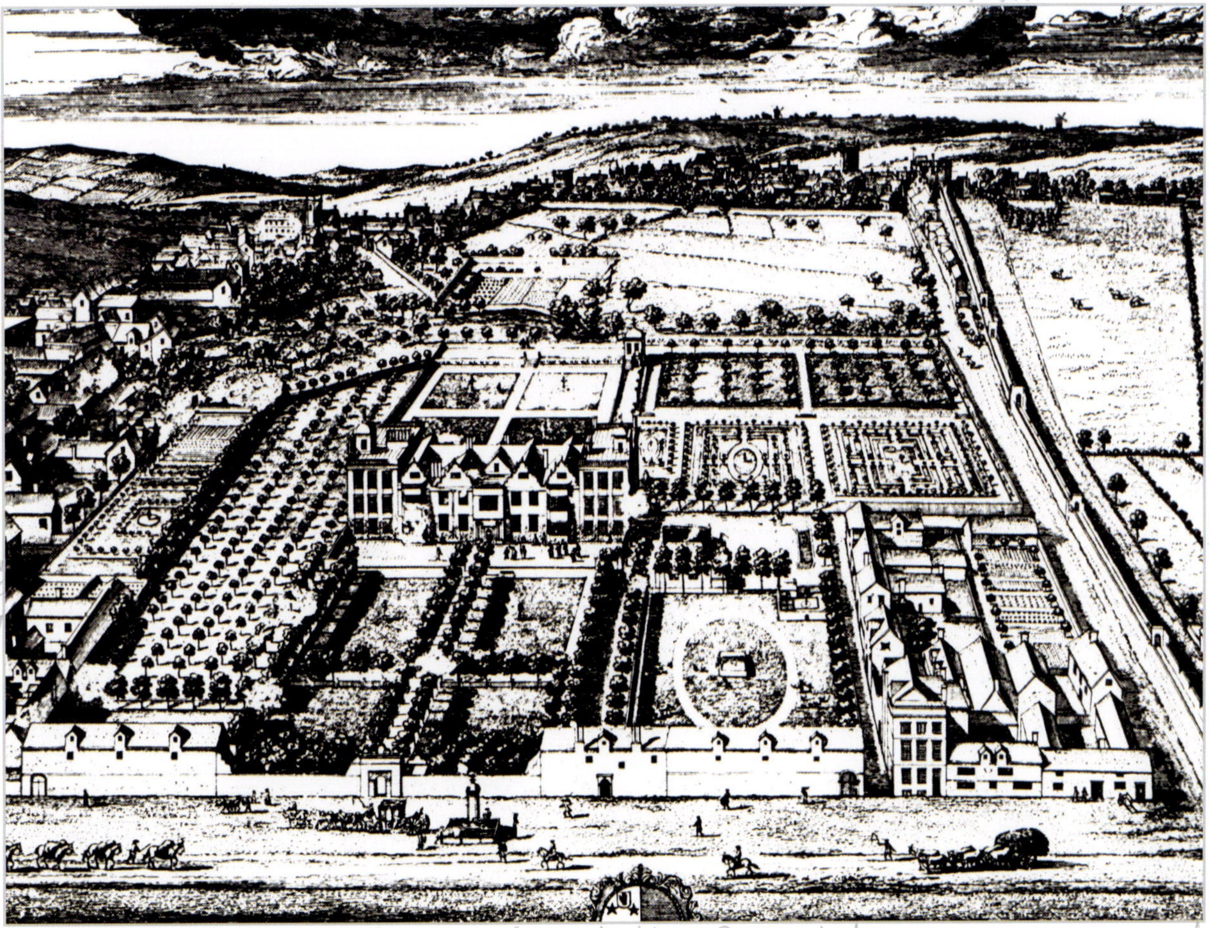

coal, something which was expanding enormously during her reign. The production of glass, iron and salt also became increasingly important in Newcastle at this time, as did shipbuilding. In the late sixteenth century the antiquarian William Camden observed that Newcastle "makes a glorious appearance, as the very eye of all the towns in this part of the kingdom; ennobled by a fine haven, where ships of great burthen lay in security. It is situate .... north of the river Tyne, over which is a fair bridge: on the left hand thereof stands the castle, and on the right the Market-place, and principal part of the city, in regard to the elegance of its buildings."

In spite of this progress, however, the early and mid-seventeenth century was a difficult time for the town. It had to withstand a serious outbreak of plague in 1636 and just before the Civil War it suffered the humiliation of occupation by the Scots (1640-41). Fighting in alliance with the Parliamentarians, the Scots again, intermittently, occupied the town between 1644 and 1647, and caused considerable damage. Charles I himself was imprisoned here (in Anderson Place) in 1646-47. Despite the town's inherent Royalist sympathies, it is said that the king was even forced to listen to extreme puritanical sermons in St Nicholas's Church, preached with the purpose of reforming him.

The restoration of the monarchy in 1660 brought renewed and developing prosperity. Newcastle's population grew to more than 15,000 and, as R.J. Buswell has suggested, "many see the 1660s as Newcastle's Renaissance in a European context [in which] the expanding economy, the growth of political power and the development of international connections, began to lay the foundation for new opportunities for urban design." It was in this context that a named architect, in the modern sense of the term, made his first appearance here. He was Robert Trollope (see p.34). Born in York in the early seventeenth century (the exact date is unknown), and a descendant of a long line of stonemasons, Trollope became an architect of genuine quality, working mainly in a slightly eccentric version of the classical style. His principal commission was the Guildhall in Newcastle (see p.34), although he also designed a number of significant manors and country houses in the North East. He lived in Gateshead, and was made a freeman of Newcastle in 1657; he died in 1686.

ST ANDREW'S CHURCH
NEWGATE STREET, NEWCASTLE, NE1 5SS

St Andrew's is the oldest church in the city centre. King David I of Scotland gave permission for the building of the church in about 1150, during a period of almost twenty years (1138-57) when Newcastle was occupied by the Scots. The church was built on the site of a previous Saxon village, while its structure may well include recycled stone from the town's even earlier Roman settlement. The church is robust, with a long low nave and a sturdy west tower. The oldest parts, including the nave, are Norman, the lower courses of which contain recycled stones from Hadrian's Wall. Inside, the delightful depressed chancel arch, with its chevron ornamentation, is also Norman, although it may have been subsequently heightened. The tower was added in the early thirteenth century.

St Andrew's has changed substantially over the centuries. It is now essentially Gothic, despite its original Norman character and the many alterations and additions made to it, in different styles. Consequently architectural interest depends largely on identifying the different phases of work. Much of the interior of the church, especially, has been altered over the last 300 years. Early in the church's history, in the thirteenth century, the chancel was enlarged and the transepts and the Trinity Chapel were added; a century later the aisles were widened, and the roof over the nave was raised.

The church was badly damaged during the siege of 1644 by the Scots, due to its proximity to the town wall, and to the questionable decision of

Left St Andrew's Church, Newgate Street, Newcastle upon Tyne, from c.1150: from the south east; the neo-Norman south transept in the foreground is by John Dobson (1844).

Right St Andrew's Church, Newgate Street, Newcastle upon Tyne: the interior looking east.

Newcastle's authorities to mount a gun on its tower. Restoration work was carried out as a consequence of this damage; new bells were installed (although not until 1726) and paid for by a public collection. The south-west porch also dates from 1726. The Georgians also provided St Andrew's with box pews and galleries, which the Victorians in their turn removed. However, the outline of an eighteenth-century arch inserted into the north wall of the nave, to assist the vision of the congregation, can still be seen. In 1844 John Dobson remodelled the south transept in neo-Norman style, while C. Hodgson Fowler, to 'modernise' the church, carried out further restoration work in 1866. Most of Fowler's work was confined to the interior, although he also renewed the windows of both aisles and, somewhat controversially, the main east window. Later Victorian and Edwardian work includes the chantry reredos (1900) by Hicks & Charlewood and the pulpit and choir stalls (1906-07) by Ralph Hedley.

The churchyard, now reduced, still contains a stretch of the town wall. Here, too, are the graves of a number of illustrious Novocastrians, including Charles Avison, the composer, and Ralph Beilby, the engraver to whom Thomas Bewick was apprenticed. Similarly, inside the church is buried the prominent local architect William Newton, who was a churchwarden here. In the nineteenth century a windmill was built in these grounds at the junction of Gallowgate and Darncrook (now St Andrew's Street). It was damaged by fire in 1895 and subsequently demolished.

THE CASTLE

NEWCASTLE, NE1 1RQ

The castle has been a prominent feature on the Newcastle skyline for almost 1,000 years and there has been a settlement in this location for at least twice that time. The substantial Roman fort of Pons Aelius, on basically the same site, guarded the river crossing from the second to the end of the fourth century A.D., when the Romans abandoned it. An eighth-century Saxon monastic village, known as Monkchester, developed from the earlier Roman fort.

In 1080, Robert Curthose, the eldest son of William the Conqueror, laid the foundations for the castle. The site was chosen for strategic reasons, with steep slopes falling away on three sides and easy access from the sea. This original 'New Castle' was probably of wood, and of motte-and-bailey type. Nothing of this structure remains above ground and any last possible traces of the motte and the bailey disappeared during the nineteenth century.

The castle changed hands several times during its turbulent early history. In 1157 Henry II regained control of it from the Scots and in 1168-78 he built a sturdier stone castle on the site. Its surviving keep is a superb example of late Norman architecture and rises to a height of over 80 feet. It was built under the direction of 'Mauricius Caementarius' (Maurice the Mason), almost certainly the same man as the 'Mauricius Ingeniator' (Maurice the Engineer) who is documented as having worked on the slightly later royal keep at Dover Castle. Most, although by no means all, of the stonework of the present castle dates from this period.

Additions to the castle in the thirteenth century included a curtain wall encircling the keep, of which parts survive to the south east, overlooking the river (see opposite page, left). A prominent part of the wall was a curved platform, sometimes known as the 'Queen's Mantle' or the 'Half-Moon Battery', projecting from the east side of the garth. Adjacent to this was a large aisled hall within the courtyard, dating from early in the thirteenth century and called the Great or King's Hall. During the middle of the century an important barbican was built, now known as the Black Gate (see p.20).

However, with the construction of Newcastle's town wall late in the century and strengthening of it in the next one, the castle's military importance declined and it began to fall into disrepair. In 1589 it was described as 'old and ruinous', although the keep continued to be used for centuries for a variety of purposes, including serving as a county gaol.

In 1618, James I leased parts of the castle to Alexander

Left The Castle, Newcastle upon Tyne, begun 1168: view of the keep from the south east.

Right The Castle, Newcastle upon Tyne: section of the south curtain wall.

Far Right The Castle, Newcastle upon Tyne: the chapel.

Stephenson, a Scottish courtier, who allowed houses to be built within the curtain wall in order to generate rental income. When, in 1808, the castle was finally taken over by the Corporation, the keep was in a sorry state. It had even been advertised in 1782 for use as a brewery or windmill, while its chapel was used as a beer cellar. The keep had no roof, the floors were dangerously decayed, and the external walls were disintegrating.

The Corporation promptly cleared the dilapidated houses and demolished the detached aisled hall (which was now sometimes known as the Moot Hall) and parts of the curtain wall, including the 'Half-Moon Battery'. In their place was built the new Moot Hall, by John and William Stokoe (1810-12, see p.76). At the same time the Corporation carried out a restoration of the keep, re-roofing it and reconstructing the battlements. Later, after the ruthless insertion of the railway (via the new High Level Bridge) between the keep and the Black Gate, necessitating the further demolition of adjoining structures, another phase of restoration to the keep was carried out from 1847, by John Dobson, for Newcastle's Society of Antiquaries, which now took possession of the building. It involved much typically Victorian re-cutting and replacement of medieval ornament, especially in the chapel and around the entrance to the (internal) Great Hall.

Hardly was this work complete when damage to the keep was caused by the Great Quayside Fire of 1854, necessitating further restoration. Additional repairs and excavations have been carried out in recent times, principally to convert the building into an exhibition space which records the castle's eventful past and displays instructive models of other Newcastle buildings. Externally, the presence of undisguised new stonework is very evident, reflecting modern 'restoration' practice.

The keep measures 62 by 56 feet. Three of the corners have square towers; the fourth tower is polygonal. The entrance to the structure is via an external stair that takes the visitor ultimately to the door of the Great Hall. Internally, there are three floors; each floor is planned around a principal room and has an apartment built into the thickness of the wall.

A chapel is located on the ground floor (see above, right) and is separated into three bays. The first two bays contain the nave and the chancel is in the third. The ceiling is rib-vaulted throughout and is decorated with chevrons and other geometric mouldings typical of Norman architecture. The bays of the nave spring from engaged columns; their waterleaf capitals are beautifully carved. Although somewhat over-restored by Dobson, the chapel is still the most complete example of Norman ecclesiastical architecture in Newcastle. The Garrison Room, adjacent to the chapel, has an enormous central pier supporting the floors above. This pier has graffiti carved into the stonework by some of the prisoners who once occupied the room.

The first-floor layout was lost in nineteenth-century alterations. Originally, on this level, there was a hall for entertaining, but the 'Queen's Chamber' does still exist, within the wall. The Great Hall and the 'King's Chamber' are located on the second floor. The Great Hall has again seen much restoration, including new clerestory windows and a barrel-vaulted roof, added as part of Dobson's work.

ST JOHN THE BAPTIST'S CHURCH
WESTGATE ROAD, NEWCASTLE, NE1 5JG

This is an unpretentious, almost rustic-looking church and was at one time a landmark helping to mark the entrance into the city from the west. It was also formerly set on the edge of attractive, semi-formal gardens (on the western part of which the Assembly Rooms were to be built, see p.62). This is in marked contrast to its present densely urban situation, with, towards Grainger Street, the church rising almost directly out of the pavement. Interestingly, St John's was Richard Grainger's parish church (there is a tablet commemorating him and his wife Rachel on the south wall of the nave), and it seems that he intended to align Grainger Street with it in order to close the vista. In the event, the street was not extended to this point until after his time, and then at a slightly different angle.

St John's has ancient origins. Its early structure is Norman, and the present nave and chancel follow the plan of the original church. The north wall of the chancel is twelfth-century; a cross-shaped mark on this wall indicates the position of a former hermitage of the same period. There is also a twelfth-century Norman window above the vestry door. The nave, north aisle, and transept are all fourteenth-century. The remainder of the body of the church is fifteenth-century (a clerestory and new roof being added then), as is the stout, rugged tower, which rises from a twelfth-century base and has a crenellated top with elaborate, crocketed finials located on each corner. Local M.P. Robert Rhodes (see p.25) paid for the tower and other improvements, his generosity being remembered in the church with a boss bearing his name.

Left St John the Baptist's Church, Westgate Road, Newcastle upon Tyne, mainly fourteenth- and fifteenth-century: view of tower from the south west.

Right St John the Baptist's Church, Westgate Road, Newcastle upon Tyne: interior looking north west.

Evidence of eighteenth- and nineteenth-century restoration can be seen both internally and externally, including the rebuilding of the chancel, and parts of the east and north walls. John Dobson undertook this work in 1848 and 1855; he also restored the church on several other occasions. Local architect John Johnstone carried out further repairs, to the roof and walls, in 1875-76. Recently there has been additional structural work done in the north transept, as well as some internal re-ordering.

The original font was destroyed by the Scots in 1644, but was replaced by the Rev. Andrew Bates in 1690. The pulpit is also late seventeenth-century and has pairs of unfluted Corinthian columns with diamond-studded arches, in the Jacobean style. Some medieval stained glass remains, re-assembled into a window in the north wall of the chancel. However, most of the stained glass is nineteenth-century, including the aisle windows by William Wailes. Twentieth-century contributions include stained glass by G.E.R. Smith and a rood beam and reredos by Charles Nicholson.

BLACK FRIARS

NEWCASTLE, NE1 4XN

The Dominicans, known as the Black Friars from the colour of their habit, spread throughout the major English towns and cities in the thirteenth century, establishing themselves in Newcastle by 1239. Black Friars was one of five friaries initially located just outside the town, but by the mid-fourteenth century it was within its walls, to the west of Newgate Street. It was formerly surrounded by orchards and gardens, still shown in eighteenth-century maps and engravings, although by 1830 these had almost completely disappeared. The original Black Friars was of the typical form of the order, having three ranges of buildings arranged around a central cloister. Its church, which was once the largest in Newcastle, formed the fourth side of the cloister, to the north (where its outline is still visible; see opposite page); it had an aisled nave, but an aisleless choir. The parts of the surviving fabric that date from the original period of construction show that Black Friars was built in a characteristically austere Gothic style.

Despite its closure during the Dissolution of the Monastries and the demolition of the church, much remains of Black Friars – the only substantial survival from what were once Newcastle's many monastic foundations. Indeed, thanks to the trade guilds of Newcastle, nine of whom, from the 1550s onwards, occupied the buildings and converted the upper floors to meeting rooms, the Black Friars complex forms probably the most complete former medieval religious house still existing in the centre of a British city. Further remodelling of the buildings took place during the eighteenth century.

The buildings that remain today are a fascinating mixture of styles from the thirteenth to the nineteenth century. Although they lay derelict for much of the twentieth century, their importance was finally recognised in the 1960s, and in 1975-81 they were sensitively restored by architects Wales, Wales & Rawson with the help of Barbara Harbottle (1931-2012), then the City Archaeologist. These structures now house craft shops, a restaurant, and the offices of the North East Civic Trust. The Trust has retained within its premises a nineteenth-century circular wooden meeting table and surrounding high-backed benches.

Externally, the remains of the church on the north side of the cloister, which is 90 feet square, have been excavated and the line of the walls can be seen.

The sense of enclosure of a medieval cloister has been re-created in part by the construction in 1991 of Jacobins Chare, to the north of the church site (see p.314); in its size and scale, this residential development properly respects the original buildings. The new courtyard is one of the quietest and most appealing public spaces in Newcastle, although now somewhat marred by the insensitive scale and detailing of nearby recent commercial development.

Left Black Friars, Newcastle upon Tyne, from 1239: from the south.

Right Black Friars, Newcastle upon Tyne: the restored cloister, from the north east.

THE BLACK GATE

NEWCASTLE, NE1 1RQ

In 1244 Henry III visited Newcastle and ordered various repairs and improvements to the castle, one of the key fortresses in the kingdom. Three years later work began on the last substantial addition to the complex, the fortified gateway now known as the Black Gate. Completed in 1250, it can be described as a barbican – an outer defence work guarding the main entrance to a castle. It was set well forward of the original entrance (the north gate), enabling defenders to readily fire on attackers who approached the west curtain wall (the most vulnerable approach to the castle, the other sides being protected by steep slopes). Such use of 'flanking fire' had become important in military architecture, and similar forward defences were built at several other royal castles around this time, for example the huge Constable's Tower at Dover (completed 1227).

The Black Gate is approximately oval in plan (50 by 34 feet) and originally consisted essentially of two large round towers with a passageway in between. There was a drawbridge at front and rear, and in the passageway was a portcullis (the grooves for this can still be seen) and gate. The ground floor of each tower was a rib-vaulted guard-room, and these survive reasonably intact.

Like the rest of the castle, the Black Gate decayed as its military importance diminished. In 1618 it was leased, along with other parts of the castle complex, to Alexander Stephenson (see pp. 14-15), who partially rebuilt it for use as a house, adding two storeys, with stone-mullioned windows, and a steeply pitched hipped roof, although for several years it was sub-let as a public house. After Newcastle was captured by the Scots during the Civil War, in 1644, the castle was seized by Parliament and the Black Gate was sold to a London merchant, Patrick Black, whose name has stuck to the building.

From the seventeenth century onwards, houses had been built to each side of the gatehouse, and the whole complex eventually became a slum tenement. In the late eighteenth century it again became in part a public house (The Three Bulls' Heads). In 1855 the jumble of buildings surrounding the Black Gate was demolished to provide access to the new High Level Bridge and the Council proposed the demolition of the Black Gate itself. However, there was strong local opposition to this, and architect John Dobson devised an impressive scheme (unexecuted) for a complete neo-medieval remodelling of the building, linking it to new Gothic-style street frontages.

Ultimately, the Black Gate was restored in 1883 by local architect R.J. Johnson for the Society of Antiquaries of Newcastle upon Tyne, which leased the building in 1882 and occupied part of it until 2009, when the Society's library and collections moved to the Great North Museum (see p.184). Johnson added an entrance footbridge – where a drawbridge had originally been – and constructed a new timber internal staircase, giving access to the upper floors. He retained the seventeenth-century pitched roof because of its antiquity and picturesqueness, rather than instating medieval-looking battlements. W.H. Knowles, another local architect, undertook additional restoration work in 1905-06, and further improvements were made at intervals later in the century.

After the departure of the Society of Antiquaries, the Black Gate lay empty until in 2013-14 it was converted into a visitor heritage centre as part of the 'Old Newcastle Project' – a scheme to increase awareness of 'the original heart of the city'. The most conspicuous feature of the conversion is an external, timber-clad lift on the north side of the building, which allows wheelchair access to all the public areas inside. These include a reception area and shop as well as exhibition and interpretation facilities.

ST EDMUND'S CHAPEL

HIGH STREET, GATESHEAD, NE8 1EP

St Edmund's Chapel was founded in 1247 and built, on what was the main road between London and Edinburgh, by Nicholas de Farnham, Bishop of Durham. It has endured despite numerous threats of demolition and is now Grade I listed. This rare example of a medieval hospital chapel was built to commemorate Edmund of Abingdon, Archbishop of Canterbury from 1233 to 1240, whose life was dedicated to relieving the suffering of the poor. In 1488 the Bishop of Durham bequeathed the chapel to the nuns of St Bartholomew, from Newcastle, who occupied it until the Dissolution of the Monasteries; after this, in 1540, it was surrendered to the Crown. St Edmund's remained Catholic in spirit, but in 1549 the Catholic missionary John Ingram was hanged, drawn and quartered outside the chapel for his beliefs.

Over the next 200 years this small chapel lost its congregation and became part of the estate of Gateshead House, the former home of the Clavering and the Riddell families, which burnt down in 1745. An Elizabethan gateway from this house is now set into the south wall of the chapel. Meanwhile, the chapel itself fell into ruin, eventually losing its roof. In the early nineteenth century St Edmund's became part of a builder's yard, but its fortunes revived and in 1836-37 it was carefully restored by John Dobson for service as Holy Trinity Chapel. At the same time, next to the chapel, Dobson built the Tudor-style Ellison Schools, although these were demolished when the large new church of Holy Trinity (by Stephen Piper) was built in 1894-96, incorporating the old chapel as its south aisle. Unfortunately, the chapel's north wall was removed during this phase of work. In 1969 Holy Trinity Church was declared redundant, having survived yet another demolition threat a few years before. It was taken over as a community facility, but the ancient chapel was partitioned off and remains in use as a parish church (including an exhibition area) to this day.

The architectural treatment of St Edmund's is typical of the Early English Gothic style. Five external buttresses support the south wall; between each buttress is a lancet window, with a dogtooth surround. The central entrance is deeply recessed and flanked by two tiers of paired blind arches, while above the entrance is another arcade, with lancet lights alternating with recesses.

Internally, a noteworthy treasure is an oaken 'bishop's chair', transferred in 1979 from nearby St Mary's Church (see p.26) and probably seventeenth-century in origin. There is also much fine Victorian stained glass by Atkinson Brothers of Newcastle, mostly representing saints and worthies, although the east window commemorates a local brewer, Thomas Tucker (d. 1891) and his daughter Eleanor (d. 1913); the west window memorialises Thomas's son, Lt Stanley Tucker, killed in the First World War in 1917.

Overall, the chapel has a beautiful simplicity of design. However, although a remarkable survival, it is overshadowed by the newer church and visually is rather 'lost' amid the bustle of Gateshead High Street.

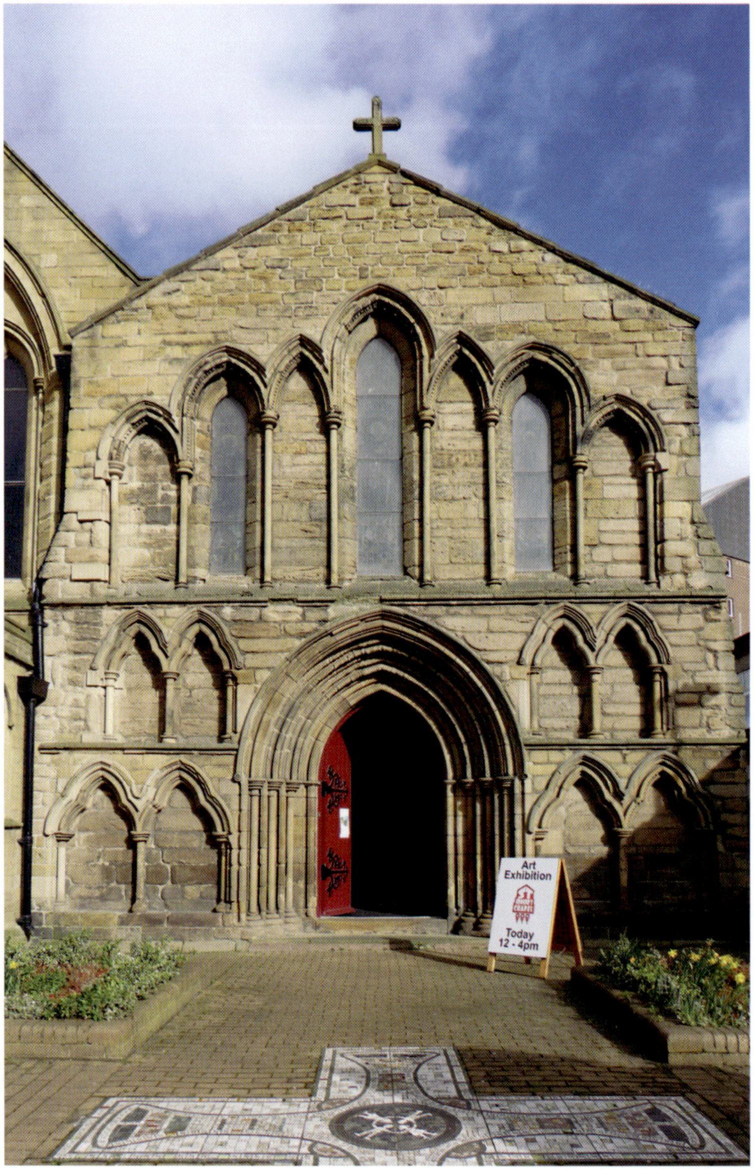

Opposite above The Black Gate, Newcastle upon Tyne, 1247-50: from the south west. Photograph Bethany Jane Robertson.

Opposite below The Black Gate, Newcastle upon Tyne: the gateway passage.

Above St Edmund's Chapel, High Street, Gateshead, from 1247: from the west.

THE NEWCASTLE TOWN WALL
NEWCASTLE, NE1 5HX

Top The Town Walls, Newcastle upon Tyne, from c.1265-80: section including the Heber Tower, from the north west.

Bottom The Sallyport Tower, Newcastle upon Tyne, as extended in 1716: from the south west.

Perhaps somewhat surprisingly, in view of the multiple subsequent developments, Newcastle still retains significant lengths of its medieval stone wall. This was originally surrounded by a substantial ditch and at one time completely enclosed the town, apart from, it seems, a stretch along the riverside between the site of the present Copthorne Hotel and the line of the Swing Bridge (which is itself on the site of the original medieval bridge). Newcastle's town wall was originally between seven and ten feet thick and was 20-30 feet high. Some surviving sections are still of considerable height, with a number of towers and turrets; these, although not complete, give a good indication of the original size. Once again, Newcastle owes a great debt to its medieval guilds and companies, who took over and at times rebuilt some of these towers for use as meeting places.

In the twelfth and early thirteenth centuries, only the castle had a fortified wall. However, as early as the twelfth century the Scots repeatedy attacked (and even occupied) Newcastle. Ultimately, therefore, permission was granted to wall the town in 1265, when presumably construction started, and its course can still be followed from existing stretches, fragments, and the lines of streets, such as Blackett Street, that were later built on the site of the wall.

Much of the wall itself is known to have been in existence by 1280. Construction probably continued until about the mid-fourteenth century; certainly it was strengthened and kept in good order during this century and the two following ones, because of the continuing threat from the Scots, on occasions at the personal behest of the monarch. Edward III ordered or funded work on the wall in 1327 and 1334, as did Henry IV in 1403 and Henry VIII in 1527. The wall was badly damaged by Scottish artillery during the siege of Newcastle in 1644, although subsequently repaired, and even later it was still significant enough defensively to receive precautionary reinforcement at the time of the Jacobite Rebellions of 1715 and 1745.

Apart from the minor gateway of the Sallyport (see below), no gates remain, all having been removed to allow for expansion and to improve access for what became the principal roadways into the town. The demolition of the wall generally had started in the 1760s with the section along the quayside, from which masonry was used to build the fine classical church of St Ann, City Road (see p.60). The process then gathered further momentum in the early nineteenth century and was largely complete by about 1830. The New Gate, standing near St Andrew's Church at the junction of Newgate Street and Blackett Street, was the last gate to be removed, in 1823; at that time it was being used as a prison. Interestingly, even at this early date there was considerable public opposition to its destruction.

The best-preserved section of the wall starts on Newgate Street in St Andrew's churchyard. There is a gap at the entrance to Stowell Street and St Andrew's Street, after which a continuous length remains along the back of Stowell Street. This stretch includes the ditch on its outside, while the lane

Right The Town Walls, Newcastle upon Tyne: section along City Road, from the north west.

Far Right The Town Walls, Newcastle upon Tyne: view of the Plummer Tower from the south west.

known as Back Stowell Street still gives an indication of the narrow passageway that formerly gave access to the wall. Along the wall, in this vicinity, are parts of towers and turrets, with some major survivals. The two most complete towers are the Durham, where Stowell Street joins Bath Lane, and the Heber. These towers have semi-circular projections beyond the external line of the wall, and still have vaulted roofs to the main rooms.

Just to the north of these two is the best-preserved tower, near the postern gate granted to the Black Friars in 1280. This is known as the Morden Tower, which has a later overhanging brick and stone upper storey built around 1700. In the eighteenth century this tower was occupied by the Guild of Glaziers, Plumbers, Pewterers and Painters, who built the extension, and used it well into the nineteenth century. The upper room is still used today by a local poetry society.

One further important stretch of the west wall still remains, along Orchard Street, preserved thanks to its location within the Federation Brewery, and revealed when the company moved across the river, leaving its buildings to be demolished. Of the eastern wall, the line can be traced but little remains.

Noteworthy, however, are the still-surviving Sallyport, or Wall Knoll Tower, on the north side of City Road, which is the last remaining gateway through the wall and dates from the fourteenth century (see opposite page, lower left), and the Plummer Tower, a little to the north, near Worswick Street (see above, right). Both of these structures received significant eighteenth-century modifications. Upon the Sallyport Tower, in 1716, the Ships' Carpenters' Company constructed a Meeting Hall in a robust, Vanbrugh-esque style, with rusticated surrounds to round-headed windows, an entrance doorway flanked by pilasters, and four corner turrets (see opposite page, lower left). By contrast, the small two-storey hall built above the Plummer Tower by the Company of Masons in 1740 (see above, right), is in a more academic Palladian style. No architect can be credited with either design.

ST NICHOLAS'S CATHEDRAL
NEWCASTLE, NE1 1PF

According to tradition, St Osmond, Earl of Dorset and Bishop of Salisbury, founded the church of St Nicholas in 1091. Nothing remains of this church, which was destroyed by fire, possibly as early as 1216. The present structure was built much later, being almost entirely of the fourteenth and fifteenth centuries. The interior dates mainly from the period c.1340-60.

Originally a parish church, St Nicholas's became a cathedral when Newcastle was elevated to city status in 1882. It has nevertheless remained essentially a large parish church, in scale and character, with the exception of its magnificent fifteenth-century lantern tower and spire, rising to a height of nearly 200 feet and dominating the Newcastle skyline.

The spire is of a rare type called a 'Scottish crown' and is a structure of both dignity and finesse (see also, chapter frontispiece). A large window of five lights is surmounted by the belfry and corner pinnacles. Behind the pinnacles project four 'flying buttresses', which in turn support a square lantern and ultimately the octagonal spire. The tower contains eight bells, three of which are medieval.

By the early nineteenth century there were fears about the tower's stability and in 1832-34 John Dobson, in collaboration with John Green, built two neo-Gothic porches on its north and south sides to support it. In 1867-70 Sir George Gilbert Scott restored the spire and underpinned the tower with a concrete foundation. Scott undertook further restoration to the cathedral as a whole during the 1870s, work that was continued after his death by his son J.O. Scott. Earlier, in 1859, Dobson had rather over-zealously reconstructed the great east window in Perpendicular style. Other alterations to the cathedral include the additions of the Georgian library and vestry, on the south side (see p.54) and, to the north east, another new library and vestry, with large hall, all in neo-Gothic style, completed to the designs of W.H. Wood in 1926.

The interior of the cathedral is serene, being generally simple and unified. The detail on the octagonal piers is sparse, with chamfered arches springing directly from piers without capitals (see opposite page, left). Much of the furnishing was removed in the sixteenth century during the Reformation. A further emptying of fittings and memorials then occurred in the late eighteenth century, not least as part of a very drastic and much-criticised 're-furnishing' by local architects William Newton and David Stephenson from c.1785, which led to the destruction of much ancient woodwork (although a fair number of miscellaneous historic items remain, for which see below).

St Nicholas's is long, rather than especially wide. Nor, internally, is the cathedral particularly high. Even so, the interior is undeniably grand, although the nave is rather dark, with the oak ceiling

Burkhard Müller, Süddeutsche Zeitung

„Wichtige Themen, ausgewiesene Autoren, Beschränkung auf das Wichtige und das Wesentliche – dazu ein günstiger Preis: das ist in der Tat das Erfolgsrezept der Reihe Wissen."
Frank Juffly, Das Buch – BücherPick

„... knappe, aber solide Nachschlagewerke ... die ihren Wert auch im Laufe der Jahre kaum einbüßen werden."
Jacques Schuster, Der Tagesspiegel

„Ein Crash-Kurs, zu bewältigen an einem Nachmittag. Auf daß niemand mehr den Historikern den Vorwurf machen kann, er habe sich nicht informieren können."
Berthold Seewald, Die Welt zu *„Die Revolution von 1848/49"*

„Wieder mal ist die Reihe Wissen um ein Glanzstück reicher geworden."
Johannes Salzwedel, Kultur Spiegel zu *„Die Gnosis"*

Die Bände haben jeweils einen Umfang von rund 128 Seiten und sind teilweise bebildert und mit Karten versehen. Die Bände kosten zwischen € 7,50[D] / sFr 13,50 / € 7,80[A] (ältere Auflagen) und € 7,90[D] / sFr 14,10 / € 8,20[A].

Innerhalb der Kapitel sind die Titel nach Themen sortiert. Ein *Autorenregister* und *„Alle Titel auf einen Blick"* finden Sie auf den Seiten 18–21.

C.H.BECK

GUT ZU WISSEN

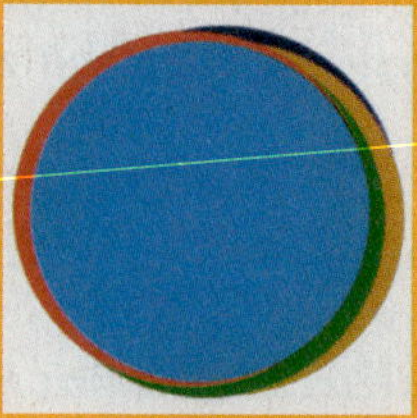

Gesamtverzeichnis
Herbst 2003

C.H.BECK
www.beck.de

absorbing the light, mainly from the clerestory of four bays of triple-light windows. The roof itself can be dated to the late fourteenth century by the heraldry on the bosses.

The stained-glass windows date mainly from the nineteenth and twentieth centuries, with the exception of a fifteenth-century round window of the Virgin and Child. This roundel is set into the east window of St Margaret's Chapel. Other medieval glass was destroyed during the Civil War. The nineteenth-century windows are of good quality and include several by the eminent local designer William Wailes.

Despite multiple depradations, the cathedral remains fairly rich in tombs, fittings and monuments. Many, as one might expect, date from the eighteenth, nineteenth and early twentieth centuries, but at the western entrance there is a splendid fifteenth-century font, consisting of a plain octagonal marble vase, bearing the arms of Robert Rhodes and elevated on a stone pedestal. The wooden font cover is slightly later, c.1500, with fine tracery and crockets. The lectern is also pre-Reformation. Prominent too are the Renaissance-style Hall (c.1631) and Maddison (c.1635) monuments (see above, right) and the magnificent Thornton Brass of 1441, which is displayed behind the altar and depicts the wealthy merchant Roger Thornton and his wife, these treasures having survived destruction by iconoclasts presumably because of their semi-secular nature. The original cathedral organ is also of considerable antiquity, having been built in 1676 by the celebrated maker Renatus Harris of London. It was reconstructed between 1881 and 1891, R.J. Johnson, the then newly appointed Cathedral Architect, re-setting it within the original case.

The elevation of St Nicholas's to cathedral status necessitated a certain amount of appropriate re-ordering in accordance with traditional usage, under the enthusiastic direction of the new Vicar, Arthur Thomas Lloyd (later the third bishop of Newcastle, 1903-07). Thus between 1884 and 1886 the high altar was enclosed within a richly carved ensemble of reredos (incorporating statues by J.S. Westmacott), choir stalls and screen, all designed by Johnson in an ornate, late Gothic style. Johnson also designed the pulpit and bishop's throne. The whole ensemble, executed by the wood-carver Ralph Hedley and the stone-carver Robert Beall, both local men of outstanding talent, is a sumptuous example of late Victorian decorative art.

Opposite Left St Nicholas's Cathedral, Newcastle upon Tyne, mainly fourteenth- and fifteenth-century: from the south.

Above Left St Nicholas's Cathedral, Newcastle upon Tyne: the interior looking east.

Above Right St Nicholas's Cathedral, Newcastle upon Tyne: the Maddison Monument, c.1635.

ST MARY'S CHURCH
OAKWELLGATE, GATESHEAD, NE8 2AU

St Mary's, formerly the town's parish church, is perched high on the southern bank of the river, between the Tyne Bridge and Sage Gateshead. There has been a church on or near this site since the eleventh century. Earlier it may have been the location of the seventh-century monastery 'Ad Caprae Caput' (at the Goat's Head), mentioned by Bede. St Mary's replaced a wooden Anglo-Saxon church destroyed in 1080 when a mob murdered Walcher, the first Norman Bishop of Durham – an event that led to savage reprisals from William the Conqueror.

Some of the stone used in building St Mary's may be recycled Roman material from structures on the southern side of the crossing at Pons Aelius. The church dates mainly from the fourteenth century, but there are some earlier elements: the oldest remains, dating from about 1200, are the round-arched southern doorway and part of the inner north wall of the chancel. On the outside of this wall an anchorage (a small chamber for an anchoress or female hermit) was built in the mid-fourteenth century. It was greatly enlarged in the seventeenth century and subsequently used as Gateshead's first school and as the meeting place of the 'Four and Twenty' prominent citizens who governed the town until 1835.

A square bell-tower was begun in 1739 by George Cansfield, an experienced master mason, to replace the now-ruinous original tower. Cansfield (not 'Causfield', as previously believed) had earlier worked for Sir John Vanbrugh at Seaton Delaval Hall and produced original designs of his own on several occasions. Even so, his expertise does not seem to have been enough to prevent problems during construction and he is said to have been ruined financially by the work. Cansfield's semi-classical tower has an upper stage (remodelled in 1773) with a pediment on each face, underneath which are round-headed arches. Other Georgian 'restorations' to the church included the insertion of sash windows, while galleries were added in 1838-39, probably by Thomas Oliver, to accommodate a growing congregation.

Before long, however, St Mary's was so badly damaged in the Great Quayside Fire of 1854 that complete demolition was contemplated. Instead John Dobson was employed to rebuild large portions of the church, which re-opened a year later. The sash windows were replaced with late Gothic-style designs and much stained glass was inserted (including work by William Wailes), although there was disappointment that the 'uncouth' tower had been kept. R.J. Johnson restored the church in 1874-76, W.S. Hicks added a reredos in 1887, and yet further restoration was undertaken, at intervals, by W.H. Wood of Oliver, Leeson & Wood (1908-22), including the addition of a south porch.

This ill-fated building was ravaged by two more fires, in 1979 (in this year it closed as a place of worship) and 1983. The fires destroyed the anchorage, the church's furnishings and the stained glass. (All the windows are now of clear glass, although some have been decorated with coloured film that imitates the effect of stained glass.) Basic repairs were carried out on the empty shell, but it was not until 1990, when it was bought by the auctioneers Phillips, that the building was brought back to life. Phillips converted St Mary's into an auction house and it was used in this way for the next decade. From 2001 to 2007 it was run as a visitor centre by Gateshead Council, who now own the building.

Following another transformation, this time at a cost of £1.2m and funded by Gateshead Council, the European Regional Development Fund and the Heritage Lottery Fund, the Grade-1 listed building re-opened in December 2008 as St Mary's Heritage Centre, 'explaining the story of Gateshead to locals and visitors alike'. The interior work done for Phillips has been removed to return the building to something approaching its former state, with a meeting room inserted at first-floor level at the east end, and a single-storey addition to the north containing toilets and other services. The main entrance is now through a large glazed Gothic arch that opens up the north transept.

An interesting structure in St Mary's churchyard is the Trollope Mausoleum, which is said to have been built by the architect Robert Trollope (see p.11) for his own use, presumably soon before his death in 1686. Square in plan, it has plain brick walls but is crowned with stonework forming a vigorous Baroque composition, with a heavy cornice, chunky corner pinnacles, and a central octagonal obelisk supported by scrollwork. The Green family, who had intermarried with descendants of Trollope, adopted the mausoleum in the mid-nineteenth century and partially rebuilt it, obliterating any inscriptions relating to him.

St Mary's Church, Oakwellgate, Gateshead, mainly fourteenth-century: from the south.

THE COOPERAGE

NOS 32-34 THE CLOSE, NEWCASTLE, NE1 3PF

Timber framing was still a popular method of construction in the late Middle Ages, although somewhat less so in the North East of England than elsewhere, given the ready availability in the region of both brick and stone. Even so, Newcastle's quayside was packed with timber-framed houses, many of which were destroyed in the Great Quayside Fire of 1854, and the Cooperage is the most complete timber-framed building from its period left in the city.

The site of the Cooperage is a prominent one: on the quayside and also at the bottom of the long stairs that connect the Close to the Castle Garth. This plot was mentioned as early as the thirteenth century; it is likely that a structure has existed on it since that time. The existing building was erected in the first half of the sixteenth century, although over its lifetime it has been much modified and enlarged. It was built as a merchant's house and for more than two centuries was passed from one merchant family to another. The functional nature of the house suggests that the owners were not as wealthy as those who owned other, more highly decorated, houses along the riverfront, for example on Sandhill.

Although it was commonplace for Newcastle merchants to use their houses for storage, it seems that this property was converted to full commercial use, as a warehouse. The building was then taken over by grocers. In 1863, a cooper called John Arthur expanded into it from his existing premises at No. 34 and the combined property stayed in the hands of his family until it was sold in 1974. Shortly afterwards the property was bought for conversion to a bar; due to the building's historic importance, few alterations were permitted.

The building's construction is comparatively simple: a four-storey timber post-and-rail frame, with curved corner bracing, sits on a stone base within a two-storey stone structure. Between the timbers are brick panels. Cruck frames, with horizontal bracing, support the roof, thus creating an uninterrupted roof space. A pair of crucks is exposed on the front facade. Beneath them is a variety of windows, including some that virtually constitute ribbon windows, easily achievable with this type of timber frame. Each floor overhangs the one below, a feature that is typical of the period, giving more space to the upper storeys and helping to waterproof the lower floors.

Left The Cooperage, Nos 32-34 the Close, Newcastle upon Tyne, mainly mid-sixteenth-century: from the south east.

Right Denton Hall, West Road, Newcastle upon Tyne, 1622: from the west.

DENTON HALL

WEST ROAD, NEWCASTLE, NE5 2BJ

The early seventeenth-century Denton Hall, sometimes known as East Denton Hall, has been since 1943 the home of the Roman Catholic bishops of Hexham and Newcastle. It is sited on an eminence facing west, adjacent to the Denton Turret of Hadrian's Wall and, when built, it would have looked along the remains of the Wall, stretching continuously to Carlisle and beyond. Its builders may well have used recycled material from the Wall. An inscription on the porch dates the building to 1622 and names the original owners as Anthony and Dorothy Errington. A later resident, albeit only on a part-time basis, was the noted London 'bluestocking' Elizabeth Montagu, whose husband inherited the house, and the lucrative coal mines that went with it, in 1758. Later still, the surgeon William Andrew I'Anson occupied the mansion from 1889 until his death in 1908, and restored it.

Denton Hall is constructed from coarse rubble stone with contrasting quoins, in a style as much Elizabethan as Jacobean. The entrance (west) facade is dominated by two large triangular gables with finials. At the head of the windows, stone band courses are used for articulation and run the full width of the facade. Each window has four individual lights, with chamfered mullions. The north and south facades each have a pair of enormous chimneys, connected back to the roof with individual gables. The interior is now of less interest, having been much altered; many of its large rooms have been subdivided and modernised.

The building is still fairly prominent within the landscape, although partly hidden by trees. However, much of its surrounding land was sold for residential development during the period c.1930-60 and Denton Hall's once-extensive grounds are now no more than a generous garden. Similarly, with the recent construction of the A1 bypass, the building has become rather isolated.

TRINITY HOUSE

BROAD CHARE, NEWCASTLE, NE1 3DQ

The area known as 'Trinity House' covers a range of buildings linked by a series of courtyards. It belongs to a private corporation, founded in 1492 and one of four similar entities operating around the coasts of England with responsibility for ports, harbours, pilotage and lighthouses. Newcastle's Trinity House was first chartered by Henry VIII in 1537. Its secluded complex incorporates almshouses, a chapel and other buildings (many of which have had a range of uses since the sixteenth century), including a rigging loft, a school and a warehouse. There is said to have been a chapel on the site since 1505, although much of what we see today dates from c.1636.

The principal access is through a Victorian, Tudor-style entrance arch (rebuilt by Thomas Oliver in 1841), into Trinity House yard, surely one of the most pleasant exterior spaces in Newcastle. A set of elegant steps leads up through an impressive doorway (1800, by local architect John Stokoe) into a fine entrance hall. Beyond is the chapel, which, despite numerous alterations, retains much early stonework. The main window in the gable is a nineteenth-century renewal, but the small, round-headed niches flanking it are from the early eighteenth century, or before. The chapel, said to have been designed on the lines of 'between decks' of an old ship, has good mid-seventeenth-century carved timber stalls, a clerk's desk and a reading desk, a pulpit, and a timber roof renewed in 1651 (see opposite page, top).

The Banqueting Hall (see opposite page, lower) dates from 1721. It is on the same level, forming the south-eastern boundary of the yard, and has a fine stuccoed ceiling and original sash windows with elliptical heads (visible in the photograph above). Also of interest is an original set of twelve late eighteenth-century comb-back Windsor chairs, possibly by a local maker.

The Board Room was rebuilt in 1791, again to the designs of John Stokoe. To the north of the yard is the three-storey former rigging loft, which originated as a medieval house; parts of it may be fourteenth-century. This loft would have been on the part of the site acquired by Trinity House in 1524, but even by this early date had become warehousing.

The fourth side of the yard is completed by a row of brick almshouses, rebuilt in 1787 with a cornice matching that of the Banqueting Hall. The property extends to two further courtyards – the 'high' and 'low' yards, with more almshouses. Between these and Broad Chare lies the former school (1753), which served until 2005 as the Trinity House Maritime Museum. Immediately to the south is the Live Theatre Company, which was established in 1973 and moved to this part of the quayside in 1982. Its premises were converted by architect Michael Drage in 1991 out of mid-nineteenth-century brick warehouses, as well as the late eighteenth-century almshouses mentioned above, all formerly part of Trinity House.

In 2006-07 the Live Theatre was extensively refurbished and extended by the architects Waring & Netts (now Space Group) to incorporate the former Museum. This work is notable for the careful repair, restoration and in some situations revealing of original early features. Combined with modern interventions, it provides new public and significantly extended backstage facilities, including a glazed tower at the centre of the building that provides a staircase, lift and circulation core to all parts of the complex, allowing daylight into the ground-floor foyer, and offering dramatic views of the quayside from the upper levels. Overall, the approach here was intended to reflect the semi-industrial nature of the original buildings, with new features mainly in galvanised steel and glass.

Left Trinity House, Broad Chare, Newcastle upon Tyne, mainly from the early sixteenth-century: view up stairs towards main entrance, by John Stokoe, 1800.

Above Right Trinity House, Broad Chare, Newcastle upon Tyne: interior of the chapel, mainly c.1636.

Below Right Trinity House, Broad Chare, Newcastle upon Tyne, interior of the Banqueting Hall, 1721.

NOS 28-30 THE CLOSE

NEWCASTLE, NE1 3RF

This is one of a number of interesting old houses remaining along the Close. Now dwarfed by the High Level Bridge, and with an eighteenth-century brick facade, the building is in fact the substantial remains of a merchant's house dating probably to the early seventeenth century. Its upper floor, above a ground-floor storage area, contains a superb long room, having close-set, plastered beams with Renaissance decoration.

Like many other buildings in the vicinity, in the 1930s this house was in the possession of Viscount Gort. He rescued items from early buildings all over the country and inserted them into similar structures that he himself owned. Therefore, as with nearby Bessie Surtees House (see p.36), not all parts of this building are original, and architects Simpson & Brown, in their 1990s restoration for the Tyne and Wear Building Restoration Trust ('Buttress'), have replaced an inappropriate rear wing with a more authentic design. Now the building has recently been converted into a high-class restaurant.

Nos 28-30 the Close, Newcastle upon Tyne, early seventeenth-century: from the north. Photograph Bethany Jane Robertson.

NO. 35 THE CLOSE

NEWCASTLE, NE1 3RN

No. 35 is the only early building to survive on the south side of the Close. It was part of a range of buildings enclosing a square and is now used as a restaurant. Although the north facade was rebuilt following the widening of the road in the nineteenth century, the remaining wings give an intriguing glimpse of an earlier seventeenth- and eighteenth-century group. The sensitive renovation of the floorscape within the courtyard, retaining the old pavers with their variety of colours and textures, creates a pleasant external space.

The building reveals its age and modifications in its varied textures of its walls (see photograph on p.2): parts are in stone, others in brick, with a timber-framed gable visible toward the riverside. There is a sixteenth-century king-post trussed roof in the east range. Until the development of the present riverside walk, the southern range was adjacent to the waterside, thereby giving direct access for the loading and unloading of goods.

35 the Close, Newcastle upon Tyne, early seventeenth-century: from the south.

WHITE HART YARD AND THE OLD GEORGE PUBLIC HOUSE

CLOTH MARKET, NEWCASTLE, NE1 1EE

The Cloth Market still gives glimpses of the character of the city before Richard Grainger's early nineteenth-century redevelopment. It was a street of mixed commercial and residential use, consisting mainly of three-storey houses principally of brick with some stone detailing. Unfortunately, the street is of interest only on the northern side, Stanegate House along the southern side being one of the many examples of mediocre 1970s redevelopment in the city.

The premises of Nos 14-16 Cloth Market, despite possessing an eighteenth-century facade, still shows evidence of building work from the sixteenth century, or even earlier. Next door in White Hart Yard are the remains of a medieval burgage lane with a worn cobbled street, the buildings on either side of the lane being formed of a patchwork of materials and periods, from seventeenth-century brickwork to early twentieth-century tiling. In this yard is The Old George, the arched entrance protected by 'glinters', i.e. granite posts built into the corners to protect the wall from damage by cartwheels. The feel of the cobbled yard as one enters from the street is still very much that of a seventeenth-century coaching inn, although the buildings themselves are an amalgam of original, recycled and later work (see above, right and left).

Above Left White Hart Yard, Cloth Market, Newcastle upon Tyne: from the north east.

Above Right The Old George public house, White Hart Yard, Newcastle upon Tyne, mainly seventeenth-century: from the south west.

THE GUILDHALL

SANDHILL, NEWCASTLE, NE1 3AF

The building now known as the Guildhall is the result of a long process of remodelling, extension and alteration by a number of (mainly local) architects including Robert Trollope (see p.11), William Newton, David Stephenson, John and William Stokoe, and John Dobson. It is a fascinating and complex ensemble.

Newcastle had a Guildhall as early as the thirteenth century, probably on approximately the present site. A building was certainly here at the beginning of the fifteenth century, when Roger Thornton (see p.25) built an adjacent charity almshouse known as the 'Maison Dieu' (indicated on Speed's Map of 1610 see p.10). We also know that at the end of the sixteenth century there existed in the vicinity a group of guild buildings and weigh-houses. Soon afterwards, the Corporation purchased the Maison Dieu to form amalgamated municipal premises, shared with the Guild of Merchant Adventurers. It is difficult to establish what proportion of these original buildings remains in the succeeding work, since they had been at least partly destroyed by fire in 1639.

Following the Corporation's decision to rebuild, Robert Trollope of York completed a commission to provide a new and costly Guildhall and Exchange, on the Sandhill, which was erected in 1655-58. As can be seen from eighteenth-century prints, this structure consisted of a rather eccentric combination of Gothic and Renaissance forms. The Corporation expended over £10,000 on the building, a five-fold increase over the original estimate, and at one point actually had to borrow money from the architect to pay for the work. Even so, they were still delighted with the outcome, noting that Trollope "had carried out the building … to the satisfaction and good liking of the Mayor and Burgesses".

Left The Guildhall, Sandhill, Newcastle upon Tyne, by Robert Trollope, 1655-58, with much later work by others: from the south. Photograph Bethany Jane Robertson.

Right The Guildhall, Sandhill, Newcastle upon Tyne: interior of the Court Room.

By the late eighteenth century the Guildhall was seriously dilapidated, through age and neglect, damage by riots in 1740, and further damage by fire in 1791. The current building owes much of its form to a series of further alterations and additions, of 1794-96, by Newton and Stephenson. Acting jointly, they removed the stair tower on the north side and replaced it with a stairway and entrance block faced with attached Ionic columns supporting a pediment above, a Palladian composition similar in form to the facade of Newton's Newcastle Assembly Rooms. This may suggest that Newton, then in failing health, was the designer, with Stephenson supervising the construction. The entrance is through a round-arched doorway flanked by round-headed niches. Trollope's elevation was refaced, with its arcading filled in and its rustication removed, and the whole north frontage was generally 'classicised' according to the taste of the late eighteenth century. In 1809, the south side of the Guildhall was also completely remodelled (see opposite page), on this occasion by John and William Stokoe, thus removing virtually any remaining external evidence of Trollope's work.

John Dobson became involved when the east end of the building was reconstructed in 1823-26. The ancient Maison Dieu was by this time much decayed, and used as a warehouse. Dobson replaced it with a semi-circular, neo-classical addition to the Guildhall complex, consisting of a covered fish market on the ground floor, with a new Merchants' Court and offices for the Town Clerk above. The bold, plain Doric colonnade on the ground floor, containing the fish market (which was walled up in 1880 following the market's conversion into a news-room), has two floors above lit by simple framed windows, rectangular on the first floor, square above. Dobson's alterations also helped to widen and improve the entrances to the quayside. A few years later Dobson designed the adjacent Watergate Building (see p.101).

Internally, much of Trollope's work does survive, particularly in the Town Court, or Court Room, with its fine hammer-beam roof (see photograph above), and in the Mayor's Parlour or Chamber with its decorated strapwork plaster ceiling, chimney piece with Corinthian columns and broken pediment above, and interesting paintings of local scenes hanging on the panelled walls. Elsewhere, on the first floor, Dobson produced a magnificent court for the Merchant Adventurers, refitting their seventeenth-century carved oak panelling and elaborate fireplace and providing a cornice and stuccoed strapwork ceiling in similar style (actually bearing the fictitious date of 1620!). The double-glazed windows were considered an innovation.

BESSIE SURTEES HOUSE

NOS 41-44, SANDHILL, NEWCASTLE, NE1 3JF

A mound of sand that accumulated on the quayside, where the Lort Burn flowed into the Tyne, became known as Sandhill. It is believed that this area has been occupied since Roman times. Prosperous merchants gravitated to it in the late Middle Ages because of its proximity to the river. The grandeur of this house and other properties on Sandhill reflected the wealth of such merchant owners, plying their wares on the quayside when Newcastle was a major port.

Built in the mid-seventeenth century, No. 41 Sandhill is best known as the scene of one of England's most romantic elopements. This intrigue in 1772 involved Bessie Surtees, the teenage daughter of a prominent banker and businessman living at the house (hence its present name). The sweetheart Bessie eloped with was John Scott, the son of a local coal-trader who went on to attend Oxford University and later, as Lord Eldon, became Lord Chancellor of England.

The building is one of the finest examples of its type in Europe: a rare specimen of well-preserved domestic architecture of the Stuart period and a superb example of a timber-framed town house. It is currently the North East headquarters of English Heritage.

Bessie Surtees House in fact represents the amalgamation of three houses on Sandhill; only two of the houses, Nos 41 and 44, form the front

elevation. The facades of the building are seventeenth- and eighteenth-century, although other parts of the structure may be even older. The house stands five storeys high, each floor overhanging the one below. The appearance of timber-framed houses of this type is that of a continuous curtain wall, formed through post and rail construction. The frame is so advanced that windows stretch completely across the facade, an arrangement not commonly seen until the early decades of the twentieth century as a result of modern techniques. The carved posts of the frame, formed into Renaissance-style elements, interrupt the full-width strips of glazing. On the upper floors the posts are remarkable in the quality of the decoration, each post being carved with five strips of reeding that resemble pieces of cord.

In 1736 the historian Henry Bourne spoke of the buildings of Sandhill having rooms of "ancient grandeur, being very large and magnificent".

Inside Bessie Surtees House are further indications of wealth: splendid moulded plaster ceilings, heavy oak panelling and ornate carved fireplaces (possibly by the same master-craftsman who was responsible for comparable ones in the Newcastle Guildhall (see p.35). Much of the interior of the house is original, although it again harbours architectural elements rescued by Lord Gort from similar structures demolished in the 1920s and 30s.

Left Bessie Surtees House, Nos 41-44, Sandhill, Newcastle upon Tyne, seventeenth-century: from the south.

Above Bessie Surtees House, Nos 41-44, Sandhill, Newcastle upon Tyne: interior of first-floor room.

THE HOLY JESUS HOSPITAL AND THE TOWER OF THE MANORS

CITY ROAD, NEWCASTLE, NE1 2AS

The Holy Jesus Hospital, City Road, Newcastle upon Tyne, 1681: from the south west.

The Holy Jesus Hospital, sometimes known as the Town's Hospital, was built to house poor freemen or freemen's widows, as well as their children who had never married. It was built in 1681 by the Corporation of Newcastle on the site of the church of the former Augustinian Friary (see opposite page), the stonework against the east end of the hospital marking the east wall of the church. In the eighteenth century the hospital adjoined two later buildings, both long since removed, the Barber-Surgeons' Hall and Sir Walter Blackett's Hospital, all fronting a pleasant field with walks.

The exterior of the Holy Jesus Hospital is simple in arrangement and the front facade is well proportioned. There are three floors, and on the ground floor 30 arches on stout square pillars run along the entire length of the building, forming a covered walkway. The arches and the piers, constructed out of moulded brickwork, create a classical effect, suggestive of Renaissance architecture. The first and second floors are defined on the front elevation by projecting string-courses; on the second floor, the window openings have timber lintels.

In Victorian times the Holy Jesus Hospital was used additionally as a poor-house and a soup kitchen. It finally closed in 1935, remaining empty for more than 30 years. Between 1971 and 1993 it served as the John George Joicey Museum, devoted mainly to the social history of Newcastle.

Subsequently, the building stood vacant for some time but is now in the care of the National Trust, and serves as the base for its Inner City Project (although at the time of writing this is scheduled for closure). Since the 1960s – when it had to survive the imminent threat of demolition – this former hospital has been crowded and almost hidden by the adjacent central motorway (east) and the Swan House complex.

Abutting the rear elevation of the Holy Jesus Hospital is a sturdy sandstone tower that incorporates the only remaining fragments of a long-vanished Augustinian Friary, built in about 1290 on the site now partly occupied by the hospital itself. The tower was probably constructed soon after the friary was closed during the Dissolution of the Monasteries (1536-41), and is sometimes known as the 'Austin Friars' Tower'. It re-uses material from the north wall of the original friary church and its sacristy.

After its closure the friary was converted into what became known as the 'King's Manor', occasionally used by Henry VIII for meetings of his King's Council of the North. The area of Newcastle within which the tower is situated is therefore known as the Manors – hence the building's alternative name of 'Tower of the Manors'. Its purpose was probably defensive. It may well have been used to store munitions, while its ground-floor room also served as a small gaol.

Within the tower, a tight stone spiral staircase provides access to the principal rooms on each of the upper floors. The ground floor now houses an interesting stone coffin found outside, to the west, within the area of the old friary church. The upper floors contain original fireplaces, and also windows, including a particularly fine one re-used from the medieval friary (although unfortunately much of its tracery has been damaged).

The Tower of the Manors ('Austin Friars' Tower'), the Manors, Newcastle upon Tyne, mid- or late sixteenth century: from the west.

ALDERMAN FENWICK'S HOUSE

PILGRIM STREET, NEWCASTLE, NE1 6SQ

This is the last remaining late seventeenth-century merchant's house on Pilgrim Street, a street which, once lined with many similar houses, was formerly the principal road north through the town, from the river bridge to the Pilgrim Street Gate. Alderman Fenwick's House has been known by this name since the early eighteenth century, although there is no evidence that Nicholas Fenwick, who inherited the building through his wife and carried out major improvements around 1700, was ever an alderman.

The house originally had an extensive 'burgage plot' garden to the rear, extending to where Grey Street now stands. A dwelling existed on the present site in the mid-sixteenth century, but the present building dates from around the 1690s, although there are indications that parts of it are earlier. Since the 1780s it has been connected internally with No. 100 Pilgrim Street, a late eighteenth-century house (seen on the left in the photograph above).

Alderman Fenwick's House is one of the earliest structures in Newcastle to be built almost entirely of brick, and is important in showing the transition to brick construction from the timber-framed type, of which, as we have seen, there are still examples on the quayside. It forms a modified 'H', with a timber staircase filling the space between the two rear wings. Fenwick's major alterations of c.1700 were probably to the Pilgrim Street front, replacing casements with more modern sash windows and creating two full-height wings supported on square columns with simple capitals, similar in style to country houses of the period (at this time he probably also embellished the front first-floor room with its splendid

Left Alderman Fenwick's House, Pilgrim Street, Newcastle upon Tyne, c.1690-1700, and adjacent eighteenth-century house (seen to the left in this photograph): from the east.

Right Alderman Fenwick's House, Pilgrim Street, Newcastle upon Tyne: the principal first-floor room.

panelling). The elevation is basically symmetrical, of six bays, although the doorway, with a projecting canopy supported on slender columns, is offset to the left. There are cornices at each floor level.

Internally, there is much of interest. The main room on the 'piano nobile' has a splendid decorative plaster ceiling that is a fine example of its period. The grand central staircase rises through the main floors and is surmounted by a delightful glazed cupola or belvedere. Externally, a balustraded walkway surrounding this feature is thought to have given the original owners of the house a view of the quayside and the river, the sources of their wealth.

Since its original construction as a merchant's house, the building has had many uses. It remained in the possession of the Fenwick family until about 1750. Then, from 1784 until 1883, it was a hotel, the Queen's Head. Its conversion into a hotel was probably facilitated by the presence of generous space behind the building, and in fact the structure was progressively extended to the rear until it reached the line of Grey Street. It then became the Liberal Club, and remained so until 1962, by which time many of the nineteenth-century additions had become derelict or had been removed.

The building was threatened with demolition and remained empty for some years. However, it was purchased by the City Council in 1974 and ultimately rescued from decay by the Tyne and Wear Building Restoration Trust. Under the Trust's auspices it has been magnificently restored by architects Simpson & Brown. It now has a new use as offices.

CHAPTER 2 THE EIGHTEENTH AND EARLY NINETEENTH CENTURIES

St Ann's Church, City Road, Newcastle upon Tyne, by William Newton, 1764-68: from the south west.

INTRODUCTION

By 1700 Newcastle was England's fourth largest town, its surviving walls a reminder of medieval power. Strategically placed, it was an important centre of consumption and trade and still very much a provincial capital, the bustle of its streets, inns and markets testifying to its continued wealth and regional impact. Around this time the traveller Celia Fiennes commented that Newcastle "most resembles London of any place in England, its buildings lofty and large of brick mostly or stone". She also stated that it had shops that "are good and are of distinct trades", while, similarly, a mid-eighteenth-century trade directory noted that "here are plenty of all things, and provisions cheap." In 1769 P. Russell confirmed in his important survey *England Displayed* that "Newcastle is eminent for its commerce, trade, and revenue."

This revenue was, of course, based largely on the coal trade. Demand for coal increased steadily during the period, for use both as domestic fuel and later for the many new industrial processes which required it. Estimates suggest that Newcastle's exports of coal rose from an already substantial 600,000 tons per annum in 1685 to almost two million tons by 1800, meeting as much as 50% of the country's demands. By this date, too, the town had about 28,000 inhabitants.

More than is often realised, the export of coal to London and the south mitigated Newcastle's geographical remoteness by facilitating contact with the capital, and the eighteenth century saw the town become increasingly sophisticated both culturally and architecturally. Newcastle's surprisingly large number of newspapers provided information about the latest London commodities and events and one of the first public libraries in the country was opened here in 1741 (see p.54). There was a high level of literacy in the town, comparable only to London according to some authorities. In 1755 the first bank in Newcastle was founded – only the second to be opened outside London – while even before this the town, thanks to its many merchants, acted as an important money-market for the area between the Tees and the Tweed.

Architecturally, the most important developments included Newcastle's Assembly Rooms, opened in 1776 (see pp.44 and 62). There had also been a series of earlier Rooms flourishing in the town from the early eighteenth century onwards. These provided the venue for the innovative series of subscription concerts started by the Newcastle-born composer and impresario Charles Avison (1709-70) in the late 1730s. The Theatre Royal in Mosley Street (now demolished) was opened in 1788 and before long two important cultural institutions in Newcastle, the Literary and Philosophical Society and the Society of Antiquaries, were founded, in 1793 and 1813 respectively. Overall, the period covered by this chapter was one of remarkable achievement in the North East, not only in art, architecture and historical research, but also in science, engineering, mathematics, music, medicine and law.

Elegant structures were being built (many, but not exclusively, by local architects); most of those still in existence are described in this chapter. As early as the 1720s Daniel Defoe had found Newcastle "a spacious, extended, infinitely populous place" (except, that is, for some of the older buildings compressed along the riverside), while around the margin of James Corbridge's *Map of Newcastle upon Tyne* of 1723 are depictions of numerous merchants' houses, recently built in fashionable classical styles (see p.44). These included Alderman Fenwick's House (see p.40). Corbridge also illustrates several important new public buildings such as the now-demolished Mansion House (1691), one of the earliest provincial structures of this type.

Also, in addition to the unique amenity of the Town Moor, which was by now used for horse racing, inner Newcastle still possessed during the eighteenth century a remarkable concentration of gardens and public spaces. On the west side of the town citizens could stroll in the attractive Forth Walk, while nearby even the new Infirmary (designed by Daniel Garrett in 1751, now demolished) was surrounded by impressive, landscaped grounds. These had been laid out by William Joyce, a Gateshead nurseryman and surveyor who also worked at Wallington Hall, Northumberland. Garrett, meanwhile, was a Palladian architect of national status, who began his career as assistant to that celebrated early Georgian arbiter of taste, Lord Burlington.

Left The Assembly Rooms, Westgate Road, Newcastle upon Tyne, by William Newton, 1774-76; engraving for John Brand's *The History and Antiquities of Newcastle upon Tyne* (1789).

Above Detail of illustration from the margin of James Corbridge's *Map of Newcastle upon Tyne* (1723).

Right R. Beilby's *Plan of Newcastle upon Tyne and Gateshead* (1788); inset: Speed's map, 1611.

The Shield Field was yet another popular open space on the other side of town. The wooded banks of the Pandon Dene (no longer in existence) also provided scope for pleasurable strolling, as did the Carliol Croft, an area of ground lying between the rear gardens of the houses on the east side of Pilgrim Street – opposite Anderson Place – and the town wall. Private gardens abounded, especially in Percy Street, Northumberland Street and Westgate Street (see p.45), while Newcastle's most important public pleasure grounds, clearly modelled on London's famous Vauxhall Gardens, were the genteel Spring Gardens, off Gallowgate, "a fine grass field, ornamented with trees" (E. Mackenzie). The nearby Public Baths of 1781 (now demolished) were also pleasantly situated, in a grove.

The Georgian era saw a steady rise in importance of provincial towns and cities, of which Newcastle was a major example. It also saw a concomitant increase in the status of the architect, and by this time a well-educated architectural profession in Newcastle had begun to emerge. William Newton (1730-98), the son of Robert Newton, a shipwright turned builder and surveyor, probably did more than anyone to develop the classical tradition in Newcastle and the North East, as perhaps pioneered by national figures like Daniel Garrett. Robert Newton (c.1703-86) had worked for Garrett during the 1740s at Fenham Hall, Newcastle, and had acted as Garrett's building inspector at the Newcastle Infirmary, on both occasions assisted by William. Also a skilled model-maker, Robert Newton soon developed the ability to produce and execute his own designs and would have passed on his knowledge to his son. In his turn, William developed from craftsman to craftsman-architect and thence to professional architect. Ultimately his status as an "eminent" practitioner became widely recognised, in no small measure due to a substantial local and regional client network, and in his later years his position in society was typified by his role as a founder-member of Newcastle's prestigious Literary and Philosophical Society.

Although William Newton is best known for his classical, mainly Palladian designs, considered later in this chapter, he also occasionally turned his hand to the 'Gothick' mode, as with his partial rebuilding of Longbenton Parish Church, Newcastle (1790-91, see p.68). Another example is his remodelling, around 1780, of the now-demolished Heaton Hall, Newcastle, a country seat of Sir Matthew White Ridley, also of Blagdon, Northumberland, and a major promoter of the Assembly Rooms. Heaton Hall was described by a contemporary commentator as "an elegant mansion, ornamented with plantations in a good taste" (see p.46). Heaton, and other present-day suburbs such as Benton, Benwell, Elswick, Fenham, Gosforth and Jesmond, were then rural villages encircling the still compact town of Newcastle itself. Other country houses in these

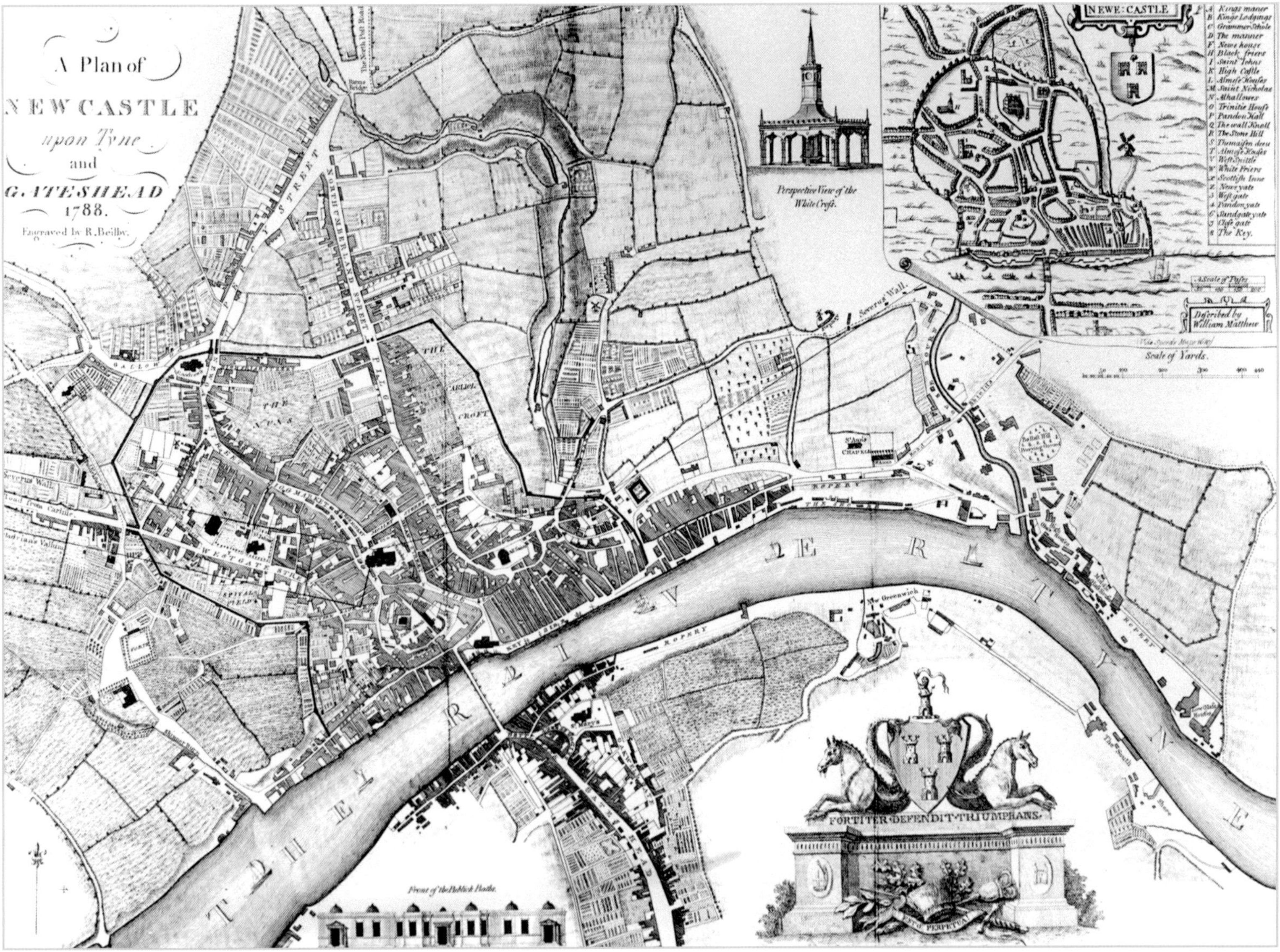

areas, also now lost, included Benton Hall (c.1760, architect unknown, see p.46'), and the late eighteenth-century Benton Park, possibly designed by Newton himself.

Links with national trends are further exemplified in the work of Newton's principal younger contemporary and successor, David Stephenson (1757-1819), the first local architect to study at the Royal Academy. Stephenson, the son of an important local builder and carpenter and just possibly a pupil of Newton, had been admitted to the Academy in 1782. Returning to set up practice in Newcastle the following year, he was responsible for the town's first Theatre Royal in 1788 (see p.46), and in the same year became semi-official Architect to the Corporation. In 1805 he was appointed Surveyor-Architect to the Duke of Northumberland, who described him as one of "the most respectable professional persons in this part of the Kingdom". For the Duke, Stephenson designed estate buildings in the county and, from 1806, the impressive New Quay, North Shields; this, however, was never completed and is now partly demolished. Later, Stephenson's pupil John Dobson (1787-1865), also partly London trained, became, from his base in Newcastle, an architect of considerable national renown. Like William Newton before him, but unlike Stephenson, Dobson developed a substantial country house practice. We shall hear much more of Dobson in Chapters Three and Four.

Also important in this era was the Stokoe dynasty of builder-architects,

best known for their work in the neo-classical and Greek Revival styles. John Stokoe (1756-1836) was the son of Wiiliam Stokoe, a master builder who died in 1802, and the father of William jnr. (c.1786-1855). John added a major extension to the Newcastle Infirmary (1801-03) and in 1803 designed the now-demolished Elswick Hall (see p.47), in Newcastle's then-fashionable 'west end'. This was later, albeit briefly, the residence of the property developer Richard Grainger (see Chapter Three). With his son William, John Stokoe was also responsible for the first Greek Revival building in Newcastle, the Moot Hall of 1810-12 (see p.76). Historians have perhaps slightly underestimated the abilities of these men. Indeed, William jnr. may well have had quite an advanced architectural training, perhaps in London or Edinburgh, and is recorded as exhibiting at the Royal Academy in 1808. However, he was soon eclipsed by Dobson, and his later career was comparatively obscure.

The trend towards classicism and fashionability developed by architects such as Newton, Stephenson and the Stokoes, was reinforced in the late eighteenth century by a limited number of municipal 'improvements'. These included the construction, in the 1780s, by Stephenson, of Mosley Street and then Dean Street (see p.47), facilitating access from the quayside. Collingwood Street, linking Mosley Street with Westgate Street (now Road), was laid out in 1810.

Even so, at this time Newcastle still retained its essentially medieval, constricted layout. Its single bridge, replaced after 1771 with a new and elegant structure by the London-based architect Robert Mylne and later widened by Stephenson, still created a difficult entrance from the river. Furthermore, Newcastle's communication routes remained generally inadequate and the town's expansion was inhibited by its encircling walls. Many of the houses in the centre were, according to the historian Bourne, "very ancient and mean" (see p.47). Opportunities for development were not always taken and much of the profit from urban and industrial activity went instead into the building of country houses by the North East's élite.

Yet as the middle classes migrated from the quayside and the old centre, so some new, high-quality residential streets and squares began to be built. Charlotte Square, under construction in 1770 (see p.61), lay just inside the walls, but these were now beginning to be demolished and in any case later developments were mainly outside them. Thus Saville Row, begun in the 1770s to run eastwards from Northumberland Street, was followed by Brandling Place, Claremont Place, Eldon Place, Eldon Row, Ellison Place, George Street, Higham Place (the first street laid out by Richard Grainger), Lovaine Place, Oxford Street, Picton Place, Saville Place, Summerhill, Swinburne Place and Victoria Square. Also, to the west, again outside the walls, there was Clavering Place (see p.65). All these typically Georgian developments, some described later in this chapter, were invariably of brick (with houses given sash windows and classical doorcases). Indeed, prior to the era of Grainger and Dobson (see Chapter Three) most domestic buildings in Newcastle were still of brick rather than of stone.

Meanwhile, what of Gateshead? During the eighteenth century this busy and modestly prosperous town quietly continued its essentially mercantile and industrial existence. It now possessed iron foundries and glassworks, and its population exceeded 8,000, but it remained greatly overshadowed by its larger neighbour north of the Tyne. Indeed, in 1769 it was described by the topographer P. Russell as "the suburb of Newcastle". However, Bottle Bank, Oakwellgate and Hillgate had become at least semi-fashionable areas. Also now located in the vicinity were several substantial landed estates, including Deckham Hall, Redheugh Hall and, the most important of them, Park House. This was owned by William Cotesworth, who laid out, or at least beautified, its splendid formal gardens. It was then rebuilt in 1730-33 by the major architect James Gibbs for a later owner, Henry Ellison. However, these buildings and their estates no longer survive and Gateshead retains comparatively little Georgian architecture.

Opposite Above Heaton Hall, Newcastle upon Tyne, 1713, remodelled by William Newton c.1783 (demolished).

Opposite Centre Benton Hall, Newcastle upon Tyne, built c.1760 for Thomas Bigge, (demolished) (© Northumberland Archives).

Opposite Below The Theatre Royal, Mosley Street, Newcastle upon Tyne, by David Stephenson, 1788 (demolished c.1836).

Above Right Elswick Hall, Newcastle upon Tyne, prior to its demolition in 1978 (© Newcastle Libraries).

Centre Right Dean Street, Newcastle upon Tyne, originally laid out by David Stephenson, c.1787-89: the upper east side.

Below Right Old timber-framed houses, now demolished, in Butcher Bank (now Akenside Hill), Newcastle upon Tyne; the butcher's premises, in the centre, were the birthplace of the noted poet and physician Mark Akenside (1721-70).

THE KEELMEN'S HOSPITAL

CITY ROAD, NEWCASTLE, NE1 2BU

This is one of three surviving buildings in Newcastle from around the late seventeenth and early eighteenth centuries to have been constructed almost entirely of brick, the others being the Holy Jesus Hospital and Alderman Fenwick's House (see Chapter One). The Keelmen's Hospital was built in 1701 by a charitable fund established by the keelmen themselves to provide support and accommodation for the elderly and sick of their fraternity and their relatives – a remarkable achievement, given the financial resources available. The keelmen, who transported goods from ships to the quayside, were exposed to a high risk of injury or death.

The hospital stands high above the road, overlooking the river, and takes the form of a cloistered square (perhaps inspired by the architecture of colleges and monasteries) with the imposing southern facade having nine bays of irregular width. The building has seen many alterations and is now a student residence. It is still reached by grand steps leading up to a pedimented doorway within the central projecting tower, which is rendered. The door is flanked by crude classical pilasters, which also flank the two floors above. This entrance bay boasts a sundial and commemorative plaque and rises to a domed clock tower standing high above the roof. On either side are brick dormer windows with scroll gables (few other gables of this type survive in Newcastle). This feature indicates Dutch influence, which is not surprising considering the trading links between the Tyne and the Low Countries.

Above The Keelmen's Hospital, City Road, Newcastle upon Tyne, 1701: from the south east.

Right White Knights, Belle Grove West, Spital Tongues, Newcastle upon Tyne, c.1700: from the south.

WHITE KNIGHTS

BELLE GROVE WEST, SPITAL TONGUES, NEWCASTLE, NE2 4LH

White Knights probably dates from just after 1700. It is a rare survival of domestic architecture of the period and thought to be the oldest continually occupied house in Newcastle. When first built, it was in the countryside, some distance from town. Originally called New House, it became a lunatic asylum in 1766 (renamed St Luke's House), run by Dr John Hall, who had as a patient John Boswell, brother of James Boswell, the biographer of Dr Samuel Johnson. When James Boswell visited his brother, he sometimes stayed with Dr Hall at his private residence in Pilgrim Street, mentioning in his diaries the pleasant walk out over fields to St Luke's House. In 1795, Dr Hall's successor, Dr Steavenson, considerably enlarged the building.

One mid-twentieth century owner of the property was Frederick Charles Pybus, an eminent surgeon at the Royal Victoria Infirmary and Professor of Surgery at Durham College of Medicine (later Newcastle University's Medical School). Pybus built up an internationally important collection of books and other material related to the history of medicine, which he housed in his library at White Knights and ultimately donated to Newcastle University in 1965.

The main entrance to the house was originally on the north side (now the rear), but is now on the garden side, and in fact the whole building has been much altered over the years, with canted bay windows added to the south facade in the early nineteenth century. Also, the section to the east of the central bay (to the right in the photograph above) was separated off from the main house during the nineteenth century to form an independent dwelling, which now forms part of the adjacent terrace. The second floor was added in 1906 to the designs of architect J.W. Taylor, producing the prominent gable with a central oriel window. This extension has an unusual structure, with steel floor beams supporting a rendered timber frame.

Internally, there is a grand central staircase and also a fine Adam-style drawing room of 1776, both of which have now been restored to their original splendour after being left in a near-derelict condition for many years. An original fireplace in the drawing room, stolen at some point during the twentieth century, has been replaced by a copy based on a photograph taken in 1907.

The property still possesses a coach house and outbuildings to the rear, which have recently been converted to an independent dwelling. Remarkably for a house so close to the city centre, White Knights also retains a large garden, bounded by an unusual eighteenth-century brick wall that is constructed in a series of curves. The modern Castle Leazes halls of residence of Newcastle University, built on the edge of the Town Moor, now dominate the view beyond.

NOS 53-75 WESTGATE ROAD

NEWCASTLE, NE1 1SG

Mention has already been made of Newcastle's considerable expansion and increased prosperity, from the early eighteenth century. Thus, although there were still areas of the town that displayed abject poverty, there were also pockets occupied by very wealthy merchants, keen to display their new or increased wealth by building opulent town houses.

Of that period, there are no finer town houses surviving in Newcastle than those built on Westgate Road. These buildings represent a departure from the earlier timber-framed houses of the quayside. Newcastle merchants, travelling around the country, not least to London, now witnessed town houses constructed out of less flammable materials such as stone and especially brick, and these became fashionable.

Westgate Road (formerly Street) is the oldest of all roads leading into Newcastle. Buildings have existed on this site since at least medieval times; indeed, this row of town houses, the majority of which date from the early eighteenth century, was built on the site of a Roman milestone. When constructed, these houses sat in semi-rural surroundings with large grounds, extending to the boundary of the town at Pink Lane. Some have seen numerous alterations, including changes to their facades. However, the now considerable variety in the individual houses only adds to the charm of the street.

The most interesting house in the row is probably that comprising Nos 55-57 (see photograph above), portions of which were used as the town's original Assembly Rooms until about 1736. At this time new premises were constructed for this purpose in the Groat Market, which in turn preceded the present Assembly Rooms. The premises forming Nos 55-57 are a little older than the others in the row and in the late seventeenth century are

known to have belonged to Sir William Creagh. Unusually for a Newcastle town house of its date, the building has a stone front – with Tuscan pilasters and a heavy eaves cornice. The grand interior includes some superb Italianate plasterwork in the Rococo style, probably dating from the second quarter of the eighteenth century.

The architect William Newton lived here for a time. Indeed, it is possible that Newton and his father, Robert, may have been involved earlier in remodelling the building after fire damage, reducing it by one storey from the four storeys (plus attics) shown in the illustration on Corbridge's map and removing a number of Baroque details to create the present, more restrained facade. They may also have been responsible for the fine interiors. The house is now part of the Newcastle Arts Centre.

Left Nos 55-57 Westgate Road, Newcastle upon Tyne, probably late seventeenth- and early eighteenth-century: from the north.

Above Nos 59-75 Westgate Road, Newcastle upon Tyne, early eighteenth-century: from the north east.

FRONT STREET

LONGBENTON, NEWCASTLE, NE12 8AH

Left House on Front Street, Longbenton, Newcastle upon Tyne, mid-eighteenth century: from the south.

Right Benton House, Longbenton, Newcastle upon Tyne, probably by William Newton, c.1770-75: from the south.

On Front Street there is a group of buildings dating from the second and third quarters of the eighteenth century. Although much altered, they still reflect the character of the formerly pleasant village of Longbenton, now an outer suburb of the city. Firstly, a sandstone farmhouse known as the Manor House stands at the Four Lane Ends crossroads, together with a group of associated farm buildings including a gin gang. In 1983 the complex was converted and extended to form flats for Nomad Housing by architects Brown Smith Baker.

Then, further to the east, are two characteristically solid, well-mannered, eighteenth-century gentlemen's residences, both of sandstone and typical of what might be termed 'builder's Georgian'. Both are two-storey and comparatively simple in plan. The smaller of the two is a still-commodious former vicarage (see photograph above), built in 1734 for the Rev. Charles Hayton (Vicar, 1734-43) and once known as North House. Altered in 1757, in more recent times it was owned by Newcastle University before being converted into private apartments in 2000.

Church House, its neighbour, is grander, was built later in the eighteenth century and is of ashlar. Both houses retain some original features, including well-proportioned sash windows, and were at one time part of the Ethel Williams Hall, a 1950s student residence of Newcastle University, although this development has now gone.

To the south is Benton House (see opposite page), a more ambitious Georgian building constructed or altered most probably around 1770-75. Admittedly its character is not immediately apparent from Front Street, as the house faces southwards and its north, or rear, elevation – doubtless considerably altered – now appears as a sandstone terrace along the main road.

Benton House has been described as a farmhouse, but this is incorrect: the south front of the house, approached along Hoylake Avenue, reveals it to be a small Palladian mansion. The building history of the house, however, is not fully documented. Reliable sources suggest that it was built in the 1740s for William Bigge II (d. 1758), a member of a prominent local coal-owning family who became High Sheriff of Northumberland in 1750, but the style of the south facade looks to be later, strongly suggesting an attribution to William Newton.

Indeed, the mansion's principal owner, Thomas Charles Bigge (1739-94), son of William Bigge II, was not only a man of considerable means but one with definite links to Newton. In 1771 Bigge followed the family

tradition in becoming High Sheriff of Northumberland and a year later married Jemima, daughter of William Ord of Fenham Hall, where Newton worked (see p.56). Thus Benton House may well have been built, or at least substantially altered, at about this time or shortly after. In addition, the design of the south facade is very similar to that of Backworth Hall, Northumberland, built by Newton for Ralph William Grey in 1778-80. Grey had married Elizabeth Brandling, the sister of Ord's wife Eleanor.

Moreover – and this was typical of the favour frequently shown to Newton by members of the local élite – T.C. Bigge himself is known to have used his various official positions to recommend him for architectural work on several occasions, as for example in his capacity as a vestryman at St Bartholomew's Church, Longbenton, in 1790 (see p.68). Bigge was also one of the proprietors of the Newcastle Assembly Rooms.

What may well have happened here is that an earlier house was indeed built around 1740; further credence for this is provided by the fact that William Bigge II purchased an estate at Little Benton from the executors of William Hindmarsh, a relative, in 1743. Later, on becoming High Sheriff and then marrying, T.C. Bigge commissioned the ever-reliable and capable William Newton to change the entrance of the house from the north over to the south side, at the same time providing the latter with a new and fashionable facade. If this was the case, it might also account for the rather 'patchwork' character of the present north elevation, some of the masonry of which could indeed be of the 1740s and so part of the original residence of William Bigge II.

In any event, the central section of the south facade of Benton House, in sandstone ashlar, is now five bays wide, with a string-course above the lower windows, and a string-sill to those of the first floor. The former entrance door, now a window, retains a pedimented porch with Tuscan columns; this feature is further emphasised at roof level by means of a broken pediment. A slight, almost unnoticeable asymmetry in this facade may be the result of adaptations forced upon the architect in the course of his probable reconstruction and extension work.

Sadly, little remains of the building's original interiors, as they were largely destroyed in a fire. By the early twentieth century, Benton House had become a golf club (remaining in use as such until the course was appropriated for housing development shortly after the Second World War). It is now a Conservative Club, incorporating shop premises to the main road.

THE THOMLINSON LIBRARY, ST NICHOLAS'S CATHEDRAL

NEWCASTLE, NE1 1DF

Left The Thomlinson Library, St Nicholas's Cathedral, Newcastle upon Tyne, by James Gibbs, 1736-41: from the south.

Right The Market Lane public house, Pilgrim Street, Newcastle upon Tyne, c.1740: from the south east.

Dr Robert Thomlinson (1668-1748), a local clergyman, donated much of his extensive private collection of books to found one of the first libraries in the country open to the public. This building, designed in 1736 by no less a figure than James Gibbs, was attached to the south side of St Nicholas's Church (now Cathedral) and incorporated a vestry at the lower level. It was paid for and endowed by Sir Walter Blackett of Wallington Hall and the library opened in October 1741. Sir Walter employed Daniel Garrett and James Paine for his improvements at Wallington, but Dr Thomlinson, who was Vicar of Whickham, was probably aware of Gibbs's similarly Palladian work at nearby Park House (1730, now demolished).

Thomlinson's will, dated 1745, approvingly notes the existence of "a handsome fabrick, consisting of two stories, for the reception of my books and those of other benefactors". In 1884 the library's contents, by then much augmented, were transferred to the Newcastle Central Library. The building here is now used as the Cathedral Choir School.

Architecturally, the Thomlinson Library is a well-mannered exercise in Gibbs's later, more Palladian manner and was the first Palladian building to be erected in Newcastle. The design of the main, south elevation is freely derived from Palladio's urban palazzo facades, such as that of the Palazzo Iseppo Porto in Vicenza, and also owes much to Lindsey House in Lincoln's Inn Fields, London, possibly designed by Inigo Jones. The library has a rusticated base, supporting Ionic pilasters, and a heavy cornice with dentil mouldings that completes the composition. Between the pilasters, at first floor level, are windows with alternating triangular and segmental pediments.

Gibbs originally planned for a ground-floor vestry apartment, below two floors each featuring a long room lined with bookselves and boasting impressive chimneypieces. The interior of the building is now comparatively simple, however, although with a number of original door and window casings. Of particular note are two magnificent doors with elaborate pediments and rich architraves. The first-floor room has a number of original details including timber ceiling panels; however, the cornicing has been removed.

Notwithstanding the aesthetic merit of this structure, it is instructive to observe the absence of any attempt by the early Georgians to conform to the style or scale of the church to which the building is attached; this presumably reflected the low esteem then generally accorded to Gothic architecture, at least in the North East.

THE MARKET LANE PUBLIC HOUSE
PILGRIM STREET, NEWCASTLE, NE1 6SG

This structure was originally an early Georgian town house. Pilgrim Street was, as we have seen, a major thoroughfare within the town and in the eighteenth century it would have been a very desirable location in which to live. Here is a surviving former town house of genuine quality. It is of brick, now painted, and dates from c.1740. Decoration is sparing, being limited to projecting window surrounds and pilasters, all in stone.

During the late eighteenth and early nineteenth centuries there was a progressive migration from the town centre to less congested locations, such as Charlotte Square and Saville Row, and then to the further suburbs beyond. Many buildings in the town centre lost their purpose and became dilapidated, and the 'Market Lane' is a good example, having almost certainly undergone several unoccupied periods.

This house has also been much altered. At some point it was separated into two units. Nor is the interior original, having been refurbished to accommodate the public house, while the facade looks to have been modified as well, especially at the junction between wall and roof. Alongside the 'Market Lane' is another Georgian building which is now a shop.

FENHAM HALL
NEWCASTLE, NE4 9XD

Fenham Hall originally dates from the fourteenth century, although little or nothing of this early structure remains. It was owned by the Knights Templar and later the Knights Hospitaller before passing via the Crown to the Riddell family, and then, in 1695, to the Ord family. In addition to the hall and associated land, the Ords owned much of the rest of Fenham, as well as other land across Northumberland.

John Ord began the present mansion in about 1744. He became Mayor of Newcastle in 1745 but died in the same year and building was continued by his brother and successor, William (d. 1768). William Ord practised as a lawyer and also married an heiress, enabling him to spend some £4,000 on his new house. This was substantially complete by 1748, but Fenham Hall is now an accumulation of facades and additions constructed over the last 250 years. In February 1908 the hall was very seriously damaged by a fire that burnt out most of the interiors (including fine plasterwork by Pietro Francini in the south block). Therefore, despite restoration, the principal interest of the building lies largely in the exterior.

Fenham Hall has three facades, all by different architects. The south facade (see opposite page, left) is generally thought to be the oldest, built in 1748 by Daniel Garrett, an architect of national status and assistant to that celebrated early apostle of Palladianism, Lord Burlington. Garrett was selected for many important commissions in the North East, including work at Blagdon Hall, Nunwick Hall and Wallington Hall, all in Northumberland. He was also responsible for the Banqueting House at Gibside, County Durham. At Fenham his two-storey facade, in ashlar, has seven bays. The three central bays support a pediment, containing the arms of the Ord family, elaborately carved by James Guthrie. The windows are of sash type. On the ground floor the windows of the central bays are within round-headed arches. Above these windows are blind tympana.

The other windows on this floor are surmounted by pediments. The composition of this facade, with its triple arches, slightly advancing three-bay centre and roofline pediment, may be derived from a design by Palladio for the Villa Saraceno, Finale di Agugliaro, near Vicenza. It is interesting to note that during this phase of construction Robert Newton worked at the hall, making bookcases, in 1751.

The front (north) facade, with wings (see opposite page), is a remodelling or replacement by Robert's son William Newton, from c.1773. An alternative date of 1788-89 has also been ascribed to this work, because documents record substantial payments made during this period to William Newton "on acct. of alterations at Fenham". Unusually for this architect, the facade is of red brick, with stone reserved for dressings and the four attached Tuscan columns that support a wide pediment. It is a sober composition of eleven bays, with the large end bays projecting as pavilions. These pavilions take emphasis away from the centre of the facade, which is somewhat less typical of Palladian architecture.

The east facade (architect unknown) is traditionally said to have been built around 1850, although recent research tends to contradict this dating in favour of something much earlier. It is also in ashlar (see above, right). Rather curiously, the style is eighteenth-century French, with window openings having depressed arches and heavy keystones, but this might just possibly result from a nineteenth-century re-facing, as opposed to new construction. The central ground-floor window looks to have originally been a door. This bay is different to the others in that its upper window is round-headed, while the aforementioned lower window is surmounted by an open segmental pediment.

In 1905 Fenham Hall was purchased by the Society of the Sacred Heart for use as a Roman Catholic teacher-training college (St Mary's). For the Society the distinguished architect Leonard Stokes added a major extension to the west, including a Grammar School, in 1906-07. Stokes was President of the Royal Institute of British Architects from 1910 to 1912, and designed many important buildings, including the Library of Emmanuel College, Cambridge. At Fenham his extension is in a bold 'Arts and Crafts classical' style, in red Flemish bond brickwork with rusticated quoins. It has various ranges, mainly of two and three storeys.

During the 1960s substantial further extensions, in a modernist idiom, were added to St Mary's College; the architect was John Cahill, of Reavell & Cahill of Alnwick. However, the college closed in 1985 and Fenham Hall is now used by Newcastle University as a student residence. At one time the Hall was surrounded by extensive landscaped grounds, now largely built over. These included a temple, possibly by Garrett, which was demolished in the 1960s, along with an original lodge to the estate.

Opposite Fenham Hall, Newcastle upon Tyne, by William Newton, c.1773 or later: the north facade.

Above Left Fenham Hall, Newcastle upon Tyne: the south facade, by Daniel Garrett, 1748.

Above Right Fenham Hall, Newcastle upon Tyne: the east facade, c.1850 or earlier.

GOSFORTH PARK ('BRANDLING HOUSE')

GREAT NORTH ROAD, NEWCASTLE, NE3 5HP

This mansion, in part of what is now Newcastle Racecourse, was originally known as Gosforth Hall, or House. It was built for the coal-owner Charles Brandling in 1755-64 to the designs of James Paine, another eminent Palladian who followed on from Garrett and again worked widely in the North East. At the time, the mansion was one of the largest Palladian houses in England. In 1769 a topographer observed that “it stands on rising ground, from which the village of Newbiggen, of Kenton, of Longbenton, and an opening between two distant hills, into the bishopric of Durham are in view” (P. Russell, *England Displayed*). Much of this vista – no doubt greatly enjoyed by Brandling and his successors – still survives (see below).

Brandling came from Felling, near Gateshead, but also owned land in Gosforth. His decision to build an impressive new seat on the north side of the Tyne reflected an expansion of his fortunes, especially as he was about to marry the heiress Elizabeth Thompson, of Shotton. He became High Sheriff of Newcastle in 1782 and two years later was elected M.P. for the town.

‘Brandling House’ is seven bays wide and three storeys high, with a rusticated ground floor. East and west wings, now somewhat altered and not shown in this photograph, symmetrically flank the main block. The windows at the centre and ends of the main floor have blind balustrades and segmental heads. The central three bays of the main front are surmounted by an open pediment. This arrangement of a projecting centre and pediment is repeated on a smaller scale in the wings. However, the whole of the building has been so altered in its details, partly to suit the needs of the racecourse, that it is difficult to gather more than an impression of the original, except perhaps from the plainer, north side.

A cast-iron grandstand was added to the south side, to the designs of S. Oswald & Son of Newcastle, when the racecourse was established in 1881, obscuring this facade. Even less sympathetic grandstand extensions were subsequently attached to the house, probably in the 1960s (and later). Similarly, little of the original, and evidently elaborate, interior survived burning by suffragettes in 1914; what remained was reconstructed in 1921.

The former estate steward’s house, across the drive from the mansion, may well be by Paine, who was perhaps also responsible for two surviving walled garden layouts on the west side of the estate, one of which is now the premises of a commercial garden centre. An original ice-house still exists near the more northern of these gardens, hidden in undergrowth. Later, in 1830, John Dobson became involved, with further alterations to the house and the design of the impressive main entrance gates (albeit now minus their original inner piers and fine wrought-ironwork) and a severe and unpretentious lodge, with smaller gates, just to the north, all on the old Great North Road. Dobson also designed the smaller lodge and gates on the east side of the estate.

With its appropriation not only for a racecourse but also for two golf courses, rather than for the usual urban development, Gosforth’s former estate retains more than a semblance of the effect of the original landscape park, possibly laid out by Paine himself.

Gosforth Park, off the Great North Road, Newcastle upon Tyne by James Paine, 1755-64: detail of north facade.

ST ANN'S CHURCH

CITY ROAD, NEWCASTLE, NE1 2AF

This church was built in 1764-68 to serve the growing population eastwards along the riverside. When it was first conceived, its congregation would have enjoyed a panorama of the Tyne valley and the countryside south of the river. Designed by William Newton, St Ann's was this important local architect's first substantial work. There had been a church on the site since 1344, but the original church of St Ann had fallen into a ruinous state and the Newcastle Corporation, which also bore the cost, decided that a "neat and commodious chapel" should be built as a replacement. In the construction, Newton recycled stone taken from the ancient town wall, a section of which along the quayside was in the process of being dismantled to facilitate access into the town. Until 1842 St Ann's, which could accommodate 600 worshippers, was a chapel of ease for All Saints' Church (see p.66).

After the Reformation, architects designing in the classical style moved away from the grand, complex churches of the medieval period to more modest, simply planned structures, with an emphasis on altar, pulpit and font. The idea was that the congregation could participate more fully in the service: "in our reformed religion, it would seem vain to make the parish church larger, than that all who are present can both hear and see" (Sir Christopher Wren). Internally, therefore, many of these classical churches were no more than simple rectangular spaces, or 'preaching boxes', without either transepts or chancels.

St Ann's, in sandstone ashlar, is in this classical, post-Reformation tradition (see also, chapter frontispiece). It is reminiscent of James Gibbs's St Martin-in-the-Fields, London (1722-26), although without Baroque detailing (for example, Newton is content to give the side walls merely plain arched recesses) and much smaller in scale. The entrance is defined by a portico of four Roman Doric columns, possibly derived from the illustrations of Roman temples in the fourth book of Palladio's celebrated *I quattro libri dell'architettura*, but here perhaps a little small for the large, blank west wall which it fronts. Just behind this, above the west end of the nave, rises a square clock tower with an urn on each corner. Two octagonal stages support an octagonal spire. The strongly classical character of St Ann's Church – there are no Christian emblems on its exterior – has prompted Richard Pears to suggest that the building may have been intended to look like a Roman temple, standing as it does near a portion of the remains of Hadrian's Wall. If this was the case, then the reference would certainly have been noted by the many antiquarian-minded viewers of the time.

The nave is rectangular with round-headed windows that now have the appearance of being set within a blind arcade, having been reduced in size during the nineteenth century. The nave walls form a parapet, behind which is a pitched slate roof. The interior is consistent with its classical form, being simple and light. At one time, with its original, larger windows, it would have been lighter still. Much of the furniture may be original, although many of the pews have been taken out, along with the original three-decker pulpit, and the capacity reduced, as a consequence of internal additions and alterations. There has also been some minor modernisation of Newton's arrangement. At the east end of the nave is a small apse that contains the altar; this is now placed in front of an ornate reredos designed by local architects Hicks & Charlewood in 1911, appropriately, but unusually for their practice, in a classical style.

Cherished by its congregation, the church, which contains a number of interesting tablets and memorials, is still immaculate both inside and out. Structurally, however, it has seen movement, with cracks running from the south-east corner of the nave and around the apse – despite remedial work carried out during the 1990s. Also, it is now somewhat hidden, overlooked by dourly utilitarian buildings from the 1960s and 70s.

Above St Ann's Church, City Road, Newcastle upon Tyne, by William Newton, 1764-68: from the south west.

Right Charlotte Square, Newcastle upon Tyne, by William Newton, from 1770: from the north east.

CHARLOTTE SQUARE

NEWCASTLE, NE1 4XF

In about 1720, work commenced on Hanover Square, Newcastle, centring on a dissenting chapel built by voluntary subscription, but this development was never finished and still less of it survives today. Thus Charlotte Square, begun in 1770 to the designs of William Newton and on land originally belonging to Black Friars, is the town's first completed formal square. Its construction was a speculation by the architect himself, who under the terms of his lease agreed to build "fashionable and commodious dwelling houses", none of which were to be less than three storeys in height. The project typified the progressive use of vacant city plots, in the eighteenth century, for the building of superior town houses and was particularly successful because of its convenient and accessible position near to the then highly fashionable Westgate Road (see p.50).

Charlotte Square is attractively elevated, with the majority of the houses being raised a storey high above Cross Street; the fourth side of the development is open to this adjacent street. The design took its inspiration from squares in London. There are three sides of houses with simple classical detailing; all are of English bond brickwork with plinths and dressings. Of special interest are the fine door cases with pediments above. The houses are not all identical, suggesting that they were built over a period of years and indeed the last house was not completed until 1777. The design of the interiors was of course supervised by Newton, but much, especially the details, was at the discretion of clients.

William Newton actually lived in the square himself, at No. 1, for twenty years, using his house "as a showcase to impress his clients with his skill and the range and quality of the workmanship that he could command" (Richard Pears). It was no accident that the architect lived in close proximity to possible and actual patrons such as members of the Carr and Ellison families, also living in the square, while representatives of the equally influential Allgood, Clavering and Ridley families had houses in nearby Westgate Road.

THE ASSEMBLY ROOMS

WESTGATE ROAD, NEWCASTLE, NE1 5XU

Newcastle's Assembly Rooms were designed by William Newton and built in 1774-76. Such buildings were used for balls, music and dancing: "We shall be at Newcastle all the winter ... there will be some balls, and I will take care to get good partners for them all" (Lydia Bennet in Jane Austen's *Pride and Prejudice*, 1813). These Rooms superseded older premises, which had been situated firstly in a house on the opposite side of the street and subsequently in the Groat Market. The site chosen for the new building was within the Vicarage gardens, near to Charlotte Square (also by Newton, see p.61), while Westgate Road (then Street) was itself one of the smartest parts of town.

The Assembly Rooms were opened in the race week, 24th June 1776, "by a very numerous and brilliant company" (Mackenzie). They soon became the place in which to be seen, to socialise and to do business, perfectly reflecting the preoccupations of 'polite society' at this time. The building is also an important indication of the wealth, prosperity and cultural aspirations of eighteenth-century Newcastle. Similarly, the general self-confidence of the Georgians is nicely epitomised by the inscription on its foundation stone, stating as it does that at this time "the polite arts, by general encouragement and emulation, [had] advanced to a state of perfection unknown in any former period".

The Rooms were paid for by public subscription at a cost of £6,000, many leading figures in the locality lending their support. As with the Newcastle Infirmary 25 years earlier, the Newcastle Hostmen were major backers of the scheme and once again some of the subscribers profited from the building work via the supply of materials. A special Act of Parliament was obtained to enable the Vicar of St John's Church to grant a lease for the building. Its proximity to St John's seemed to suggest that the venture had ecclesiastical approval, although at the time there were complaints about the fact that the Assembly Rooms were situated so near the church, on what had been church land.

Left The Assembly Rooms, Westgate Road, Newcastle upon Tyne, by William Newton, 1774-76: from the west.

Right The Assembly Rooms, Westgate Road, Newcastle upon Tyne: the ballroom.

Of its type, the building is one of the finest in the country. Its bold and symmetrical facade, with simple windows located between columns and with two lower wings framing the central block, is typical of its designer in being essentially Palladian, not least in the composition of the central block. However, here we also find the use of the recently discovered Greek, rather than the Roman, Ionic order (as published by Le Roy in 1758 and by Stuart and Revett in 1762) for the capitals of the substantial attached columns supporting the pediment, surely reflecting a new, increasingly popular neo-classical taste.

The lateral windows on the first floor are set within shallow, semi-circular arches, while extra emphasis and verticality is achieved by pairing the columns at the sides. Further impact in the facade is provided by the use of rustication at ground-floor level, although this is somewhat reduced by the presence of a later canopy (1882) over the entrance.

From the outset the Assembly Rooms were expensively furnished and fitted out. The interiors are designed in a version of what was then the highly fashionable neo-classical style of Robert Adam (something perhaps encouraged, like the use of Grecian features on the facade, by Newton's cultured and knowledgeable patrons). Certainly in scale and quality these interiors surpass those of any other non-domestic building of the period in the region. There are two suites of rooms, over two floors. The centrepiece is the great ballroom on the first floor; its ornate plasterwork and lavish chandeliers (the central one was made at the local Close Glassworks) are of outstanding quality (see photograph above). Access to this room is via a fine staircase.

With comparatively few buildings of its kind still in existence, Newcastle's Assembly Rooms must be seen as an architectural treasure of national or even international significance. The building is Grade 1 listed and, importantly, is still used as a place of assembly and enjoyment for the people of Newcastle.

THE FORMER WINDMILL
CLAREMONT ROAD, NEWCASTLE, NE2 4AL

Left The former Windmill, Claremont Road, Newcastle upon Tyne, by John Smeaton, 1782: from the east.

Opposite Above Clavering House, Clavering Place, Newcastle upon Tyne, attributed to William Newton, c.1784: from the north west.

Opposite Below Former Friar House, Clavering Place, Newcastle upon Tyne, attributed to William Newton, c.1790: from the west.

This rare surviving windmill building is a well-known curiosity and landmark within the area of Spital Tongues. It was built in 1782 by the eminent engineer John Smeaton, best known as the designer of the Eddystone Lighthouse. The mill is a 'smock' type, with an octagonal base and horizontal timber boarding. Its sails were removed in the 1920s. The mill has windows cut into the base, above which are ornate canopies giving views in all directions. The base of the mill now appears to be built into the end block of a later brick terrace. This block was a golf clubhouse for many years until the adjacent dual carriageway was built, separating it from the golf course on the Town Moor. This was then moved to another part of the Moor and a new clubhouse built, with the windmill being converted by architect Tom Falconer into offices and studios. The building was later used as a clothing design studio, before being recently converted into an orthodontist's practice by architects Howarth Litchfield.

CLAVERING HOUSE AND THE FORMER FRIAR HOUSE

CLAVERING PLACE, NEWCASTLE, NE1 3NG

Clavering House and its neighbour Friar House, both attributed to William Newton, constitute all that remains of the once-fashionable Clavering Place, developed towards the end of the eighteenth century. In their heyday these houses would have enjoyed the benefits of fine views of the Tyne valley. Unfortunately, the area in which they stand was cut off from the main part of the city by the development of the railways and so became part of the essentially industrial location now known as the 'Stephenson Quarter', currently being redeveloped (see page 142).

Clavering House was built in about 1784 and takes its name from its most famous resident, Sir Thomas Clavering of Axwell (although Sir Thomas also occupied a house in Westgate Road). It is an attractive Georgian town house typical of the period, having red English bond brickwork, ashlar dressings, and a Welsh slate roof. The flat, central portion of the facade is an interesting composition: slim vertical windows frame a grand entrance with a wide doorway set between pilasters supporting a pediment. Above the entrance are blind panels, on either side of a window with an arched head.

Friar House is another substantial Georgian property, built around 1790. In the early nineteenth century, R.H. Williamson, Recorder of Newcastle and Chancellor of County Durham, acquired the property and lived there until his death in 1835. Although different in style from its neighbour and less refined, this two-storey house is almost equally interesting, being similar in manner and scale to the surviving Georgian brick town houses situated opposite the Newcastle Assembly Rooms (see p.51). Constructed of brick, its five-bay facade has an impressive entrance: a deep fanlight sits above two slender doors, with Tuscan pilasters supporting an architrave. At the rear a large Venetian window dominates the elevation, being designed originally both to light the main staircase and to make the most of the view of the large garden, now occupied by the former Turnbull's Warehouse (see p.196).

Friar House lay semi-derelict for many years but in 2012 was sensitively restored and converted into a fourteen-suite 'aparthotel'. This was done by architects MawsonKerr, who were able to maintain the character of the building by respecting the original room arrangement, keeping many of the interior details including coving, staircase, fireplaces, and old kitchen ranges, and improving the hard landscaping at the front.

ALL SAINTS' CHURCH

THE QUAYSIDE, NEWCASTLE, NE1 3UF

This is without doubt one of the finest architectural sights in Newcastle, an elegant late eighteenth-century structure positioned on a site high above the quayside and once dominating the major gateway into the city across the Tyne. All Saints', said at the time of its consecration to "convey the highest ideal of magnificence and grandeur", was designed by David Stephenson to replace a medieval church on Pilgrim Street (formerly the main north-south route through the city). Although the church is now almost completely enclosed by an unsympathetic 1960s office development, its upper parts – especially its spire – still provide the focal point of some of the finest views in many parts of Newcastle.

In 1786, after decades of unsuccessfully trying to repair it, the authorities invited three prominent local architects to report on the condition of the dilapidated medieval church then on the site, also known as All Saints'. A proposal by William Newton to restore this Gothic building was rejected (even he conceded that it was unsafe), and the church was duly pulled down. Newton's colleagues John Dodds and David Stephenson had favoured replacement and the latter then won a competition for this with a version of the present design.

Newton stood aside from the competition, probably for reasons of professional integrity, in view of his opposition to the scheme. However, Dodds did enter, as did the little-known W. Bell and J. Jopling and, more importantly, the major provincial architect Thomas Harrison, then of Lancaster. Harrison's proposal, featuring a semi-circular space fronted by a Doric portico with classical steeples at either side, was extremely novel, seemingly too much so for the building committee. Yet it may have paved the way for the acceptance of Stephenson's ambitious scheme, although – perhaps fortunately for the building's appearance – the favoured architect was still obliged to replace the dome indicated on his original design with a spire. This feature was not completed until 1796, although the church itself was consecrated in 1789.

All Saints' is most unusual in plan, with the body of the church being oval. This form has precedents in the Italian Baroque, but in certain respects the building is much more akin to the austere, post-Reformation, Wren-inspired 'preaching box' type of church, with box pews at ground level and galleries supported on Doric columns. Curiously, however, a contemporary observer noted that All Saints', which could accommodate up to 2,000 worshippers, "has the disadvantage to which all circular buildings are subject – that of drowning the voice of the preacher, and rendering it impossible for those who are seated at any distance from him to hear his discourse distinctly".

The exterior of the church is very finely finished throughout and abounds in fashionable neo-classical details, "selected", according to another contemporary commentator, "from the purest models of antiquity". These details include flutings, mouldings, urns, swags and Coade stone panels – elements absent in the more conservative work of Stephenson's older colleague and rival, William Newton. The tower and spire of All Saints' are placed above the church front, again in the fashion of St Martin-in-the-Fields in London by James Gibbs, and particularly well executed here. In fact, the overall plan of All Saints' is subtly adapted from an alternative design for St Martin's by Gibbs, which also utilises an oval. This unexecuted scheme dates from about 1720 and was published in 1728 in Gibbs's *Book of Architecture*, the most influential architectural treatise of its time. Stephenson's design may also owe something to that of the recently completed St Andrew's Church, Edinburgh (by Andrew Frazer), which also has an oval interior.

The main body of All Saints' is fronted by a portico with four Greek Doric columns – a very early use of this form, albeit in this case with slightly more Roman proportions – supporting a pediment. This arrangement, incidentally, superseded Stephenson's original design, abandoned because of cost, which would have featured a colonnade of coupled Ionic columns. The square tower behind and above has pediments above 'Wyatt' windows (another neo-classical feature absent in Newton's work). The simpler upper section of the tower has round-arched windows, partly blind, and then tapers dramatically to a slender octagonal glazed storey above the clock level, with diagonal corner bases for the detached, coupled columns supporting in turn the base of an open balustrade. There is a further octagonal stage with single corner columns, and a tall spire in the form of an obelisk. The composition of the steeple is exceptionally sophisticated and in its upper portions has a delightful, light, open-work character. In its own terms it is a noble successor to the medieval lantern tower of St Nicholas's Cathedral (see p.24).

Entrance into the building is via imposing stone steps, through the portico and into a lobby, or vestibule, beneath the tower. This lobby forms a circular domed space, flanked by what were originally a chapel and vestry, with the doors into the 'nave' straight ahead. On entering the nave, the axis changes unexpectedly, with the altar located in the shallow apse to the east (right) rather than straight ahead. The typically Georgian demands of symmetry and proportion mean that there is also a matching projection on the west side of the nave. Similarly, the overall length of the building (less the portico) is one and a half times its width (excluding the projections), while the chapel, vestibule and vestry are all equal in width, which is the same as the diameter of the lateral projections (apses) of the nave. Throughout the interior, the woodwork, including the columns, is of very finely finished mahogany. Many wealthy local benefactors contributed to both the construction and the furnishing of the church, which was built at the unusually high cost of £27,000.

All Saints' is one of Newcastle's most important buildings, not only for the quality of its workmanship in both wood and stone, but also for its location and very fine design. Neglected for many years, and, hard though it is to believe, seriously threatened with demolition in the 1960s, it was deconsecrated. In the early 1980s, however, it was well restored by architects Pearce, Howe & Murray to form offices and an auditorium for an educational charity. In 2001 it was re-consecrated as a church for the use of a breakaway Anglican group.

Left All Saints' Church, the Quayside, Newcastle upon Tyne, by David Stephenson, 1786-96: from the south.

Above All Saints' Church, the Quayside, Newcastle upon Tyne: view of the interior showing gallery.

ST BARTHOLOMEW'S CHURCH
STATION ROAD, LONGBENTON, NEWCASTLE, NE12 8AN

Left St Bartholomew's Church, Station Road, Longbenton, Newcastle upon Tyne, substantially rebuilt by William Newton in 1790-91: from the south.

Right Former Stables (Coxlodge Hall), the Drive, Gosforth, Newcastle upon Tyne, 1796 (detail): from the south.

Sitting within its large churchyard and with its rather horizontal, slightly squat proportions and comparatively plain stonework, St Bartholomew's could easily be taken for a typical Northumbrian medieval church – and indeed so it once was, until the dilapidated ancient structure was taken down and the church rebuilt, at least in part, by William Newton (1790-91). It is interesting to note that there was again a connection with the local landowner Thomas Charles Bigge, who was a member of the parish committee which contracted with Newton (see p.52).

Of Newton's work, however, only the north wall of the present nave and the attractive battlemented tower, with its stumpy spire and endearingly simplified pinnacles, survive. The tower contained a staircase leading to a western gallery, now removed (it does not seem that there were ever nave galleries). The Georgian 'Gothick' style of the tower is not only unusual for this area, but also offers a clue as to the approach Newton might have adopted in restoring and repairing the medieval All Saints' Church, on the quayside (see p.66), had he been granted his wish to do this a few years before.

Newton rebuilt the nave of the church illustrated here to a slightly larger size than the original, creating a rather plain, aisleless 'preaching-box' with three round-headed sash windows on the south side, probably matched by similar apertures on the north. Repairs to its walls had to be made as early as 1842, as a result of cracks caused by mining subsidence.

Meanwhile, the original chancel had been retained for reasons of economy, against parishioners' wishes; later, its floor was belatedly raised to match that of the new nave in 1838. To judge from a late eighteenth century print and a sketch by local artist G.B. Richardson of c.1840, both showing Newton's reconstruction, this was a rugged old structure with a large 'Palladian' window at the west end – probably inserted by Newton – but because of dilapidation it was rebuilt in 1855 to create the present chancel (architect or contractor unknown). This, in a plain but locally appropriate lancet style, was paid for by Balliol College, Oxford, owners of the church and lands in the parish since 1340.

St Bartholomew's became more essentially Victorian in character when in 1874 R.J. Johnson added a five-bay south aisle with a contiguous organ chamber (overlapping a third of the length of the chancel), all in a restrained and again appropriate Perpendicular style. Johnson may also have been responsible for the similarly styled windows in the north wall of the nave, and the west wall of the tower. The attractive little south porch that accords so well with the earlier fabric dates from 1885 while the choir vestry of 1888 is by W.S. Hicks. In complete contrast to the rest of the architecture, an octagonal church hall (designed by A. White) is an uncompromisingly modern addition of 1980, attached on the north side of the nave.

The church's overall internal effect is serene and surprisingly spacious, the arcade having chamfered arches springing from octagonal capitals, and with a large, matching Gothic arch leading into the chancel. Inside, too, are numerous interesting monuments, some dating back to the sixteenth century, and tablets. The font is Victorian (1857), as is the stained glass in the south window of the organ chamber, representing the Baptism of Christ, the Crucifixion and the Last Supper. The glass is attributed to Hardman of Birmingham (1855) and once formed the west window of the rebuilt chancel. Its transfer was undertaken in 1902 by architect W. Ellison Fenwicke, who at the same time installed the elaborate carved oak reredos.

FORMER STABLES AND LODGE

THE DRIVE, GOSFORTH, NEWCASTLE, NE3 4AH

A street name (The Drive) commemorates the existence of Coxlodge Hall, a large mansion which was demolished in 1939. The street was originally the driveway to the Hall. A few buildings survive from the estate, namely a small lodge on the Great North Road, the remains of the walled garden now forming part of the boundaries to twentieth-century housing, and the fine original stable block of 1796, the date of construction of the Hall itself. This former stable block, now used as offices, is built of local sandstone in a classical style, with nine bays and a pedimented centre surmounted by a clock tower.

The lodge is similar in style but may be slightly later than the stable block. It is a simple single-storey building, constructed out of ashlar, with curved bays containing segmental windows to the south, flanking the entrance door. It was extended in the 1960s with a severe, flat-roofed, modernist pavilion, typical of its period and designed by Harry Wood, a lecturer at the Newcastle University School of Architecture at the time. This structure, however, has recently been replaced as part of a complete renovation of the lodge in contemporary style.

Coxlodge Hall itself was built by Job Bulman, a medical doctor originally from Gateshead who had made a fortune in colonial India and whose name was originally given to this part of present-day Gosforth ('Bulman Village'). The architect of Coxlodge Hall is unknown. The Hall passed out of the family in 1832, before being severely damaged by fire in 1877. It was then rebuilt in Victorian classical style and by the 1930s had become a private school.

ST NICHOLAS'S CHURCH

CHURCH ROAD, GOSFORTH, NEWCASTLE, NE3 1XR

There had been a church on this site, serving the Gosforth parish, since medieval or even Saxon times. However, because of the needs of a greatly increased congregation, the old and probably dilapidated building was removed and a new church built in 1799, to a design by the local builder-architect John Dodds. Job Bulman of Coxlodge Hall (see p.69) was one of its patrons. St Nicholas's is one of the few new churches in Newcastle to date from the second half of the eighteenth century, the others being St Ann's on City Road, St Bartholomew's, Longbenton, and the very much grander All Saints', all discussed earlier. All except St Bartholomew's are in the classical style.

In its original form, St Nicholas's shared with St Ann's a straightforward plan, featuring a west tower with a stone spire, rectangular nave with a projecting apse, and a west gallery. However, although St Nicholas's had a much deeper apse, overall both its form and design are simpler and plainer. The building is of sandstone ashlar, with recessed, round-headed windows.

Since 1800 the church has undergone many alterations. Fortunately, these have been generally sympathetic. Between 1818 and 1820 John Dobson added galleried north and south aisles, supported on Tuscan columns with segmental arches, and a new south doorway, which was

blocked in later alteration work. Dobson also built a Tudor-style sexton's cottage (now demolished) in the churchyard. A porch was added on the south side of the church in 1833, while a north porch followed as part of restoration and other work done in 1884 (by R.J. Johnson). Stained glass features the work of Wailes, Kempe, Swaine Bourne & Son, and Evetts.

By the late nineteenth century the church had again become too small for its congregation and so, in 1913, it was extended eastwards and northwards by Hicks & Charlewood, using the same details as Dobson for columns and arches. At this time the galleries were removed. In 1959 a new vestry was added, partly as a war memorial, by F.W. Harvey, formerly Education Architect of Newcastle.

St Nicholas's remains an interesting and unusual parish church, its classical style, as with All Saints' and St Ann's, contrasting with the medieval Gothic survivals and numerous Gothic Revival structures found elsewhere in Newcastle and Gateshead. It is set in a large churchyard containing many interesting tombs and monuments.

Left St Nicholas's Church, Church Road, Gosforth, Newcastle upon Tyne, by John Dodds, 1799, with later work by John Dobson and Hicks & Charlewood: from the south.

Above St Nicholas's Church, Church Road, Gosforth, Newcastle upon Tyne: the interior looking east.

FENHAM BARRACKS

BARRACK ROAD, NEWCASTLE, NE2 4NP

James Johnson and John Sanders designed Fenham Barracks, built on land taken from the Town Moor, in 1803. This was during the Napoleonic Wars, when there was fear not only of invasion from abroad, but also of sedition at home. Johnson and Sanders were not local men, being Architects to the Barrack Department of the War Office in London (Sanders in fact had been a pupil in the capital of the celebrated architect Sir John Soane). It has also been suggested that their designs were supervised by no less a figure than James Wyatt, in his capacity as Architect to the Board of Ordnance. Certainly the Newcastle Barracks conformed to a standard national type.

They were completed in 1806 and originally formed an enormous complex, mostly demolished during the 1970s. Two Georgian blocks remain, although these differ in scale. The smaller is two storeys in height and seven bays wide, while the larger (see photograph above) is of three storeys, and twelve bays wide. Both blocks, built of English bond red brickwork on a plinth of coarse rubble, have a band course at sill height for articulation. These structures are functional and, naturally, military-looking, although not without charm.

The larger block has a plinth the height of the ground floor and at first-floor level has arched windows on the north and south facades, the first

and last within blind arches. This detail is repeated on the shorter east and west facades, with a doorway within the central arch. On the west facade the entrance is on the first floor, with a sandstone staircase for access. The smaller block repeats these details, although its arched windows are on the ground floor and the size of the plinth is reduced. It also has a fine doorway with engaged Tuscan columns supporting an open pediment. Above the door is a semi-circular fanlight.

Also noteworthy are the blocks originally used as an office, and as a guard-house, which were constructed as part of the defensive wall surrounding the barracks. Single-storey, with sandstone ashlar fronts, these structures stand like sentinels on either side of the entrance (see photograph above). They have imposing, windowless facades on to Barrack Road. Each has a gabled chimney-stack overhanging the pavement and a low-rise extension behind the defensive wall. Their rear elevations are constructed of brickwork, with windows that would have originally looked out on to a cobbled courtyard. This part of the former barracks complex is now used as a bar and restaurant.

Left Fenham Barracks, Barrack Road, Newcastle upon Tyne, by James Johnson and John Sanders, 1803-06: the larger block, from the north.

Above Fenham Barracks, Barrack Road, Newcastle upon Tyne: the Guard House and Office, from the south.

SUMMERHILL SQUARE, GREENFIELD PLACE AND ST ANNE'S CONVENT

NEWCASTLE, NE4 6EB

The area of Summerhill, behind Westgate Road, is a delightful pocket of tranquillity on the edge of the city centre. Here a secluded development of fine domestic architecture from the late Georgian period contrasts with the bustling Westgate Road, less than 50 yards away. The Irish Quaker Charles Bragg named the area Summerhill, after a Quaker development outside Dublin. In the very early nineteenth century he constructed a south-facing house where St Matthew's Church now stands (see p.176). Some of the original walls of this house can still be seen to the rear of the church.

To the east of Bragg's house more late Georgian houses were built, the first of which again dates back to the early nineteenth century. The development expanded to form what is now known as 'Summerhill Square', with other streets growing out from the square. The location was perfect for well-off families, who bought or leased the houses to be near the town, but not within its squalor. Fresh air was almost guaranteed as the south-westerly prevailing wind blew chimney smoke away to the northern and eastern suburbs.

The houses are all typical of their period, with walls built out of garden wall and English bond brickwork. They also have basements in sandstone ashlar, floor and sill banding, and stone lintels over the window openings. All the houses have attractive door cases that differ slightly in grandeur and detail. Also, the houses themselves vary in scale, being of either two or three storeys; the larger ones have decorative wrought-iron balconies (see photograph top left). Within the overall discipline of classicism, this diversity only adds to the charm of the development.

Internally, the rooms are generous and many of the houses have retained original features such as grand staircases, lit by elongated windows to the rear. By contrast, the square's enclosed garden is disappointing. It consists of little more than a lawn. However, its effect is somewhat improved by the stepped topography of the site and the high-quality, wrought-iron fencing that surrounds the garden.

On the south side of the square lies Summerhill Grove, where we find a slightly later building, namely St Anne's Convent (see opposite page, left), the first religious house to be established in Newcastle since the Reformation. The Sisters of Mercy came to Newcastle from Liverpool in 1855 at the invitation of William Hogarth, Bishop of Hexham and Newcastle.

Above Left Summerhill: Greenfield Place, Newcastle upon Tyne, early nineteenth-century: view of three-storey terraced housing showing balconies from the south.

Below Left Summerhill: Summerhill Terrace, Newcastle upon Tyne, early nineteenth-century: view of two-storey terraced housing from the west.

Right St Anne's Convent, Summerhill, Newcastle upon Tyne, originally a house designed by Ignatius Bonomi, c.1826, extended by Dunn and Hansom, c.1870: from the south west.

A convent was initially opened in Westgate Hill and the Sisters operated there until 1870, when they purchased a house called The Priory in Summerhill Grove. This house, originally built c.1826 by Cuthbert Rippon of Stanhope Castle to designs by the Durham architect Ignatius Bonomi, making a rare excursion north of the Tyne, was now converted into a convent by the Sisters. In 1878 the prominent local Catholic architects Dunn & Hansom added a second floor to the house and designed a modest chapel, which is in a conventional Early English Gothic style, its elevations pierced by simple lancet windows.

As completed, the convent consists of an L-shaped residential block with an attached chapel framing three sides of a small yard. The house is in the 'Tudor-Gothic' style, contrasting with the rest of the architecture in and around Summerhill Square, with delicate tracery in the ground floor windows and with dormers enlivening the roofscape. The main entrance is set beneath a stepped wall with a stone cross finial. The whole complex is built of sandstone with roofs of Welsh slate. In 1987 the Sisters, who also ran a school from the time of their first residence until 1983, moved to Nos 7 and 8 Summerhill Grove, next door, with the former convent being converted into sheltered housing. The Sisters still offer day facilities for the handicapped, the disabled and the elderly.

THE HOUSE OF RECOVERY

BATH LANE, NEWCASTLE, NE4 5SQ

The former House of Recovery was built in 1804, by an unknown architect, as a fever hospital, located on the edge of town. Its cost was £1,800, paid for by subscription, its purpose being to protect against epidemics. The building housed sufferers of cholera, typhoid and smallpox, all of which were rife in some parts of Newcastle at the time and, indeed, subsequently. It closed as a hospital in 1888, becoming a storage depository for nearby schools.

Although the building has character, it is of a somewhat morose kind, perhaps in keeping with its original purpose. Designed in a restrained, almost functional classical style and built of stone, it has three storeys and five bays, the middle three projecting slightly. The windows of the upper two floors are of simple, rectangular sash type with sandstone lintels. The openings on the ground floor are more distinctive, being located within blind arches. The building, which was restored in 1988 for the North of England Museums Service, is now somewhat hidden by the recent Citygate development.

Above The House of Recovery (the Fever Hospital), Bath Lane, Newcastle upon Tyne, 1804: from the south.

THE MOOT HALL

CASTLE GARTH, NEWCASTLE, NE1 1RQ

The Moot Hall is one of the most austere and imposing buildings in Newcastle. In an elevated position high above the quayside, it was designed in 1810 as the Northumberland County Court and Prisons by the father-and-son partnership of John and William Stokoe (although the drawings are signed by John alone). It derives its name from the old Moot Hall (see p.15) within the Castle Garth, which it replaced.

It is, for the most part, a correct and remarkably up-to-date exercise in the newly fashionable Greek Revival style, the severe, minimally decorated classical idiom that became popular from the end of the eighteenth century. It is the first example of its kind in Newcastle, although, perhaps influentially, the gentleman amateur architect Sir Charles Monck had used the same style most impressively for his home, Belsay Hall, about twelve miles to the north west, a few years before.

The Moot Hall is of two storeys with a basement on the front (north) side and in effect has three storeys on the south (this is because the ground slopes down, and the basement therefore increases in size towards the rear). The Moot Hall is built of high-quality sandstone ashlar, and has on the main (north) facade, eleven bays, one projecting at each end; the central three are protected by a grand portico. The windows, in plain reveals, are of fine proportions. The only decorative elements for the bulk of the facade are a string-course placed at the head of the lower windows and below the sills of the upper ones, together with a further string-course above the windows and in line with the bottom of the triglyphs of the portico. The whole elevation is surmounted by a bold cornice and parapet, completely hiding the shallow pitched roof.

The portico enlivens the whole elevation. Six steps lead up to four Greek Doric columns, correctly fluted and standing directly on the stone pavement without bases. Above the capitals are a lintel and a string-course, with triglyphs and metopes beneath a cornice and a triangular pediment. The central two columns of the portico are more widely spaced, evidently to improve access. This feature was considered a solecism by John Dobson and other later architects.

The Moot Hall was designed with a similar southern portico, this time having six columns, but the spaces between the columns were closed in during the mid-1870s by the architect William Crozier of Durham, with windows being inserted in the blank bays. Crozier also re-organised the interior, incorporating much rich Victorian decoration. Internally many features remain from both this re-organisation and from the building's original design, including the cells. In 1980 the Moot Hall was converted into a Crown Court and sensitively restored by the Napper Collerton Partnership (now Napper Architects). This work was carried out under the supervision of W. R. Foster.

THE VILLA REALE
OFF SANDYFORD ROAD, NEWCASTLE, NE2 1NP

Located just outside the city centre, this small mansion was designed by John Dobson in 1817. It is one of the few authentic 'villa'-type designs, by him, or any other architect, still surviving in the city, and is also one of his earliest. Designed, in the Greek Revival manner, for Captain John Dutton, it has a Doric portico probably showing the influence of at least two recent buildings in the area, Sir Charles Monck's Belsay Hall, Northumberland, and the Moot Hall in Newcastle itself, by John and William Stokoe (see opposite page). Dobson's earliest known work, the Royal Jubilee School in City Road, Newcastle (1810-11, now demolished), was also Grecian.

The austerity of the Villa Reale's design is overlaid by ideas of 'Picturesque' planning, as shown in the varied facades, suggestive of earlier villas by Sir John Soane and James Wyatt. This variation includes, for example, the combination of the porticoed entrance, with the semi-circular bay on the garden side. There is also still some suggestion of the original 'Picturesque' landscaping, possibly by Dobson himself, in what is left of the wooded grounds of 'Sandyford Park'. The Villa Reale later became a convent. It now forms part of the Chapman House development, a campus that contains the Junior Department of Newcastle High School for Girls, and within the school is known as 'Dobson House'.

Left The Moot Hall, the Castle Garth, Newcastle upon Tyne, by John and William Stokoe, 1810-12: from the west.

Above The Villa Reale, off Sandyford Road, Newcastle upon Tyne, by John Dobson, 1817: from the south west (the area of light-coloured wall indicates the position of a conservatory, added later and recently removed).
Photograph Anna Flowers.

JESMOND TOWERS (FORMERLY WEST JESMOND HOUSE)

JESMOND, NEWCASTLE, NE2 3QE

This house, overlooking Jesmond Dene, has a complex history of alteration and extension, for the most part sympathetic. Although much of what we now see is later, it reminds us that during the late Georgian period, after the 'Gothick' of the mid-eighteenth century, various versions of the Gothic or 'Tudor-Gothic' styles were becoming popular. These were seen as romantic alternatives, albeit occasional ones, to the prevailing orthodoxy of classicism, and Jesmond Towers remains a fine example of 'picturesque' Gothic, in the tradition of Vanbrugh, Robert Adam, Nash and Smirke.

The initial phase of construction of what was then West Jesmond House, in 1817, was by John Dobson for Sir Thomas Burdon. This was an important early commission for the architect, since Burdon was an influential Newcastle figure at the time. Dobson's work, now largely hidden by later construction, was in the 'Tudor-Gothic' style, reminiscent of work by Sir Robert Smirke, and by Dobson himself at Cheeseburn Grange, Northumberland (c.1813).

It appears from drawings prepared for a later remodelling by Thomas Oliver jnr. in 1869, for a new owner, the shipbuilder Charles Mitchell, that Dobson's early, three-storey north facade was essentially symmetrical, with octagonal corner turrets. It was also originally fronted by a grand terrace overlooking the Dene.

Much of Dobson's slightly later work of 1823-27, for Richard Burdon Sanderson, is still visible on the south front, the main section having a central tower with castellated gabled wings. The corner turrets and mouldings are more highly decorated than those of the first phase, and the windows now have tracery in a mixture of Gothic styles. The central section boasts a double-height oriel window.

Oliver added an extra storey to the north front, while the south front received another tower, with Dobson's single-storey linking block gaining another floor. Square and canted bay windows were also added, as well as a new wing. In 1884-85 Mitchell commissioned his now favoured architect, T.R. Spence (see p.190), to add a Gothic-style picture gallery as a further additional wing to the house (seen on the left in the photograph, left). This contained Mitchell's varied and substantial art collection, including both Old Masters and modern works (now dispersed). A surviving Gothic-style lodge, with banded stone, was also built, on the north side of the estate. Used by tradesmen, this gave access on to Jesmond Dene Road.

Oliver's remodelling, together with Spence's further enlargements (the latter executed by the prominent Newcastle building firm of Messrs. Walter Scott), created the rambling Gothic building we see today. Internally, there are Gothic details in the stone arched entrance hall, chimney-pieces and balustrading of the south staircase. Arts and Crafts and even proto-Art Nouveau features, including some fine stained glass designed by the architect, are present in the later portions added, or altered, by Spence and complement the earlier neo-Gothic work. For example, the top-lit former picture gallery has an ornately moulded frieze, stencilled decoration, and richly carved oak doors, by Ralph Hedley. Hedley, later to be employed by Mitchell and Spence at St George's Church, Jesmond (see p.190), was also responsible, with his assistants, for some exceptionally fine carving in the entrance hall, central staircase (now removed), and the former billiard room, library and picture gallery.

Following the death of Charles Mitchell's son and successor, incidentally a noted amateur artist (see p.191), the family sold the house in 1912 to the Daughters of Wisdom (Les Filles de la Sagesse), who founded a convent and then established La Sagesse School in the premises. During their tenure Spence's ornate picture gallery was used as the School Hall. In 2008 the closure of the school was announced, and the site sold. Since then the buildings have been empty, but work is now in progress to renovate them and develop the site for largely residential purposes.

Jesmond Towers (formerly West Jesmond House, later
La Sagesse School), Jesmond, Newcastle upon Tyne,
by John Dobson, 1817, with later work by others: from the south.

NOS 6, 7 AND 8, HIGHAM PLACE

NEWCASTLE, NE1 8AF

This short street, now truncated by modern development and almost hidden away between a nightclub and the Laing Art Gallery, is notable for three surviving town houses (Nos 6, 7 and 8), which date from c.1819-20. They were part of an attractive terrace which was built, as his first independent work, by the celebrated builder and entrepreneur Richard Grainger for Alderman William Batson, a prominent Methodist. Grainger, of course, went on to be responsible for major developments in the town (see Chapter Three). He may have designed, as well as built, this conventional terrace.

Solid and unpretentious, these houses by Grainger are constructed of dark brick with stone details. Three storeys high with an attic, they are typical of many houses surrounding the town centre at that time. A few of these remain, sometimes much altered, such as the slightly larger examples in nearby Ellison Place.

One of the three houses in Higham Place illustrated here, No. 6, was formerly the headquarters of the Northern Architectural Association, a society of architects founded in Newcastle in the middle of the nineteenth century by John Dobson and others. This organisation, still in existence as a small charity, was one of the forerunners of the Royal Institute of British Architects, which also occupied the premises for many years. The interiors of these houses are mostly much altered and display little original character.

Nos 6, 7 and 8 Higham Place, Newcastle upon Tyne, built by Richard Grainger, c.1819-20: from the south west.

BRUNSWICK METHODIST CHAPEL

BRUNSWICK PLACE, OFF NORTHUMBERLAND STREET, NEWCASTLE, NE1 7BJ

John Wesley, the founder of Methodism, made numerous visits to Newcastle and the North East, and some of his activities are noted on plaques in Northumberland Street (at the site of the 'Orphan House', his original chapel) and on the east quayside. Indeed, he said of Newcastle that there was "no other place in Great Britain comparable to it for pleasantness". The Brunswick Chapel dates from 1820-21 and, according to the historian Mackenzie, was designed by W. Sherwood, closely following the plan of a similar building by him in Hull. Sherwood, whose name is little documented, was almost certainly a builder rather than an architect, even though the Brunswick is the earliest, largest and most impressive of the many nineteenth-century Methodist chapels on Tyneside.

The chapel is hidden away behind Blackett Street and Northumberland Street and, with the right-hand bay of its impressive classical facade now masked by a much later utilitarian brick extension to Fenwicks department store, some of its original grandeur is lost. The facade is of brick, with five bays, the central three projecting, with a pediment above. Each bay has a round-headed opening at ground and first floor levels; in the centre is a simple columned porch and imposing entablature.

Internally, the chapel once housed a large congregation; it has a fine curved balcony supported on columns, all in plain but well-finished timber, and facing the pulpit and organ. However, this space is now lost, as during the early 1980s a floor was constructed at gallery level and a suite of offices inserted into the ground floor (the main area of which is now used for community purposes), leaving just part of the upper level as the chapel.

The Brunswick Methodist Chapel, Brunswick Place, off Northumberland Street, Newcastle upon Tyne, by W. Sherwood, 1820-21: from the east.

CHAPTER 3

LATE GEORGIAN, TO c.1840

The Ouseburn Viaduct, Byker, Newcastle upon Tyne, by John and Benjamin Green, 1837-39 (detail): from the south east.

INTRODUCTION

In the early nineteenth century, in the wake of rapid population growth and the Industrial Revolution, progress was being made all over the country on new streets, residential developments, churches, and public and institutional buildings. North East England – where enormous wealth accrued through the export of coal, with transport industries developing rapidly to facilitate this – contributed fully to this 'age of improvement'.

For example, the expansion of Gateshead during the 1830s and 40s can be charted via the laying out of good-quality terraced housing on Bensham Road and Walker Terrace (see p.123). This process was also marked by the construction of a number of villas and mansions on the edge of town (see p.146), especially along the Durham Road, where industrialists were buying up land. Terraced housing was also built along substantial portions of this road.

But the most important developments were once again in Newcastle itself. Initially, these expanded on the middle-class streets that had been built outside the eastern walls from the 1770s onwards, and followed the construction of New Bridge Street (1812). With the middle classes increasingly retreating to the suburbs – the truly wealthy moved to the surrounding villages, now more easily accessible via improved roads – the Pandon Dene Bridge (see p.84) was important in that it opened up new land conveniently placed for the town centre.

Thus, on the west side of the Dene, in Picton Place, were built fashionable villas, many now of stone. Some were designed by John Dobson (see p.46). On both sides of New Bridge Street, beyond the Dene, high-quality semi-detached and terraced houses were laid out, including the semi-detached Ridley Villas of c.1823, again probably by Dobson. In addition, the builder and entrepreneur Richard Grainger (1797-1861) had by now emerged on to the scene with his nearby Higham Place development (see p.80).

Notwithstanding this substantial building activity, Newcastle's expansion was still inhibited by its medieval street pattern and encircling walls, which also formed an obstacle to the physical movement of resources. Moreover, the scale and appearance of the overcrowded, dilapidated and insanitary buildings of the old town were incompatible with the idea of progress. By contrast, Grainger's major new streets were to be clean, wide, well paved and spacious, facilitating the movement of people and goods and symbolising both Newcastle's economic success and a new spirit of civic pride.

Meanwhile, within the old walls lay the thirteen acres of neglected ground comprising the 'Nuns' Field' (from the original Nunnery of St Bartholomew) and the historic manor of Anderson Place (see p.11), to which Grainger's first major developments were necessarily peripheral. Thus, in 1824 Blackett Street (now largely redeveloped) was laid out just to the north of this site, planned jointly by Dobson and his former pupil Thomas Oliver to replace a section of the old town wall (see p.85). It was followed by Eldon Square, on the northern side of Blackett Street (see pp.85 and 86) and, over to the west, Leazes Terrace, both of unprecedented monumentality. These developments by Grainger dramatically enhanced the classical tradition of Newcastle street architecture, while the now-demolished Royal Arcade, a commercial building by Dobson of 1831-32 at the junction of Pilgrim Street and Mosley Street, reinforced the air of fashionable elegance that the entrepreneur was bringing to the town.

However, Grainger was soon to go further in laying out a whole new commercial and residential city centre in the area of the Nuns' Field and Anderson Place. The acquisition of this largely vacant site, in July 1834, the demolition of Anderson Place itself and the purchase and removal of adjoining property to the south, enabled the area to be developed as an architecturally coherent entity. Splendid classical streets soon took shape, with the development largely complete within about six years. Grainger had already presented to the Council a scheme involving a major new street (now Grey Street) running from Dean Street to the eastern end of Blackett Street. Four lateral streets linked eastwards with Pilgrim Street and westwards to what is now upper Grainger Street, the last-named being one of a quadrilateral of streets containing a new market (see below). The most northerly of these was to become Clayton Street, connecting with Grainger's earlier Eldon Square development.

Left The Bridge over Pandon Dene, Newcastle upon Tyne (built 1812, demolished 1865). An engraving of 1821.

Right Thomas Oliver's *Plan of Newcastle upon Tyne and Gateshead,* 1830 (reduced version).

This was essentially the scheme as carried out (see p.85). Not everyone approved, particularly those who lamented the destruction of many picturesque old buildings. Thus, for example, the topographer Stephen Oliver wrote in 1835 that "at the present time, building and improving appear to be all the rage in Newcastle, and if certain speculative architects had their way there would not be one stone of the old town left above another, but all would be rebuilt from cellar to garret according to the said projectors' standard of invariable modern taste." Even so, as a result of the implementation of the above redevelopment scheme, Newcastle became "the best designed Victorian town in England and indeed the best designed large city in England altogether" (Nikolaus Pevsner, *The Buildings of England: Northumberland*, 1957).

Who, then, were the men who planned, designed and contracted these new developments? Grainger himself played the pivotal, entrepreneurial role, and planned the arrangement of most of the new streets. The son of a quayside porter, he had set up as a builder in 1816 and before long was purchasing and developing property. He achieved success largely through his own efforts, although he was greatly helped financially by an advantageous marriage to the daughter of a prosperous leather-merchant. He also had the consistent backing of John Clayton, the influential Town Clerk of Newcastle. Later in his career, after narrowly avoiding bankruptcy thanks to Clayton's intervention, Grainger undertook an ambitious redevelopment of the west end of Newcastle, centring on his own residence, Elswick Hall (see p.47), but this scheme was not altogether successful and was never brought to completion.

Grainger himself was often accorded the title of 'architect' in his own lifetime and subsequently, and no doubt reserved the right to approve designs. However, he was too astute not to know his own limitations and for the central redevelopment he carefully divided the architectural work between several different, but all highly capable, local practitioners, namely Dobson, John Green and his son Benjamin, John Wardle and George Walker (the last two being Grainger's own salaried architects). This procedure no doubt reflected his desire for overall control. Meanwhile, Grainger was also fully supported by two other capable, trustworthy and highly respected professionals: Thomas Bryson, at the time Town Surveyor for Newcastle, acted as his foreman and clerk of works, while Thomas Brown, a prominent member of the House Carpenters' Company, superintended the building operations.

Grainger's new central layout contained not only the 'Grainger' Market, designed by Dobson, and the Theatre Royal, by the Greens (both buildings replacing earlier structures located elsewhere), but also the Central Exchange, designed by Wardle and Walker. These two architects were also responsible for most of Grey and upper Grainger Streets, with their intersections, the two further streets linking Grey and Pilgrim Streets, and the plainer but still dignified Clayton Street. The lower east side of Grey Street was the work of Dobson, while Grey's Monument, at the northern end of the street, was designed by John and Benjamin Green. All these developments are examined later in this chapter.

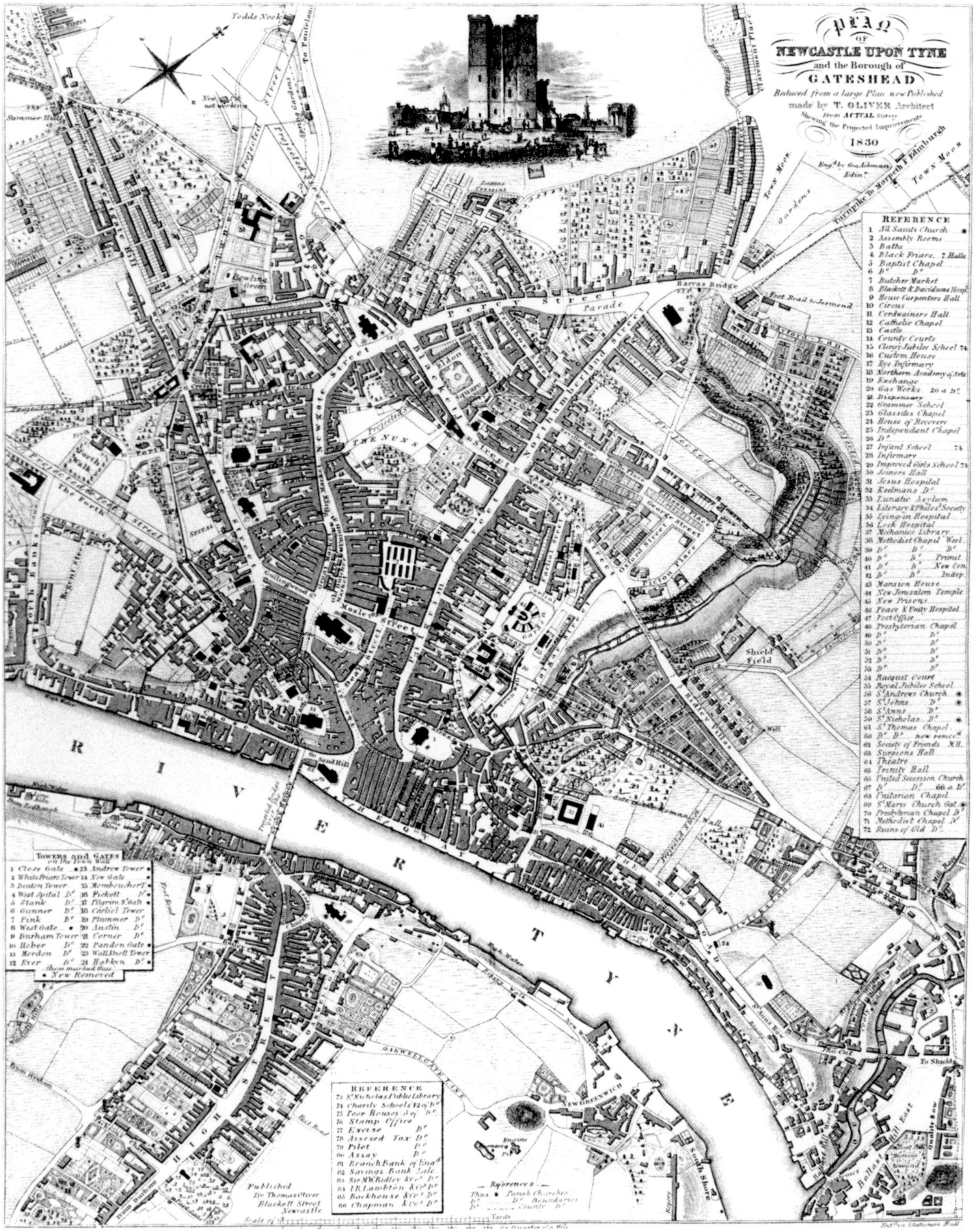
PLAN OF NEWCASTLE UPON TYNE and the Borough of GATESHEAD
Reduced from a large Plan now Published made by T. OLIVER Architect
From ACTUAL Survey
Shewing the Projected Improvements
1830
REFERENCE
TOWERS and GATES on the Town Wall
RIVER TYNE
Percy Street
Barras Bridge
Shield Field
Todds Nook
Summer Hill
Published By Thomas Oliver Blackett Street Newcastle

Left Eldon Square, Newcastle upon Tyne, by John Dobson, 1825-31, largely demolished; engraving of the square as originally designed, produced for E. Mackenzie's *A Descriptive and Historical Account of the Town and County of Newcastle upon Tyne* (1827).

Right *Plan of the Towns of Newcastle upon Tyne and Gateshead, Shewing their Recent and Proposed Improvements*, by John Wardle and George Walker, 1844 (© the Literary and Philosophical Society of Newcastle upon Tyne).

Of the architects employed by Grainger during the progress of the central redevelopment, and at other times, John Dobson was by far the most eminent. From his base in Newcastle Dobson produced over 400 works of virtually every building type. Many of his urban buildings have unfortunately been demolished, but more of his numerous villas and country houses in the region survive. Highly regarded as a neo-classicist, Dobson was also a competent exponent of the adaptable 'Tudor-Gothic' style. In the ecclesiastical field he pioneered the Gothic Revival in Newcastle and elsewhere in the North East.

Born near North Shields, Dobson was the son of a prosperous market gardener and occasional landscape designer. After an apprenticeship (c.1804-09) with David Stephenson (see p.45), Dobson studied painting and architecture in London before returning to set up practice in the North East in 1810. Over the course of a career of more than 50 years, he achieved a remarkable level of professional integrity and competence, being noted not just for his technical and constructional expertise, but also for his unusual sensitivity in the siting of his buildings. Ultimately his practice became very substantial, with clerks, draughtsmen and several pupils.

Despite Dobson's very large output, many of his schemes and designs remained unbuilt (or were executed in considerably altered form). Thus, for example, a plan he himself evolved for the redevelopment of central Newcastle (c.1824), based on the construction of a classical square and 'civic palace' on the Anderson Place site, was eventually superseded by Grainger's more commercial scheme. To this Dobson contributed but, as we have seen, by no means exclusively.

Of the other architects to have been employed by Grainger during his career, Thomas Oliver (1791-1857) was perhaps the most important, even though after the substantial commission for Leazes Terrace (see p.99), he did little or no further work for the developer. Indeed, the number of other buildings which can be ascribed to Oliver generally is small, although 'Gibson Town', a development of artisans' houses between New Bridge Street and the City Road, Newcastle (1836-48, largely demolished), was a major work.

Oliver began independent practice in 1821, after which he was soon employed to undertake surveys for the Newcastle Corporation and also for the Liverpool and Manchester Railway Company. His first significant architectural work was a pair of fashionably stone-fronted houses on the west side of Northumberland Street, Newcastle, dating from 1824 and now demolished. Nowadays, Oliver is best known not only as the architect of Leazes Terrace but also for his superb engraved maps of Newcastle, of 1830, 1844, 1849, 1851, and (issued posthumously) 1858. One of his sons, Thomas jnr. (1824-1902), became a noted later Victorian architect in the North East (see Chapters Four and Five).

An architect who for a time threatened rivalry to both Dobson and Oliver was John Green (1787-1852). He began as a carpenter and builder in Corbridge, Northumberland, and did not set up in Newcastle (as architect and civil engineer) until 1820. From about 1837 until his death he was in partnership with his son Benjamin (1813-58), a pupil of no less a figure than A.C. Pugin (father of A.W.N. Pugin) and an expert in Gothic design. In addition to their work for Grainger, the Greens produced a rejected design for a high-level bridge at Newcastle in 1839, based on the

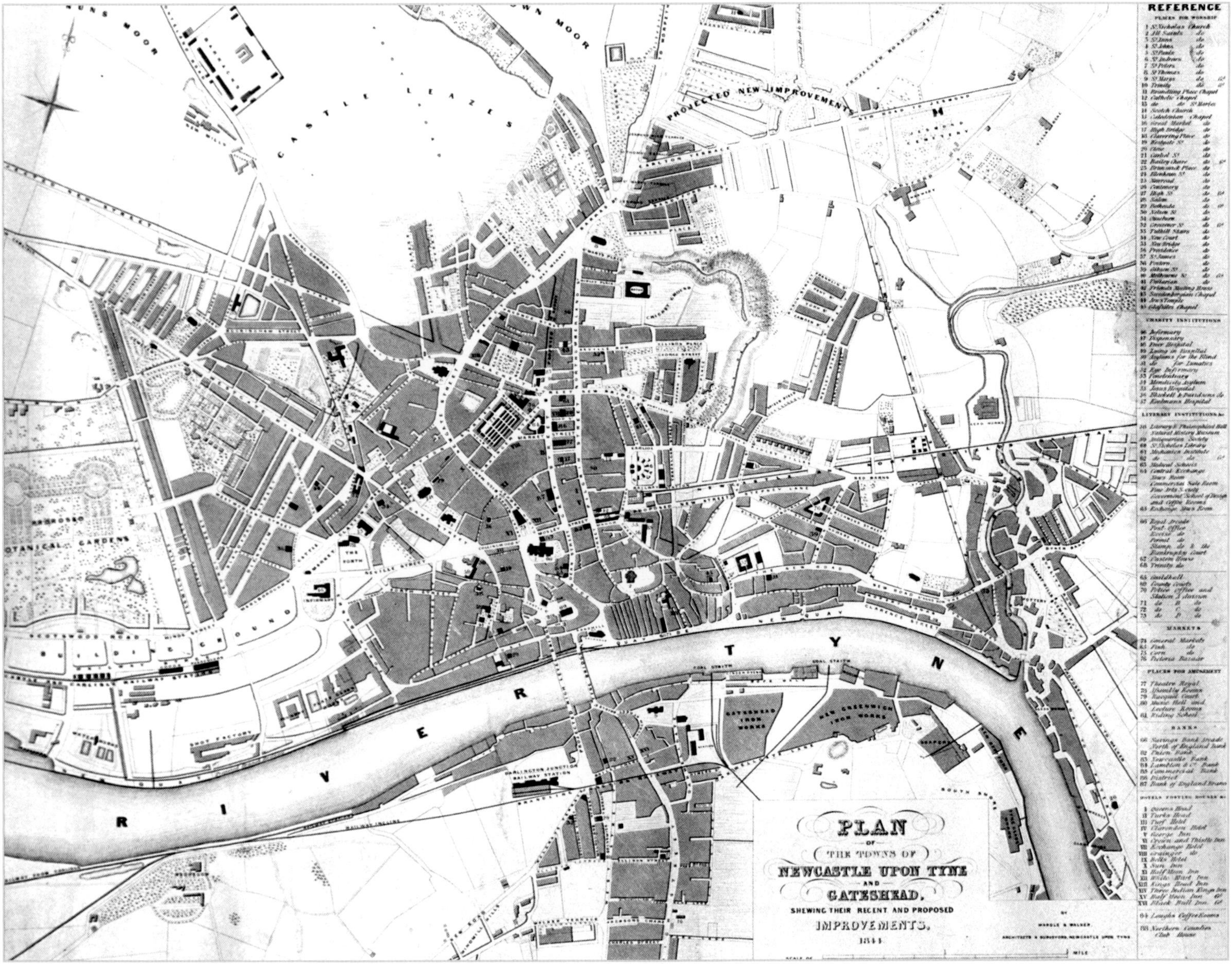

same laminated timber principle as their pioneering Ouseburn Viaduct (see p.120), as well as many small and conventional neo-Gothic churches. They also designed numerous attractive 'Tudor-Gothic' stations for the Newcastle and North Shields, and Newcastle and Berwick, Railways (from 1835 and 1846 respectively).

Of John Wardle (c.1795-1860) and George Walker (fl.1834-63, d.1886), Grainger's principal architects for the central redevelopment of Newcastle, between about 1834 and 1841, comparatively little is known. This is especially true of their early careers, although it is recorded that Walker had been a pupil of John Green. After their period of work for Grainger, they set up in partnership, but this never really took off and by 1851 they were working independently. In view of their obvious ability, it is curious that neither man produced much in the way of major later work.

What is certain, however, is that the immense contribution of Grainger and the talented architects he employed in creating what became known as 'the city of palaces' made this a truly memorable period in Newcastle's architectural history. The distinctive style of architecture that they produced gave rise to the popular description 'Tyneside Classical'.

THE LITERARY AND PHILOSOPHICAL SOCIETY

WESTGATE ROAD, NEWCASTLE, NE1 1SE

Above The Literary and Philosophical Society, Westgate Road, Newcastle upon Tyne, by John Green, 1822-25: from the north.

Right The Literary and Philosophical Society, Westgate Road, Newcastle upon Tyne: interior of library, by F.W. Rich, 1893-94.

Newcastle's Literary and Philosophical Society was founded in 1793. It was an early example of a society created to improve knowledge via discussion, lectures, demonstrations and the availability of a library for its members. In its earlier years it particularly encouraged scientific research and debate. Such inventions as the Davy miner's safety lamp (1815) and Swan's electric light bulb (1879) were demonstrated before its members.

The Society moved premises several times until, in 1821-22, it acquired the grounds of Westmorland Place, a former home of the Earls of Westmorland, located between Westgate Street (now Road) and the recently constructed Collingwood Street. It resolved to erect a building with "a stone front, and a handsome entrance and staircase at the end fronting the street", all "at a cost not to exceed £4,000".

An architectural competition was immediately organised. This was won by John Green, although the design as executed, replacing a seventeenth-century house formerly on the site, seems to have been based on a combination of elements from several alternative schemes put forward by him. It is almost certain that John Dobson also offered a proposal, now lost, which was probably rejected on grounds of expense. Ironically, the building as erected cost over £13,000.

The Society's new premises opened in 1825 and initially included meeting rooms, a library of 8,000 volumes, a librarian's room, a lecture room, and also the Museum of Natural History. This arrangement persisted until the museum moved to its new-built home, the Hancock Museum, now the Great North Museum (see p.184), in 1884. A contemporary view was that "a worthy shrine has been erected in which to deposit the works of the ancient sage and the modern genius" (W. Collard & M. Ross).

The 'Lit & Phil' building was originally free-standing. It has an elegant facade of sandstone ashlar largely in the Greek style, although with some residual Palladian elements, three storeys high and three bays wide, under a moulded cornice and pediment. The ground floor is rusticated and has a central, recessed doorway, flanked by Greek Doric columns, with a window on either side. The two upper floors are articulated by four plain Doric pilasters, supporting an

entablature and pediment. The sash windows of the main storey are tall, with moulded surrounds and cornices, the central cornice being supported on brackets. The second-floor windows are much smaller, and are square, with projecting sills.

Internal modifications to the building were soon required. The lecture room was enlarged in 1836, before being completely remodelled by Dobson in 1859-60 at the expense of Sir William (later Lord) Armstrong. Dobson's work was removed during a reconstruction in 1966. A new library wing – now obscured by the adjacent, early twentieth-century office building known as Bolbec Hall – was added in 1885-89 to the designs of A.B. Gibson. This, as well as the installation of electric lighting, was again funded by Armstrong, one of the Society's most enthusiastic members and supporters.

On the night of the Society's centenary celebrations (7th February 1893), the building suffered a disastrous fire. Armstrong yet again generously opened his purse and now brought in his own architect, F.W. Rich, who designed the magnificent new interior, with its ornate staircase and fine library. With its glazed, iron domes, and spiral staircases leading to a gallery with fine wrought-iron balconies, the library is especially memorable. Particular attention was now paid to fire-proofing, with the insertion of reinforced concrete floors. The building re-opened in October 1894.

JOHN DOBSON'S HOUSE

NEW BRIDGE STREET, NEWCASTLE, NE1 8AN

John Dobson's House, New Bridge Street, Newcastle upon Tyne, by John Dobson, 1823 (seen to the left in this photograph): from the south.

This house (seen on the left in the photograph above) dates from 1823. It is the only one remaining from a group of detached villas built after the new bridge over the Pandon Burn was constructed by John Stokoe in 1812, and located to the west of what is now the central motorway (east). The bridge itself lay just outside the town wall and opened up new land for suburban development.

It is difficult nowadays to appreciate the quality of this house, which is currently – at least for the moment (see below) – in use as a nightclub, amongst its later, twentieth-century extensions and with its plain ashlar now insensitively painted over. However, its original, block-like form is still clearly visible, illustrating the understated simplicity of Dobson's neo-classical style. The severity of the street facade, which is the least altered element, is enhanced by the placing of the original entrance to the side.

The house is of three bays and has three storeys and a basement. The ground floor on the surviving street elevation has tall windows, each surmounted with a flat pediment supported on consoles; above these are square windows beneath a deep cornice, with the top floor above. This cornice is supported by shallow pilasters at the corners (the right-hand one partly obliterated by an extension) and sits above a fine honeysuckle frieze. Dobson himself modelled the pattern for this in clay. The square windows of the top floor are completely plain, with the roof hidden behind a parapet.

Internally, very little of Dobson's work survives. A long garden behind the house, which once contained the architect's substantial collection of architectural fragments and antiquities, has also disappeared.

At the time of writing there are plans, endorsed by English Heritage, to demolish the adjoining nightclub (built in 1921 and for many years known as the Oxford Galleries) apart from its classical-style portico. Under these proposals, three tower blocks of seven, nine and eleven storeys, containing accommodation for students, will take the nightclub's place. The Grade II listed former John Dobson's house will be redeveloped as a stand-alone villa, probably serving as a restaurant and café-bar; it is also proposed to restore its original ashlar stone finish and remove a current twentieth-century extension.

HOUSES ON SHERIFF HILL

GATESHEAD, NE9 5SJ

The name 'Sheriff Hill' is derived from the meetings of Newcastle sheriffs with judges from Durham, who came north to hold assizes from as early as the thirteenth century. At that time the area was little more than moorland. Later it became wealthy due to its rich coal seams, mines being opened towards the end of the eighteenth century. The enclosure of Gateshead Fell in 1822 led to a further increase in population around Sheriff Hill and to the construction of a number of good early nineteenth-century classical houses. At one time all the houses in this vicinity would have enjoyed fine views of the Tyne valley.

Home House (see right, top) is sited on Kells Lane. It is symmetrical (apart from a later dormer window) and constructed out of sandstone, with coarse rubble masonry to the sides and rear, and high-quality ashlar at the front. The roof is of Welsh slate, with chimney-stacks at either end of the ridge. There is a moulded eaves cornice. Five stone steps lead to the entrance; above the door is an attractive oblong fanlight.

Thornlea (see right, lower) is situated off Church Road, in the shadow of St John's Church (see p.92). It was originally the service wing of Sheriff Hill Hall, a substantial villa built in 1823-24 by John Dobson for the businessman and industrialist Matthew Plummer. This was a typical example of the many villas and small mansions constructed on the fringes of Newcastle and Gateshead in the early nineteenth century for the 'nouveaux riches', by Dobson and other architects, usually, like Sheriff Hill Hall, in a rather severe neo-classical style. Most of these houses have disappeared. Sheriff Hill Hall itself was largely demolished c.1967, after being occupied for some years by Gateshead High School.

Typically for its architect, Thornlea is constructed of sandstone ashlar; it has a hipped roof of Welsh slate with two central chimney-stacks, also in ashlar. There is a gabled extension at the east end, built of random rubble, and presumably later.

Above Right Home House, Sheriff Hill, Gateshead, c.1822: from the west.

Below Right Thornlea, Sheriff Hill, Gateshead, by John Dobson, 1823-24: from the west.

ST JOHN THE EVANGELIST'S CHURCH

CHURCH ROAD, LOW FELL, GATESHEAD, NE9 5RB

The Church of St John the Evangelist dates from 1824-25 and was designed in the neo-Gothic style by John Ions (c.1785-1826), a builder-architect of Gateshead. He died young and this is his only significant building. It is said that Ions received some assistance in his design from Ignatius Bonomi (1787-1870), a contemporary of John Dobson and the leading architect in County Durham at that time (see p.75). There is evidence that John Stokoe may have also been involved in the design.

St John's was built for what was then an expanding community, many of the surrounding houses being of a similar date. The church is beautifully sited, originally in a semi-rural position, with its tall, slender spire – said to have been suggested as a landmark feature by the eminent local clergyman and historian John Hodgson of Heworth – rising from a crenellated tower. Overall, however, it is an essentially functional building, without transepts and conceived as a Gothic 'preaching-box'. Contrasting with the lofty spire is the low, wide nave, supported by buttresses. Each bay of the nave has a window with rudimentary tracery; elsewhere, decoration is limited to the hood mouldings over each window. The church's entrance is to the south, overlooking the large graveyard, which contains a number of interesting tombs and monuments.

The interior of the church is spacious and of impressive quality. Much of it is original, with the exception of work carried out during a recent refurbishment in order to provide additional administrative rooms. A first-floor gallery survives and the woodwork, especially that of the altar, the gallery and the timber-panelled ceiling, is some of the finest of its period in the North East. St John's is in immaculate condition. Held in high regard by its congregation, it is a fine structure worthy of their respect.

THE FORMER LYING-IN HOSPITAL

NEW BRIDGE STREET, NEWCASTLE, NE1 8AL

Left St John the Evangelist's Church, Church Road, Low Fell, Gateshead, by John Ions, 1824-25: from the south.

Right The former Lying-In Hospital, New Bridge Street, Newcastle upon Tyne, by John Dobson, 1825: from the north.

Newcastle's former Lying-In Hospital was built in 1825-26 as a maternity hospital or 'asylum' for poor, married, pregnant women, superseding earlier premises in Rosemary Lane. At first, its rules of admission were strict. It could accommodate twelve patients only, and these had to have a letter of recommendation and a marriage certificate. The building is aligned at an angle to the street because it originally backed on to the then-existing town wall.

Designed by John Dobson, it was one of his first public works to be built in the 'Tudor-Gothic' style, a form the architect also favoured for some of his country house designs around this time. It is a rectangular structure, having ashlar masonry on the front elevation and coursed rubble to each side, and with a hipped roof. The front elevation has three bays, with the central bay recessed slightly and the rather unprepossessing entrance door dominated by a large oriel window above. The bays on either side have windows on the ground floor and large blank niches above, all with Tudor-style drip mouldings and Perpendicular and Decorated Gothic details to the openings.

Overall, the hospital is not one of Dobson's more impressive designs. It is uncharacteristically tentative in the arrangement of its elements, and its details are somewhat rudimentary throughout. However, it was built on a limited budget (it cost only £1,550, with Dobson also giving his professional services free) and at a time when, for public buildings, the neo-Gothic style was in its infancy. In addition, the building certainly appealed to people at the time, being described as "chaste, plain and substantial".

The former Lying-In Hospital closed in 1923. Later, it was used as the BBC regional headquarters for many years, and received several extensions during that time. In the early 1990s these were removed to reveal Dobson's original structure, when 'Portland House', a new office complex on the corner of New Bridge Street and John Dobson Street, was built around it. Some argue, perhaps rightly, that this more recent development is unsympathetic and dominating. However, Dobson's building was at least retained, something that probably would not have happened a decade or two earlier.

ELDON SQUARE
NEWCASTLE, NE1 7JB

Regrettably, the Georgian terrace that we see today is merely the eastern wing of what was originally a much larger, three-sided residential development. This was built (1825-31) on the north side of Richard Grainger's newly constructed Blackett Street. For its construction Grainger used for the first time what became his preferred building material: fine ashlar masonry. At the time, town houses in stone were rare in Newcastle; earlier Georgian developments, such as Charlotte Square, had been constructed largely out of brick, with stone used sparingly for details, if at all.

Eldon Square was the first and one of the finest of the Corporation's nineteenth-century ventures into large-scale town improvement with Grainger. It was the city's first really substantial, formal scheme and must have seemed remarkable to contemporary observers for its size, uniformity and quality of construction. Architecture of this status reflected the upgrading of Newcastle at this time into an even more major trading centre. Rich merchants and industrialists were now driving the economy forward and a new type of architecture was required to reflect and affirm this progress.

For the design of Eldon Square, Grainger initially called on Thomas Oliver, who conceived a square of spacious town houses with an attractive communal garden. However, John Dobson was then asked for his opinion and ultimately the square was built with his elevations. The architecture was characteristically grand and neo-classical, having shallow pilasters at the ends of the blocks for articulation and very tall windows at piano nobile level. The facades had a prominent horizontal accent in the form of a bold cornice beneath the attic storey.

The slightly longer northern range was planned to differ from the other blocks in having a central projection, with an Ionic portico as well. This was never built, although a feature whereby the last five bays at each end form 'pavilions', via the use of pilasters, was retained. Dormers were added to parts of this range around 1900. Surrounding all the houses, and the ornamental garden, were high-quality wrought-iron railings, with honeysuckle motifs resembling those of the cast-iron balconies on the house facades. Some of this original fencing still survives. Although the garden itself had largely disappeared by the early twentieth century, some compensation is provided by the presence in the centre of the square of a fine First World War memorial dating from 1923, with an equestrian statue of St George and the Dragon by Charles Hartwell on a pedestal designed by Cackett & Burns Dick.

During the 1960s, the Council decided to demolish Eldon Square. Its precinct was to be retained as an open space, but surrounded by a major new shopping complex, with a high-rise hotel (designed by the celebrated Danish architect Arne Jacobsen) on the western side. This scheme received the enthusiastic support of the then Council Leader, T. Dan Smith, who seems to have particularly disliked the square. When challenged by conservationists, Smith's supporters on the Council stated, ludicrously, that "it is only the buildings surrounding the square that will be removed".

In the event, this scheme for the redevelopment of Eldon Square was abandoned in 1971 in favour of one based on the present Eldon Square shopping centre, designed by architects Chapman Taylor & Partners in 1972 in conjunction with Wilfred Burns, then the city's Chief Planning Officer, and subsequently updated (see p.295). Ironically, even with its later modifications, this shopping centre still occupies only a small part of the area of the original square, which has been retained as an open space; nor at first did the structure even have a principal entrance from this space. Meanwhile, the survival by default of the square's eastern wing, isolated, and now dwarfed by acres of brown brickwork, only serves as a reminder of a crude and unnecessary loss.

However, recent alterations have to some extent succeeded in re-animating the square. These alterations include a formal re-ordering of the square's landscaping, the building of café and restaurant units on the north and west facades of the modern Eldon Square development, and the provision of a major new entrance to the complex.

Eldon Square, Newcastle upon Tyne, by John Dobson, 1825-31: the surviving eastern wing.

ST THOMAS THE MARTYR'S CHURCH

BARRAS BRIDGE, NEWCASTLE, NE1 7PF

Designed by John Dobson, St Thomas's is a church without a parish and is doubly unusual in being governed by a Body Corporate of Master and Wardens. Constructed in 1827-30 to serve the expanding population of Newcastle, it replaced a much smaller, medieval chapel, demolished to widen the entrance to the old Tyne Bridge, and was built on, or near, the site of yet another antiquity, also now demolished, St Mary Magdalene's Hospital. The church, funded partly by the Corporation (who required an Act of Parliament to build it) and partly by public subscription, was planned to seat 1,300 people at an estimated cost of £6,000.

Its original surroundings were attractively semi-rural, near the northern end of the Pandon Dene (hence the 'Barras Bridge', which crossed it), with high-quality suburban development beginning to be laid out just beyond. Indeed, as late as c.1900 substantial gardens lay to the east of the wooded precinct of the church, before the eastwards extension of St Mary's Place and the building of the present City Hall and Baths. Even now, St Thomas's retains something of its former park-like situation, despite the felling of some ancient trees in recent years.

Its design was selected from three alternative schemes placed before the Corporation in July 1827, two by Dobson and one by John Green. It is not known why Dobson was allowed to submit two designs, but his second one, which is lost, may well have been classical. The character of Green's design is unknown. Dobson produced a model of the successful scheme.

St Thomas's is one of Dobson's earliest ecclesiastical works, and was also the first neo-Gothic church in Newcastle. It is in a rather free Early English style. While far from authentic, the design has individuality and perhaps represents a slight advance on many of the rather similar 'Commissioners' Gothic' churches of the time and, overall, is a fine example of early nineteenth-century ecclesiastical architecture. Gothic in style but not in feeling, it exudes a Georgian lightness and elegance which, for some, contrasts favourably with certain more archaeologically 'correct' interpretations of Gothic later in the century, such as Dobson's own Jesmond Parish Church (see p.148).

Left St Thomas's Church, Barras Bridge, Newcastle upon Tyne, by John Dobson, 1827-30: from the south west. Photograph Bethany Jane Robertson.

Right St Thomas's Church, Barras Bridge, Newcastle upon Tyne: the interior looking east.

The main entrance to the church is at the west end, in line with the nave – a typically Georgian feature – beneath a tall tower with a balustraded Gothic parapet. The tower is also surmounted by pinnacles, as are the flying buttresses which support it and the other buttresses flanking the side aisles.

The interior of the church was planned simply, in a way that still reflected the Georgians' emphasis on the congregation's ease in following the service (it served an Evangelical congregation). It is rectangular, with merely a recess, rather than a traditional chancel, for the altar, and side aisles that are almost the same height as the nave. The slender columns dividing the aisles from the nave, and supporting the springing for the stone-ribbed vaults, are remarkably delicate, and represent an early use of iron construction.

However, the building's light and airy interior, possibly modelled on the hall-choir of London's Temple Church, was somewhat compromised by Dobson's own addition of galleries in 1837, even though they were allowed for from the start. After this, the church seated 1,673 worshippers. The stained glass of the east windows (by George Baguley) dates from 1881, at which time a new screen was inserted, along with new pulpit, lectern and reredos, all to the designs of J.W. Dyson.

There has also been some modern re-ordering. Indeed, at the time of writing, a further re-ordering is being planned "in order to benefit the wider community and to allow the congregation to grow in the future". Three options have been developed for public consultation, of which the most far-reaching are the second and third. Their main suggestions are for the creation of an additional entrance from the south side, and of new rooms below the galleries, for use when the main central area is occupied. The galleries themselves – to be linked by a glass bridge – would also become fully accessible, potentially accommodating exhibition and meeting spaces.

ST MARY'S PLACE

NEWCASTLE, NE1 7PQ

This range of housing on the south side of St Mary's Place, overlooking and complementing St Thomas's Church (see p.96), provides another example of John Dobson's 'Tudor-Gothic' work. Built around 1829-30, possibly for Richard Grainger, it consists of a terrace of houses with basements, steps up to the main floor, and two further floors above. The top floors have gables above the windows, breaking the roof-line, while string-courses emphasise each floor level. This symmetrical terrace was originally terminated at each end by a projecting wing. However, the western wing, at the Northumberland Street junction, has been largely replaced by a piece of late twentieth-century pastiche.

Even so, and despite many other alterations made especially to the ground floor to incorporate a variety of shops and offices, the terrace remains an elegant and restrained composition. The gables of the top floor are particularly successful in relieving an otherwise rather bland facade. Overall, St Mary's Place is a more successful essay in the 'Tudor-Gothic' idiom than Dobson's slightly earlier Lying-In Hospital (see p.93). It is also a rare example of a street frontage designed in any form of Gothic style.

St Mary's Place, Newcastle upon Tyne,
by John Dobson, c.1829-30: from the north east.

LEAZES TERRACE

NEWCASTLE, NE1 4LZ

Leazes Terrace, Newcastle upon Tyne, by Thomas Oliver, 1829-34: from the north west.

Leazes Terrace dates from 1829-34 and was designed for Richard Grainger by Thomas Oliver. With Eldon Square, it was the finest and most ambitious residential development yet built in Newcastle, comparable in quality to the best contemporary work in London, Edinburgh, or Glasgow. It is built of fine ashlar in what was then a rural setting on the edge of town; the east and north facades still look over Leazes Park (created from part of the Town Moor in 1873).

The overall effect is not unlike that of John Nash's grandiose villas and terraces in and around London's Regent's Park, also dating from the early nineteenth century. However, to the west, Leazes Terrace is now uncomfortably overshadowed by the concrete east stand of the St James's Park football ground (see pp.324-325).

Unlike the squares of London and Edinburgh, and nearby Eldon Square, Leazes Terrace turns outwards rather than inwards. It also forms a subtly inexact quadrilateral rather than a precise rectangle (there are 84 bays on the east side, 69 on the west, 21 on the south and 20 on the north). The inner court, now used for car parking, consisted originally of service yards, accessed through two segmental-arched carriage entrances on the main, east facade. Each house in the terrace was originally fronted by a flower garden or shrubbery, protected by iron railings.

The composition of this very large terrace, which has three main storeys above a semi-basement, exhibits great dignity and grandeur and, like many other 'Tyneside Classical' street frontages, is based on the 'palace front' system of design. Thus there are projecting bays at the centre and ends of the long (east and west) facades, with Corinthian pilasters at the centre, and at the corner bays. These elements also feature exquisitely moulded cornices and friezes. However, so long are these facades that their overall effect can be appreciated only at a distance, now possible from Leazes Park alone. No doubt there were pressures on the architect to make the development as large – and hence as potentially profitable – as possible.

The windows of the terrace are simple and well-proportioned. On the first floor these are protected by cast-iron balconies, sadly now missing on the east side overlooking Leazes Park. The north and south facades are particularly interesting for the way in which the detailing of the stonework and cornice 'steps up' through the projecting wings and central bay, counterbalancing the sloping ground.

For many years much of the terrace was utilised by Newcastle University as a student residence, the remainder being under-used and badly in need of repair. However, it has now been well restored and cleaned. Students still occupy the south side, with the rest of the building having been converted into private apartments. In these there is still some sense of former grandeur, particularly where the original staircases have been retained.

LEAZES CRESCENT

NEWCASTLE, NE1 4LN

In complete contrast to the grand Leazes Terrace is Leazes Crescent, an adjacent development to the north west of Percy Street laid out from 1829, again by Thomas Oliver for Richard Grainger. However, it is one of the entrepreneur's more unusual developments, because of the smallness of its scale and for its use of stucco in imitation of stone, rather than ashlar masonry. The Crescent contains what were described as "neat dwelling houses" (W. Collard & M. Ross) and demonstrates what Grainger could do on what was for him a rare excursion into artisans' or lower middle-class housing.

Because of the use of stucco, this two-storey terrace has a 'Regency' quality, resembling similar work of the period in, for example, London and Brighton. It features a deep cornice, below which is a delicate frieze (although this is now incomplete), and has bay windows at the terminations. Doorways are simple with round arches to most of the windows, and the whole composition ends in a fine curve to the road junction.

A little to the north and east of the Crescent lies the separate St Thomas's development, off Percy Street (see p.124). This was built of brick with stone dressings, probably from c.1840, and is much more typical of 'Tyneside Classical' architecture. During the 1960s both the St Thomas's development and Leazes Crescent itself were saved from demolition only by the vigorous action of local residents and conservationists.

Above Leazes Crescent, Newcastle upon Tyne, by Thomas Oliver, from 1829: from the north.

Right The Watergate Building, Sandhill, Newcastle upon Tyne, by John Dobson, 1830: from the south west.

THE WATERGATE BUILDING

SANDHILL, NEWCASTLE, NE1 3RG

On the quayside, between the Guildhall and the Swing Bridge, stands the Watergate Building, a commercial structure designed by John Dobson in 1830. It is now partly used as flats. The Swing Bridge occupies the position of Newcastle's earlier medieval and Georgian bridges, and the Watergate Building was erected on the site of the medieval chapel of St Thomas the Martyr, which stood near the bridge-head.

This chapel had been demolished, in 1827, to improve access and was replaced by St Thomas's, Barras Bridge, a neo-Gothic design at the north end of the city (see p.96). By contrast, the Watergate Building is in much the same classical style as the slightly later Grainger development in and around Grey Street, if somewhat plainer.

The Watergate is a tall building, in ashlar masonry, curved and later extended. The front on to Sandgate curves round to meet the present bridge. This facade has recessed horizontal joints within the ground-floor masonry, with shop fronts, now housing a bar, between doorways at each end. Above are two storeys beneath a cornice, with a further storey above. The projecting end bays have Tuscan pilasters, and a cornice above both ground and second floors; here the uppermost windows are pedimented. A truncated pyramidal slate roof surmounts each end bay.

The south facade has one-and-a-half floors below a cornice that joins that of the Sandgate side, with the floors and cornice above in line with those of the main facade. The asymmetrically arranged windows, which also vary in size, and the obvious changes in the stonework, show that the building has undergone a number of alterations and extensions not apparent from the north. The flats on the south side offer spectacular views over the river.

The Watergate Building is a good and quite rare example of late Georgian commercial architecture. It is comparatively utilitarian in character but, in a manner typical of its designer, makes good use of its site, in this case through the design of its attractively curving street facade.

BENWELL TOWERS (LATELY THE MITRE PUBLIC HOUSE)

BENWELL LANE, NEWCASTLE, NE15 6LX

Benwell Towers (formerly Tower) dates from 1830-31. John Dobson designed it in 'Tudor-Gothic' style for a colliery owner, Thomas Crawhall, probably incorporating the remains of an earlier house. It is a country house in scale and status, an important landmark from the era when Benwell was an independent, rural village.

The present building is perhaps the third or fourth on the site. The first was a tower-house constructed in the early thirteenth century. Of this, little is known, although it is said to have belonged to the priors of Tynemouth. The few surviving records suggest that it was of three storeys with an embattled parapet. In the sixteenth or seventeenth centuries a manorial wing was attached to this tower, while in the mid-eighteenth century the house was re-fenestrated, and further extended by means of a three-storey block. All this is evidenced from surviving sketches and plans from this period, as well as from a series of watercolour paintings by the prominent local artist J.W. Carmichael, done around 1830, just before the building was taken down.

By now Benwell Tower had become the seat of the Shaftos, a family of wealthy merchants and landowners keen to exploit Benwell's rich coal seams. Members of the family are buried within the grounds. Robert Shafto (d. 1780) was High Sheriff of Northumberland in 1754, when he evidently contemplated having the property rebuilt by the architect James Paine. The project was never carried out, but at about this time, or soon afterwards, a chapel that stood to the south of the property was removed, because it allegedly spoiled the view.

By the early nineteenth century the house had become ruinous, as a result of neglect by a later owner, the infamous adventurer Stoney Bowes (also the husband and tormentor of Mary Eleanor Bowes, the heiress of Gibside, County Durham). For its new owner, Thomas Crawhall, who demolished the building, Dobson offered several reconstruction schemes, all asymmetrical in plan and having a variety of irregular silhouettes. The house as constructed emerged as a simplified but still 'Picturesque' amalgam of these. It has a continuous crenellated parapet, central turret, and rectangular windows with chamfered mullions and square hood mouldings above. It is said to adopt much the same plan as the previous building, suggesting that old foundations were re-used.

Crawhall had little time to enjoy his new residence, dying in 1833. Benwell Tower was put up for sale but after a short interval was let, firstly to Joseph Anderson, a solicitor, and secondly (until 1880) to the glass manufacturer John Sowerby. By now the property had another owner, the banker John William Pease, who had acquired it in 1864 and shortly afterwards built on another part of its estate his new residence Pendower Hall (see p.156). In 1882 Pease gifted Benwell Tower, together with its gardens and seven acres of land, as the bishop's residence for the newly created diocese of Newcastle. Diocesan Architect R.J. Johnson added a richly decorated, Perpendicular-style chapel in 1887 (seen on the right in the photograph, left). Later, after service as a fire station during the Second World War, the mansion was converted into a public house and restaurant (The Mitre) before being used as the setting for the youth club at the centre of the popular television series *Byker Grove* (1989-2006). At the time of writing it is empty and its future uncertain.

Considering its varied history, the building's interior is remarkably intact, although some inappropriate alterations have been made. For example, what was a fine staircase is now masked by a stage set. Even so, most of the rooms are still spacious, with grand marble fireplaces, much oak panelling, and heavily ribbed ceilings with Tudor-style bosses.

Tradition has it that the celebrated landscape designer Lancelot 'Capability' Brown laid out the gardens of Benwell Tower during the eighteenth century. In fact, there is very little surviving physical evidence of Brown's possible involvement, although the building is still surrounded by the residue of an attractively wooded estate. However, Brown was almost certainly consulted about work done at Benwell during the 1730s. This was again for Robert Shafto, almost certainly the same man as mentioned above; he inherited the estate from his father, also called Robert, in 1735 and was soon making considerable improvements to both house and estate.

Moreover, nineteenth-century maps show to the east of the house a substantial park with clumps of trees in the style of Brown and – perhaps suggesting the later, more 'picturesque' involvement of Dobson – a wooded 'rookery' behind the mansion to the north and west, as well as a lawn in front. The sale particulars of 1833 refer to "the recent embellishments of the park and pleasure grounds". The lawn was separated from the park by a ha-ha, presumably an eighteenth-century feature and one which was frequently used by Brown.

Benwell Towers (lately The Mitre public house), Benwell Lane, Newcastle upon Tyne, by John Dobson, 1830-31; additions by R.J. Johnson, 1887: from the south east.

ST JAMES'S CHURCH

BENWELL LANE, NEWCASTLE, NE15 6RR

Left St James's Church, Benwell Lane, Newcastle upon Tyne, by John Dobson, 1831-32, later enlarged: from the north west.

Above The tomb of Richard Grainger (d.1861), St James's Church, Benwell Lane, Newcastle upon Tyne.

Right The Dispensary, Nelson Street, Gateshead, probably dating from the 1830s: from the north.

St James's, built in 1831-32 in a then-rural situation, was John Dobson's first neo-Norman church. However, his use of the style (then viewed as a useful, occasional alternative to the Gothic) was at this stage rather tentative. Indeed, the building was, with its undecorated arches, still essentially classical. Moreover, it was planned as a typically Georgian rectangular 'preaching-box' without aisles, transepts or chancel and with the main entrance leading into a square, centrally placed tower.

This arrangement was not unlike that of Dobson's earlier church of St Thomas's, Barras Bridge (see p.96), although, unlike St Thomas's, St James's has been very substantially altered over the years. At St James's there was also a small vestry on the north side of the tower, while inside the church there were originally galleries both at the west and in the nave, extending to the fourth bay. The ground floor was totally occupied by seating.

The nave is a generous space, although its interior is dark, as a result of the small size of the windows; in this respect, perhaps, it does recall original Norman architecture. The roof is supported on queen-post trusses with ornate tie beams. The arcades have a series of round-headed arches that spring from circular piers.

St James's was originally built as a chapel of ease, becoming a parish church in 1843. As the population of the area rapidly increased, so the church was significantly enlarged, for the most part in a similar neo-Norman style; the original chapel became the chancel of the re-built church. Hicks & Charlewood added the spire, clock, porch and baptistery in 1895 and, in 1903, the north aisle. The south aisle (now converted into a church hall) is earlier, dating from 1879-80.

The churchyard is large, having been substantially extended in 1900. It contains the graves of many eminent local figures. These include John Buddle, an innovating mining engineer who had donated land for the construction of the church, the industrialist William Cookson, Arthur Lloyd, third bishop of Newcastle (1903-07), and most importantly the entrepreneur Richard Grainger, referred to so frequently in this book.

Grainger lived for a time at nearby Elswick Hall (now demolished, see p.47). He died in 1861 and is buried in a T-shaped enclosure surrounded by Gothic-style railings. His decision to be buried at this church is testimony to the status that the village of Benwell once possessed. For many years Grainger's tomb (see above, right), a worthy resting-place for such an important Novocastrian, sat rather anonymously, surrounded by the results of vandalism. However, in 2011 it was splendidly restored to its original condition by Newcastle City Council to commemorate the 150th anniversary of Grainger's death. The project was winner of the restoration category at that year's Lord Mayor's Design Awards.

THE DISPENSARY

NELSON STREET, GATESHEAD, NE8 1NY

This building was originally designed as a substantial private house, probably in the 1830s, before being bought by Gateshead Corporation in 1855 to assist in preserving public health. It remained a dispensary until 1947 and was then used by the town's Housing Department until the recent reorganisation of social housing. It is now occupied by a travel company.

A fine example of late Georgian classical design, this is a noble survival in an area of much redevelopment. Of two storeys, it is constructed from light red brick, with stone dressings. The entrance is flanked by engaged, square, Tuscan columns, below an entablature. The roof is of Welsh slate, with paired stone brackets elegantly supporting deep eaves. The sash windows have stone wedge lintels and sit between brick pilasters with stone capitals. A pilaster at each corner provides an effective accent.

THE FORMER CUSTOMS HOUSE

QUAYSIDE, NEWCASTLE, NE1 3DE

Left The Customs House, the Quayside, Newcastle upon Tyne, refaced by Sydney Smirke, 1833: from the south east.

Right The former administration block of the General Hospital, Westgate Road, Newcastle upon Tyne, by W.H. Dunn, 1882: from the south east.

The Customs House was originally built in 1766 to cater for expanding traffic on the Tyne, moving from earlier premises near Sandhill. Although some internal features survive from the mid-Georgian period, the building's main interest now lies in the fact that it was attractively re-fronted in 1833 by the noted architect Sydney Smirke. He was the son-in-law of John Dobson and the younger brother of Sir Robert Smirke, designer of the British Museum (Sydney Smirke subsequently added the Museum's splendid domed Reading Room). The Newcastle Customs House is a fine example of minor official architecture of the period.

Smirke's new facade replaced, or re-faced, an earlier, plainer one of brick and is in a well-considered Renaissance style, reminiscent of sixteenth-century Italian palazzi. It has a symmetrical five-bay elevation on three floors. The ground floor is rusticated with round-arched windows and a shallow porch framing the entrance door (with royal arms above). The tall, well-proportioned windows on the first floor are framed by pilasters and are pedimented. Square windows to the top floor are surmounted by a cornice and solid balustrade. The interiors have mainly been modernised. The building now serves as barristers' chambers.

THE GENERAL HOSPITAL

WESTGATE ROAD, NEWCASTLE, NE4 6BE

Newcastle General Hospital grew out of the Newcastle Union Workhouse. As the city's population increased during the early Victorian period, so too did the number of people who were reliant on workhouse support. In 1834 the Poor Law was passed and several existing workhouses within the town centre were consolidated into a purpose-built institution, the Newcastle Union Workhouse. It was built outside the town, at the top of Westgate Hill. This site was chosen in order to limit the number of 'undesirables' within the central area, thereby reducing crime and disease; an alternative site in the Scotswood Road area offered for sale to the Board of Guardians by Richard Grainger in 1837 had been rejected. If a workhouse had been built here, it would have become part of Grainger's visionary Elswick development (see p.84).

As constructed, the workhouse's facilities included workshops, dormitories, a dining hall, an administration block and a lying-in ward. The early building history of this institution is unclear, but it is now thought likely that John Green jnr. (see p.145) designed it, or at least the majority of it, and the workhouse opened in 1839 or shortly thereafter.

Later, Newcastle's Board of Guardians extended the facilities of the workhouse to include an infirmary to treat sick people from the 'lower classes' generally. George Walker, better known for his earlier work for Richard Grainger, is recorded as having designed an infirmary, together with school buildings and yet more dormitories, in 1854, although exactly how much of this work was carried out is unclear. What is certain is that a substantial new 'Poor Law Infirmary' was built in 1868-70 to the designs of Septimus Oswald of Newcastle. This was in Gothic style and consisted of buildings around three sides of a quadrangle. It housed 200 patients, with male wards at the west and female at the east, and cost £14,000.

A new administration block by W.H. Dunn was added in 1882 (see photograph right) and a substantial extension to the infirmary opened in 1914; isolation wards had been added five years earlier by architects Newcombe & Newcombe. During the First World War the workhouse buildings and part of the infirmary were occupied by the military and used for treating soldiers who had venereal disease.

From c.1921 to 1931 the complex was known as the Wingrove Hospital. It was then incorporated into the City General Hospital, which opened in 1931, expanding its provision so as to accommodate over 800 beds. Many of the former workhouse buildings (which had been extended in 1897-98, and then reconstructed by Newcombe & Newcombe in 1902-03) were integrated into the new hospital, although some were demolished, including the old infirmary itself.

The surviving buildings from the original workhouse are mainly simple, utilitarian structures but W.H. Dunn's administration block is much more architecturally ambitious – a distinctive presence on Westgate Road. It is symmetrical and extremely long, with the central seven bays projecting. There are two main storeys and a basement. These have rather spare classical detailing, but the attic storey in the roof is more elaborate and eye-catching, with volutes framing the prominent dormer windows.

After the first edition of this book was published, the NHS decided to sell the site of the former General Hospital, and in 2010 accident and emergency services were relocated to the Royal Victoria Infirmary. Working with Newcastle University and the supermarket firm Tesco, the Newcastle NHS Foundation Trust has the aim of redeveloping the site to provide a 'Campus for Ageing and Vitality', alongside a large Tesco store. After considerable local opposition, revised plans for this scheme, overseen by Napper Architects, were approved in 2011. At the time of writing, although some of the buildings from the hospital are still in use, many are empty and not being maintained. None, however, has yet been demolished.

JESMOND (OLD) CEMETERY

JESMOND ROAD AND SANDYFORD ROAD, NEWCASTLE, NE2 1NL

Left Jesmond Cemetery, Newcastle upon Tyne, by John Dobson, 1834-36: the Jesmond Road entrance, from the north west.

Right Grey Street, Newcastle upon Tyne, from 1834: the west side, by John Wardle and George Walker, looking south.

The rapid expansion of the city in the early nineteenth century, coupled with the rising mortality rate through cholera, meant that an increase in cemetery provision was required. In 1834-36 John Dobson was employed by the Newcastle General Cemetery Company to design this cemetery, one of his finest surviving works.

The cemetery is triangular in layout and bounded by a high stone wall. The main entrance is on Jesmond Road (see photograph above). This is a highly imposing composition, featuring a powerful arch with square towers on either side, flanked by chapels. The style is essentially Greek Revival, although the arch is a Roman feature. The excellent ashlar stonework is given a horizontal emphasis by the use of recessed joints, and there is also fine ironwork with acanthus details.

The southern entrance, on Sandyford Road, features two massive, square gate piers, the upper parts of which evoke the shape of a sarcophagus. These structures exemplify Dobson's remarkable talent for creating powerful block-like forms, in this case almost as much Egyptian as Grecian in their monumentality. Each pier has an entrance for pedestrians running through it. Just inside the entrance is a simple neo-classical stone lodge with a pitched roof.

Both entrances to the cemetery have been compared to the work of Karl Friedrich Schinkel, the great German neo-classicist, and were much admired by the nineteenth-century architectural and horticultural writer J.C. Loudon, who considered them to be among the finest and most appropriate of their kind. Sir Albert Richardson, a noted authority on Georgian architecture, found “superlative merit” in their design, while to a modern critic they are “grandly original, severely noble and uncompromisingly stark” (J.S. Curl). Loudon, meanwhile, would also have approved of Dobson's informal layout and planting within the cemetery, with trees, shrubs and pathways. The cemetery also contains numerous excellent funerary monuments, including the Archibald Reed Monument, an elaborate Gothic shrine designed by Dobson himself in 1843.

Dobson’s initial scheme for the cemetery was even grander. This had its main orientation running east to west, with a colonnaded mausoleum in the centre and an obelisk at, or near, the eastern entrance. A central dome would have surmounted the main pair of chapels (to the west).

Despite neglect and numerous demolition threats to its chapels and gates over the years, Jesmond remains the North East’s finest cemetery. Appropriately, it contains the graves of several important local architects, including Dobson himself, William Stokoe, Thomas Oliver and John Green, although these are all unexpectedly modest. The chapels were converted into offices in 1978 and housed the Tyne and Wear Archaeology Unit for some time. They are now vacant.

GREY STREET

NEWCASTLE, NE1 6EE

Grey Street was the key part of Richard Grainger's redevelopment of central Newcastle, which was made possible by his purchase of Anderson Place in 1834. However, there is evidence that Grainger was making plans for the street as early as 1831. It was designed to attract what the developer himself called the "most opulent consumers", who now lived in the upper town. From the start it featured a series of prestigious shops, offices and showrooms, with housing above.

Initially, Grainger had intended to make Grey Street the principal north-south route through the town, planning to extend it northwards to Barras Bridge and the Great North Road. However, for reasons that remain unclear, this ambitious scheme was never carried out. Even so, the street as built still provided a new and important link between the upper and the lower town.

Grey Street was essentially a continuation northwards of Dean Street up to Blackett Street. Its construction was by no means straightforward. For example, it involved the removal of the comparatively modern Theatre Royal on Mosley Street, replaced by the current building in Grey Street itself (see p.114). In addition, the even more recent Butchers' Market north of Dean Street was replaced, again at the developer's expense, by the present Grainger Market (see p.112). Further design problems included the desire or need to follow the site of the Lort Burn, especially at the southern end; the necessity for deep cellars and much building up of the road (Grainger himself commented on the enormous effort he had expended in levelling the ground); the requirement to cut across the medieval High Bridge Street linking Pilgrim Street with the Bigg Market; and the fact that the new street had to rise through a significant slope to Blackett Street.

The response to these difficulties led to the construction of one of Europe's finest streets. The fact that it was built largely on the line of the Lort Burn, which was now filled in and culverted, led to the street's slightly curving layout; this was therefore both fortuitous and intentional, since Grainger is known to have desired a "picturesque effect".

This subtle layout is best appreciated by walking upwards from Dean Street on the west side, where the slope and the curve suggest something interesting just out of view. Rounding the curve, the grand portico of the Theatre Royal is suddenly revealed, followed by the dramatic vista created by Grey's Monument and the rounded corners of the Central Exchange Building, with its strongly modelled domes. Later insertions and alterations notwithstanding, Grey Street was considered by Nikolaus Pevsner to be "one of the best streets in England" and it was voted the finest street in the country in a national radio poll of 2002.

Its stately, four-storey, classical elevations, articulated at times by orders, are by John Wardle and George Walker, apart from those on the east side between Shakespeare Street and Mosley Street, which are by John Dobson, while the Theatre Royal is by John and Benjamin Green. Architecturally, the street is conceived as a series of long, symmetrical blocks of uniform height, stepping down the slope and given extra variety by the curving line of the street itself. These frontages have projecting accents centrally and at the ends. There are plain sections between the 'pavilions', while the 'pavilions' themselves are adorned with pilasters or attached columns on the first and second floors. At the junctions between streets are wings with pilasters, which are returned around the corners to give completeness and depth to the facades.

This way of grouping individual buildings to create a series of 'palace fronts' had been a popular means of generating civic presence since the work of John Wood the Elder in Bath during the early eighteenth century. Grainger was specifically inspired by the later Edinburgh New Town development, and even more by the recent 'Metropolitan Improvements' in London undertaken by John Nash between 1811 and 1827. There is, for example, a distinct resemblance between Grey Street and London's Regent Street, even in the latter's redeveloped form.

King C.I imprisoned on this site 1646-7 Poll

Left Grey Street, Newcastle upon Tyne: the west side, looking north west.

Right Grey Street, Newcastle upon Tyne: the Lloyds Bank Building, by John Wardle and George Walker, 1838-40: from the west.

Particularly notable within Grey Street is the section on the west side, from Mosley Street up to High Bridge Street, where some of the facades have giant Corinthian pilasters or columns rising through the main two floors with a heavily moulded cornice above. One such example is the former Bank of England branch office premises, the design of which, by Wardle and Walker, is said to have been approved by no less a figure than the Bank's own architect, Professor C.R. Cockerell.

Above Market Street, occupying the triangle between Grey Street, Grainger Street and Market Street, is the Central Exchange Building (see p.116). On the east side, Dobson's elevations below the Theatre Royal have been much altered, but still reveal the basic composition of central block with columns, balanced by plainer wings with projecting 'pavilions'. Here the design is generally more complicated and elaborate.

Among the other buildings on the street, that of Lloyds Bank (see photograph above) on the east side near the Grey Monument, originally housing the Northumberland and Durham District Banking Company, is particularly finely ornamented and well composed. Dating from 1838-40, it has nine bays, the middle three recessed, with Corinthian columns and pilasters rising from the first floor to a powerful cornice above; the ground floor has Tuscan pilasters. As a plaque on its Market Street elevation indicates, the building occupies the site of the demolished Anderson Place (see p.11). Grainger originally intended the building to be new Law Courts and Civic Offices, but after his proposal was rejected by the Council (one of his first significant setbacks), he had the fully worked-out design, by Wardle and Walker, adapted for use as a banking-house. Substantially modernised and remodelled inside in recent years, the structure now boasts an impressive, top-lit atrium. The buildings to the north of the Lloyds Bank premises, on the same side of the street up to the junction with Blackett Street, are all later but largely respect the scale and organisation of the original street.

THE GRAINGER MARKET

NEWCASTLE, NE1 5JQ

The Grainger Market, designed by John Dobson and opened in October 1835, played an important part in the commercial success of Richard Grainger's central area redevelopment and was the first major building to be completed within it. It is contained within a block of four terraces, on Grainger Street and Clayton Street to the east and west, and on Nelson Street and Nun Street to the north and south, respectively. As elsewhere in Grainger's redevelopment, the frontages are all in ashlar masonry, with central 'pavilions' and projecting wings at the corners. However, although the effect of these frontages is still palatial, they are somewhat plainer than those, for example, in Grey Street.

Above shops on the ground floor are two floors with rectangular windows separated by a string-course and surmounted by a cornice. On the longer east and west fronts there are attic floors with square windows above the cornice and stone balustrading above the central bays. The main elevation to Grainger Street also has Corinthian pilasters to the central pavilion and wings, with their bases starting above the shop fronts and rising to a cornice (see photograph above). The north and south facades have no attic floor, just a continuous stone balustrade above the cornice.

The shop fronts within the facades have been much altered over the years, but recent developments under the 'Grainger Town Partnership' have led to replacements with more restrained Georgian and Victorian-style designs, although these still show significant variations in quality. The top floors, empty for many years, are now being re-occupied as flats.

Behind the street facades lies the market itself, built to replace an earlier market located near Dean Street. It has fourteen entrances from the surrounding streets, each located to fit in with the overall design of the facades. This very large market, about two acres in extent and defined externally by by 50 and 46 bays on the long sides and 34 on the short ones, was much praised when it opened. It was considered "superior to in extent, convenience, and elegance, to any in Great Britain" (W. Collard & M. Ross).

It is divided into two parts. The eastern section, originally the meat market, has four aisles lit by clerestory windows running from north to south, with four arched, transverse aisles containing market units. The western section, originally the vegetable market, is 57 feet wide and was designed to be largely open-plan, although with narrow side aisles. Its impressive timber roof, partially supported by cast-iron columns, was destroyed by fire in 1901 and replaced by the present railway station-like arched system with lattice girders (see right, top). Earlier, in 1880, Borough Engineer John Fulton had carried out improvements to the market (now patrolled by wardens to ensure standards of decorum and hygiene) to include better lighting and ventilation as well as washing facilities.

Many authentic features in the market still survive, including the public weighing-room and a Marks & Spencer's Penny Bazaar, opened in 1895, which has original fittings (see right, lower). A refurbishment programme of 2003 exposed more original detail. It also reduced the number of static stalls in the original vegetable market and replaced them with a café and events space, where a regular arts and crafts market is now held.

Left The Grainger Market, Newcastle upon Tyne, by John Dobson, 1835: the eastern elevation on Grainger Street.

Above Right The Grainger Market, Newcastle upon Tyne: interior; the roof is a replacement of 1901.

Below Right The Grainger Market, Newcastle upon Tyne: interior with Penny Bazaar, 1895.

THE THEATRE ROYAL

GREY STREET, NEWCASTLE, NE1 6BR

The Theatre Royal, by John and Benjamin Green, is the greatest public building on Grey Street, located at a key point on its curve and designed with a grand portico to maximise its impact. The building was a replacement for the earlier Theatre Royal on Mosley Street (designed by David Stephenson), which was demolished under a much-disputed agreement whereby Richard Grainger provided a new theatre as well as paying its proprietors a cash sum. The removal of the old theatre provoked considerable public opposition, and the memory of it remains in the name Drury Lane, a little alley near the foot of Grey Street.

The Greens were appointed architects of the new theatre as early as September 1834 but do not seem to have produced plans for some eighteen months. The building, which opened in February 1837, occupies the frontage of the block facing on to Grey Street, between Market and Shakespeare Streets. It generally follows the classical conventions of the rest of the street, although it does not have a rusticated ground floor. The Corinthian pilasters on the end bays start from plinths on the ground floor, which help form a visual base for the whole building, and terminate with an entablature supported by brackets, beneath an elaborate balustrade. In the end bays are large windows flanked by Tuscan pilasters, with balconies below and pediments above; the pediments in turn are surmounted by square attic windows with moulded surrounds. Each of the inner, adjacent bays, on either side of the portico, have two large windows; the lower ones, with pedimented heads, rise straight from the plinths, while, unusually for Grey Street, the upper ones are round-headed, with moulded surrounds supported by pilasters.

The central section behind the portico, more Victorian than Georgian in the way that it dominates the pavement, is elaborately glazed with round-arched windows, with the main entrance doors below. The portico, the only one in the Grainger central development, is formed by pilasters on the wall surface and six columns set forward. These columns all have finely carved Corinthian capitals and are on bases following the line of the plinth of the main building. Above is a simply moulded architrave below a triangular pediment containing the royal arms, superbly carved in the round by Christopher Tate of Newcastle; at the apex is the base for a statue, intended to have been of the actress Sarah Siddons, which was never completed.

The theatre-goer originally entered through the portico into a two-storey rotunda beneath a dome, with "a circular stone gallery supported by richly ornamented stone cantilevers". Local architects John Johnstone and William Newcombe carried out unspecified alterations and improvements in 1857 and 1891 respectively, before the theatre's interior was gutted by fire in November 1899.

Over the next two years the interior was completely reconstructed by Frank Matcham of London (1854-1920), the most famous theatre architect of his time. Matcham enlarged the auditorium and created a magnificent Rococo-style decorative scheme with plasterwork by De Jong. The original character of Matcham's auditorium was respected and enhanced during an extensive restoration and remodelling of 1987-88 by architects Renton Howard Wood Levin, with interior designer Clare Ferraby. This work was funded by the City of Newcastle with assistance from the then European Economic Community, Tyne and Wear County Council, the Arts Council and English Heritage. The theatre was extended behind the stage into other buildings within Grainger's development along Market Street and Shakespeare Street (also by John and Benjamin Green), providing greatly increased storage, practice space and artists' accommodation. In addition, the entrance foyer was enlarged and a second staircase was inserted to give access to all levels of the auditorium. This new configuration replaced the old separate entrance and staircase to the 'gods' provided by Matcham.

This reconstruction re-created a traditional theatre, one of the largest and finest in Britain, intended to satisfy the needs of both modern theatre-goers and numerous major touring companies, including Opera North and the R.S.C. Since then such has been the success of the Theatre Royal that in 2011 a further remodelling of its public areas took place. This was undertaken by Sansome Hall Architects Ltd, who went back to Matcham's original designs, and replaced much that had been removed or damaged. In addition, the seating, lighting and air conditioning were replaced to give twenty-first-century levels of comfort, while access and toilets were also improved. The theatre now seats approximately 1,300 people.

Opposite The Theatre Royal, Grey Street, Newcastle upon Tyne, by John and Benjamin Green, 1836-37: from the south west.

Above The Theatre Royal, Grey Street, Newcastle upon Tyne: interior of auditorium, by Frank Matcham, 1901. Photograph Sally Ann Norman.

THE CENTRAL EXCHANGE

GREY STREET, GRAINGER STREET AND MARKET STREET, NEWCASTLE, NE1 5AF

The Central Exchange was built by Richard Grainger in 1836-38, to the designs of John Wardle and George Walker, to occupy the triangular plot at the meeting of Grey, Grainger, and Market Streets. Grainger offered the new building as the town's Corn Exchange, but the Newcastle Corporation, which was perhaps beginning to feel threatened by his prolific output, rejected it. It was also felt that the location was unsuitable, since a Corn Exchange should be nearer to the other markets. Therefore, in 1838 the Corporation built a Corn Exchange (by John and Benjamin Green) in the Bigg Market, on Middle Street. This was later incorporated into John Johnstone's Town Hall building of 1855-63 (see p.128); the whole structure was demolished c.1969.

Grainger's Central Exchange became instead a subscription newsroom, i.e. premises where subscribers could read a selection of newspapers, including the standard London publications. It opened in 1839. The enormous space that would have been used as the market trading-floor was now dedicated to its new purpose. It proved to be a very popular and profitable facility, a contemporary account stating that "few provincial towns in the world possess a hall combining such magnificent dimensions, elegant proportions, and convenient arrangements" (W. Collard & M. Ross). The Exchange also contained coffee-rooms and apartments, looking over the surrounding streets, while its cellars (used as air-raid shelters during the Second World War) and basement service road, were considered advanced features.

Built of high-quality ashlar masonry, the Central Exchange is a noble composition that deals beautifully with its awkward, triangular site. Its sides are comparatively plain, although the central sections project and are articulated by Tuscan pilasters between each window. However, the corners of the building are turned, with effortless grace, by means of rotundas, each articulated with engaged Corinthian columns and capitals through the first and second floors. Each rotunda also has an attic floor, effectively accented by an elaborate cornice, above which scrolled brackets support a ribbed dome surmounted by finials of exuberant Prince of Wales feathers, cast in copper. This magnificent treatment of corner features, with the curve surmounted by a dome, became characteristic of much Newcastle architecture until at least the early twentieth century.

Unfortunately, the Central Exchange was forced to close in 1867 as a result of a serious fire. It was re-opened three years later under new management, again as a newsroom, but with additional facilities designed by local architect William Parnell, including an art gallery and later a concert hall. In 1886 a smoking-room was constructed within the newsroom and in the 1890s a very early commission for architects Cackett & Burns Dick (see Chapters Five and Six) resulted in part of the gallery being converted into a small vaudeville theatre.

By 1900, when unexecuted plans were put forward to convert part of the premises to a restaurant and hotel, the establishment rivalled any private cultural club in the country. However, a year later the building was again ravaged by fire and did not re-open until 1906. Oswald & Son of Newcastle designed the present 'Central Arcade' (see p.228), with offices above, which replaced the former interior. At street level there are now continuous shop frontages with associated space on the first floor. In 2004 the building's upper floors were imaginatively converted into luxury flats by GWK Architects (now part of ADP).

The Central Exchange, Grainger Street elevation, Newcastle upon Tyne,
by John Wardle and George Walker, 1836-38: from the west.

NELSON STREET

NEWCASTLE, NE1 5AW

Left Nelson Street, Newcastle upon Tyne, by John Wardle and George Walker and others, c.1836-38: from the west.

Right The Lord Collingwood public house, Clayton Street, Newcastle upon Tyne, probably by John Wardle and George Walker, c.1836-38: from the east.

Far Right The Duke of Northumberland public house, Clayton Street, Newcastle upon Tyne, probably by John Wardle and George Walker, c.1836-38: from the south.

Nelson Street, situated to the north of the Grainger Market, was built c.1836-38. The street's north side is now in effect a facade to the modern Eldon Square shopping centre. However, this frontage probably still contains a greater variety of elements than anywhere else within the Richard Grainger central development (albeit partly because of later insertions and alterations), prompting speculation that not only John Wardle and George Walker, but also other architects, including John Dobson, may have been involved.

Nos 8 and 14 Nelson Street have an Italianate quality and were designed as wings to each end of the original street. Their side windows have flat, carved pediments, while a central window has a pediment on scrolls, below a balustrade. A later shop front has been sympathetically inserted into No. 8, while No. 14 (the former Dispensary, and almost certainly the work of Dobson) possesses what is believed to be an original ground floor.

Between these two buildings are the former Music Hall and Lecture Room premises, having a completely different character in that they have round-headed windows, unusual for architecture sponsored by Grainger. Also, each has a round-headed entrance door (with pediment above), which is placed to the side, rather than in the centre. The Cordwainers' Hall (1838), with its fine 'Egyptian' lettering, is at the west end of the street, which is terminated by a semi-circular bay.

Like Nun Street, its counterpart on the other side of the Market, Nelson Street links Grainger Street with Clayton Street, originally conceived as an important part of the Grainger plan of vistas and terminations. Formerly, Clayton Street continued past the end of Nelson Street, to give a view north into Eldon Square (see p.94). The entrance to the present Eldon Square shopping centre has now blocked this vista, but the termination to Nelson Street itself still remains in the shape of the fine Lord Collingwood public house (see opposite page).

THE LORD COLLINGWOOD AND THE DUKE OF NORTHUMBERLAND PUBLIC HOUSES

CLAYTON STREET, NEWCASTLE, NE1 5PU

The Lord Collingwood (see above, left), now sadly an amusement arcade, and The Duke of Northumberland (see above, right) public houses were designed and built for Richard Grainger c.1836-38, almost certainly by John Wardle and George Walker. They were intended to be identical, closing the vistas at the ends of Nelson Street and Nun Street respectively, although they now seem more like adjuncts to the latest extensions to the Eldon Square development.

Built of sandstone ashlar masonry, their fronts are dominated by an arrangement of two full-height, semi-circular bay windows, which sit either side of a central entrance. At both pubs these originally featured two free-standing columns and two pilasters supporting an entablature, but The Duke of Northumberland's entrance has been remodelled and reduced, marring the effect of symmetry; access is now through the curved side bays, which serve as semicircular lobbies.

The interiors of these buildings have been much refurbished, and the former Lord Collingwood has had its original ground-floor windows and doors replaced by modern 'frameless' glazing. Nevertheless, they still retain much of their dignity.

THE OUSEBURN VIADUCT

BYKER, NEWCASTLE, NE6 1PG

This impressive structure dates from 1837-39, and is a splendid manifestation of the innovative engineering spirit of the time (see also, chapter frontispiece). It has nine arches, spanning a distance of 918 feet across the Ouseburn valley, at a height of 108 feet above the stream. The two outer arches at each end of the viaduct are of stone, while the inner five arches are of ribbed, composite construction; each composite arch is now (see below) constructed out of six curved 'I' iron sections, braced together with horizontal ties.

The viaduct was designed for the Newcastle and North Shields Railway by the talented local father-and-son partnership of John and Benjamin Green. As well as being first-class architects responsible for such commissions as Newcastle's Theatre Royal, the Greens were also pioneering engineers, although it was John, the father, who provided most of the expertise in this aspect of their work.

The Ouseburn Viaduct was the first structure in the country to use – initially – laminated timber sections, pinned together and bound by diagonal braces, to form its composite arches. This system "excited the surprise and admiration of all persons possessed of scientific and mechanical knowledge" (W. Collard & M. Ross) and, for it, the Institute of Civil Engineers awarded John Green the Telford Medal in 1841. The construction of the viaduct also involved the innovative use of mobile cranes.

The timber sections of the structure were removed in 1867, the arches being rebuilt in iron, although this was allowed for by the initial design. At this time the original piers were retained, as were the approaches. Later, in 1887, the viaduct was widened to accommodate two further tracks. During the first year of the viaduct's existence, more than 600,000 passengers travelled across it.

GREY'S MONUMENT

GREY STREET, NEWCASTLE, NE1 6JG

This famous monument was built in 1838 to close the vistas culminating at the point where Grey Street and Grainger Street meet at their junction with Blackett Street. The monument was dedicated to Earl Grey, the Prime Minister who successfully piloted through Parliament the Reform Bill of 1832, and who was also a Northumberland landowner. The Monument reflected a change (from September 1836) in Richard Grainger's initial thinking, for he had originally planned to call what is now Grey Street 'Upper Dean Street' and envisaged at its head a very different monument, consisting of a female figure on a pedestal. Similarly, he now abandoned another earlier idea, namely that for a large and rather incongruous Gothic church on the upper west side of Grainger Street.

The monument as built, of millstone grit stone on a base of local sandstone, was paid for by public subscription, organised by a committee chaired by William Ord, M.P. for Newcastle. Designed by John and Benjamin Green, it is a Roman Doric column, with its base 147 feet high including its base. The column is hollow, housing a staircase of 164 steps up to a railed platform, which is occasionally opened to the public. On a pedestal above the platform is a large (thirteen feet) Portland stone statue of Earl Grey, clad in robes. This was carved by E.H. Baily, a Royal Academician who was also responsible for the similarly placed figure of Lord Nelson in London's Trafalgar Square.

In 2000, the 'Grainger Town Partnership' finished a programme of cleaning and restoration of Grey's Monument. The structure is still at the heart of the city's shopping area and remains one of the best vantage points from which to appreciate Grainger's redevelopment of central Newcastle.

Left The Ouseburn Viaduct, Byker, Newcastle upon Tyne, by John and Benjamin Green, 1837-39 (detail): from the south east.

Right Grey's Monument, Grey Street, Newcastle upon Tyne, by John and Benjamin Green, 1838: from the north.

CARLTON TERRACE AND OTHER TERRACES

JESMOND ROAD WEST AND GREAT NORTH ROAD, NEWCASTLE, NE2 4PD

From about 1830 onwards the area to the east of the Great North Road, north of Barras Bridge, was laid out with high-quality suburban terraces, built of brick with stone detailing. However, much of this elegant development was destroyed by the creation, in the 1960s, of the central motorway (east). The earlier houses, along the Great North Road itself and Jesmond Road, as well as in Victoria Square, further to the east, were probably the finest.

Victoria Square dates from c.1845; it is now very severely truncated by the motorway. However, Carlton Terrace (c.1840), on the north side of Jesmond Road, survives complete and is a splendid design by John Dobson of the 'palace front' type (see photograph above). Its three-storey composition is treated as a self-contained architectural whole, in which the total effect is greater than the sum of its parts. The terrace has projecting and slightly raised central and end sections, and a continuous stone band above the first and second floors. The end sections are further accented, having Tuscan pilasters supporting a cornice above paired brackets. The western end block consists of a larger residence. It does not have a front door opening on to the street, but instead possesses an elaborate, three-bay entrance facade looking to the west.

Carlton Terrace aside, the best remaining section of the development is the slightly earlier range across the road, which has the address Jesmond Road West. This terrace dates from the early 1830s and is very probably also by Dobson, although some of the houses now have later, bay windows. It has been refurbished and converted into luxury dwellings. Meanwhile, its composition very effectively turns the corner into the Great North Road, of which Nos 14-20 still retain most of their honeysuckle-patterned, cast-iron balconies, similar to those in old Eldon Square and Leazes Terrace.

TERRACED HOUSING

WALKER TERRACE, GATESHEAD, NE8 1EB

These two-storey terrace houses on Walker Terrace, Gateshead, are of particularly high quality. They date from 1842-43 and are constructed of local, pinkish brick with sandstone dressings. Each house has five bays, with the exception of the end houses; these the (unknown) architect cleverly rotated by 90 degrees so that their fronts face on to the adjoining roads and the side elevations terminate the terrace. Each house has an individual roof of Welsh slate, with interesting paired brick chimney-stacks. The effect is almost that of a series of adjoining villas.

The houses (now used mainly as offices) step down the slope toward St Joseph's Church (see p.150) and are built on sandstone plinths. Their centrally placed entrances, also of sandstone, are comparatively grand, with Tuscan pilasters supporting an entablature. The doors are generally panelled, with rectangular fanlights above. The ground-floor windows have sandstone surrounds connected to plinths. Each house has a front garden retained by sandstone walls, with attractive stone gate piers.

Opposite Carlton Terrace, Newcastle upon Tyne, by John Dobson, c.1840: from the south west.

Above Terraced houses, Walker Terrace, Gateshead, 1842-3: from the west.

THE ST THOMAS'S DEVELOPMENT

OFF PERCY STREET, NEWCASTLE, NE1 4LG

St Thomas's Crescent (see left, above), Square, Street and Terrace (see left, below), dating probably from the very late 1830s or early 1840s, form a coherent development of small-scale brick houses that epitomises the modest but civilised terraced constructions of this period. Inspired, if not designed, by John Dobson, these houses are in a simplified version of the 'Tyneside Classical' style.

The houses have basements and rubble sandstone rear walls to the yards behind. Steps lead up to the front entrances, which have pilasters and stone architraves. The windows are simple but well-proportioned, with stone sills and lintels. The corner buildings have brick pilasters rising from the ground floor to an eaves cornice. On St Thomas's Street, a segmental arch gives access to what was originally the coach yard. This whole group of buildings was well restored by architects Barnett Winskell for North Housing in 1982. The reinstatement of the cast-iron railings was a particularly welcome feature of their work.

Above Left St Thomas's Crescent, Newcastle upon Tyne, late 1830s or early 1840s: from the north east.

Below Left St Thomas's Terrace, Newcastle upon Tyne, late 1830s or early 1840s: from the north west.

BONDED WAREHOUSES

THE CLOSE AND HANOVER STREET, NEWCASTLE, NE1 3RF

These large bonded warehouses between the Close and Hanover Street are said to have been constructed between 1841 and 1844 for a Mr Amor Spoor, who may well have undertaken the building work and even the design work himself. However, an attribution to Thomas Oliver has also been suggested. Built of plain brick, with a regular pattern of round-arched windows, these impressive structures are fine examples of the 'functional tradition' of late Georgian and early Victorian architecture, even though a significant part of them had to be demolished after two disastrous fires in 2000.

On the Hanover Street side, the warehouses followed the curve and fall of the street (see above, right), with triangular brick pediments creating a vigorous roofline. The cobbled street itself retains strips of granite, placed to support the weight of waggons. Down on the Close, the buildings stand seven storeys high, their plain brick elevations, on ashlar plinths, giving a cliff-like appearance (see above, left). They had tall, rusticated sandstone archways as entrances.

In 2006 these unlucky buildings were further damaged by fire, resulting in more demolition. The remaining parts of the warehouses have been converted into flats by Napper Architects, with somewhat unsympathetic modern blocks replacing the demolished sections.

Above Left Bonded Warehouses, the Close, Newcastle upon Tyne c.1841-44, converted to flats, 2007-8: view from the riverside, from the south west.

Above Right Bonded Warehouses, the Close, Newcastle upon Tyne: the remaining section on Hanover Street, from the north.

CHAPTER 4

EARLY AND MID-VICTORIAN, TO c.1880

Saltwell Towers, East Park Road, Gateshead, by William Wailes, from 1862 (detail).

INTRODUCTION

During the Victorian period, with the vast expansion of urban areas, there was an enormous increase in building activity in Britain. Newcastle and Gateshead were no exceptions to this. Between c.1800 and c.1850 their populations rose from about 28,000 to 75,000, and from around 8,500 to 30,000, respectively – in no small measure due to immigration. Surrounding villages were being rapidly swallowed up and there was further decentralisation of the wealthy from the ever more crowded old town centres.

Coal mining remained the staple revenue earner, but newer industries developed rapidly along both banks of the Tyne, with heavy engineering and shipbuilding being important on the Newcastle side (Armstrong's Elswick works were especially noteworthy) and iron founding, metal fabrication and chemical manufacture likewise prominent in and around Gateshead.

Similarly, George Stephenson and his son Robert established the world's first locomotive workshop in Forth Street, Newcastle, as early as 1823, and the works expanded as the demand for railway rolling stock increased. The building of the High Level Bridge and Central Station from 1846, leading to the expansion of the railway network northwards towards Edinburgh, changed the character of this area between the railway and the river. Formerly part of the western development of residential housing outside the walls (see p.46), the area became a site of major manufacture for the new railway age (see p.142). However, cut off from the city by the station and the railway, it suffered decline in the latter part of the twentieth century.

Alongside all this growth of urbanism and industry, and acceleration of engineering progress, the Victorian period also saw a concomitant rise in the size and status of the architectural profession. This was reflected locally in the formation, in 1858, of the Northern Architectural Association, which is now incorporated into the Royal Institute of British Architects. Appropriately, John Dobson was elected its first President. During the early to mid-nineteenth century, Newcastle alone had a dozen architects and architectural practices, a larger number than most comparable towns. This figure rose to no less than 70 by 1900. Such was the volume of work available that some architects, although by no means all, began to specialise in one particular field of practice.

At this time most of the architectural work in Newcastle and Gateshead was, with some important exceptions, still reserved for local men (albeit almost invariably working in nationally accepted styles). This was much less the case with comparable urban centres such as Manchester and Liverpool. Thus it is significant that buildings as major as the town halls of both Newcastle and Gateshead were designed, in 1858 and 1868 respectively, not by prominent national figures, but by the Scottish-born local architect John Johnstone (c.1814-84). Newcastle's town hall (see p.128) stood opposite the Cathedral of St Nicholas; it was demolished c.1969.

Meanwhile, following the re-organisation of local government in 1835, building work in towns and cities was increasingly driven by the activities of municipalities and other official (and commercial) bodies, rather than by individuals, however entrepreneurial. Similarly, boards and institutions were now tending to supersede the earlier private or aristocratic patron, with architectural commissions being decided by committee and the choice of architect arrived at by open competition.

The churches, too, in all their increasingly multifarious denominations, were very active in this period, which was one of unprecedented religious revival, as well as population growth. For a time, both before and after the Education Act of 1870, they were a major provider of schools, as well as of other social facilities. The Nonconformists were particularly successful in reaching into the new, working-class areas. Church architecture itself flourished, in both Gothic and classical styles.

Suddenly, the activities and methods of someone like Richard Grainger, so dominant in the period discussed in Chapter Three, seemed characteristic of a passing age. In the late 1830s Grainger had been at the zenith of his wealth and influence. Abruptly, however, the newly reformed Newcastle Council became less accommodating; perhaps he had become too successful for his own good. Soon he over-reached himself and his career began to go downhill amid accusations of financial impropriety.

Left The Town Hall, Newcastle upon Tyne, by John Johnstone and W.A. Knowles, 1858-63, now demolished (© the University of Northumbria at Newcastle).

Right Thomas Oliver's *Plan of Newcastle upon Tyne and Gateshead*, 1851.

After c.1840 he made comparatively little contribution to Newcastle's development.

Of the various architects Grainger employed, Thomas Oliver and John and Benjamin Green, were all dead by 1858, while John Wardle and George Walker returned to the comparative obscurity from which they came. Yet the ageing but indefatigable John Dobson was still busy during the first half of the period covered by this chapter, and actually produced one of his greatest works, the Newcastle Central Station. This, even though completed in reduced form, is an example of nationally significant monumental classicism. However, Dobson's last years were clouded by the death, in the Great Quayside Fire of 1854, of his talented son Alexander, a promising architect destined to succeed him. His hopes of an architectural dynasty remained unfulfilled. A small consolation might have been the fact that some of his former assistants, like Thomas Prosser and Johnson Hogg, went on to become successful practitioners during the period under review.

Dobson's practice was purchased at his death in 1865 by Thomas Austin (1822-67) and his partner R.J. Johnson (1832-92). The latter went on to make a very significant contribution to the architecture of Newcastle and the North East. Other important members of this younger generation of local practitioners included William Parnell (d. c.1886) and A.M. Dunn (1832-1917), who from 1871 to 1893 worked with E.J. Hansom (1842-1900) as Dunn & Hansom.

The industrial and residential expansion of Newcastle and Gateshead came at a considerable environmental cost. Both urban areas were becoming increasingly congested. In central Newcastle most of the many public spaces accessible in Georgian times (see Chapter Two) had been built over by 1850 (see p.129). Historic structures suffered too, in spite of antiquarian concerns. For example, the venerable Hospital of St Mary the Virgin was demolished to allow for the widening of Neville Street in 1845, while later, in 1880, the ancient Carliol Tower of the town wall was removed to make way for the new Public Library in New Bridge Street (itself now demolished). The fact that this was a fine classical building, designed by Newcastle's Borough Engineer and Property Surveyor, A.M. Fowler, cleverly incorporating Thomas Oliver jnr.'s former Mechanics' Institute of 1866 at its west end (see p.130), did little to appease the growing number

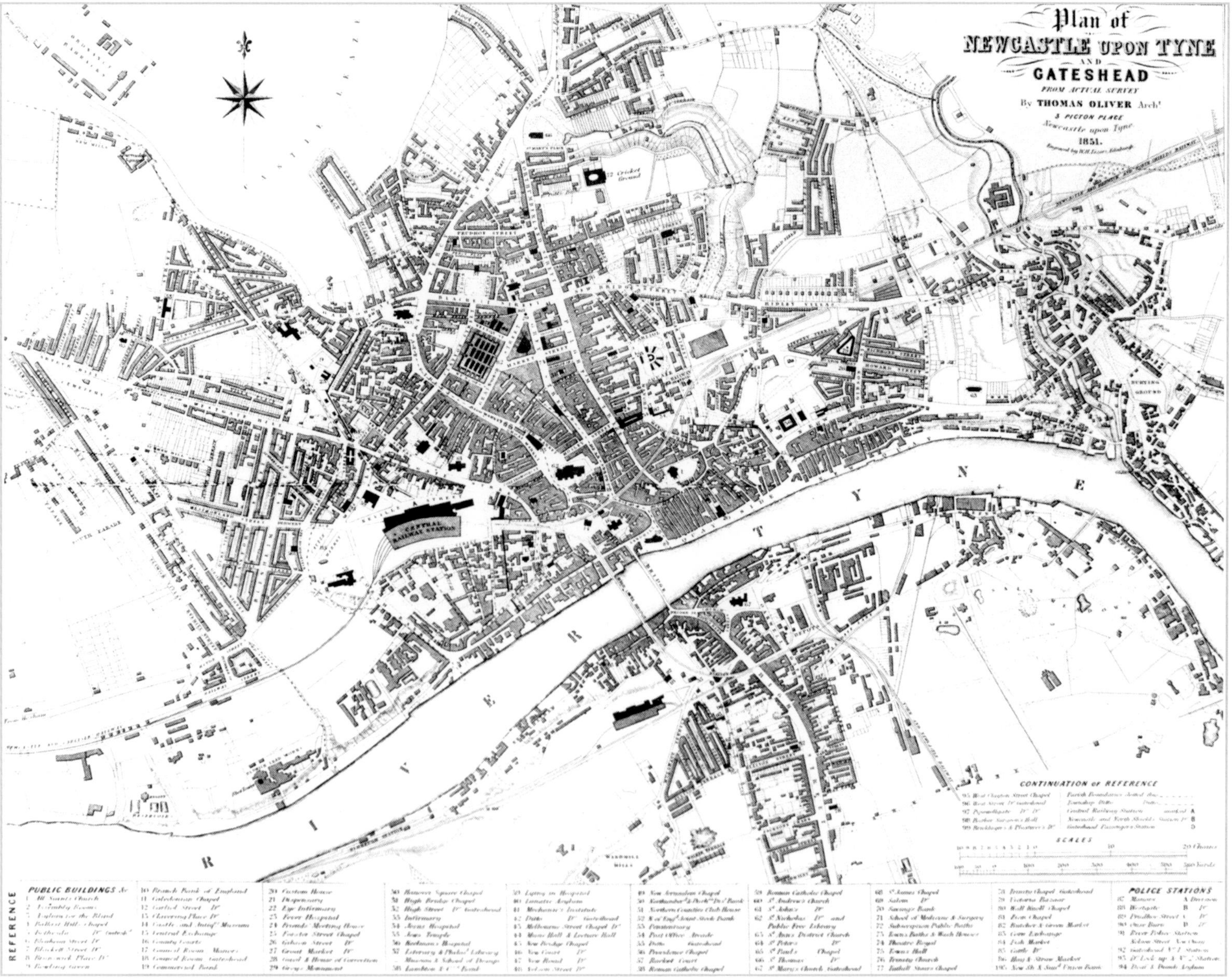
Plan of
NEWCASTLE UPON TYNE
AND
GATESHEAD
FROM ACTUAL SURVEY
By THOMAS OLIVER Arch^t
3 PICTON PLACE
Newcastle upon Tyne
1851.
CONTINUATION of REFERENCE
SCALES
PUBLIC BUILDINGS &c
REFERENCE
POLICE STATIONS
RIVER TYNE

of conservationists now centring on the Society of Antiquaries, the Architectural and Archaeological Society of Durham and Northumberland, and the Northern Architectural Association.

In Newcastle, despite urban expansion and the demolitions that went with it, some areas, such as the comparatively modern residential precinct west of Pandon Dene and north of New Bridge Street, were still fairly pleasant at this time. Ellison Place, for example, had attractive gardens, while other private gardens in this vicinity led down to the Dene. Like many nineteenth-century villa gardens in Newcastle, these contained trees and shrubs, perhaps with a few architectural features, all traversed by winding paths in the now-fashionable 'gardenesque' style. However, the lowest stretches of the Pandon Dene, near the Tyne, were now insanitary and before long its whole course began to be filled in, mainly for railway, warehouse and residential development.

Near to this lies the Ouseburn valley, originally forming part of the township of Byker. This interesting area of the city, once a luscious and picturesque landscape, was initially used primarily for agriculture. Industrial development began to develop from the seventeenth century. At first its scale did not despoil the valley's natural beauty, but the spread of the Industrial Revolution in the nineteenth century changed the valley beyond recognition. There was an explosion of activity as industrialists moved into the area, attracted by cheap land with good access to a watercourse, and there followed an enormous influx of working people into the valley, looking for employment. Poor-quality housing was erected to accommodate them; many lived in cramped dwellings, cheek by jowl with tanneries, slaughterhouses and glue works on Stepney and Byker Banks. Despite Sir William Armstrong's involvement in the development of the district – he built a bridge over the Ouseburn in 1875-76 – the valley's fortunes began to wane as early as the latter part of the nineteenth century, as the quantity of goods being transported by water diminished because of competition from the railways. Over the next century much of the area's building stock was demolished. However, there is still a considerable amount of infrastructure remaining from the Industrial Revolution period, including a number of bridges and viaducts that sail elegantly over the valley, adding a dynamic and vertical dimension to the scene (see for example page 120).

Overall, Newcastle had become notorious for the unhealthy conditions endured by many of its inhabitants. Grainger's improvements, however splendid, had made little impact upon these problems. His developments were not philanthropic and had been concentrated in a central zone where maximum profit and prestige could be achieved. Cholera epidemics were still frequent and a report of 1861 referred to Newcastle's "narrow, dark and filthy entries", "undrained chares", "ill-paved streets" and "badly kept roads". *The Builder* magazine described the town as "one of our greatest disgraces in respect of filth". These problems were not helped by the fact that the rather frugal Newcastle Council was often reluctant to use even the powers it had to improve social conditions.

Gateshead was no better. Here the population was increasing faster than the rate of house-building. As a result, working-class living conditions were deteriorating, especially in some of the notorious cul-de-sacs between the High Street and Oakwellgate. Moreover, the Tyne, once well wooded and enriched with flowering shrubs, was now the second-busiest river in Britain. It was also heavily polluted by industry.

Not surprisingly, there soon began to be agitation for the provision of public, or 'people's', parks. By the 1860s such parks existed in London and most large provincial towns, although not in Newcastle or Gateshead. Here such amenities were slow to be provided, again partly because of cost. In Newcastle, it was even suggested that working-class people ought to be able to use some of the new urban cemeteries, being laid out during the 1850s (see p.145), for their recreational walks, while, paradoxically, another major impediment to progress seems to have been the existence of the Town Moor. Many in authority believed that the Moor was one of the finest public parks in the country and therefore new ones were unnecessary. This argument ignored the fact that the Moor was at that time suitable only for riding on and so beneficial mainly to the better-off; it was also comparatively inaccessible to the growing industrial communities of the burgeoning east and west ends of town.

Public pressure finally paid off and in Newcastle Leazes Park opened in 1873, carved out of the Town Moor. Other parks soon followed. Between 1878 and 1880 Heaton Park was created through the purchase of the attractive former Heaton Hall estate, with its wooded grounds sweeping down to the Ouseburn valley below. At the same time the adjacent Armstrong Park was added to it following its donation to the city by Lord Armstrong. The sequence was completed in 1883 when he made a gift to the city of Jesmond Dene, landscaped for him by the naturalist and occasional landscape designer John Hancock. The contemporary Elswick Park, in the west end, also passed into public ownership as a result of private philanthropy, as did to some extent Saltwell Park in Gateshead, opened in 1877.

As one would surmise from the above account of mid-Victorian developments, Newcastle and Gateshead possess a wealth of architecture from this period. Despite many demolitions, it has not been difficult to select for this chapter a range of examples which illustrate and typify its richness, eclecticism and decorativeness. Indeed – as for that matter with Chapter Five – a number of other very worthy buildings could have justified inclusion but for the limitations of space and the need not to unbalance the overall content of this book. All the many styles of mid-Victorian architecture are represented, although the range of neo-Gothic secular (not ecclesiastical) buildings is admittedly limited – in contrast to other northern cities, such as Manchester, Liverpool and Leeds – probably because of the strong classical tradition established earlier by Dobson and his local contemporaries and predecessors.

The Laing Art Gallery (by Cackett & Burns Dick, 1902-04) and the former Public Library (by A.M. Fowler, 1878-82), incorporating (to the left) the Mechanics' Institute (by Thomas Oliver jnr., 1866), New Bridge Street, Newcastle upon Tyne; of these, only the Laing Art Gallery now remains (© Newcastle Libraries).

ST MARY'S CATHEDRAL (R.C.)

CLAYTON STREET WEST, NEWCASTLE, NE1 5HH

A.W.N. Pugin (1812-52), the famous Gothic Revival architect best known for his contribution to the design of the Houses of Parliament in London, designed St Mary's Roman Catholic Cathedral in 1842. It was built, in local stone, by his favourite contractor, Myers & Wilson of Hull, at the rather low cost of just over £10,500. The original budget had actually been less than £7,000. Funds had been laboriously raised through donations and by public subscription, many members of Newcastle's large but impoverished Catholic community contributing a halfpenny each.

Even so, the commission stipulated that the building was to be "large and handsome", and in the Decorated Gothic style of the period of Edward III, "when Christian architecture attained the most consummate beauty". In addition, it had to be capable of seating 1,200 people.

Earlier, with the greater religious toleration of the late eighteenth and early nineteenth centuries, Roman Catholic worship had re-started under the auspices of the priest James Worswick, who operated in a small brick church behind his house in Pilgrim Street. An altar from this church is now in St Dominic's Church, New Bridge Street (see p.163). It was Worswick who in 1842 acquired the land for the new cathedral, but he died a year later. He is buried in a vault in the nave.

St Mary's was completed in 1844, except for the magnificent tower. This was started by Pugin up to a height of fourteen feet and completed in modified form in 1872 by the distinguished local architects Dunn & Hansom, who also added the spire (the total height being 223 feet), paid for by the Dunn family. When the diocese of Hexham and Newcastle was created in 1850, St Mary's became a cathedral.

Rather unusually for Pugin, the design is rectangular rather than cruciform. The cathedral has no transepts, and even the chancel, which is not expressed externally except for a very slight projection, is subsumed within the two easternmost bays of the nave. This creates a very open effect, which is now exaggerated by the removal of Pugin's rood screen and side choir screens during a modern re-ordering.

The building also has very generous aisles, which are nearly as wide, and as high, as the relatively narrow nave (see opposite page, top left). There is no clerestory. The overall arrangement is therefore not unlike that of a 'hall-church' or triple-naved church, a type sometimes found in continental Gothic architecture and here reflected in the cathedral's largely symmetrical, three-gabled exterior.

This plan-type was occasionally favoured by Pugin for churches with potentially large congregations, as at St Mary's, although there was no attempt to include galleries, which he abhorred. In addition, budgetary factors and the restricted and enclosed nature of the site almost certainly helped to shape the design, Pugin himself noting that "a low church would appear crushed and mere aisles without gables would never answer."

These factors, as well as the need to utilise the whole site, probably also accounted for the decision to place the tower laterally at the south west.

Left St Mary's Cathedral (R.C.), Clayton Street West, Newcastle upon Tyne, by A.W.N. Pugin and others, from 1842: from the south east; the statue of Cardinal Hume (unveiled 2002) is by Nigel Boonham.

Right St Mary's Cathedral (R.C.), Clayton Street West, Newcastle upon Tyne: the interior looking east.

Far Right St Mary's Cathedral (R.C.), Clayton Street West, Newcastle upon Tyne: chapel with stained glass by William Wailes.

The tower now dominates the whole composition, for the exterior of the cathedral generally is comparatively plain, with large expanses of flat ashlar relieved mainly by buttresses and by some fine Decorated-style window tracery.

Of St Mary's, a Victorian commentator, while describing the exterior as "ineffective" (before the tower and spire were completed), proclaimed that "the enrichments of its style are lavish in the interior, which exhibits in every part refinement and elegance". Altars of Caen stone were designed by Pugin and made by Hardman of Birmingham, one of his trusted manufacturers, who were also responsible for the pulpit and font. Many of the windows, too, are of similarly exceptional quality, especially those designed by Pugin himself. These were well made by the local designer and manufacturer (and admirer of Pugin) William Wailes, who gained national recognition as a consequence of this work.

Good examples are the richly coloured east windows. The central one depicts the Tree of Jesse and is flanked by windows of the Good Shepherd and of the Virgin with Saints George and John, to the north and south respectively. There is also much good later Victorian stained glass, by Wailes and others (see above, right), as well as three Arts and Crafts-style windows by J.L. Nuttgens in the Blessed Sacrament Chapel. During the Second World War several of the cathedral's windows were blown out; fragments of these windows were recycled into their replacements, while others were replaced by modern stained glass.

Pugin himself designed much of the church furniture and metalwork, the latter being fabricated by the firm of Hardman. The carving throughout the building is also of good quality, especially that of the altars, which were again designed by Pugin and made of Normandy stone (see above, right). The encaustic floor tiles are also of note. In 1881 Dunn & Hansom restored and redecorated the cathedral with the help of the firm of Lavers, Barraud & Westlake; the tiled frieze around the nave, which is inscribed with the names of local saints, dates from this period.

Over time, the cathedral has developed into a substantial ecclesiastical precinct, with several extensions. In spite of these and other alterations, the structure remains surprisingly cohesive. George Goldie added a chapter room and library in 1851, while Pugin's son and successor, E.W. Pugin, added the Tudor-style clergy house in 1858; this itself was extended by A.M. Dunn in 1869. The baptistery chapel dates from 1902. Much later, in 1980-88, architects the Napper Collerton Partnership (now Napper Architects) undertook a major restoration programme, as well as adding to the meeting accommodation and the clergy's residence. As part of this restoration, the cathedral was redecorated using colours favoured by Pugin.

More recently, another major renovation programme has been taking place, in phases, since 2009. This is under the direction of the present Cathedral Architect, Kevin Doonan (contractor: Stephen Easten Specialist Building Ltd), and includes: the re-tiling of the whole floor surface; a re-ordering of the sanctuary; a reinstatement of the Lady Chapel, with restoration of its reredos; the refurbishment of pews; the installation of new brass railings for the sanctuary; and improved lighting. Most, if not all, of the above work has now been completed, the tilework consisting of a mixture of tiles salvaged from the original floor and carefully cleaned prior to relaying, and new ones, albeit laid in a different pattern to the original. Earlier, Doonan had added a glazed screen, bookshop and porch to the Clayton Street West elevation (1998-2003).

At the time of writing, yet more work is planned for the future, including the addition of a substantial choir gallery at the west end which will accommodate a new and "grand" three-manual pipe organ built by Kenneth Tickell & Company. The present organ will be sold and the space it currently occupies opened up to permit a clear view of the Blessed Sacrament Chapel. In addition, the nave west window will be re-glazed.

NOS 40-44 MOSLEY STREET

NEWCASTLE, NE1 1DF

This distinguished commercial building, adjacent to St Nicholas's Cathedral, dates from c.1845. John and Benjamin Green designed it for the Newcastle Joint Stock Bank. It has the appearance of a Roman or Venetian High Renaissance palazzo. This Renaissance style of architecture was becoming increasingly popular in the early Victorian period for the growing number of new public and institutional buildings, such as banks, clubs, offices, libraries, museums and town halls.

The former Joint Stock Bank is four storeys high and square in plan. On each of its two street facades it is five bays wide (although their ground floors have been marred by the insertion of twentieth-century shop fronts). One of the facades is on Mosley Street; the other forms the east side of St Nicholas's Square, which the building helped to define as a dignified public space (subsequently enhanced by the installation of Sir Alfred Gilbert's splendid Queen Victoria Monument in 1903). The rusticated ground floor has tall, round-arched windows. There are round-headed windows on the first floor too, separated by moulded pilasters. Above this floor is a stone balcony. Giant Ionic attached columns between the windows of the two upper levels support an entablature with a heavy bracketed cornice. The windows on the second floor are pedimented.

Nos 40-44 Mosley Street, Newcastle upon Tyne, by John and Benjamin Green, c.1845: from the south west.

ST CUTHBERT'S (FORMER) CHURCH

BENSHAM ROAD AND DERWENTWATER ROAD, GATESHEAD NE8 1US

During the early nineteenth century the population of Bensham rose rapidly. Bensham had become a popular place to live as a result of its attractive position overlooking the Tyne; in addition, land here was considerably less expensive than in Newcastle. However, there was no church to serve this expanding suburb, Gateshead's first, until St Cuthbert's was built in 1846-48 to the designs of John Dobson as a chapel of ease to St Mary's, Gateshead (see p.26). It became a parish church in its own right in 1865.

Its comparatively modest cost of £2,000 was raised through public subscription, with a grant from the Incorporated Church Building Society and a donation from the prominent local landowner and politician Cuthbert Ellison. The site for the church was given by the Askew family.

This is a mature Dobson design and is an advanced version of his earlier St James's, Benwell (see p.104), which is now greatly altered. Like St James's, it is in the neo-Norman style and has a five-bay nave. However, St Cuthbert's seems to have been specifically inspired by a beautiful twelfth-century church at Barfreston, Kent, which Dobson had recorded during a sketching tour.

St Cuthbert's has a finely carved 'chancel' arch, reminiscent of the one in St Andrew's, Newcastle (see p.12), although beyond this arch is not so much a proper chancel as a substantial apse, within which the altar is located.

Externally the church forms a compact and well-designed composition. It has a 'transitional'-style tower (with a modest spire) at the south west, with the west wall having triple windows under a single arch. The north aisle was a later addition of 1875, in an appropriate neo-Norman style. In its heyday, worshippers at St Cuthbert's could admire its simple and well-proportioned interior, with excellent stained glass by William Wailes and slender shafts rising between the side windows to support the timbers of the roof.

A contemporary account said of St Cuthbert's: "occupying so prominent a site, the edifice will be seen from various and distant points, and will form a pleasing and interesting feature in a locality of great natural beauty". The natural beauty may have gone, but the church still stands as a landmark for miles around. Moreover, at least until the 1980s, it remained a spiritual and architectural focal point in what had long become a seriously underprivileged area.

More recently, however, the church suffered badly from subsidence, steadily lost its congregation and in the early 1990s was forced to close. It was declared redundant and stripped of its fittings and furniture. Sadly, too, it was badly vandalised and was even threatened with demolition. Ultimately St Cuthbert's was sold by the Church Commissioners in 2007 and is now privately owned. A floor has been added to provide rentable office accommodation in the roof space, where many original features, including exposed roof beams, have been carefully retained. A basement floor is being opened up for use as an art gallery.

St Cuthbert's Church, Bensham Road and Derwentwater Road, Gateshead, by John Dobson, 1846-48: from the south.

THE HIGH LEVEL BRIDGE
GATESHEAD AND NEWCASTLE, NE1 1RQ

The High Level Bridge (1846-50), one of the great nineteenth-century engineering feats, supports both rail and road traffic, but its paramount importance was in bringing the railway from London across the Tyne to Newcastle and thence ultimately to Edinburgh and beyond. It thus ended Gateshead's brief period as the railway terminus. The bridge also had the effect of bringing trade directly into the higher part of Newcastle, leading to the development of St Nicholas's Street and thus increasing even further the accessibility and prosperity of Richard Grainger's new commercial centre.

The idea for such a bridge was by no means new. Between 1835 and 1844, for example, at least ten unexecuted proposals had been drawn up for a high-level bridge across the Tyne, most of them on, or near, the line of the present bridge (some incorporating into their structures the then-existing Georgian bridge) and similarly combining road and rail links. John Dobson, John and Benjamin Green, Grainger himself, Thomas Oliver and even the famous engineer Isambard Kingdom Brunel were among those putting forward such schemes. There had been even earlier proposals.

In the event, the High Level Bridge formed part of an overall plan that included the construction of Newcastle's Central Station (see p.138). The bridge was designed by Robert Stephenson, with the able assistance of Thomas Harrison, later Engineer-in-Chief of the North Eastern Railway Company, as executant engineer. The architectural treatment was by Francis Thompson, assisted by Edward Harwood.

The railway line across the bridge was completed by August 1849. Queen Victoria and Prince Albert crossed the bridge (and stopped) on their way back from Scotland on 28th September and are said to have admired the view. However, there was no official opening ceremony. The roadway was opened in February 1850.

The bridge gives 118 feet of clearance above low water. Its width is just over 39 feet, and its length just over 750 feet across the river itself. Divided into six main spans, each of just under 125 feet, the bridge is supported on pairs of elegantly tapering, ashlar piers; these are joined together laterally by arches just below the lower deck and, to reduce weight, are also hollow above the water-line.

During construction, James Nasmyth's newly invented steam hammer was used to drive massive timber piles into the silt of the river bed, to support these piers. The contractors, Rush & Lawton, transported over 50,000 tons of the hardest and most durable locally quarried stone to the site. However, the special lime and mortar that they used had to be sourced from as far afield as Dorset.

The High Level Bridge's rail and (lower) road decks are of both cast- and wrought-iron construction, involving shallow arches that spring between the masonry piers and support the cast-iron 'I' sections holding up the upper deck; this in turn is tied vertically to the lower deck. The ironwork used was of the highest quality and was fabricated by Hawks, Crawshay & Sons, of Gateshead, whose yard was situated where the Baltic Centre for Contemporary Art (see p.316) now stands.

Although its foundations had to be repaired and strengthened in 1919, and its metallic structure reinforced three years later (in order to receive tramcars), the bridge survived remarkably unaltered until 2005, when it was closed for a major programme of strengthening and repair. This work continued until 2009, when, resplendent in its original paintwork colour (cream, to resemble stone), the bridge re-opened. Admittedly, this was for pedestrian and restricted traffic only, although trains continue to use the upper level. The restoration work received a Europa Nostra award in the same year.

The High Level Bridge, Gateshead and Newcastle upon Tyne,
by Robert Stephenson and Thomas Harrison, 1846-50: from the north.

THE CENTRAL STATION

NEVILLE STREET, NEWCASTLE, NE1 5DH

Left The Central Station, Neville Street, Newcastle upon Tyne, by John Dobson and others, from 1846: the portico, from the west.

Right The Central Station, Neville Street, Newcastle upon Tyne: interior. Photograph Kristen McCluskie

Far Right The Central Station, Neville Street, Newcastle upon Tyne: the Centurion Bar, by William Bell, c.1892-94.

Designed by John Dobson, Newcastle's Central Station was opened, after three years of building work, by Queen Victoria and Prince Albert on 29th August 1850, although not in its complete form. A vast amount of land and property had been appropriated for its construction, including the area of the Forth, mentioned in Chapter Two, and part of the old town wall.

The station was built as one large terminal to consolidate the needs of several railway companies, and houses over two miles of platforms, the longest of which extends to 445 yards. It was also the first structure of its kind in Europe to be built with all its platforms covered. Taken as a whole, this station is perhaps the finest in the country: a marvel of Victorian engineering and probably Dobson's greatest architectural achievement. Thus the architectural historian Andrew Saint could not but admire its "gracious curving platforms and iron and glass within, like York further up the line, but infinitely grander outside in its armour of muscular Italianate sandstone classicism" (*Architecture Today*, 64, 1996).

Stylistically, the station's use of arches, vaults and bold detailing typifies the Victorians' move away from Greek classicism, with its plain walls and strictly rectangular openings, to the grander and more eclectic Roman and Renaissance styles. Sometimes, as here, these styles could be effectively combined.

Dobson's original design for the main facade of the station on Neville Street was of great nobility. Dating from 1846, it was conceived as two parallel porte-cochères, the outer forming a projecting central portico, having groin-vaulted ceilings of stone, with a circular light at each intersection. The architect himself keenly anticipated "the grandeur of the effect produced by an arcade and portico of this length".

However, to save money following a financial crisis that hit the railway companies in 1848, the front portion of the station had to be substantially redesigned. In addition, it became necessary to incorporate a suite of offices for staff transferred as an economy measure from York. Dobson produced a second, more attenuated design for the facade (c.1849-50), which retained the central portico from the first design as a single porte-cochère. However, even this remained unbuilt.

In the event, the front of the station was not completed until 1862-63. It finally took the form of a simplified version of what was essentially the second project, scaled down yet again by Dobson in conjunction with his former assistant Thomas Prosser, now Architect to the North Eastern Railway Company. Thus the portico as built has pilasters instead of coupled columns and lacks the groined vaults originally proposed. Even so, it retains the seven huge arched bays, and, although less rich in detail,

it still exhibits a good deal of the scale, dignity and grandeur of the earlier designs. Just inside the main entrance are roundels with portrait reliefs of Queen Victoria and Prince Albert, flanking King Edward VII.

The corner pavilions at the extremities of the facade are particularly impressive compositions, reminiscent of Vanbrugh and the English Baroque. But the 'wings' stretching between these structures and the central portico, although powerful, are less convincing and perhaps reflect the compromises forced upon the architect. They have a rather curious arrangement of large, semicircular windows on the first floor rising starkly from a flat and wide entablature, above pairs of rectangular windows separated by pilasters.

The facade of the Central Station lies alongside the tracks, unlike, for example Lewis Cubitt's contemporary King's Cross terminus in London, the entrance giving no hint of the astonishing train shed that lies behind. This, like nearby Grey Street, has a sweeping curve along its length. Its roof has three 60-foot spans of segmental curved 'I' sections, the central one higher than the other two. These form wrought-iron bowstring arches, which sit on slender, cast-iron columns. Double-pitched glass roof lights, at the centre of the spanning arches, provide natural light for the platform area. The overall effect is both functional and elegant. The station interior also benefits from unexpected views of the castle from the main platform, looking south.

Dobson used technology that was revolutionary for its day; it was also extremely influential. Probably in collaboration with Robert Stephenson, he invented a new method of making curved roof ribs by means of passing wrought iron between bevelled rollers. A model of the Central Station roof, exhibited by Dobson at the Great Exhibition of 1851, won him an Honourable Mention. All the ironwork of the station was fabricated by J. Abbot & Co. of Gateshead.

The station was subsequently extended to the south and west, mainly between 1892 and 1894, by William Bell, who followed Prosser as Architect to the North Eastern Railway Company. Bell also added two further spans to Dobson's roof, which look compatible but are of a different design. The same architect also remodelled the First Class Refreshment Room (now the Centurion Bar, see above, right), creating a sumptuous interior, now restored (c.2005), in the same style as his work in the adjacent Station Hotel (see p.143). It has some of the best Burmantofts faience in the country.

In 2013-14 the firm of Ryder Architecture carried out a major redevelopment of the station. Working closely with Network Rail and the City Council, Ryders have improved the whole passenger experience through the provision of better waiting accommodation, toilets and signage, as well as modern retail and leisure facilities. In addition, the 1980s 'High Tech' ticket office has been demolished and replaced by a much less obtrusive, more rectilinear structure intended for retail use. Most importantly, this new structure does not interfere with the run of original columns. The mighty porte-cochère has been pedestrianised, with its arches now enclosed by frameless glazing, set inside the main structure and thus designed to be practically invisible. Major works to the public realm outside the station are also projected, in order to improve pedestrian and vehicular movement on arrival at and departure from the station.

THE FORMER RIDING SCHOOL

NORTHUMBERLAND ROAD, NEWCASTLE, NE1 8ST

This austere building, on the south side of Northumberland Road, was built as a Riding School for the Northumberland Yeomanry in 1847. It is by John Dobson, although the comparatively routine nature of the design suggests it might have been largely the product of his office.

Unusually for a public building by Dobson, it is of brick, although with a stone plinth and details. It is a functional structure, suitable for equestrian instruction, consisting originally of a large, barn-like space, with exposed brickwork and timber trusses and lit by a series of high-level, seven-light windows on the west side. These windows are separated by piers and are of unorthodox design, being semi-circular with deep stone sills and surrounds, and integrated keystones.

Externally, the narrow front facade has three tall, round-arched recesses with dressed sandstone surrounds framing square and round-headed windows inset within them. Above the central panel is a linked circular window. There is a stone string-course at the springing of the arches which, with the stonework along the gable, forms in effect a triangular broken pediment. This string-course continues at the sides to form a plain cornice.

Disused for many years, the structure was effectively restored and converted into teaching accommodation for Northumbria University by architects Ainsworth Spark in 1991. Its interior has been subdivided and the roof hidden, but the basic fabric remains.

THE 'CLUNY' WAREHOUSE (THE FORMER PLUMMER'S FLAX MILL)

OUSEBURN, BYKER, NEWCASTLE, NE1 2PQ

Conveniently located and with direct access to the Tyne for transportation by barges, the lower Ouseburn valley became noted for the manufacture of glass, pottery and metal products and retains a rich heritage of industrial architecture. Of particular interest are the former warehouses and factories on or near the banks of the Ouseburn itself.

The finest of these buildings is the former Flax Mill, designed by John Dobson in 1847-48 for the industrialist Robert Plummer. Here linen was spun, but only until 1859, when increasing competition from cotton forced the building to close. It later became a flour mill. In 1930 the firm of Macpherson's converted it into a warehouse known as the 'Cluny' (from their popular brand of Scotch whisky).

Although Dobson designed comparatively few industrial buildings, he worked on these structures with just as much care as on his other commissions, believing that they could, and should, be monumental and dignified. With its sandstone walls rising sheer above the river, and its restrained classical detailing, the Cluny perfectly exemplifies this approach. It is five storeys high including an attic (which looks to be a later addition), and twelve bays wide, with an additional entrance bay. Tall, flat-arched windows give views across the valley.

There are few finer Victorian industrial structures in the North East, for, "by a simple treatment of common material, a fine architectural effect is produced" (M. Dobson, *Memoir of John Dobson*, 1885). At one time the former mill possessed a particularly well-proportioned factory chimney, but only the base of this survives. The building now contains non-profit-making studios and workshops; to the rear is a brick annexe, which houses The Cluny public house.

Left The former Riding School, Northumberland Road, Newcastle upon Tyne, by John Dobson, 1847: from the north west.

Right The 'Cluny' Warehouse (the former Plummer's Flax Mill), Ouseburn, Byker, Newcastle upon Tyne, by John Dobson, 1847-48 (the right-hand building in this photograph): from the east.

THE FORMER STEPHENSON LOCOMOTIVE WORKS

SOUTH STREET, NEWCASTLE, NE1 3PE

As mentioned in the Introduction to this chapter, the pioneering railway engineers George Stephenson and his son Robert established the world's first locomotive workshop in Forth Street, Newcastle, in 1823. Although the works were much altered and then finally abandoned at the beginning of the twentieth century, it is still possible to see part of them as they were developed between 1848 and 1867 on nearby South Street, where an existing early nineteenth-century house was also incorporated into the works.

Adjacent to this, the tall, round-headed windows and large entrance door, with a huge cast-iron lintel above, show the extent of the workshop, part of which was incorporated within an adjacent builders' merchants' premises, now unoccupied. A later glazed wall and the glass roof of the boiler shed can be seen from the west side. Internally, cast-iron columns support heavy timber roof trusses, originally providing a large open space for locomotive assembly.

The complex was derelict for many years, but the Robert Stephenson Trust has now restored the house as offices, with a display of rooms from Stephenson's day, and converted the workshops into an exhibition venue. In line with this improvement, the whole surrounding area, contained to the south of the Central Station and bounded by the High Level Bridge and the railway to the west, has now become known as the 'Stephenson Quarter' in belated recognition of its importance in the development of the railways. It is the subject of a major development of new commercial and residential buildings, together with the retaining and refurbishment of key buildings associated with the Stephenson's and later railway works, and for the improvement of pedestrian links with the city centre.

THE ROYAL STATION HOTEL

NEVILLE STREET, NEWCASTLE, NE1 5DH

Left The former Stephenson Locomotive Works, South Street, Newcastle upon Tyne (overall complex, from 1848): from the north west.

Right The Royal Station Hotel, Neville Street, Newcastle upon Tyne, by John Dobson and others, from 1851 (the portion designed by Dobson is seen to the right in this photograph): from the north east.

The original Station Hotel, now comprising the western ten bays of the present building (except for their top two floors), was initially designed by John Dobson in 1851. It continued the facade of the station to the east, and offered direct access to the platforms at the rear. However, because of the financial crisis which also caused the postponement of the construction of Dobson's great station portico (see p.138), the hotel was not built until 1862-63, and then in a slightly modified design by Thomas Prosser. Previously, hotel accommodation had been within the station itself.

In 1892-94 the hotel was greatly extended to the east by the North Eastern Railway Company Architect William Bell. Thus the Dobson-Prosser section of the building lies to the right of the present main entrance. It was originally four storeys high (subsequently being raised to match the later extension) and has alternate segmental and triangular pediments to the first-floor windows.

Bell's huge extension is of five storeys with attics. The facade has eleven bays, in addition to a projecting entrance section which links it to the earlier Dobson-Prosser work. The first-floor window pattern of this earlier section is repeated, although interrupted by three canted bay windows, three storeys high (these may be later additions and, if so, extremely well done). The entrance block has three floors lit by triple windows below a cornice and a steep, double-hipped roof, complete with parapet and a pedimented aedicule that echoes the forms of the dormer windows elsewhere on the roofline.

The entrance itself, beneath a cast-iron canopy, is approached by steps and leads into a splendid entrance hall and staircase lit by an ornate chandelier. The interior is generally very grand, with some of the public rooms containing magnificent Burmantofts faience tiles on the walls, supplied by the Leeds Fireclay Co. and much admired at the time.

THE CENTRAL PUBLIC HOUSE
HALF MOON LANE, GATESHEAD, NE8 2AN

This ornate Victorian public house was built in 1854 to the designs of Matthew Thompson, for Alderman J. Potts, a local wine merchant. It deals splendidly with its awkward, triangular site, alongside the railway line. The building is mainly of three storeys, tapering to a 'flatiron', east end, although its west end is two-storey, stepping down towards a railway arch. The building has recently been successfully restored, after being in danger of demolition for some time, and retains much authentic Victorian character both inside and out.

The ground-floor elevation of The Central is almost Baroque in character and is particularly striking, with a high plinth supporting an arcade with protruding keystones. The arches are separated by powerfully rusticated Ionic pilasters that support a heavy cornice; the arches themselves spring from smaller pilasters. The north facade has a number of fanlights with original stained glass.

The upper floors are plainer, but still vigorous in the treatment of their two- and three-light windows, which have chamfered stone mullions. The roof is low pitched, in Welsh slate. Inside the building there is a superb panelled ceiling.

The Central public house, Half Moon Lane, Gateshead, by Matthew Thompson, 1854: from the east.

BENTINCK VILLAS, BENTINCK ROAD
NEWCASTLE, NE4 6UR

Bentinck Road was laid out in the mid-nineteenth century to connect Elswick Road and Westgate Road, both primary routes into Newcastle from the west. Bentinck Villas and the adjoining Bentinck Terrace, on the east side of Bentinck Road, are also from this period.

The construction of these properties, for prosperous families, provides further evidence of the progressive depopulation of the town centre at this time. It is also interesting to note how the epithet 'villa' could now be applied to dwellings that were quite modest, especially in comparison to their grand Georgian predecessors.

These two-storey classical villas are built of pinkish brick with what are now painted stone dressings. A number have been extended into the roofspace, compromising their elegance with poor-quality dormers. The floors are separated on the facade by a stone band, while the (sash) windows have stone surrounds. The entrances have engaged Tuscan columns supporting an entablature, a popular form in Newcastle. The main cornices are supported on carved brackets; above the cornices are deep, plain parapets, behind which are pitched roofs of Welsh slate. The front gardens have boundary walls in ashlar and retain their original wrought-iron fencing.

The interiors of these houses are impressive, with tall and generous rooms. Many still possess their original plasterwork, crafted by the highly accomplished Ralph Dodds, well known for his work for John Dobson in some of Northumberland's finest country houses.

Bentinck Villas, Bentinck Road, Newcastle upon Tyne, from c.1850: from the west.

ALL SAINTS' CEMETERY

JESMOND ROAD, NEWCASTLE, NE2 1NL

All Saints' Cemetery, Jesmond Road, Newcastle upon Tyne, by John Green jnr., 1855-56: from the south.

All Saints' was one of a number of municipal cemeteries built between 1855 and 1858 in what were then the outer suburbs of Newcastle. Other examples include St Andrew's (Tankerville Terrace, Jesmond), St John's (Elswick Road, Elswick) and St Nicholas's (Wingrove Avenue, Fenham).

All Saints' dates from 1855-56 and lies nearly opposite the main entrance of Jesmond (Old) Cemetery, designed by John Dobson about twenty years earlier (see p.108). A comparison shows the extent to which taste had changed during the early Victorian period. Whereas Dobson's main cemetery entrance is in a severe and dignified Greek Revival style, with gates and chapels conceived as a whole, the design of All Saints' Cemetery is entirely Gothic, with much carving and embellishment, and its two chapels are well set back from the entrance gateway. Here, too, the planting is much less intricate and ornamental than at Jesmond Cemetery.

The architect of All Saints' Cemetery, John Green jnr., was the nephew of John Green and the cousin of Benjamin Green, both much better known than himself. Even so, he was distinguished enough to have succeeded to the Presidency of the Northern Architectural Association after Dobson's death in 1865. He is also known to have completed a number of works begun by his cousin Benjamin, whose health had become uncertain well before his premature death, in an asylum, in 1858. However, Green jnr. designed this cemetery independently.

Its entrance gateway is set within a large, heavily moulded Gothic arch, beneath a tall gable with tracery-like carving. There are smaller gables at right-angles on either side. Although the ensemble is flanked by low walls containing the pedestrian entrances and end piers, it still looks curiously isolated, somehow suggesting that it is the surviving piece of a larger structure.

The separate chapels within the cemetery grounds (which were extended to Osborne Avenue in the early 1900s) are arranged symmetrically on either side of the entrance road. Each is built to a simple T-shaped plan in coursed, squared sandstone, with windows in Decorated Gothic style, and steeply pitched slate roofs. Each chapel also has a delicate turret, with a spire, at the south end. Only the western (Anglican) chapel is still in use for funerals.

HEATHFIELD

DURHAM ROAD, GATESHEAD, NE9 5AP

Left Heathfield, Durham Road, Gateshead, by John Wardle, 1856: from the south west.

Right St Paul's Church, Havelock Street, Elswick, Newcastle upon Tyne, by John Dobson, 1857-59: from the south.

Heathfield is one of a number of substantial houses and villas built in this vicinity during the mid-nineteenth century for prosperous industrialists and professional people, who were attracted by the clean air and semi-rural surroundings. John Wardle designed this two-storey property in 1856 for J.W. Swinburne, a solicitor who was Town Clerk of Gateshead. Wardle is of course better known for his earlier contribution to Richard Grainger's redevelopment of central Newcastle (see Chapter Three), but by now he was concentrating mainly on domestic buildings, working in partnership with his son John jnr.

Heathfield is in a restrained neo-classical style, consistent with most of Wardle's other commissions, and is symmetrical, with a protruding central block between two wings. This central block, illustrated here, has four bays, with two canted bay windows. The wings are comparatively plain; the one to the right appears to have been somewhat altered, probably when general modifications were made to the house around 1900.

Effective use is made throughout of the local Gateshead sandstone. The building has unusually deep eaves, elegantly supported on paired brackets, a feature also found at the earlier former Dispensary building in the centre of Gateshead (see p.105).

The interior of the house can no longer be seen as an entity, having been recently subdivided into Council-owned flats. Even so, it retains some high-quality original plasterwork, including a number of decorative roses and cornices, and several impressive Victorian fireplaces.

When first built, Heathfield was noted for its splendid garden, laid out in romantic Gothic style with artificial hills and waterfalls, and entered from the main road through a still-surviving gateway featuring monumental arches on either side. These have Tuscan entablatures surmounted by imposing lions, facing each other, carved by Anthony Kell and John Lamb Burnie. Much of the garden survived until the Second World War, but little of it now remains.

ST PAUL'S CHURCH

HAVELOCK STREET, ELSWICK, NEWCASTLE, NE4 6JT

This sturdy church is a late work by John Dobson, dating from 1857-59. For the most part in a simple Early English Gothic style, it is typical of the many plain and rather functional churches then being built in the new urban and industrial areas, invariably subsidised by the Government-backed Incorporated Church Building Society. Here as elsewhere much of the terraced housing once surrounding the church has been replaced with high-rise development.

A limited budget forced the architect to make numerous concessions in the design, which he seems to have regretted. Even so, the church's external massing is undeniably impressive and Dobson incorporated as much detail as he reasonably could in the circumstances. He also provided a generous nave, lit by clerestory windows with plate tracery, for the large congregation.

However, St Paul's has only a recess rather than a proper chancel, a point for which Dobson was criticised at the time. The church also lacks a spire, although there is an attractive polygonal turret on the south-west corner. Buttresses, between which are pairs of lancet windows, support the aisles. Over each lancet is a hood moulding, running into a string-course. The west facade of the church has two lancets surmounted by a rose window and a gable cross, while the east end boasts a particularly fine five-light window (by Morris & Co.).

The interior finish features plaster with ashlar dressings above timber boarding and a dado. The nave arcades are stately, with delicately carved spandrels that rise to support a splendid open timber roof. A vestry in Gothic style was added to the church, c.1908, by A.B. Plummer, then the Newcastle Diocesan Architect and Surveyor.

St Paul's closed in 2006 but was taken over by the Life Transformation Church in 2009. Much needed structural repair is planned.

JESMOND PARISH CHURCH

NEWCASTLE, NE2 4DJ

John Dobson was commissioned in 1857 to design this church, the first to be built in what was soon to become a rapidly expanding and affluent suburb. Funded by public subscription, at a final cost of nearly £6,500, it commemorated a celebrated local pastor, Richard Clayton (1802-56), and was initially known as the Clayton Memorial Church. The aim was to ensure the continuation of Clayton's ultra-Evangelical ministry, conducted at St Thomas's, Barras Bridge (see p.96), which it has succeeded in doing right up to the present day, and to testify to "the veneration and affection of a bereaved congregation for their departed minister".

This very late design by Dobson shows him working in a more distinctly Victorian Gothic Revival idiom. Thus the church combines the Decorated Gothic style with Dobson's more usual Early English, so that there is now a good deal of elaborate window tracery and sculptural enrichment. The large east window is particularly fine, while the west end features a rose window and gable cross. On the exterior of the church there are prominent gargoyles, together with hood mouldings that terminate in expressively sculpted heads of prophets, kings and saints (see opposite page), a treatment found in other late Dobson churches.

Yet the overall design is still curiously old-fashioned. There is no proper chancel, and the church actually has galleries (the western gallery was removed in 1907, at which time the north and south galleries were re-fronted), something very unusual for this date. These features were specifically demanded by the building trustees, who required a church to reflect Evangelical principles, with an open, auditory plan, having a central pulpit and a communion table behind it at the east end, and seating no fewer than 800-900 worshippers on the ground floor alone.

Inside the church, the surviving longitudinal galleries are carefully placed between two tiers of aisle windows, thus avoiding the problems caused by Dobson's enforced insertion of galleries at St Thomas's, Barras Bridge, twenty

Opposie page Jesmond Parish Church, Newcastle upon Tyne, by John Dobson, 1857-61: from the south east.

Left Jesmond Parish Church, Newcastle upon Tyne: detail of exterior carving on south elevation.

years earlier (see p.97). At Jesmond Parish Church the galleries flank a well-proportioned nave with stately arcades and delicately carved stone shafts rising through the spandrels to support a fine timber roof. The present oak communion table and limewood reredos of the Last Supper, based on the celebrated painting by Leonardo da Vinci and carved by Ralph Hedley under the direction of R.J. Johnson, date from 1890; Hicks & Charlewood added choir stalls, again carved by Ralph Hedley, in 1901.

Initially the church had plain glass, although this was steadily replaced with stained glass after 1868. The original stained glass of the east window (by George Baguley, 1877) was destroyed in an air raid of 1941, being replaced in 1956 with glass designed by Lawrence Lee. There is other stained glass by Baguley, and by Atkinson Brothers of Newcastle.

Perhaps because of its unorthodox character, this sturdy, vigorous building is one of Dobson's finest churches. The massive, rather squat tower, unexpectedly placed at the south-east corner, was intended to be higher, with a spire. It is pinnacled (additional pinnacles were taken down in 1963) and at the upper level has pairs of windows on each side. Admittedly, the position of this tower results in a rather unsatisfactory composition at the east end, especially with the later addition of a polygonal vestry to the north east by R.J. Johnson in 1874.

The south elevation is more effective. The tiers of windows lighting the side aisles are set in gables at right-angles to the main roof, expressed externally as a series of bays separated by buttresses. Each bay has a pair of windows, the lower being square-headed and those within the gables, pointed. This same arrangement also applies to the north elevation, although this is largely masked by church hall buildings added in the 1920s. The south elevation includes an entrance porch.

When Jesmond Parish Church was consecrated in 1861, it was surrounded by open fields, which were soon to be filled with fine suburban terraces and villas. Sadly, the church is now uncomfortably bounded on the south by the adjacent inner-city motorway (east), as it carves its way through Jesmond towards the coast.

ST JOSEPH'S CHURCH (R.C.)

HIGH STREET WEST, GATESHEAD, NE8 1LX

Built in 1858-59 to the designs of A.M. Dunn, himself a Roman Catholic, this was the first established Roman Catholic church in a town where sectarian controversy had been prevalent and was financed largely by public subscription. It was also the product of ceaseless campaigning by a Father Betham, who had set up a Catholic ministry in Gateshead in 1850, at first using a warehouse in Hillgate. Such, it seems, was the apathy of local Anglicans that Betham soon had the temerity to call himself the Vicar of Gateshead.

St Joseph's is a substantial design in what became Dunn's preferred Decorated Gothic style. It is constructed of coursed, dressed sandstone above a rock-faced stone basement. The church is in many ways typically High Victorian, but has a slightly unusual arrangement of nave, aisles, chancel, and south transept only. Moreover, the transept is short, and so too is the chancel, which has more the character of an apse. A tower or spire, never built, seems to have been intended to occupy the north-west corner of the building.

Almost no original internal fittings remain at St Joseph's as a result of a modern re-ordering, but the unified scheme of stained glass of c.1870, probably by William Henry Atkinson, a pupil of William Wailes, is noteworthy. The windows behind the high altar represent Saints Edward, Henry, Patrick and Cuthbert, with the Virgin and St Joseph in the centre.

St Joseph's Church (R.C.), High Street West, Gateshead, by A.M. Dunn, 1858-59: from the north west.

GARTH HEADS INDUSTRIAL DWELLINGS

GARTH HEADS, NEWCASTLE, NE1 2JE

This is a severe and functional building, rather resembling a warehouse. Four storeys high with a central, six-storey block, it was the first housing of an institutional nature provided in Newcastle for industrial workers and was funded by philanthropists rather than by the Corporation. John Johnstone designed the building in 1869 for the Newcastle upon Tyne Improved Industrial Dwellings Co. Ltd; it was opened in 1870 and extended in 1878. Originally there was no internal sanitation in the dwellings. However, two WCs were provided on each landing and there were communal washhouses in the courtyards.

The dwellings are constructed of brindled brickwork in English bond, with ashlar sills and keystones (now painted). The severity of the design is relieved by mouldings that articulate the floor levels and pilaster-like strips that rise through all floors of the main facade. In addition, the corners of the building are chamfered, with three blank windows, while the eaves have a decorative brick cornice. On either side of the main entrance are infilled openings that were originally part of shop units.

Nerwcastle Corporation bought the building in 1968 and recently it has undergone a major conversion into student flats. There have been numerous other alterations to it over the years, but nevertheless, some original internal details remain.

Garth Head Industrial Dwellings, Newcastle upon Tyne, by John Johnstone, 1869-70; extended 1878: from the south west.

THE NORTHERN COUNTIES SCHOOL FOR THE DEAF

GREAT NORTH ROAD, NEWCASTLE, NE2 3BB

This rather forbidding Gothic Revival structure is the earliest and most northerly of three important institutional buildings set back from the Great North Road and situated just to the north of Brandling Park. The others are the former Northern Counties Orphan Asylum (see p.181) and the slightly later former Fleming Memorial Hospital for Sick Children (see p.193). They are all different, but are in typically Victorian historicist styles and also collectively give an impressive indication of the period's wealth, both public and private.

The building illustrated here is situated next to St Andrew's Cemetery and was initially known as the Northern Counties Institution for the Deaf and Dumb. Dating from 1860, it was designed by Johnson Hogg, in association with T.W. Goodman of London, for an organisation that had been founded in 1838 and now required larger, purpose-built, accommodation. Hogg had started his career as a stonemason. He later became an assistant to John Dobson, before setting up as an independent architect, c.1857.

The building is of local sandstone with red sandstone details and was originally accessed via a lodge and impressive gates. Its west facade, on the Great North Road, originally contained the main entrance, placed beneath a tower. This facade, its composition now significantly compromised by the addition of an attic floor above the main hall with a flat-roofed dormer, modern windows and a timber fascia, has five bays to the north of the entrance tower, and four bays to the south. Stairs lead up to a Gothic-arched doorway in the tower, which itself rises through the steeply pitched roof of the main building. At first-floor level, the bays to the north have large Gothic windows in a free Decorated style, lighting the main hall. On the ground floor are triple pointed-arched windows below a projecting double stone band. The bays to the south are more domestic in character, with canted bay windows on two floors and a gabled attic above. An attractive lodge on the south-west side dates from 1879.

Extensions and modifications to the institution's main block not already mentioned include those by W.L. Newcombe, in 1893-94, and Stephen Piper, in 1905, the latter for new school premises. In addition the main entrance to the institution is now reached from Tankerville Terrace, on the east side, via a complex of buildings in various styles. All these changes have reduced the impact of the original design.

The Northern Counties School for the Deaf, Great North Road, Newcastle upon Tyne, by Johnson Hogg and others, from 1860: from the north west.

SALTWELL TOWERS

EAST PARK ROAD, GATESHEAD, NE9 5AX

Left Saltwell Towers, East Park Road, Gateshead, by William Wailes, from 1862: from the south west.

Right Phoenix House, No.18 Sandhill, Newcastle upon Tyne, by William Parnell, 1863: from the north west.

Saltwell Towers (see also, chapter frontispiece) was designed and built, as his own house, by the eminent local stained glass designer and manufacturer William Wailes (1808-81). Greatly influenced by the Gothic Revivalist A.W.N. Pugin (see p.133), Wailes worked in a similar neo-medieval idiom and was already an experienced designer when he set up in full-time practice in 1840. He was responsible for windows in both of Newcastle's cathedrals. After 1861 his firm continued as Wailes & Strang until c.1915.

Although he had his workshop in Bath Lane, Newcastle, Wailes preferred to live in rural settings. He initially purchased 60 acres of land between East Park Road and West Park Road, Gateshead, where he built his first house, South Dene Tower. Of red and white brick, this castellated, 'Tudor-Gothic' property (demolished in 1956) anticipated the design of Saltwell Towers, which is built of similarly polychromatic brickwork and is asymmetrical, with a highly romantic skyline formed of towers, turrets and battlements – all very much as the great contemporary critic John Ruskin, another champion of the Gothic Revival, would have advised.

Wailes later leased South Dene Tower to Robert Coltman Clephan, a noted collector of medieval armour, and bought a considerable quantity of additional land in the vicinity. Here, from 1862, he constructed Saltwell Towers, north of the earlier house and centrally placed on a raised terrace within the enlarged plot. It was a perfect vehicle to display his talents in stained glass design. However, his windows here do not survive. Similarly, nearly all the elaborate, neo-Gothic furniture and woodwork designed for the house by the gifted, if eccentric, Newcastle carver Gerard Robinson has also disappeared.

Wailes surrounded his new mansion with fine, decorative gardens, said to have been laid out by John Hancock (see p.131). In 1876 Wailes sold these gardens to Gateshead Corporation for £32,000 for use as a public park, on condition that he could continue to live in Saltwell Towers until his death. W.B. Kemp of Birkenhead redesigned the park, which opened to the public in 1876.

The house was then leased to a number of tenants, until taken over by the Corporation. It was used as a hospital during the First World War and then as a museum from 1932 to 1969. Unfortunately, however, it was subsequently allowed to fall into decay, with much of the exterior brickwork crumbling and most of the interior woodwork being lost to dry rot. More recently, Gateshead Council secured a grant of £10 million from the Heritage Lottery Fund for a major restoration of both house and gardens from 1999. Saltwell Towers, fully refurbished and with the addition of a well-considered modern extension, re-opened in 2004 and is now a visitor centre for the park. The gardens have been replanted with Victorian varieties.

PHOENIX HOUSE

NO. 18 SANDHILL, NEWCASTLE, NE1 3AF

Originally known as Queen's Buildings, Phoenix House was designed by local architect William Parnell in 1863 for the Royal Insurance Company, whose coat of arms is still visible. It now houses restaurants with flats above them.

The building, in sandstone ashlar, formed part of the slightly belated redevelopment (c.1858-63) of Newcastle's quayside, following the Great Fire of 1854. Initially, John Dobson was employed by the Corporation to re-plan the area in 1855-56, but after a lengthy series of delays the redevelopment was finally undertaken by Ralph Walters, a Newcastle-born entrepreneur then resident in London. His layout largely followed Dobson's street plan, if not his proposed elevations. However, a valuable proposal by Dobson to link the quayside with the upper town was unfortunately abandoned.

The main entrance to Phoenix House, on the corner of the Side and Queen Street, is placed within a well-considered curve. This corner elevation has coupled, giant Corinthian columns rising through the first and second floors, round-arched windows in the attic floor, and some rich relief carving, including the coat of arms mentioned above. The treatment of this curved corner is perhaps a respectful response to Dobson's earlier semi-circular extension to the Guildhall (1823-26), which stands nearby. However, the subsequent change in taste, from neo-classical severity to Victorian grandiloquence, is very evident.

A basement sloping down the hill supports the ground floor. It has seven bays on this side (but more elsewhere) containing large windows, separated by Tuscan pilasters supporting a continuous cornice above. The end bays of the two upper floors are separated by pilasters; between the central five bays are giant attached Corinthian columns supporting a deep entablature and dentilled cornice, below a further attic floor.

BENWELL DENE HOUSE

BENWELL LANE, NEWCASTLE, NE15 6RU

Alfred Waterhouse, architect of such archetypal Victorian masterpieces as Manchester Town Hall and London's Natural History Museum, designed this asymmetrical 'Tudor-Gothic' dwelling in 1864. It was built for the banker and antiquarian Dr Thomas Hodgkin, the architect's brother-in-law and, incidentally, business partner of John William Pease, who lived at nearby Pendower Hall (see p.156). Much less decorative than many of Waterhouse's other commissions, Benwell Dene House nevertheless still shows his characteristic control. Originally it was also beautifully sited, on the northern banks of the Tyne, although it now sits within a poorly maintained external space containing a number of more modern buildings.

The house is one of a number of substantial properties that were built in close proximity, many architecturally rather similar. They are mostly now demolished, but were formerly owned by wealthy industrialists and professional men who chose to live in or near the then-fashionable villages of Benwell and Elswick, with their clean air, spectacular views across the river and good transport links to Newcastle. Other such houses that are still in existence include (in addition to Pendower Hall), Benwell Hill House (which later became St Cuthbert's Grammar School and now houses various small businesses and charities), the somewhat earlier Benwell Towers (see p.102), and Elswick Lodge, all built in various versions of the 'Tudor-Gothic' style.

The house illustrated here is two storeys high, with an attic storey within the steeply sloping roof. On its completion, in 1866, Hodgkin gave, in his own words, a "sumptuous supper" for the workmen employed in building the house, which is finely constructed of hammer-dressed sandstone on an ashlar plinth and with ashlar dressings around the openings.

The plan of the house is irregular, with wings and annexes protruding from a principal range that runs east-west, parallel with Benwell Lane. This gives the building a picturesque architectural character, additionally achieved by the prominent use of a multitude of gables, dormers and chimneys, while the roof itself is covered with graduated slates, with serrated ridge tiles and stone copings. All the windows have chamfered mullions and stone lintels.

When Hodgkin retired in 1894 to live in the splendid keep of Bamburgh Castle, Northumberland (by arrangement with Lord Armstrong), he wrote of his Benwell residence: "it is a terrible wrench to leave this dear house". The mansion soon became the Royal Victoria School for the Blind. At this time, too, Waterhouse designed a new wing for it, while Hodgkin donated its substantial gardens for use as a public park and, in his own words, "to save the place from the ravages of the builder". Thus the attractively wooded Hodgkin Park, sloping gently down towards the Tyne, was formally opened in 1899; it was extended in 1907-08.

THE FORMER COUNTY COURT BUILDING

NO. 52 WESTGATE ROAD, NEWCASTLE, NE1 5XU

The County Court was built in 1864-65 to the designs of Charles Reeve, a Government architect, in what had been part of the grounds of St John's Vicarage. It is a dignified, five-bay, three-storey composition, again demonstrating the Victorians' predilection for ornate, neo-Renaissance styles in much of their public and commercial architecture.

As with its more famous neighbour, the Newcastle Assembly Rooms, the building's facade is constructed of fine ashlar masonry with the rear elevations for the most part of brick. Its architectural language is reminiscent of Renaissance palazzo design; both the rustication around the windows and door on the ground floor, and the keystones decorated with masks, are devices used by the Italian master Palladio.

A cornice with a dentil moulding gives further articulation, dividing the ground floor from the first; a string-course, integrated with the upper window surrounds, separates the first floor from the second. Another cornice, larger and with brackets, effectively completes the facade.

The building continued to serve as the County Court until the much larger Law Courts, on the Newcastle quayside, were finished in 1990. There is still a courtroom within, but it has lost its original fittings and is no longer used. A firm of solicitors now occupies the premises.

Opposite Benwell Dene House, Benwell Lane, Newcastle upon Tyne, by Alfred Waterhouse, 1864: from the south.

Above The former County Court Building, No. 52 Westgate Road, Newcastle upon Tyne, by Charles Reeve, 1864-65: from the south west.

PENDOWER HALL

WEST ROAD, NEWCASTLE, NE15 6PP

The Quaker banker John William Pease, who also owned Benwell Towers (see pp.102-3), built this house in 1865-66 and moved into it with his wife, Helen Maria, and their four children shortly afterwards. They would have greatly enjoyed the building's up-to-date facilities, including gas lighting, as well as its park-like grounds, which offered fine views of the Tyne valley to the south.

The 'Tudor-Gothic' Pendower Hall, with its multiplicity of gables, dormers and pointed arches, looks very like the slightly earlier Benwell Dene House (see p.154). This similarity, coupled with the fact that the latter mansion was owned by Pease's friend, business partner and also brother-in-law, Thomas Hodgkin, has prompted an attribution to Alfred Waterhouse. However, this cannot be proved, so curiously for a building of this quality, the architect of Pendower Hall is unknown.

What is nevertheless certain is that in 1885 R.J. Johnson was employed to make substantial additions to the house; these included a magnificent library in neo-Jacobean style (see below), with other interiors reflecting an Aesthetic Movement influence. Despite later institutional use – by Newcastle City Council from 1920 to 2012, as a special school and then a teachers' centre – much of Johnson's work survives. At the time of writing, however, Pendower Hall is empty and disused. The future of this Grade II listed building, which has the additional historical significance of being sited close to Hadrian's Wall, is currently under consideration by Newcastle City Council and English Heritage.

Above Pendower Hall, West Road, Newcastle upon Tyne, 1865-66, with additions by R.J. Johnson, 1885: from the south east.

Right Pendower Hall, library by R.J. Johnson, 1885.

THE MILL VOLVO (FORMERLY THE JOURNAL) TYNE THEATRE

WESTGATE ROAD, NEWCASTLE, NE1 4AG

The Tyne Theatre and Opera House, as it was originally called, was designed by William Parnell and built in 1866-67. Its backers included the local politician Joseph Cowen, Thomas Forster, a solicitor, and the celebrated actor-manager George Stanley. Although overshadowed by the grander, more conspicuous Theatre Royal (see p.114), what is now the Mill Volvo Tyne Theatre actually had at the time of its opening a larger capacity than its competitor in Grey Street and its contribution is still of great significance. It is the oldest working Victorian theatre in the country and also possesses the most complete set of stage machinery from the period (designed by the notable stage carpenter William Day of Liverpool), with a complex system of bridges, traps, flies and other devices. Like the Theatre Royal, it is Grade I listed.

Although Parnell had no previous experience in theatre design – his practice featured primarily factories, offices and warehouses – he produced a structure with excellent acoustics, thanks partly to an internal lining of wood (fabricated by joiners J. & W. Lowry). The elegant auditorium has three tiers of balconies, accommodating about 3,000 people; the stage is 50 feet deep. Originally, a painting above the proscenium depicted "Britannia Giving her Blessing to the Arts".

Externally, the building's front facade is constructed of an unusual, but effective, combination of white glazed bricks with sandstone dressings. The composition is for the most part Italianate and has handsome, Renaissance-style arched windows on the second floor, below a string-course and a heavy cornice supported by decorative stone consoles.

After alterations and improvements of 1892-93 by local architects Oliver & Leeson (including the construction of the popular Winter Garden Tea Rooms and a red-brick addition to the front right), the theatre became the Stoll Picture House in 1919, when cinemas were beginning to rival theatres in popularity. The specialist theatre architect Frank Matcham undertook the conversion. The building remained a cinema until 1974, when it was restored to its former use, re-opening as the New Tyne Theatre three years later. On Christmas Day in 1985 a disastrous fire destroyed much of the stage and the proscenium arch, but fortunately the auditorium was not destroyed and the theatre was carefully restored by the New Tyne Theatre Trust. Since 2002 the theatre has been run by the management group SMG Europe. It changed its name in 2012 when the car dealership Mill Volvo became its new sponsor.

The Mill Volvo (formerly The Journal) Tyne Theatre, Westgate Road, Newcastle upon Tyne, by William Parnell, 1866-67: from the north east.

ST NICHOLAS'S HOSPITAL

JUBILEE ROAD, GOSFORTH, NEWCASTLE, NE3 3XT

Initially known as the 'Newcastle upon Tyne Borough Lunatic Asylum, Coxlodge', St Nicholas's Hospital dates originally from 1866-69. Located in the suburb of Gosforth, it consists of a large group of buildings surrounded by much open space, typical of the mental institutions of the time. Soon after its opening it was able to accommodate 250 patients.

In earlier times, the hospital presented a long, mainly two-storey profile towards Salters Road. The arrangement included a main building, designed by W.L. Moffatt, an Edinburgh-based architect who specialised in this kind of institutional work, and eastern and western ranges subsequently added by local architect A.B. Plummer in 1885. Their elevations are now largely obscured by later extensions and additions, some with squat, Italianate towers. There are also some detached blocks and pavilions.

At its opening, the original main building (see left) was described, perhaps somewhat fancifully, as "Palladian, simple in its details, but effective in its character". It is in coursed sandstone, with smoother window surrounds and details, and a prominent central clock tower with a pyramidal roof topped by an ironwork balustrade. The north facade of this block has a central projecting section with heavily recessed joints and projecting cornices above both the ground- and first-floor windows. A round-headed entrance door, placed between two pilasters, is reached via a pair of curved ramps with heavy stone balustrades.

An additional eastern range consists of a series of two-storey pavilions with south-facing verandas, while further large extensions in a similar classical style were added in 1895-1900 to the designs of J.W. Dyson of Newcastle. These extensions cost the then enormous sum of more than £200,000 and include a notable recreation hall and theatre, with large, round-headed windows and an impressive proscenium arch. This is decorated with Art Nouveau-style Doulton tiles depicting female figures in flowing robes, floating amid trees and flowers, designed by W.J. Neatby and dated to 1896. Yet further extensions included a nurses' home and an isolation block, added by Dyson, c.1912-13.

In 1920 the institution was re-named the City of Newcastle Mental Hospital, before becoming St Nicholas's Hospital in 1947. The high walls have been lowered, with a large part of the grounds sold for housing and commercial use. Some of the hospital outbuildings were converted into apartments during the 1990s by architects JDDK (Jane Darbyshire & David Kendall). However, the main buildings are still occupied and the hall is frequently used by local theatrical groups.

There have been a number of recent additions to the hospital facilities, including the Bamburgh Clinic, by MAAP Architects, which won an R.I.B.A. award in 2008. This new provision, part of the secure area for highly vulnerable patients, is successful in that it maintains the required level of security, but does so in a humane and sensitive way. Thus the building is organised around a series of landscaped courts, relating to each of the three wards, which are linked by a double-height corridor around each court. This arrangement gives access to the patients' rooms, which look outward to give the occupants a sense of privacy. The communal areas provided have to be more materially robust, but overall the scheme radiates a sense of care for both the occupants and the staff.

THE FORMER GATESHEAD TOWN HALL

WEST STREET AND SWINBURNE STREET, GATESHEAD, NE8 1HE

Left St Nicholas's Hospital, Jubilee Road, Gosforth, Newcastle upon Tyne: the original main building, by W.L. Moffatt, 1866-69 (detail): from the north west.

Right Gateshead Town Hall, West Street and Swinburne Street, Gateshead, by John Johnstone, 1868-70: from the south west.

Following the re-organisation of local government in 1835, many new town halls were built throughout Britain, constituting important expressions of civic and municipal pride. Gateshead Town Hall is an excellent example. It occupies a prominent, if sloping, site to the north of the town centre and still dominates the skyline from the High Level Bridge. Before its construction, in 1868-70, the Corporation occupied premises on Oakwellgate and then near the old railway station.

The Town Hall was designed by John Johnstone, following a competition of 1867, which R.J. Johnson also entered, receiving second premium. The project was delayed because of budgetary concerns. Following a number of enforced re-designs, Johnstone eventually completed a scaled-down building costing £12,000. It included offices, committee rooms, a council chamber, police and fire stations, and a magistrates' court; there was also, typically, a large hall for public events. To have financed and built such a complex must be seen as a considerable achievement for a town that was far from affluent.

The building is of sandstone ashlar, in an eclectic Italianate style not untypical of Victorian town hall architecture generally. Its main facade on to West Street is symmetrical, with a repeated rhythm created by sets of paired windows. A higher, central entrance block protrudes for emphasis. Here a cornice separates the comparatively plain ground floor from the first floor, which features three powerful, double-arched windows.

Reliefs representing Commerce, Industry and Justice, as well as a surmounting figure of Queen Victoria, form part of a balustraded parapet, separated from the main portion of the facade by a heavy dentil cornice. The stonework also features some heraldic carving, emblematic of the town. At ground-floor level, engaged columns flank a small, centrally located entrance. In front of the building stands an ornate cast-iron clock tower, made in 1892 by Gillett & Johnston of Croydon. It was restored by Gateshead Council in 2001.

The Town Hall remained in use until 1986, when the Council moved to a new, much larger and purpose-built Civic Centre on Regent Street. The older building was largely empty for some years, although it did host a number of functions, and its interiors are for the most part intact. Much of their fine Victorian stained glass (and some from the 1930s), depicting figures, emblems and themes relating to the locality, still survives and other features of note include the pillared entrance hall, and two grand staircases leading up to the former Council Chamber, with its intricate, patterned ceiling. On the southern side of the building is the spacious and impressive public hall, which is noted for its good acoustics; it has a high, arched ceiling and a wealth of decorative plasterwork.

The nearby Sage Gateshead (see p.320) has recently taken over the management of the building as a venue for intimate performances and a centre for community music.

THE SWING BRIDGE

GATESHEAD AND NEWCASTLE, NE1 3RQ

This superb bridge across the Tyne was built by the famous engineer Sir William (later Lord) Armstrong, between 1868 and 1876 (although work actually commenced in 1864, on the building of a temporary bridge to ensure continuity of passage). Armstrong probably also had a major hand in the design, although John Ure, Engineer to the Tyne Improvement Commission, is officially credited with this. Armstrong was certainly one of the main beneficiaries of the construction of the bridge, since it allowed the large ships built at his Elswick works to pass downriver.

The Swing Bridge replaced Robert Mylne's bridge of 1775-81, a nine-arched stone structure that was still in good condition but which had become an obstacle to river traffic. Mylne's bridge followed the line of the previous medieval bridge and probably that of the yet earlier Roman crossing of Pons Aelius. During the construction of the Swing Bridge, the repeatedly re-used foundations of all three predecessors were exposed, while two Roman altars from a shrine dedicated to the gods Neptune and Oceanus, built to protect the original bridge, were dredged from the river.

In its day, the Swing Bridge was the largest structure of its kind in the world. It is a marvel of engineering. Cantilevered on cast-iron rollers, its central portion will turn on its own axis to rest above, and in line with, a central stone platform. Armstrong fabricated the bridge's wrought-iron structure and its hydraulic machinery; the Tyne Improvement Commission was responsible for the foundations and abutments.

In its open position, the bridge provides two clear passages along the river, each 95 feet wide. Perched on top of the bridge is a panopticon-type enclosure giving the operator a 360-degree view of the river and of any approaching ships. Although still in perfect working order and continuously manned, the bridge is now seldom opened because of the paucity of traffic travelling on the Tyne. Even so, since first opening the bridge has allowed nearly half a million vessels to pass through.

The Swing Bridge, Gateshead and Newcastle upon Tyne, by John Ure, 1868-76: from the north east. Photograph 2006.

THE FORMER NORTHERN COUNTIES ORPHAN ASYLUM

GREAT NORTH ROAD, NEWCASTLE, NE2 3BB

The first component of this complex is an attractively composed design by R.J. Johnson of Newcastle in an advanced free Jacobean style (see right, top), often favoured by this architect in his later years for collegiate and institutional work. The structure, situated just to the south of the Northern Counties School for the Deaf (see p.151), opened in 1869 as the Abbott Memorial Building of the Northern Counties Orphan Asylum, initially just for girls. Funds had been donated by Mrs J.G. Abbott.

Of red brick with stone details, it was intended to have "the appearance of a handsome mansion". It has two main storeys with attics and a fine, symmetrical facade with projecting gabled wings fronted by canted bay windows. There is also a good first-floor ironwork balcony between the wings.

The separate Jane Philipson Orphanage (for boys) was soon added to the south (see right, lower). This was funded by the Philipsons, another wealthy local family, and was designed by G.T. Redmayne of Manchester, who used for the most part local red brick, with contrasting stone details in the window arches and other features.

The Philipson Orphanage is essentially neo-Gothic, although with a profusion of round arches, and is much more 'picturesque' than Johnson's earlier block. Indeed, and curiously, it could easily pass for an earlier structure. Its asymmetrical cruciform plan includes a tall entrance tower at the south-west corner matched by a projecting main gable, also on the west side; this has a large, tripartite, round-headed window in the top floor.

An inscription above the main door dates this second Orphanage to 1873, although the architect's drawings are dated 1874 and the building opened in 1876. In 1883-85 Johnson returned to add the neo-Gothic Adamson Memorial Chapel, again in red brick with stone dressings and with a fine, Perpendicular-style west window. The chapel effectively linked the Abbott and the Philipson Orphanages but is now demolished.

During the Second World War the whole institution was taken over, in stages, by the Maternity Hospital and the buildings were substantially remodelled. The Hospital officially re-opened in 1950, re-named the Princess Mary Maternity Hospital. This in turn moved to new accommodation in Newcastle's Royal Victoria Infirmary in 1993.

The whole complex has now been successfully converted into apartments by architects Stringer & Jones. This project involved the construction of new residential buildings in a sympathetic style, linking the original blocks and forming an attractive enclosed court.

Top The former Northern Counties Orphan Asylum, Great North Road, Newcastle upon Tyne, by R.J. Johnson, 1869: from the north west.

Above The former Jane Philipson Orphanage, Great North Road, Newcastle upon Tyne, by G.T. Redmayne, c.1873-76: from the north west.

JESMOND DENE BANQUETING HALL LODGE

JESMOND DENE ROAD, NEWCASTLE, NE7 7BA

In 1860 Sir William (later Lord) Armstrong, who was then residing at his house Jesmond Dean (now demolished) on Jesmond Dene Road, commissioned John Dobson to design a Banqueting Hall in which to entertain his distinguished visitors. The Hall, in Italianate style, was built near the house, on the edge of what was soon to become the industrialist's private park, Jesmond Dene. In 1869-70 the Hall was extended by the important London architect Norman Shaw, then about to begin work on Cragside, Armstrong's famous country house near Rothbury in Northumberland.

At one time the Banqueting Hall housed paintings, sculptures and even a water-powered organ. Although the Hall is now a roofless ruin, and not illustrated in this book, its small gatehouse-cum-lodge, another part of Shaw's work of 1869-70, still remains. This lodge is a 'Tudor-Gothic'-style building in rock-faced stone (emblazoned with Armstrong's initials). With its large, arched gateway, gables projecting from a steep slate roof, and tall stone chimneys, it anticipates the pleasant informality of early Arts and Crafts architecture.

Jesmond Dene Banqueting Hall Lodge, Jesmond Dene Road, Newcastle upon Tyne, by R. Norman Shaw, 1869-70: from the south west.

ST DOMINIC'S PRIORY CHURCH (R.C.)

NEW BRIDGE STREET, NEWCASTLE, NE1 2TP

St Dominic's Priory Church (R.C.), New Bridge Street, Newcastle upon Tyne, by A.M. Dunn, 1869-73: from the north.

A.M. Dunn designed this large and impressive church in 1869. When Cardinal Manning opened the church in 1873, it was described as being in the "German Romanesque" style. Certainly, the well-travelled Dunn had been making first-hand studies of German (and French) Romanesque architecture around this time. However, the building also has Gothic features and so can perhaps best be described as 'transitional style'. The attached brick and terracotta Priory was added by Dunn, now in partnership with E.J. Hansom, in 1887.

The construction of this church marked the return of the Dominicans to Newcastle after more than 300 years of exile following the Dissolution of the Monasteries. Now the monks began to provide financial support for the many people in the vicinity who lived in abject poverty. Their building also became a spiritual centre for the town's many Irish Catholic immigrants and even today St Dominic's continues to be active within the community, although the threat of vandalism restricts the times when it can open its doors to worshippers.

The design of the church was influenced by thirteenth-century Dominican architecture. The exterior is of coursed sandstone and the treatment is robust, with a powerful north (ritual west, see below) facade rising sheer above New Bridge Street. A substantial wheel window, located high up on this facade, floods the nave with light; the clerestory has triple lancet windows, with one sequence within each bay. Externally, the wheel window is placed above delicately carved, interlocking blind arcades, either side of a damaged statue of St Dominic. However, these arcades are now partly masked by a stark, modern entrance lobby.

Because of the constraints of the site, the church is oriented north-south, rather than east-west, so that the ritual east end, with the altar, is at the geographical south end. The rich interior, with walls of exposed polychrome brick and stone, contains much heavy, typically High Victorian carving. The neo-Gothic choir stalls (by Edward Blore, 1827) were originally in Peterborough Cathedral; they were salvaged and brought to the church by a parishioner during the 1890s.

NEVILLE HALL

WESTGATE ROAD, NEWCASTLE, NE1 1SE

Left Neville Hall, Westgate Road, Newcastle upon Tyne, by A.M. Dunn, 1870-72: from the north west.

Right Neville Hall, Westgate Road, Newcastle upon Tyne: the Wood Memorial Hall.

Neville Hall was purpose-built in 1870-72 for the North of England Institute of Mining and Mechanical Engineers, which had hitherto occupied temporary premises. Following the passing of the Government Inspection Act in 1850, local industrialists had established the Institute of Mining Engineers in 1852 (the Mechanical Engineers joined later, in 1866). Their principal aim was to promote education and technological advance in order to prevent explosions and accidents in mines.

The Institute's new building was sited on land acquired from the then School of Medicine (which at first occupied part of the premises itself, as did the College of Physical Sciences and the administrative department of the Blyth and Tyne Railway Co.). Originally the land had been owned by the Nevilles, Earls of Westmorland, hence the building's name. It was designed by A.M. Dunn, a committed Gothic Revivalist much influenced by Pugin (see p.132), and, unusually for Newcastle in the secular field, is a full-blooded example of High Victorian Gothic.

This style was perhaps chosen to help establish the Institute's distinct identity and to make a strong visual contrast with its classical neighbour, the Literary and Philosophical Society (see p.89). Dunn probably obtained the commission because of his expertise in the Gothic style and also possibly because his father, Matthias Dunn, was a prominent member of the Institute.

Neville Hall is a noble and decorative structure, having two full storeys, together with an attic storey above a continuous Lombard frieze. Dunn cleverly manipulates the fenestration on each floor to give expression to the facades, which are also heavily buttressed. Impressive trefoil dormers light the attic floor, while the first-floor windows have decorative, blind tympana and are flanked by columns carved with free foliage patterns. The ground-floor windows, which by contrast are rectangular rather than pointed, have richly carved surrounds. In addition, cornices and string-courses are used to further accent the elevations: for example, a continuous, carved band separates the ground and first floors. The main entrance to the building is on the north-west corner, flanked by Shap granite columns and located within an elaborately carved bay.

On the ground floor are offices, while the principal room on the first floor is the Wood Memorial Hall. This houses the Institute's library and is one of the finest examples of Victorian neo-medieval interior design in the

North East. It is a more than worthy testimonial to the great mining engineer Nicholas Wood (1795-1865), mentor of Robert Stephenson and first President of the Institute (1852-56).

A high and beautifully lit space, the Hall has skylights within the elaborately curved ceiling and boasts a splendid, west-facing stained-glass window by Cooke of London (commemorating heroes of mining and engineering). The Hall also contains a wealth of rich carving in stone and wood, both naturalistic and heraldic, as well as gilding, patterned ornament, and vibrant contrasts of materials throughout (see photograph above).

Appropriately, the Wood Memorial Hall is dominated by a shrine-like statue of Wood himself, by Edward William Wyon, while the coupled polished marble shafts that support the transverse arches bracing the roof have shields inscribed with Wood's monogram. An embattled cornice and carved string-course (by Roddis of Birmingham) and two heavily carved stone fireplaces on the north side provide further enrichment. The general decorative opulence of this great room, which has elements drawn not only from the Gothic but also from the Romanesque style, accords perfectly with the doctrines of John Ruskin regarding decoration and the use of materials.

The exterior of Neville Hall as a whole, with its picturesque use of Prudham stone banded with contrasting red sandstone, is equally Ruskinian. Moreover, at one time the building was further embellished with pairs of carved stone birds, above the dormers, as well as a statue of a miner with his Davy lamp. These are all now removed, but they powerfully reflected Ruskin's specific encouragement of architects to make use of sculptural adornment.

The panelling and balconies at mezzanine level in the Wood Memorial Hall were inserted in 1902 by local architects Cackett & Burns Dick, who at the same time remodelled the Institute's semi-circular Lecture Theatre, reached from the ground floor. They also installed its present mahogany furniture and fittings, in the fashionable Edwardian neo-Baroque style.

The Institute has maintained its educational role ever since it opened and still presents lectures and educational workshops with the aim of advancing technological knowledge. It also hosts regular events and lectures organised by various local learned societies.

THE FORMER NATIONAL PROVINCIAL BANK

MOSLEY STREET, NEWCASTLE, NE1 1DF

The former National Provincial Bank, Mosley Street, Newcastle upon Tyne, by John Gibson, 1871-72: from the north west.

From the 1870s, Collingwood and Mosley Streets developed into Newcastle's financial axis as banks and insurance companies erected impressive branch buildings. Some of these were national firms who used their own architects, as in this case with the.employment of the specialist and highly accomplished bank architect John Gibson (1817-92). Gibson, here assisted by local architect William Glover, later President of the Northern Architectural Association, acting as clerk of works, designed over 40 branches for the firm, including six in the North East. The National Provincial Bank was founded in 1833 and established one of the first nationwide branch networks in Britain. In setting up a Newcastle branch, the firm was keen to acquire a site "in the immediate proximity of Mr. Grainger's handsome Grey Street" (quoted by I.S. Black). This was achieved with the purchase of a site at the corner of Mosley and Dean Streets.

John Gibson had formerly worked as an assistant to Sir Charles Barry (1795-1860), giving him a thorough knowledge of classical and Renaissance styles, and went on to receive the R.I.B.A. Gold Medal in 1890. Here Gibson's building, of 1871-72, was designed in the Italian Renaissance style, drawing inspiration from the palazzi built by mercantile families such as the Medici.

Its rusticated base gives an impression of strength and also resolves the problem of the sloping site. The ground floor, also rusticated, has windows with red granite shafts. *The Builder* of October 1898 commented, "The refined and dignified National Provincial Bank … is the only building which we remember to have seen in which the introduction of polished red granite shafts seemed to be an improvement, by giving a touch of life without destroying the repose of the composition." Meanwhile, the upper storeys are adorned by giant pilasters and, as in Gibson's other branch buildings, the name of the firm and the date of its establishment are carved on the crowning entablature.

The building's splendid exterior, setting the tone for future development in Collingwood and Mosley Streets, masks a complex division of public and private space – just as a Renaissance palazzo often had both business and residential accommodation. A public banking hall occupied the ground floor, while the upper storeys were utilised for commercial and legal purposes, also housing residential quarters for a clerk and messenger. Exuding High Victorian splendour, the public offices were embellished with Honduran and Spanish mahogany and Minton floor tiles.

The building, now privately owned, has been converted for use as an eating and drinking establishment during the day and a bar at night, initially as The Lodge then from 2014 as a steakhouse. The interior has been much altered, but the decorative ceiling, pilasters and dividing columns of the former banking hall have been retained.

THE FORMER GENERAL POST OFFICE
ST NICHOLAS STREET, NEWCASTLE, NE1 1RH

The former General Post Office was designed in 1873 and opened in 1876. It is one of the most impressive examples in the city of the ornate and grandiloquent classicism so often utilised for mid-Victorian public and commercial buildings.

James Williams, the Architect to Her Majesty's Office of Works, successfully conveyed a sense of Baroque grandeur in this four-storey, three-bay structure, especially through the effect of the recessed, double-height central entrance; this has giant Doric columns and pilasters rising through the two lower floors below Corinthian pilasters on the levels above.

The side bays on the two lower floors have a window to each floor, with heavily moulded surrounds. The upper floors adopt the same rhythm. The third-floor windows are the plainest; those on the second floor have pediments, the central one above the entrance being segmental and supported by attached columns. The whole dramatic composition is enhanced by heavy rustication at the corners, and by a deep cornice at the eaves.

The building closed as a post office in 1993 and lay empty until 1997, when it was bought by Red Box Design Group and sensitively converted to mixed use, including flats, the group's own offices, and the headquarters of R.I.B.A. Enterprises, the business arm of the Royal Institute of British Architects. In December 2013 R.I.B.A. Enterprises bought the freehold of the building and the following year announced plans for its comprehensive remodelling and refurbishment.

The former General Post Office, St Nicholas Street, Newcastle upon Tyne, by James Williams, 1873-76: from the north east.

ST HELEN'S CHURCH

BELLE VIEW BANK, LOW FELL, GATESHEAD, NE9 6BR

St Helen's is a fine Gothic Revival church in the Early English style, constructed out of rock-faced sandstone with ashlar details. Set in a pleasantly wooded churchyard, it dates from 1874-76 and was designed by John Wardle jnr. Before it was built, those wishing to attend worship in Low Fell were presented with a strenuous climb to St John the Evangelist's Church on Sheriff Hill (see p.92). St Helen's cost £13,000, which was paid in full by Edward Joicey, a colliery owner living at Whinney House, Low Fell, who also gave the necessary land.

The church was built to accommodate 500 parishioners. This number was later reduced to 330 as a result of interior alterations, although for the most part the building remains in its original form. Its cruciform plan, typical of the High Victorian period, features the usual nave, chancel and transepts.

Internally, fine, plain arches lead into the transepts, while the impressive nave has a fine, medieval-style open timber ceiling, supported on exposed truss sections and arched braces. The lower and more intimate chancel, entered through a comparatively ornate arch, has a beautiful arcade of Caen stone with trefoil-headed arches on single shafts of Frosterley marble, and an unusual, semi-octagonal apse, illuminated by excellent stained-glass windows by William Wailes. Indeed, the windows throughout are of particularly good quality; some of the best stained glass designers of the time, and subsequently, were employed here, including Wailes & Strang, Edward Burne-Jones (working for Morris & Co.), George Baguley and Charles Kempe. The reredos, erected in memory of Edward Joicey in 1884, features three quatrefoil-shaped panels of Caen stone, while the octagonal, panelled font is another splendid example of Victorian decorative design.

The entrance to St Helen's is through the base of the tower, attached to the south aisle. The fine broach spire rises off a square belfry that contains two original bells, cast by John Warner & Sons in 1876. A row of contemporary almshouses lies to the north of the church.

St Helen's Church, Belle View Bank, Low Fell, Gateshead, by John Wardle jnr., 1874-76: from the south.

THE FORMER TYNE STEAM SHIPPING COMPANY OFFICES

THE QUAYSIDE, NEWCASTLE, NE1 3UQ

Dating from 1875, and designed by R.J. Johnson, this typically ornate commercial structure is one of the finest Victorian buildings on Newcastle's quayside. It is five storeys high and occupies the narrow plot between King Street and an alleyway called Plummer Chare. Its eclectic classicism has been likened to that of the Northern European Renaissance and certainly, for example, with the three prominent gables defining the attic storey, there seems to be a reference to Dutch architecture – perhaps because the shipping company did much of its trade with Holland.

The building is executed in fine ashlar and its architectural language is both delicate and controlled. Johnson uses a cornice to define each floor, while Tuscan, Ionic and Corinthian pilasters on the ground floor, first and second floors, and third and fourth floors respectively, provide further vigorous articulation to the facades. The entrance is located under a richly decorated arch, with the Newcastle coat of arms carved in the tympanum. The building is now a restaurant.

Above The former Tyne Steam Shipping Company Offices, entrance on King Street from the west. Photograph Bethany Jane Robertson.

Right The former Tyne Steam Shipping Company Offices, the Quayside, Newcastle upon Tyne, by R.J. Johnson, 1875: from the south west.

THE FORMER SAILORS' BETHEL

HORATIO STREET, NEWCASTLE, NE1 2PE

'Bethel' is a Hebrew word meaning 'house of God' and it has been applied in English to various types of place of worship. The Bethel Union (a forerunner of the Mission to Seafarers that flourishes today) was a Christian organization that supported sailors, fishermen and their families. In the nineteenth century the growth in the number of river workers, keelmen and fishermen on the Tyne rapidly increased the membership of the Union in Newcastle. Permanent premises for worship and welfare were needed and a site was identified on the corner of Tyne Street and Horatio Street, close to the Newcastle quayside. This was leased by the Local Authority to Councillor William Stephens, a leading member of the Bethel Union and an influential fundraiser for the building of this new Sailors' Bethel.

The building, designed in 1875 by local architect Thomas Oliver jnr., is on a steeply sloping site, having two storeys on Horatio Street and one to the rear on Tyne Street (an old cobbled street now serving as a private road for new apartments). A modest but worthy exercise in High Victorian Gothic, even boasting some gargoyles, the Bethel is largely of red brick, with ashlar banding, and originally consisted of one main block containing a Nonconformist chapel on the first floor, with an entrance bay to the west. There is a doorway on Horatio Street at ground level beneath a quatrefoil window, and a further entrance at the rear on Tyne Street (now the main entrance to the building).

The chapel has three Gothic windows on each side and a three-sided, gabled apse lit by a traceried east window, with a steeply pitched hipped roof surmounted by a flèche. This is an unusual feature for Newcastle, and makes the Bethel a prominent landmark on the quayside.

The building, which cost £2,000, was opened to members and seamen in 1877. In 1900 a Sunday School room was added to the west side by local architects Oliver, Leeson & Wood. After the Second World War the Bethel served as a Danish Chapel for a time before closing in 1949. It then changed use several times before becoming offices for a design company, following a sensitive conversion in 1991. There is a painting of the building (1965) by L. S. Lowry in Newcastle's Laing Art Gallery.

The former Sailors' Bethel, Horatio Street, Newcastle upon Tyne, by Thomas Oliver jnr., 1875-77: from the south east.

BENSHAM GROVE

BENSHAM ROAD, GATESHEAD, NE8 1PU

Bensham Grove is a large stone house built, or remodelled, by Joshua Watson, a Newcastle cheesemonger who came from a longstanding Quaker family and who bought the plot around 1803. Watson's son, Joseph, was a solicitor and noted political orator. He in turn was the father of Robert Spence Watson, who inherited the property in 1874 and lived in it with his wife Elizabeth for nearly 40 years. A nationally recognised lawyer, philanthropist and political activist, Spence Watson was President of the National Liberal Association from 1890 to 1902 and was for many years the Honorary Secretary of Newcastle's Literary and Philosophical Society. A noted patron of the arts, he was visited at the house by many eminent artists and designers, mostly from the Pre-Raphaelite circle. These included Ford Madox Brown, Dante Gabriel Rossetti, William Bell Scott and William Morris (with whom he also became linked through his left-wing political activities).

The Spence Watsons commissioned Morris & Co. to redecorate their house, c.1875. The Arts and Crafts-style interiors which resulted, particularly on the ground floor, give the building its main interest. Morris & Co. provided fireplaces, tiles and carving, but most notable is the stained glass (see right, lower). This includes, for example, four images of medieval-style figures playing musical instruments in the upper lights of the dining room bay window, designed by Edward Burne-Jones. Upstairs, in the principal bedroom, are roundels with heads of Saints Hilda, Cuthbert and Bede, and the poet Caedmon.

Externally, Bensham Grove is of solid but unremarkable appearance. The west facade has a prime aspect looking out over the Tyne valley. The addition of bay windows during the Victorian period breaks the basic symmetry of the arrangement. So too does a large brick extension that might be either Victorian work or part of an earlier structure retained as a service wing. The house has been aptly described as "an informal, comfortable home, high-minded and light-hearted at the same time" (D. Potter). Above all, it constitutes a rare example of important work by Morris & Co. in the North East.

Robert Spence Watson died in 1911. After the death of his widow, Elizabeth, in 1919, the building was left to Gateshead Corporation for use as a permanent centre for adult and working-class learning; it is now also a community facility.

Top Bensham Grove, Bensham Road, Gateshead: from the south west.

Above Bensham Grove, Bensham Road, Gateshead: stained-glass window of St Cuthbert, by Morris & Co., c.1875.

THE MANSION HOUSE

FERNWOOD ROAD, JESMOND, NEWCASTLE, NE2 1TJ

The Mansion House in Fernwood Road is the official residence of Newcastle's Lord Mayor. It is the third building in the city to have fulfilled this role and has an intriguing and complex history, having originally been built as two separate houses.

Newcastle's original Mansion House was built in 1691 in the Close, on a quayside site near the present Copthorne Hotel (see p.315) and amply fulfilled the important civic function of displaying Newcastle's wealth and power to visiting dignitaries and merchants. However, the new town council, formed under the Municipal Reform Act of 1835, came to view the historic Mansion House as an expensive luxury and, despite protests from local people, it was vacated two years later and its contents auctioned off; the building itself was destroyed by fire in 1895. By this time No. 1 Ellison Place was being used as the city's Mansion House.

The present Mansion House is an amalgam of two semi-detached villas built by the shipowner Benjamin John Sutherland in 1876. The designs were probably provided by John Gibson, an architect based in Grey Street, Newcastle, although surviving plans confirm only that he advised Sutherland on the positioning of the houses within their grounds. Designed in a 'Tudor-Gothic' style, the houses were named Thurso House and Kelso House, reflecting the fact that the Sutherland family hailed from Scotland. Benjamin John Sutherland himself resided at Thurso House, while the neighbouring villa was rented out to business associates.

Sutherland's son, Sir Arthur Munro Sutherland, was born in 1867 and followed his father into the shipping business. After making his fortune, he purchased the two houses and converted them into one grand property in 1910-12. The alterations, by an unknown architect, were extremely well executed, ensuring that the two buildings blended seamlessly into a unified composition.

During the course of the alterations, the wooden eaves were replaced with a castellated stone parapet, which enhanced the building's dignity. Paired lancet windows were added to the outer gables, illuminating the attic space within, which would have provided accommodation for servants. A bold entrance porch was added to the former Thurso House, featuring a wide Tudor Gothic arch between crenellated turrets. The Sutherland coat of arms was displayed above the arch, together with the family motto Sans Peur – 'without fear'. To complement this addition, a double-height bay window was added to the frontage of the former Kelso House. Sir Arthur purchased and demolished several neighbouring properties in order to create extensive grounds for his residence.

Internally, walls were removed to form a stately suite of rooms. A splendid entrance hall was created, the walls of which were lined with rich wood panelling that features classical pilasters and stylised faces. This hall is dominated by an ornate staircase with a seahorse emblem on the newel post, a motif derived from Newcastle's coat of arms. The fireplace is again surrounded by superb oak panelling, a facsimile of woodwork dating from 1658 that the magnate had discovered behind a brick wall in his father's former office at No. 38 Sandhill, Newcastle. Using craftsmen and timber from his ships, he now produced an exact copy for his own residence. The ceiling is embellished with Jacobean-style plasterwork based on that in the original Mansion House.

Sir Arthur became Lord Mayor of Newcastle in 1918 and made many donations to the city. When he died in 1953, he bequeathed his house to Newcastle, exclaiming, "it is a lovely house and I hope it will prove worthy of the city of my birth."

The Mansion House, Fernwood Road, formed by amalgamating two semi-detached villas in 1910-12: from the south east.

THE FORMER UNION CLUB

WESTGATE ROAD, NEWCASTLE, NE1 1TT

This opulent former gentlemen's club was designed by M.P. Manning in 1877 and was erected at a total cost of no less than £40,000. It is an inventive building, in the newly popular French Renaissance style (an alternative, neo-Gothic design by Alexander & Henman of Stockton and Middlesbrough was rejected), and almost certainly influenced the design of John Johnstone's later Newcastle and Gateshead Gas Company Offices (see p.186), which stand nearby. Above a comparatively sober ground floor, the facade increases in complexity as it rises, culminating in a rich and varied skyline, with numerous decorative gables, dormers with pediments, cornices and slender chimneys.

In its heyday the club was frequented by some of Newcastle's most powerful citizens, including Sir William Armstrong, Joseph Cowen, Isaac Lowthian Bell and Richard Burdon Sanderson, operating as a wealthy and cultivated elite. Appropriately, therefore, the entrance hall was lit by stained-glass windows depicting cultural heroes such as Chaucer, Spenser, Shakespeare and Milton, along with allegorical representations of Poetry and Music. On the first floor were the club's principal rooms, with bedrooms for club members above. Accommodation for servants was provided on the third floor.

After closing as a club, the building stood empty for decades and was threatened with demolition. The interior suffered badly, many of the original internal finishes being lost to neglect and water damage. A number of conversion schemes, some of them grossly inappropriate, were proposed, but eventually a successful refurbishment of the ground and first floors was carried out for the J.D. Wetherspoon chain of public houses.

Architects Lawrence Beckingham Field were careful to retain what original and period features remained. The tiled entrance and central staircase (with fine late Victorian stained glass) are impressive, as are the reception rooms, now used for drinking and dining. From 1970 the former Union Club suffered by being adjacent to Westgate House, an out-of-scale modern building, but this was demolished in 2006 by its owners OneNorthEast.

The former Union Club, Westgate Road, Newcastle upon Tyne, by M.P. Manning, 1877: from the south.

DURHAM ROAD BAPTIST CHURCH

GLADSTONE TERRACE, GATESHEAD, NE8 4DY

This church was built in 1877-78 to the designs of Thompson & [W.H.] Dunn of Newcastle and is an impressive structure in the classical 'preaching-box' tradition, still favoured even at this late date by some Nonconformist sects. These denominations were often, although not always, keen to signal their distinct identity via the use of the classical style, at a time when both Anglicans and Roman Catholics now favoured a neo-Gothic mode.

The church is constructed of narrow courses of banded sandstone with dressings in ashlar. The entrance facade is quite complex. At ground-floor level a three-bay arcade springs from squat columns, forming the lower part of an Italianate composition of two storeys overall, surmounted by a pediment supported on giant Tuscan pilasters. An unusual, round-headed window, not unlike the 'Wyatt' window type popular during the neo-classical period, sits above the entrance. It is crossed by a string-course – running right across the inner part of the facade – supported within the window aperture itself by two delicate column-mullions.

On either side of the entrance bays are lower, rounded corners with balustraded parapets. The five-bay, lateral elevations to the nave lack the complex detailing of the west facade. However, with their segmental-headed windows at first-floor level and round-arched windows below, they are still quite elegant.

The interior of the church is simple and light, as one might expect for a place of Nonconformist worship. At first-floor level there are fine timber stalls with elaborate balustrades, running full-length on both sides of the nave. To the rear of the building, connected by a single-storey link, is a two-storey schoolhouse; this accords well with the church in terms of style and materials.

Left Durham Road Baptist Church, Gladstone Terrace, Gateshead, by Thompson & [W.H.] Dunn, 1877: from the north.

Right The former Maling 'B' Pottery, Walker Road, Ouseburn, Byker, Newcastle upon Tyne, 1878: from the south west.

THE FORMER MALING 'B' POTTERY

WALKER ROAD, OUSEBURN, BYKER, NEWCASTLE, NE6 1AB

The former Maling 'B' Pottery is a good surviving example of Victorian industrial architecture. Its founders moved their long-established pottery from Sunderland to Newcastle in 1817 and started production at a site on the Ouseburn. In 1859 the Ford 'A' Pottery was built on what became known as Ford Street. This was followed in 1878 by the Ford 'B', now known as the Maling 'B' Pottery, near St Lawrence's Square, which at the time was the largest integrated pottery in Britain. It incorporated significant innovations in the design of the workshops and up-to-date protection against fire, although its architect is unknown.

The Maling 'B' Pottery expanded to occupy a five-acre site, with its own goods yard beside the railway. The main buildings were originally U-shaped, with ancillary structures including crushing mills, kilns and workers' facilities such as a canteen. In the late nineteenth century the works had upwards of 1,000 employees, mostly women.

The pottery closed in 1963, when it was partly demolished. However, large sections remain. Particularly impressive, if starkly utilitarian, is the main, four-storey block, constructed of brick with a few stone details for lintels and quoins. It has large, regularly spaced windows along its considerable length. There is also a large, double-storey entrance through to a cobbled yard, sloping to an upper level. Several workshop ranges survive within the yard, as does a central building. This has a fine clock tower with stone quoins and a pyramidal slate roof topped by an open lantern; it was built as a fire station for the factory, with offices above, and now serves as a café.

The whole complex now houses a series of small independent workshops that are rented out for creative businesses. An undistinguished new building was completed in 2009, on a cleared site, to accommodate further companies.

ST MATTHEW'S CHURCH
SUMMERHILL STREET, NEWCASTLE, NE4 6EJ

St Matthew's is one of the most impressive churches in the North East. A magnificent building of great refinement, in the late Decorated Gothic style, it provides an excellent example of the unfailingly pious and scholarly work of one of Newcastle's most capable nineteenth-century architects, R.J. Johnson, and of his talented successor, W.S. Hicks (of the celebrated practice Hicks & Charlewood).

The church was begun to the designs of Johnson in 1878, for what was then a mixed congregation encompassing both rich and poor. Despite donations, lack of funds caused numerous delays in the construction. Although consecrated in 1880, this ambitious church was still lacking its western aisle bays and outer aisles eight years later. Ultimately, the building was completed after Johnson's death (1892) by Hicks & Charlewood, who added the tower in 1894-95 and finished off the western aisle bays and outer aisles in 1900-05. The parish hall was added in 1906-07 by C.S. Errington.

St Matthew's is hemmed in by the terraced houses of the Summerhill area, except to some exent at the west end, where one can have a better view of the centrally placed tower, rising in full glory. Originally, because of the constricted nature of the site, the intention was to angle the tower into the south-west corner of the church. The tower as built is one of Hicks's finest inspirations. It is beautifully proportioned, tapering slightly as it ascends. Topped with battlements and four pinnacles, it forms a prominent landmark on the western edge of the city.

The interior of the church is finished in dressed red sandstone, a material more usually associated with the north west of England. The church is wide, rather than long, with double aisles, its spaciousness emphasised by the integration of nave and chancel. The nave piers have capitals that increase in decoration towards the chancel,

where Hicks designed the elaborate reredos (1895-96) in memory of Johnson. Charles Kempe was responsible for the superb stained glass of the large Jesse window of 1899, situated in the east wall, behind the high altar.

The lectern dates from 1900, but it resembles and perhaps consciously recalls the magnificent early sixteenth-century example in St Nicholas's Cathedral, Newcastle. Other furnishings and decorative details are similarly opulent. Indeed, in the best High Anglican tradition, there seems to be a deliberate, and successful, attempt within the design of this church to emulate the grandeur and detail of a cathedral.

Left St Matthew's Church, Summerhill Street, Newcastle upon Tyne, by R.J. Johnson and (later) W.S. Hicks, begun 1878: from the south.

Above St Matthew's Church, Summerhill Street, Newcastle upon Tyne: the interior looking east.

THE FORMER FISH MARKET

THE CLOSE, NEWCASTLE, NE1 3RQ

Newcastle's Borough Engineer and Property Surveyor, Alfred M. Fowler, designed this grand, neo-Baroque building in 1878-80. It was one of several major works he completed in the city (see p.128). These commissions were typical of the frequent use by the Corporation of its own surveyors and engineers for important civic buildings, leading to considerable disquiet among local independent architects.

This fish market took over the function of John Dobson's Guildhall extension of 1823-26, which was now closed in at ground-floor level (see p.34). The idea was to profit, much more than hitherto, from the substantial local fishing industry and to take advantage of a site that offered an almost unique proximity to both the riverside and railway lines. Built of brick with stone details, Fowler's building is a spacious, single-storey structure (erected by local contractor Walter Scott), originally containing the open-plan market hall itself. It is symmetrical, seven bays wide and three deep. Its lateral (east and west) facades have central openings flanked by circular windows.

More prominently, on the main (river) facade there are tall, round-arched windows with keystones, divided by rusticated pilasters, on either side of a central archway flanked by heavily blocked columns. These columns support a stone entablature, cornice and pediment, all creating a fashionably Baroque effect. Facing the river, this central ensemble is surmounted by a carving of Neptune, the sea god, along with figures of North East fisherfolk and King Coal (by sculptor George Burn), while just below, on the elaborate wrought-iron entrance gates, are displayed the arms of the city, suggesting powerful, proprietorial authority.

The building has a low hipped roof with a ridge ventilator, ensuring a constant circulation of air. This was just one of many design features that emphasised hygiene, sanitation and efficiency. Also, as with the Grainger Market (see p.112), new standards of Victorian respectability had to be observed: for example, the use of abusive, obscene and profane language was prohibited.

With its contrasting red brick and exuberant stonework, the former Fish Market is a potent symbol of the wealth and confidence that were characteristic of Victorian Newcastle. During the 1990s it was converted into offices, which involved the insertion of a mezzanine floor. The building is now a nightclub.

THE CROWN POSADA PUBLIC HOUSE

NOS 31-33 THE SIDE, NEWCASTLE, NE1 3JE

With its largely unaltered interior, The Crown Posada is one of the most intimate and atmospheric of the city's surviving nineteenth-century public houses. Dating from 1880, it was designed by local architect W.L. Newcombe for the brewer John Sanderson. It has a bold, strongly articulated facade, giving it substantial presence considering its fairly narrow frontage.

The building is of sandstone ashlar above a grey granite plinth, with three floors and a gabled attic. It is four bays wide, the two side bays projecting slightly. On the ground floor, Tuscan pilasters separate doors on each side (which are panelled, with over-lights) from the fine stained-glass windows of the two central bays. Above are panels with swags, while an entablature supports a dwarf balustrade to the first floor. There are pediments above the first-floor windows, both curved and triangular, while the second-floor windows are surmounted by architraves. Above, a moulded cornice supports the decorated dormers of the attic storey, in the centre of which is another balustrade.

Internally, the public house is unusually long and narrow, with a 'snug' at the front behind a partition. The fine timber panelling and slightly later Pre-Raphaelite-style stained glass (by George Baguley) add to the quality of the interior (see below).

Left The former Fish Market, the Close, Newcastle upon Tyne, by A.M. Fowler, 1878-80: from the south.

Far Right The Crown Posada public house, Nos 31-33 the Side, Newcastle upon Tyne, by W.L. Newcombe, 1880: from the north east.

Right The Crown Posada public house, Nos 31-33 the Side, Newcastle upon Tyne: stained-glass window, by George Baguley.

CHAPTER 5

LATE VICTORIAN AND EDWARDIAN, c.1880-1914

St George's Church, Osborne Road,
Jesmond, Newcastle upon Tyne,
by T.R. Spence, 1886-88: detail of chancel.

INTRODUCTION

During this period the urban and industrial expansion of Newcastle and Gateshead, described in Chapter Four, continued apace. Especially noteworthy was the enormous growth of shipbuilding on the northern side of the Tyne, highlighted by the launch, in 1907, of the *Mauretania*, then the largest and fastest liner in the world. However, ominous signs of starker times to come included the closure of two major Gateshead companies, the metal fabricators Hawks, Crawshay & Sons and J. Abbott & Co., in 1889 and 1909 respectively. Even so, housing was now being laid out at an even faster rate than ever before. By the early twentieth century the population of Newcastle was 215,000, while that of Gateshead, now a large and sprawling borough, had reached 105,000.

Between about 1880 and 1914 large numbers of grid-like terraced streets, built of brick and slate, sprang up around the older central zones of Newcastle and Gateshead. These were almost invariably laid out by industrialists (for their workers) or by other private developers. Thus Byker, Heaton and Walker, in the east of Newcastle, and Benwell, Elswick and Fenham in the west, still have extensive areas of artisan housing of this type. So too do the areas on either side of Gateshead's Durham Road, while much of nearby Bensham is similarly laid out. For the middle classes, larger terraced houses, usually with substantial bay windows, were also being built in the more affluent suburbs, as for example in Jesmond and Gosforth, Newcastle (see p.231).

In both Newcastle and Gateshead, many 'houses' of this period are in fact flats: the distinctive 'Tyneside flat' is an ingenious (and virtually unique) two-storey terraced arrangement whereby one household lives above another, each having its own individual front (and back) door. Such dwellings can be identified, on closer inspection, by their double front doors; one leads into the downstairs flat, comprising two bedrooms, a living room and scullery, the other into its upstairs counterpart, possessing an additional bedroom above the front entrance.

There are many variations. Good surviving examples of the less expensive, flat-fronted type can be found in Walker Road, Newcastle. A more elaborate version, with bay windows and small front gardens, can be seen in the streets around West Jesmond Metro Station, such as Lavender Gardens, Sunbury Avenue and Glenthorn Road (see p.182). Other examples lie off Durham Road, Gateshead, in the vicinity of St George's Church (see p.190), and in many parts of Bensham. Unusually for an English city, by 1911 as many as 44% of Newcastle's population lived in flats. In Gateshead the proportion was even higher, at 62%.

One striking consequence of this enormous growth of residential accommodation was an equivalent increase in church building. This was given further impetus by the powerful independence of the increasingly numerous and well-subscribed Nonconformist denominations, which often led to the construction close to one another of visually similar, but spiritually and socially very different, churches and chapels. At the same time, provision for Roman Catholics also expanded, not least in response to substantial Irish immigration, especially in the more industrial areas.

Even the Church of England, hitherto seen as overwhelmingly middle-class, underwent a major re-organisation with the formation of the Diocese of Newcastle in 1882. Its first incumbent was E.R. Wilberforce, a 'muscular Christian' and member of a great Victorian philanthropic family. True to type, he saw the need to carry the Church's mission into the new industrial areas. He created new parishes and in 1883 set up a highly successful Building Fund for new churches. Within ten years this fund had raised £100,000. Wilberforce personally threw his weight behind the enterprise, demanding, "who will come forward and give a church for God and God's poor?" In this way, he encouraged major private benefaction, so crucial for the construction of some of the magnificent new churches (and, for that matter, that of numerous public and institutional buildings of the period) described in this chapter.

Thus, although there was a comparative paucity on Tyneside of neo-Gothic secular buildings, the situation continued to be very different in the case of ecclesiastical architecture. Here an existing Gothic Revival tradition reached a splendid climax in the hands of such eminent local figures as R.J. Johnson and A.M. Dunn (of Dunn & Hansom), whose earlier work we encountered in Chapter Four. Also important in this

context was Johnson's pupil W.S. Hicks (1849-1902), of the distinguished local practice Hicks & Charlewood.

Reflecting national practice, architects in Newcastle and Gateshead now tended to specialise in work for a single religious denomination. Accordingly, we find Johnson and Hicks building almost exclusively for the local Anglicans – both men held, successively, the important post of Diocesan Architect of Newcastle – while Dunn & Hansom became the preferred architects of Tyneside's Roman Catholic establishment. This pattern of employment invariably reflected the religious affiliations of such architects. For example, both Johnson and Hicks (a licensed Lay Reader), were devout Anglicans who routinely prayed over their designs. What is more, like many of their contemporaries, these architects – both of them noted for their antiquarian pursuits – now began to embrace the hitherto neglected Late Decorated and Perpendicular English Gothic styles, with their limitless potential for elaboration, richness and ornament. These were qualities that were now increasingly required and affordable, while the belated popularity of these late Gothic styles perhaps also reflected a new sense of Englishness and of a continuous Anglican heritage.

In addition, these architects' emphasis on highly crafted decorative elements, and their frequent use of local materials, anticipates many features of Arts and Crafts architecture, into which the very late Gothic Revival ultimately merged. Indeed, Hicks – who was also a noted poet and essayist – actually practised several of the crafts and enjoyed carving in wood and stone. Of Hicks, who was President of the Northern Architectural Association, 1890-92, it was deservedly said at the time of his premature death that "he was a man of lofty ideals, and was not only a master of art but had also early in life set himself a high standard of professional morality ... it was not sufficient for him that a thing was 'good enough', it must be the best that he and his colleagues could do."

Hicks's mentor Johnson had been a pupil of no less a figure than Sir George Gilbert Scott and was an early and influential pioneer of a more reverently conservative approach to restoration. More varied in his practice than Hicks, who was primarily an ecclesiastical specialist, Johnson in his architecture reflects not only an affinity with mainstream developments but also a typical late Victorian desire to create a range of appropriate and identifiable building types. Thus, in addition to his churches, Johnson designed numerous public and commercial buildings in Newcastle and elsewhere in a variety of mainly classical styles, such as the 'Queen Anne' (see below). Like Dobson before him, he became the leading architect in the North East, achieving a substantial measure of both regional and national renown. So too, to a slightly lesser extent, did Dunn & Hansom, who prospered sufficiently to open an additional office in London in 1880.

The eclecticism and opulence of late Victorian and Edwardian architecture was perhaps never better displayed than in the period's commercial buildings. These sought to be elaborate as well as efficient, outshining their neighbours. This effect is seen to good advantage in the new business district that now evolved just to the north and east of Newcastle's Central Station. In this district, Dean, Mosley, and Collingwood Streets began to be rebuilt with massive banks and offices, designed by such distinguished Newcastle practitioners as Johnson and the firm of Oliver, Leeson & Wood. Also to be found in this vicinity is a building by Alfred Waterhouse, a major national figure (see p.200). However, most of the important architectural work in Newcastle and Gateshead still remained firmly in the hands of the thriving local profession.

The architecture of the late Victorian and Edwardian period seems, with hindsight, to have been largely founded on a desire to abandon the rigidities of the earlier classic and Gothic Revivals. The intention was to move away from revivalist 'historicism' (not that this was ever mere copyism, as used to be thought) towards a form of modernity. But the transition was to be achieved through evolutionary, rather than revolutionary, means. One approach was to try to create new architectural styles, such as the so-called 'Queen Anne'. Another was to combine, in new and unusual ways, several styles within the same building; this led to the term 'Free Style' being coined to characterise much of the architecture of the time. In fact, even the 'Queen Anne' was really an amalgam of several idioms. Built of brick with stone details, and usually with white-painted windows, this highly fashionable architecture combined Dutch and vernacular elements with features from actual Queen Anne buildings of the early eighteenth century. As evidenced in this chapter, the popularity of the style was based on its adaptability. Classical in form but Gothic in feeling, it was comparatively informal, with a hint of domesticity. It could serve very effectively for schools, hospitals, libraries, commercial buildings, and of course above all for domestic architecture.

The Arts and Crafts Movement and the Art Nouveau style also provided important new directions. The former proposed a renewed commitment to hand craftsmanship and principles of good design based on fitness for purpose and the correct use of materials; the latter created innovative, sinuous, decorative forms based ultimately on nature. At the same time there was also a new interest in the neo-Baroque, perhaps reflecting Britain's burgeoning imperial grandeur. This style was often combined with Arts and Crafts elements and made much use of architectural sculpture, another feature of the period.

One common factor in nearly all the architecture of this time was its emphasis on decoration. Inexpensive, high-quality labour was available to the late Victorians and Edwardians and in addition they did not hesitate to employ superb individual artists, designers and craftsmen. They also built to last. The building industry remained essentially craft-based, even though architects were now incorporating into their designs new and improved materials like steel and reinforced concrete, as well as the most up-to-date technical services. This combination of craftsmanship and technological advance, together with ample funding made possible by the wealth of the country at this time (especially in the North East), ensured an unsurpassed standard of building construction.

In spite of its seemingly obvious merits, the inventive and confident architecture of this period – not just in Newcastle and Gateshead but elsewhere in the country and even abroad – has long been unjustly neglected, perhaps because of its apparent unorthodoxy. However, there are signs that its qualities are beginning to be properly valued once again. Almost certainly this architecture would have developed further, in all kinds of interesting ways, but for the cataclysm that was so soon to come: the First World War.

'Tyneside flats' in Oakland Road, Jesmond, Newcastle upon Tyne.

THE GREAT NORTH MUSEUM: HANCOCK (FORMERLY THE HANCOCK MUSEUM)

BARRAS BRIDGE, NEWCASTLE, NE2 4PT

Left The Great North Museum: Hancock, Barras Bridge, Newcastle upon Tyne, by John Wardle jnr., 1880-84: from the south.

Right The former Dame Allan's School and Master's House, Northumberland Road and College Street, Newcastle upon Tyne, by R.J. Johnson, 1882-83: from the south west.

Built in a dignified but for its date a decidedly old-fashioned neo-classical style, this is perhaps the last building in Newcastle that continued the remarkably persistent 'Tyneside Classical' tradition of John Dobson and his contemporaries earlier in the century. Indeed, as Michael Johnson has argued, it seems again to invoke a key attribute of Newcastle's cultural identity – the long-standing association between Greek antiquity and intellectual pursuits. The museum was designed by John Wardle jnr. (the son of Richard Grainger's collaborator John Wardle) for the Natural History Society of Northumberland, Durham and Newcastle upon Tyne, one of Newcastle's major cultural institutions, when it moved from the Literary and Philosophical Society's premises. However, the eminent local naturalist and ornithologist John Hancock, after whom the museum was named, was largely responsible for planning the internal layout. This is notable for a sequence of three very large, top-lit exhibition halls.

Construction work started in 1880 and the building was opened on 20th August 1884 by the Prince and Princess of Wales. It is of fine sandstone ashlar. The cost was more than £42,000, mostly donated by benefactors, including Col. John Joicey and Sir William (later Lord) Armstrong, a friend of Hancock. Lady Armstrong also made a private donation.

The main facade of the museum looks towards the Great North Road and Barras Bridge, as does the impressive Armstrong Monument (see below). The facade has broad stone steps leading up to an entrance section of five double doors, with windows above, set between giant Tuscan pilasters. The composition is completed by large, projecting bays at each side; these have similar pilasters framing blank panels below and windows above. Placed above a cornice is a parapet, largely concealing the roof, which displays on its central section the museum's former name, prominently carved in low relief in bold sans serif lettering. The Armstrong Monument, inaugurated in 1906, features a bronze statue of the industrialist by sculptor Hamo Thornycroft, standing upon a plinth designed by local architect W.H. Knowles and placed just outside the museum's boundary wall.

The museum underwent a major refurbishment, extension, and internal reorganisation of the exhibits as part of the extensive redevelopment of the Newcastle University Campus, following the adoption of a master plan by Terry Farrell Architects (now Farrells, see p.305). It closed in 2006 and re-opened in 2009 as The Great North Museum: Hancock. Here, work by Purves Ash (now Tench Maddison Ash) with Sir Terry Farrell involved a substantial extension to the rear of the original building, to improve facilities and provide more exhibition space to house additional exhibits moved from the University's Museum of Antiquities (now demolished, see p.195), and Shefton Greek collection. The library collection of Newcastle's Society of Antiquaries was also re-located to the new Great North Museum, from the Black Gate (see p.20). The internal re-ordering has opened up the main exhibition area and re-established the sense of light and space given by the original glazed rooflights, which had been sealed off as part of earlier work. Moreover, with the housing of Greek, Roman, Egyptian and natural history exhibits all together in the same building, the Great North Museum: Hancock is, in the words of Sir Terry Farrell himself, "almost like the great London museums all in one".

THE FORMER DAME ALLAN'S SCHOOL AND MASTER'S HOUSE

NORTHUMBERLAND ROAD AND COLLEGE STREET, NEWCASTLE, NE1 8ST

Designed by R.J. Johnson and dating from 1882-83, this was the third new building for Dame Allan's School, an institution that grew out of the Charity School of St Nicholas, originally founded by Dame Eleanor Allan in 1705. Dame Eleanor was the daughter of a local goldsmith and widow of John Allan, a Newcastle tobacconist. She purchased land in Wallsend and established a school for 40 boys and 20 girls.

Constructed of thin bricks with stone details, and with a wooden oriel and bay windows and a heavy wooden cornice, Johnson's building is in the then-fashionable 'Queen Anne' style. In contrast to contemporary Board Schools (see, for example, page 199), it exudes a middle-class domesticity indicative of the higher social status of its mostly fee-paying pupils. The building, comprising two blocks, features two square four-storey towers – topped by 'umbrella' domes – that flank the main, arcaded entrance of the school section and dominate the west facade. Two stout Tuscan columns sit in the centre of the entrance. Above this is an oriel window beneath a gable. On the western wall of the former Master's House is a fine statue of Dame Eleanor set within an aedicule.

The south facade of the Master's House section, appropriately more domestic in character, has two bay windows on the ground floor, on either side of the entrance facing on to Northumberland Road. The north and east facades of the complex are less interesting, being dominated by a modern extension that attempted to complement Johnson's work.

Of the original structure *The Builder* wrote in 1898, "It is difficult to believe [it] is not old work ... the detail throughout is remarkably good, and the character preserved without a flaw." Dame Allan's School moved to bigger premises in Fenham in the 1920s. The main building above is now occupied by the City Social Services, and the former Master's House by Northumbria University and the Law Society.

THE FORMER WENGER'S STORE

(ORIGINALLY THE NEWCASTLE AND GATESHEAD GAS COMPANY OFFICES), GRAINGER STREET, NEWCASTLE, NE1 5JG

The Newcastle and Gateshead Gas Company offices building was designed by John Johnstone and built in 1884-86. In the mid-1960s it became Wenger's Department Store. It is the last building – and also probably the finest non-classical-style building – on Grainger Street, before St John's Church. A flamboyant edifice in the French chateau style of the seventeenth century, it is somewhat alien to the more sober classicism of Richard Grainger's earlier central redevelopment slightly to the north, yet it is possibly the best building on Grainger Street. Significantly, this street was extended southwards to this point only in 1868, and then not as Grainger had originally proposed.

We have already referred to the work of Johnstone (see pp.150 and 159). Eclectic even by Victorian standards, he was well known for his love of detail and decoration. Thus an array of pediments, dormers, finials and turrets are here arranged to form a dramatic roofscape that lifts the skyline of the whole area. The former Wenger's Store has a prominent corner position and its facades are accented by string-courses and a variety of window forms, including oriels.

The building has a steel frame, an advanced feature for its day; this enabled the architect to create an unusually open and light interior. However, many years without an occupier following the closure of Wenger's Store in the 1970s left the whole structure seriously dilapidated. Thankfully it is in use again, as a wine bar.

The former Wenger's Store (originally the Newcastle and Gateshead Gas Company Offices), Grainger Street, Newcastle upon Tyne, by John Johnstone, 1884-86: from the south west.

THE FORMER GATESHEAD PUBLIC LIBRARY

SWINBURNE STREET, GATESHEAD, NE8 1AX

The former Gateshead Public Library, Swinburne Street, Gateshead, by John Johnstone, 1885: from the north.

The former Gateshead Public Library is part of a complex of civic buildings, including the (former) Town Hall, built on an eminence between Swinburne Street and Nelson Street. Designed by John Johnstone, also the architect for the Town Hall itself (see p.159), the library was built in 1885. It forms the centrepiece of a group of Victorian municipal buildings constructed at various times and by various architects, originally containing a post office, a bank and a building society.

The Public Libraries Act of 1855 enabled the Corporation to increase taxes to pay for books and buildings. However, the Library's construction was delayed by budgetary problems and by opposition to the free library movement. These problems meant that the building was not finally completed until just after Johnstone's death (in 1884). Its budget was extremely limited, yet the architect still managed to incorporate an art gallery at first-floor level.

The Library is a symmetrical composition, built of local sandstone, with two main storeys and an attic storey above. Like its neighbour, the Town Hall, it was designed in an eclectic and decorative Renaissance style, for the most part Italianate. It also contains some Baroque elements, for example the vigorous pedimented surround of the central dormer window of the top floor.

The interior of the building has four primary rooms per floor. The front rooms are illuminated by large, round-headed windows on the ground floor; at first-floor level they are lit by rectangular windows, set back behind a Composite order that supports a cornice with ornate dormers above. The central entrance is round-arched, placed below a broken pediment supported on large, decorative consoles.

Such was its popularity during the later Victorian period that eventually the library was unable to cope with demand and so in the early twentieth century the authorities built another library, on Prince Consort Road (see p.239). The Swinburne Street building is now used by local arts organisations.

ALL SAINTS' CHURCH

WEST AVENUE, GOSFORTH, NEWCASTLE, NE3 4ES

All Saints' was designed by R.J. Johnson, in his now-preferred late blend of Decorated and Perpendicular Gothic styles, but in its proportions and slightly simplified details it perhaps reflects the influence of his architect friend G.F. Bodley. It was consecrated in 1887, construction work having begun two years earlier under the auspices of contractors Amos Gray & Co. (see p.190). Situated in an affluent and expanding suburb, the church is appropriately grand, spacious and opulent. Even so, and despite generous donations from the local Cochrane family, funds remained short during its construction and the building was still being fitted out in 1891. The square, battlemented west tower was added five years later in 1896, by Johnson's last partner, A. Crawford Hick – although it was built essentially to the design provided by the senior architect.

The nave has five bays, with the aisles and clerestory lit by square-headed widows with Perpendicular tracery, separated by high buttresses. There is a battlemented parapet above the clerestory. Internally, the nave is unusually wide, giving a deliberate balance of verticals and horizontals. There is also a tall chancel arch with a choir screen crafted by the distinguished local woodcarver Ralph Hedley, who also did much other fine carving in the church, especially in the choir. However, in the case of the reredos and screen (installed in 1889 and 1891 respectively), Hedley specifically executed Johnson's designs. Hicks & Charlewood added aisle screens in 1901.

The majestic, Decorated-style east window has seven lights and contains richly coloured stained glass by Heaton, Butler & Bayne. Other stained glass is by Powell of Whitefriars. The east window was intended to be seen, in the words of the architect himself, "as a jewelled background for the rich lacework of the screen". The elaborately traceried west window is also Decorated Gothic in style. Other furnishings include the font and cover (1906), dedicated to William Cochrane.

All Saints' is a good example of the late Victorian ecclesiastical response to middle-class suburban development. It is also splendid testimony to what a fellow-architect described as Johnson's "earnest-minded search for whatsoever things are honest and lovely".

Left All Saints' Church, West Avenue, Gosforth, Newcastle upon Tyne, by R.J. Johnson, 1885-87: from the west.

Above All Saints' Church, West Avenue, Gosforth, Newcastle upon Tyne: the interior looking east (photograph: Russell Baston).

ST GEORGE'S CHURCH
OSBORNE ROAD, JESMOND, NEWCASTLE, NE2 2TF

Located at a bend in the road, behind a green flanked by trees, this is one of the largest and most richly decorated churches in the North East, and one of the most impressive in the entire North of England. It was designed by T.R. Spence (1845-1918), who was also responsible for the attractive adjacent church hall and the original vicarage (demolished in the late 1960s, see p.293), all carefully grouped around a 'village green'. The church was built of local sandstone from North Brunton quarry by Amos Gray & Co. and consecrated in October 1888. It was intended to serve a particularly affluent portion of the prosperous and expanding suburb of Jesmond (the population of which had trebled during the preceding 30 years, to almost 8,000). Indeed, in this instance the expense of pew rents would have largely excluded the working classes.

St George's was funded by Lord Armstrong's business partner, the shipbuilder Charles Mitchell, who spent more than £30,000 on its construction and insisted on a private entrance for his own and his family's exclusive use; this led into the morning chapel (on the north side of the church). Mitchell also donated the site, as well as the 'village green' fronting the church – on condition that it was never built on. The idea for such a grand building arose from discussions between the shipbuilder and his friend Somerset Pennefather, then Vicar of Jesmond Parish Church and later of St George's. The art-loving Mitchell (appropriately commemorated by Sir George Frampton's remarkable sculptural monument in the north aisle of the new church) insisted on complete control in all matters of design, proclaiming that "the House of Prayer and God's House should be exceedingly magnifical." Mitchell also commented: "I have built a great many ships, and I have put the best material in them from one end to the other; I am now building one house for God, and I wish to put the best material into that." According to Canon Pennefather, "that was the secret of his life; the best had to be done."

St George's Church, Osborne Road, Jesmond, Newcastle upon Tyne, by T.R. Spence, 1886-88: from the south west.

Accordingly, Mitchell engaged as architect the little-known but highly sophisticated Spence, who was the Secretary of the Newcastle Arts Association and a friend and contemporary of his son, Charles William Mitchell, a talented amateur artist and important promoter of local art education. Spence had recently undertaken major work at Mitchell's nearby residence of Jesmond Towers (see p.79).

Spence worked in Newcastle for only about ten years, from c.1876 to c.1886, before moving to London. Although St George's Church reveals him as an architect of great distinction and originality, it is the only significant building he designed. He was primarily a decorative designer and painter; his exhibits at the Royal Academy included, for example, such fashionably arcane historical subject-pieces as *Telemachus at the House of Menelaus* (1898) and *The Surrender of Capua* (1903). He was influenced by the Pre-Raphaelites, who had strong links with the North East, and was connected with the Arts and Crafts Movement via the Art Workers' Guild. He was also associated with the Aesthetic Movement and was a pioneer in England of Art Nouveau.

Externally, St George's Church is for the most part conventional (albeit with some passages of quite exotic relief carving, by Robert Beall of Newcastle), evidently reflecting John Ruskin's advocacy of the "English earliest Decorated" Gothic style. The plate-traceried clerestory windows of the tall nave can be seen above the side aisles, which are lit by paired lancets. Surmounting the two-light west window is a band of relief carving with stylised, natural forms. However, the chief feature is an unusual and very lofty (154 feet) Italianate bell-tower, a feature likely to have been specifically favoured by Mitchell. Attached to the south-east corner of the church, this tower has paired lancet openings, an open arcade for the bells and a steep pyramidal roof surmounted by a cross. It dominates the view northwards along Osborne Road and forms one of Jesmond's (and Newcastle's) major landmarks.

Internally the building is even more of a surprise (although Neil Moat, in his recent major study of the church, sees less of a dichotomy between exterior and interior). The first impression is not just of almost cathedral-like size, but also of colour, most unusual for the period. The church consists of a large nave, north and south aisles, chancel, western baptistery, organ chamber, clergy and choir vestries, and a morning chapel to the north east. Apart from large areas of plain wall surface above the nave arcades – seemingly intended for fresco or mosaic – the whole interior is decorated. The roofs are stencilled and painted in subdued colours (by C.S. Wardropper of Gosforth), the floors are mosaic (by Rusts of Battersea) and there is much fine marble inlay and glazed tilework, all complementing the splendour of ornate woodcarving, elaborate metalwork and lustrous contrasts of materials such as alabaster, copper and onyx.

The carved oak-work of the pulpit is by Ralph Hedley of Newcastle (well known to Spence and Mitchell through his additional activities as a painter and membership of the Newcastle Arts Association), as are the pair of oak screens facing on to the choir. Meanwhile, Hedley's local and seemingly equally capable compatriots Robson & Sons were responsible for the organ chamber and morning chapel screens, as well as (almost certainly) for the splendid free-standing litany desk. The metalwork in the church was executed by Shirley & Co. of London.

The intricate relief blind tracery on the west wall is in Caen stone and was carved, in two stages, again by Robert Beall with the possible assistance of his son, also Robert. This incorporates a bronze figure of St George – said to be by Spence himself – below a large window depicting the Last Judgement, by J.W. Brown of London. Also at the west end is the font, of Mexican onyx with columns of red jasper. The intricate and richly coloured windows in the aisles and baptistery are by Spence and were made by the Gateshead Stained Glass Co. (formerly Sowerby & Co.), as was all the other stained glass. Their iconography is characteristically complex; indeed, it has been said, albeit perhaps a little fancifully, that all the known symbols of Christian art can be found within the church.

The magnificence of Spence's scheme of decoration reaches a climax in the chancel (see chapter frontispiece), an effect further emphasised by the absence of transepts. Here the altar and reredos of costly Pavonazza marble, carved by local craftsmen Emley & Sons, are surmounted by three mosaic figures of the risen Christ with Saints Gabriel and Michael (by Charles William Mitchell) below a Nativity window (again by J.W. Brown). These are flanked by large areas of Art Nouveau mosaic decoration and then, on both side walls of the chancel, by large, frieze-like mosaic figures of the Twelve Apostles, the work of Charles William Mitchell and reflecting an Early Christian or Byzantine influence, perhaps specifically from Ravenna. Also in the chancel are attractive roundels by G.W. Rhead (in tilework) and by Heywood Sumner (in gesso). Spence's employment of these and other additional designers and craftsmen was typical of the Arts and Crafts Movement's collaborative approach – although Spence remained firmly in charge in all matters of design.

The whole ensemble at St George's is not only extremely elaborate but also artistically advanced for its period. Thus the flowing curves of the chancel wall patterns, echoed in the aisle and baptistery windows and the intricate ironwork of the church gates (by Alfred Shirley, and bearing the exhortation, 'Do all to the Glory of God'), are early examples of, or at least foreshadow, the decorative features of Art Nouveau. Similarly, the emphasis on mosaic decoration exemplifies the growing influence of Byzantine art characteristic of the time. Importantly, too, St George's reflects the overall influence of the Aesthetic Movement, with its philosophy that art was as important for its own sake as for any religious message it might convey. More than anything, it was this approach that "imbued St George's with a uniquely mysterious poetry appropriate to its role as a modern place of worship" (Neil Moat).

THE SUTHERLAND BUILDING

NORTHUMBERLAND ROAD, NEWCASTLE, NE1 8JF

The architects of the Sutherland Building of Northumbria University were Dunn, Hanson & Dunn (this well-known local practice having taken A.M. Dunn's son, Archibald jnr., into partnership in 1887). The building was originally designed in 1887 as the Durham College of Medicine, i.e., the Medical School of the University of Durham. Subsequently it became the Dental School of Newcastle University. It is a grand brick structure (with some stone and terracotta details) in an exuberant Tudor style: there are flat-headed Perpendicular-style windows, with elaborate mullions and transoms, and the usual array of prominent gables and chimneys. These features are reminiscent of traditional Oxford and Cambridge collegiate architecture, as is the building's basically quadrangular plan. An extension containing laboratories, additional lecture theatres, a gymnasium and a caretaker's house was added in 1906.

The Sutherland Building has two entrances: a main one facing Northumberland Road and a subsidiary one on College Street. The main entrance rises into a crenellated tower, again suggestive of a college gatehouse, with oriel windows above its elaborate, arched doorway. Internally, there is a splendid entrance hall with a fine oak staircase leading to the first floor. Here we find the principal room of the building, used by the University for receptions and lectures. It has a Tudor-style interior with wainscoted walls and a barrel-vaulted ceiling with splendid decorative plasterwork.

THE FORMER FLEMING MEMORIAL HOSPITAL FOR SICK CHILDREN

OFF BURDON TERRACE, JESMOND, NEWCASTLE, NE2 3AE

This attractive, English Renaissance-style structure was built in 1887-88 on a site formerly occupied by the Newcastle Cricket Club, between the earlier Abbott and Philipson Orphanages (see p.161) and Brandling Park. It was paid for by John Fleming, a local solicitor, in memory of his wife, and was opened by Lord Armstrong. Its construction allowed the Children's Hospital, founded in 1863, to move from Hanover Square to this healthier, more open site near the Town Moor.

The Fleming Memorial Hospital was designed by the London practice of Quilter & Wheelhouse, who obtained the commission following a competition. It is of red brick, with string-courses, quoins, window surrounds and other details in local stone, all beneath steep, slated roofs and tall brick chimneys. On the main facade there is an eye-catching tower which houses the main entrance. The Hospital was closed in 1987, when the facilities were moved to the Royal Victoria Infirmary (see p.214). Subsequently, the entire premises were well restored and converted into a business centre.

Left The Sutherland Building, Northumberland Road, Newcastle upon Tyne, by Dunn, Hansom & Dunn, 1887: from the north west.

Above The former Fleming Memorial Hospital for Sick Children, off Burdon Terrace, Newcastle upon Tyne, by Quilter & Wheelhouse, 1887-88: from the west.

NEWCASTLE UNIVERSITY

THE ARMSTRONG BUILDING, THE KING'S HALL AND QUADRANGLE, NE1 7RU

The Armstrong Building (see above, right) of the then Durham College of Science is the earliest of the buildings on the site of what is now Newcastle University. A College of Physical Sciences had been set up in Newcastle in 1871 and incorporated into the University of Durham in 1874. Its premises were in Westgate Road. Lord Armstrong laid the foundation stone of the new Armstrong Building in 1887 and the College adopted his name in 1904. The architect selected (without a competition) was R.J. Johnson, who devised a quadrangular plan that is still at the core of the University.

For the Armstrong Building itself Johnson adopted a Tudor-Jacobean collegiate style, using brick with stone details, in which he was already well practised (see p.188). At the same time he prioritised all necessary practical and technological requirements, stating that "in no case has utility been sacrificed to architectural effect". His planning, based on exhaustive studies of existing colleges and laboratories, ensured that the physics and chemistry departments were self-contained, while making the most functional and up-to-date use of materials throughout. Thus, for example, the laboratories were lined with glazed bricks for ease of cleaning and their floors were supported on brick piers to minimise vibration. The building was also one of the first to make large-scale use of electricity.

The Armstrong Building has large windows with stone mullions and an impressive entrance through to the internal courtyard, via the 'Royal Jubilee Exhibition Tower'. This tower commemorated Queen Victoria's 1887 Jubilee and is now seen to better advantage than for many years following the recent demolition of the University's Museum of Antiquities, which used to obstruct the view. It is placed within the eastern block, originally containing lecture theatres and engineering laboratories. Following R.J. Johnson's enforced retirement through illness, the Armstrong Building was completed in 1892-94 by local architect Frank West Rich. Rich introduced a few Art Nouveau details into the design, which makes an interesting comparison with the Sutherland Building, now of Northumbria University (see p.192), built at much the same time to serve as the Durham College of Medicine.

Another prominent local architect, W.H. Knowles (see pp.128 and 211), completed the Armstrong range in 1904-06, developing Johnson's original plans in the same Tudor-Jacobean style, again in red brick (although slightly lighter in colour) with stone details. However, some Art Nouveau touches have again been introduced and there is also a strong Baroque flavour, as well as much architectural sculpture (by W. Birnie Rhind), highly characteristic of this slightly later period (see p.239).

The outline, but little more, of Johnson's proposed culminating western block survives in Knowles's elevations on to what is now Queen Victoria Road (see above, left). Here the main entrance lies beneath an ornate tower, of which the first two storeys are in stone, with the doorway flanked by Ionic columns supporting a broken pediment. Above the pediment is a round-headed window set behind more paired columns.

The octagonal corner turrets of the tower start at second-floor level, framing two further floors of windows, stone mullioned and square headed, that are flanked by yet more columns and finished by a segmental pediment. Above this, the tower, which forms a major city landmark, rises to a stone belfry.

Internally, the entrance opens into a fine central hall with two circular, balustraded openings in the ceiling, looking down from the upper floor and supported on shallow, segmental arches above paired marble columns. The visitor proceeds through this attractive space into the impressive King's Hall, where graduation ceremonies and other formal events, as well as concerts and performances, take place.

This hall has a medieval quality, with high timber wainscoting, a 'minstrels' gallery' and a hammer-beam roof. More modern touches include stained glass by T.R. Spence (see p.190), excellent Art Nouveau metalwork and delicate figures, in a similar style, executed in relief within the plasterwork of the roof. These figures were executed by the Arts and Crafts-inspired Newcastle Handicrafts Company. The hall also incorporates a fine organ, whose case was designed by Bruce Allsopp (1912-2000), formerly of the Newcastle University School of Architecture.

The University quadrangle is bounded to the south east by the Arches (see right, top), the formal entrance into the quadrangle from Barras Bridge. Originally built for the School of Art, it was designed by Knowles in 1911 and is again of red brick with stone dressings in the Tudor-Jacobean style. It is battlemented and pinnacled to accord with the details of the Armstrong Building itself.

On the north-east side of the quadrangle is an interesting range of buildings of a more domestic scale, again by Knowles. The Hatton Gallery is entered via a grand stair and columned doorway, while the School of Architecture (see right, lower), with mullioned bays and a steeply pitched roof, has two elaborate entrances, reflecting the fact that it was originally designed as two Schools, those of Agriculture and Bacteriology. The range is completed by the former University Library of 1923-26 (now a Language Centre), by A. Dunbar Smith. This continues the theme of brick construction and has a large, tiled, hipped roof – very much in the Arts and Crafts influenced 'neo-vernacular' style of the early twentieth century. The junction formed by the north side of the quadrangle and Queen Victoria Road is filled by the Percy Building, a classically inspired structure of 1958 (architect: Professor W.B. Edwards).

There have been major changes around the Armstrong Building as part of architect Terry Farrell's master plan for the reorganisation of the campus, commissioned by the University in 2002 (see p.305). The road in front of the Arches, known as King's Walk, has been pedestrianised and, as already mentioned, the Museum of Antiquities, an early post-war red brick building designed by the University's Professor W.B. Edwards and formerly attached to the south side of the Arches, has been demolished. This building housed the University's Roman collection, now re-located to the Great North Museum (see p.184). In its place a new paved and landscaped area, with seating and examples of public sculpture, has been created and the imposing east elevation to the Armstrong Building has been properly revealed. Curiously, however, this has also meant that the Arches now lacks a balancing element to the left as viewed from the street and so seems to form a rather unsatisfactory entrance to the quadrangle beyond. The very pleasant layout and planting of the quadrangle itself – created just after the Second World War by the planner Professor J.S. Allen, again of the University – has been updated with new trees and stone paving.

Opposite Left The King's Hall, etc. (Newcastle University), Queen Victoria Road, Newcastle upon Tyne, by W.H. Knowles, 1904-06: from the south west.

Opposite Right The Armstrong Building (Newcastle University), R.J. Johnson and others, from 1887: from the south east.

Above Right The Arches, Newcastle University, by W.H. Knowles, 1911: from the south east.

Below Right The School of Architecture, etc. (Newcastle University), by W.H. Knowles, from 1913: from the north west.

THE FORMER TURNBULL'S WAREHOUSE

HANOVER SQUARE, NEWCASTLE, NE1 1NA

This must be one of the most striking buildings in Newcastle, and it is one of the first that the visitor sees when crossing the River Tyne by railway. Towering above Hanover Square on the west side of the High Level Bridge, it was originally a printing works for Messrs Robinson & Co., before being taken over as a warehouse. The enormous windows were to provide light for the printing processes, and the solid timber floors, designed for the weight of the machinery, were supported on cast-iron columns.

In red brick with discreet stone details, the structure was conceived by local architect F.W. Rich as a multi-storey industrial palace with towers, gables and buttresses. At the same time, much of its architectural language is classical, relating to the style known as 'Queen Anne'.

The northern section was built first, in 1888, and was then extended southwards towards the river in 1896-98, as Robinson's evidently acquired an earlier adjacent building. The character of this later portion is slightly more utilitarian. The striking tower on the east facade (1898) was the last element to be built, giving the dramatic skyline that we see today. The huge lettering proclaiming "E. & F. Turnbull Ltd" high up along the sides of the building refers to a later occupier.

The building has now been imaginatively converted into luxury apartments by architect Bill Hopper, who has retained many of the original features, including much tiling. The apartments that share the stupendous river views through the huge, south-facing windows are considered by many to be the most desirable in the whole of the city; the building is reputed to house the first 'million-pound apartment' on Tyneside.

THE ALLIED IRISH BANK

COLLINGWOOD STREET, NEWCASTLE, NE1 1HE

Left The former Turnbull's Warehouse, Hanover Square, Newcastle upon Tyne, by F.W. Rich, from 1888: from the east.

Right The Allied Irish Bank, Collingwood Street, Newcastle upon Tyne, by R.J. Johnson, 1888-91: from the north west. Photograph Bethany Jane Robertson.

As shown by earlier examples in this book, the eminent local architect R.J. Johnson worked in various versions of the 'Queen Anne', neo-Jacobean, and classical styles. Here he again shows his versatility in this refined and scholarly design of 1888, inspired by Italian Renaissance palaces. Constructed originally for the Quaker-based Bank of Hodgkin, Barnett, Pease, Spence & Co. (founded in 1859), and, following their move from rather cramped premises in Newcastle Town Hall, the building opened in 1891. Shortly afterwards it was described by *The Builder* magazine as "a composition of the highest excellence". A modern writer (Andrew Greg) has astutely observed that it "evokes the spirit of the Medicis in the new commercial heart of Newcastle".

This immensely solid, eleven-bay building is constructed of high-quality sandstone ashlar, on a granite plinth. It is made to seem almost free-standing by the clever setting back of the lower, one-bay wings. The Renaissance-style window details, so important to the overall effect, show the additional influence of the eighteenth-century architect James Gibbs (see p.47). There is rustication around the windows on the ground floor, which have prominent keystones; the first-floor windows have alternating triangular and segmental pediments. The top floor is comparatively plain but is surmounted by a highly decorative cornice below a roof balustrade with ball finials. The central entrance to the bank is an impressive composition in its own right, crowned by a segmental pediment with a carved tympanum.

Internally, the spaces were carefully planned, combining mercantile and domestic elements in a manner that was again typical of the Renaissance. Originally there were bullion rooms in the basement, a banking hall on the ground floor, and dining and sitting rooms for the directors – who had personally selected Johnson as architect – on the first floor. The second floor had a series of bedrooms together with a caretaker's kitchen. The banking hall, entered via a richly decorated lobby, has Ionic columns and is still largely intact, despite the insertion of a mezzanine that reduces the impact of the space.

Johnson had made substantial additions to bank director John William Pease's Benwell residence, Pendower Hall, three years before (see p.156), while fellow-director Thomas Hodgkin (see p.154) was, like Johnson, an active member of Newcastle's Society of Antiquaries. A noted enthusiast for the Italian Renaissance, Hodgkin almost certainly played a significant role in choosing both the architect of the bank and the architectural style used – so different from the neo-Gothic idiom that was usually favoured by Quaker patrons.

ST MICHAEL'S CHURCH (R.C.)

WESTMORLAND ROAD, ELSWICK, NEWCASTLE, NE4 7RE

Left St Michael's Church (R.C.), Westmorland Road, Elswick, Newcastle upon Tyne, by Dunn, Hansom & Dunn, 1889-91: from the south west.

Right The former Ouseburn Board School, Albion Row, Newcastle upon Tyne, by F.W. Rich, 1891-93: from the south.

The church of St Michael and All Angels was designed by Dunn, Hansom & Dunn. Built in 1889-91 in the Decorated Gothic style, it is the finest church in Newcastle by this distinguished local practice. An opulent and large-scale design, "the detail of which is learned and the vertical character very impressive" (*The Builder*), it displays a mature understanding of Gothic forms.

Rising from a compact, cruciform plan, with a square chancel, St Michael's has an impressive, octagonal crossing tower, clearly reminiscent of the great tower of Ely Cathedral (see also, St Chad's, Bensham, p.212). St Michael's is also abundantly decorated with projecting gargoyles, recalling those of Albi Cathedral in southern France, which the elder Dunn sketched in 1879.

The nave has six bays and is well lit by a generous clerestory, and by substantial windows to the east and west, both with superb, curvilinear tracery. The aisles are supported by heavy buttresses, separated by pairs of lancets with hoods.

The interior of the church has a splendour made possible only by generous donations, as for example from the Liddells of Prudhoe Hall, Northumberland. The building cost about £20,000. There is much excellent carving, including the high-quality alabaster reredos, and fine woodwork by Ralph Hedley of Newcastle. Angel corbels line both the chancel and the arcades (which have alternating round and octagonal piers), while within the open lantern are large figures of popes and saints.

Other decorative elements include the stained glass of the west window of 1891 by N.H.J. Westlake, appropriately depicting St Michael, seen amid much vivid imagery that includes a grotesque devil. The equally fine east window, by Atkinson Brothers, of Newcastle, who were also responsible for most of the other windows, illustrates the Parable of the Sower in the four upper lights and Christ on the Way to Calvary in the four lower. A contemporary description in *The Building News* praised some of the figures for their "surpassing beauty and sweetness".

St Michael's is superbly sited on a hill, commanding the landscape in the manner of a medieval cathedral and originally dominating the steep, densely packed terraces where the industrial workers of Elswick, with their high proportion of Irish Catholics, lived. The terraces, laid out from 1883, have now been largely replaced by crude modern tower blocks. These reduce the impact of the church, which has also become rather isolated.

THE FORMER OUSEBURN BOARD SCHOOL

ALBION ROW, NEWCASTLE, NE6 1LL

The former Ouseburn School was designed by F.W. Rich, for the Newcastle School Board, and was built in 1891-93. It cost just over £17,000, a very considerable sum for that period. The building is one of the finest on the east side of Newcastle and is a prominent local landmark. At the time of its construction Rich's sons, Edmund and Roland, had recently completed their architectural training and had entered their father's office as assistants. They may well have contributed to the design. Edmund died in 1930, only a year after his father, but Roland continued to practise until after the Second World War.

The school has three ranges enclosing a yard and is built of red engineering brick with sandstone dressings. Its architectural language is eclectic and experimental. However, the building is essentially in the 'Queen Anne' style, with strong classical elements, although cleverly avoiding complete symmetry. It may be compared to the slightly later, and less exuberant, Westgate Hill School (see p.203).

Two five-storey towers, with elaborate, Japanese-style, pagoda-like roofs (functioning also as ventilation outlets), are the dominant feature. It has been suggested that Rich designed the towers in this way, quite unofficially, to catch the eye of Japanese dignitaries and business delegates travelling up the Tyne on their way to Lord Armstrong's Elswick works. The Japanese were some of Armstrong's best customers, while Rich was a consulting architect to Armstrong. There was in any case a considerable vogue for 'japonisme' at this time. In addition, the building displays a strong Dutch influence, particularly in the prominent and extravagantly curling gables.

The school is recognised not only for its somewhat idiosyncratic architectural language but also for having been an institution that played a vital role in the social and educational development of people in the Byker area. Not surprisingly, it is protected by a Grade II* listing. The school closed c.1977, leaving the building vacant for a long period (except for partial use as a storage depot). Following restoration during the 1990s, it is now used as a business development centre.

THE FORMER PRUDENTIAL ASSURANCE COMPANY OFFICES

MOSLEY STREET, NEWCASTLE, NE1 1DE

This building is one of two in the city designed by Alfred Waterhouse, a nationally known architect (see p.154). Located on the corner of Mosley Street and Dean Street, the building uses in its construction an interesting mixture of red sandstone (a rare material in Newcastle), polished granite and red brick. It has a steel framework and was built in 1891-97 by the local contractor Walter Scott, with some modifications in 1898-1900.

Waterhouse, departing steadily although perhaps not entirely from his earlier Gothic Revival manner, designed most of the larger 'Prudential' offices in the ever-growing towns and cities of mid- and late Victorian Britain. These buildings established a recognisable house style. This example, although opulent, is by no means the most grandiose. However, it does show genuine originality, incorporating an eclectic variety of Northern European Renaissance features, including stone-mullioned windows, turrets and gables. It is also effectively adapted to its sloping site, through its strong basement storey (which has good wrought-iron grills).

The corner entrance is set in a canted bay that rises through the full height of the building and is surmounted by rudimentary turrets and a Dutch gable. Impressive though it is, however, this way of turning the corner is perhaps not quite as successful as the curve-and-dome system much loved by Tyneside architects and developers from Richard Grainger onwards.

Internally, the tall, arched main banking hall, now a café, is accessed via a vestibule and has colourful Burmantofts faience tiles in delicate shades of green and yellow. The remainder of the building is still used as offices.

ST GEORGE'S CHURCH

DURHAM ROAD, GATESHEAD, NE8 4AJ

Left The former Prudential Assurance Company Offices, Mosley Street, Newcastle upon Tyne, by Alfred Waterhouse, from 1891: from the west.

Right St George's Church, Durham Road, Gateshead, by Stephen Piper, 1894-97: from the south west.

This large church was built in 1894-97 to the designs of local architect Stephen Piper. It replaced an earlier, temporary church on the site. St George's is prominently located, facing the town's main war memorial, and is a robust and rather stern composition in the Early English Gothic style, built of coursed rubble with dressed stone details. Its grandeur of scale and impressive massing accord well with late Victorian taste, but otherwise its design is rather untypical of the period, lacking as it does the elaborate decoration of the now-preferred late Gothic styles.

The entrance is deeply recessed at the foot of a sturdy south-west tower which, unusually, has a gabled roof. The tower also features octagonal pinnacles rising from a setback buttress on each corner. The main window of the church's west end, facing on to Durham Road, sits above three gabled chapels and comprises a group of five lancets set within a blind recess. Two large, stepped buttresses support this western facade, framing both the main window and the chapels. The nave is without clerestories but is illuminated by two groups of triple lancets, each set within blind arches. The transepts are wide, expressed externally on both the north and south sides by large gables.

The treatment of the church's spacious and well-proportioned interior, which was designed essentially for preaching, is consistent with the exterior. It is comparatively undecorated, being finished in stucco with stone dressings. This effect accords with the church's Evangelical character, which successive vicars have maintained to this day. Much of the glass is clear-float.

The chancel is aisleless, and is as high and as wide as the nave. The transepts, which are cross-vaulted, are wide and shallow, while the lofty arcade has arches springing directly from square piers without capitals; these piers have chamfered corners. The ceiling is simply but attractively detailed in oak. Much of the furniture of the church is original and the organ of 1901, by the nationally renowned builder Father Henry Willis, is especially fine.

The elaborate, Perpendicular-style reredos, by Ralph Hedley, was installed a few years after the church itself was built. It is not entirely in keeping with the rest of the interior, but it does incorporate a notable and highly naturalistic relief of the Last Supper that ranks as one of Hedley's most impressive works.

JESMOND DENE HOUSE

JESMOND DENE ROAD, NEWCASTLE, NE2 2EY

Jesmond Dene House, on the southern side of Jesmond Dene, was originally designed by John Dobson in 1818 as a neo-Gothic residence (known as Black Dene House) for Dr Thomas Headlam, an influential local physician and politician. It probably resembled the same architect's nearby West Jesmond House (later Jesmond Towers, see p.78). Dobson worked on the house again in 1822 and in 1851 made substantial alterations to it for a new owner, William Cruddas. However, Dobson's work has almost completely disappeared as a result of later rebuildings and the character of the house is now essentially late Victorian.

Captain (later Sir) Andrew Noble (1831-1915) was a ballistics expert and a key figure in Lord Armstrong's Elswick Works. He became Vice-Chairman of the company in 1883 and ascended to the Chairmanship when Armstrong died, aged 90, in 1900. Noble bought the house in 1871 and, much influenced in many ways by his employer, commissioned Norman Shaw to make significant alterations and extensions. Shaw was then working for Lord Armstrong at Cragside in Northumberland and his work at Jesmond Dene House reflected a similar 'Tudor-Gothic' approach, featuring prominent gables, pitched roofs and tall chimneys. The house also contained a private laboratory for Noble's scientific experiments.

Anything remaining of Dobson's work was finally obliterated by F.W. Rich, who once more rebuilt the house, in 1896-97. Here again Noble followed Lord Armstrong's lead in using the latter's consulting architect. Rich created a 39-room, Tudor-style mansion, suitable for receiving foreign dignitaries, adding features that included a Gothic porch, a magnificent great hall with a superbly carved chimneypiece (and minstrels' gallery) and a new west wing. The drawing room features an inglenook with William De Morgan tiles.

Stylistically, Rich, who was also responsible for Noble's nearby Real Tennis Court (see p.211), essentially continued Shaw's approach at Jesmond Dene House, with much use of half-timbering, buttresses, oriel windows, and elaborate internal panelling while also introducing a slight Arts and Crafts influence.

Jesmond Dene House has been much altered internally and was used as a special school for many years. It recently underwent a sensitive conversion into a 'boutique' hotel and specialist restaurant (opened 2005). The architects were JDDK.

WESTGATE HILL SCHOOL

WESTGATE ROAD, NEWCASTLE, NE4 6NY

Left Jesmond Dene House, Jesmond Dene Road, Newcastle upon Tyne, rebuilt by F.W. Rich, 1896-97 (shown undergoing conversion to a hotel): from the south east.

Right Westgate Hill School, Westgate Road, Newcastle upon Tyne, by Dunn, Hansom & Fenwicke, 1896-99 (shown before recent alterations): from the south.

Westgate Hill School is a late work by the distinguished local practice that had now become Dunn, Hansom & Fenwicke. It is typical of their larger 'Board Schools', many of which are now demolished. Indeed, it was the largest example of its type in Newcastle. Built to house 1,520 pupils, it cost £24,000 and is a prominent feature in the landscape, especially when approaching from the east. It occupies the former site of Gloucester House, once the home of an affluent local tailor.

Dating from 1896-99, the school is an impressive, composition in an institutional 'Queen Anne' style, featuring both classical and Dutch-inspired forms. Constructed predominantly from red engineering brick, with terracotta mouldings, the building has a central block with two flanking wings. Three enormous Dutch-style gables dominate the front elevation on to Westgate Hill. The outer two are stepped, while the central one has scrolls and a date plaque, surmounted by a finial.

The central block has a rusticated stone base and the upper storeys have arched windows between brick Tuscan pilasters. The treatment of the wings is similarly inventive. Each had large arched windows on the ground floor, with rectangular sash windows above; at second-floor level high arched windows are closely flanked by rectangular ones – a feature somewhat reminiscent of Palladian architecture. The attractive caretaker's lodge, which is built of brick and terracotta tiles, is also worthy of note.

Great care was taken with the functional and hygienic planning of the school. In order to save space, stairwells, rather than corridors, form the principal communication routes within the building (although the classroom ceilings were high, to ensure the circulation of air). The stairwells are faced with glazed brick to prevent wear and tear and to facilitate cleaning. The playground was enclosed on three sides only, to provide better light and ventilation, while, as was standard Victorian practice with school buildings, there were separate entrances for boys and girls – in this case in different streets.

Westgate Hill School was opened on 4th September 1899 by Alderman W.H. (later Sir William Haswell) Stephenson, a prominent Methodist and public benefactor (see p.230), not least to the Newcastle School Board. His speech contained the pious hope that the school would "bring to bear upon the rising generation an influence which would deter them from drunkenness, gambling, wantonness, and scribbling and writing on public buildings".

In 2012 Westgate Hill Primary School moved to a new building nearby, and in 2013-14 the Victorian building was given a major refurbishment before returning to use as a school. Externally the main change is that the arched windows on the ground floor of the wings have been removed, forming open arcades.

THE FORMER NEWCASTLE BREWERIES OFFICES

PERCY STREET, NEWCASTLE (THE 'BRUCE BUILDING') NE1 4LE

These former offices of Newcastle Breweries were built in 1896-1901 to the designs of local architect Joseph Oswald (son and partner of Septimus Oswald) who, incidentally, was a shareholder in Newcastle Breweries, which provided him with many commissions. The structure is sometimes known as the 'Bruce Building', because it occupies the site of the former Percy Street Academy, Newcastle's first college, founded in 1806 by John Bruce. It is in a bold and eclectic neo-Baroque style, with English Renaissance details. The ground floor is executed in red sandstone above a granite plinth, while the upper floors are of red brickwork with sandstone details. These contrasts of building materials are typical of late Victorian architecture. So too is the building's overall asymmetry.

The curved north corner is surmounted by a turret with a copper dome, while the main Percy Street facade has on the ground floor four round-headed windows (with a central oculus) and a narrower entrance bay to the south. A complex, asymmetrical arrangement at first-floor level features three oriel windows supported on brackets, with three more conventional windows flat to the wall, all surmounted by richly carved lintels. A string-course divides the first floor from the second, with the parapets of the oriels becoming balconies to the windows above them.

Higher still, above a deep cornice, is a pair of elaborately shaped, Flemish-style gabled dormers, cleverly placed just off-centre, with oculi and sandstone details. The building's end elevations culminate in gables that are similarly fashioned and decorated. Tall, red brick chimneys rise from the steeply pitched, tiled roof. Internally there is much faience, by Burmantofts of Leeds, in the entrance hall and staircase area, with stucco decoration to ceilings and friezes; there is also some interesting emblematic stained glass. The former boardroom is panelled in mahogany. At the time of the building's opening, a local newspaper enthused: "There has just been exposed to public view, the hoardings being removed, one of the finest blocks of buildings of its kind which Newcastle can now boast of – Newcastle or any other town, I warrant you" (quoted in B. Bennison and J.P. Merrington, *The Centenary History of the Newcastle Breweries Ltd*, *1890–1990,* 1991).

At the rear of the building is a fine classical arch that led into the brewery yard. Just through the arch can be seen a flat-roofed brick extension to the main building that also incorporates an unusual cylindrical structure, in metal; this ensemble is thought to have been a Second World War look-out shelter.

In the 1950s the building was compulsorily purchased from the brewery to provide space for the expansion of King's College (now Newcastle University). It was occupied by University departments for many years, but was empty for some time and was sold on to a private company in 2013. At the time of writing there are plans to convert the upper floors into residential accommodation, with the ground floor being reserved for commercial use. This work is due to commence late in 2014, under the project-management of architects Elborn Design.

The former Newcastle Breweries Offices, Percy Street, Newcastle upon Tyne, by Joseph Oswald (Oswald & Son), 1896-1901: from the east.

COLLINGWOOD BUILDINGS

COLLINGWOOD STREET, NEWCASTLE, NE1 1JF

Local architects Oliver & Leeson designed Collingwood Buildings, erected in 1897-99 and initially containing shops, offices and a hotel. It seems that the building was not successful as a hotel and in 1903 Cackett & Burns Dick of Newcastle created the impressive banking hall of new owners Barclays Bank, adapted from the original hotel ground floor.

Occupying an acutely angled corner site between Collingwood Street and Pudding Chare, and designed in a free, neo-Baroque style, the building is constructed out of sandstone ashlar, with porches in contrasting grey granite. It is has four main storeys with an attic storey above; this has a mansard roof with a free composition of gables and pediments. Giant pilasters of a Composite order provide accent to the facades at first- and second-floor levels.

The complex is also notable for its impressive sequence of arched shop fronts, which provide wonderful views into the banking hall. The entrance is on the building's semi-circular corner, set back behind Tuscan columns. This whole corner arrangement is excellently handled, as is so often the case with Newcastle's Victorian commercial architecture, and terminates with a grand dormer (originally intended to be a turret, with a wrought-iron balcony). The building has been well described by Michael Johnson as rising up like the prow of a ship.

The interior of this hall is as opulent as any in the city, reflecting its status as a former local bank headquarters. Lined with marble, it has mahogany fittings by Waring and Gillow of Lancaster. Enormous Corinthian columns support an impressive stucco ceiling, decorated by G.G. Laidler of Newcastle. After a long period without an occupant, the banking hall has been refurbished as a bar and restaurant, with minimal impact on the space. This work was mainly limited to finishes and furniture. Above the banking hall are offices, originally used for bank administration. At one time there was also a directors' retiring room on the first floor.

Collingwood Buildings, Collingwood Street, Newcastle upon Tyne, by Oliver & Leeson and (later) Cackett & Burns Dick, from 1897: from the south west.

ST GABRIEL'S CHURCH

HEATON ROAD, HEATON, NEWCASTLE, NE6 5QN

We have already seen several examples of the versatile, inventive, and sometimes unorthodox work of Lord Armstrong's consulting architect, F.W. Rich (1840-1929). Rich, who also worked extensively for the Duke of Northumberland, was said towards the end of his life to be the oldest practising architect in the country. His busy and important practice made him quite a wealthy man. Rich was also a very active member of the Northern Architectural Association: he became President in 1897 and remained involved in its affairs right up to the end.

Curiously, although entering the architectural profession as early as 1863, in the office of William Parnell, and setting up independently in 1872, Rich enjoyed the most creative phase of his career during his 50s and 60s, a time when he designed St Gabriel's and other buildings discussed in this chapter. This was possibly thanks to the fresh input of his talented sons, Edmund and Roland, his assistants from the early 1890s.

Rich could successfully turn his hand to the opulent classicism required by many commercial clients (he was, incidentally, a great admirer of the earlier 'Tyneside Classical' tradition), as well as being a master of the more eclectic styles characteristic of the late Victorian and Edwardian periods. St Gabriel's, which as far as is known is Rich's only church, shows him to be also a remarkably assured and capable exponent of the neo-Gothic style (here mainly the Decorated and Perpendicular).

St Gabriel's – always traditionally 'High Church' in its persuasion – was built to serve the rapidly expanding although then still semi-rural suburb of High Heaton. It occupied land donated by Lord Armstrong, who was no doubt responsible for the choice of architect, for he also reserved the right, and exercised it, to approve the plans. These initially indicated a Gothic design, with nave, one aisle and tower, to hold 500-600 people (later increased to 1,000).

Another well-known Tyneside benefactor, Miss Emily Matilda Easton of Felling (see p.213), gave funds towards the construction of the church, which, replacing a temporary iron structure, was begun in June 1898. The nave and south aisle were consecrated in September 1899, but the chancel, tower (minus the pinnacles originally intended), north aisle and north transept, together with the Arts and Crafts-style vicarage at the west end of the church (1901), required a further six years to complete. The materials used throughout are snecked local sandstone and Lakeland slate, and the builder was Walter Baston, later a churchwarden at St Gabriel's; he is commemorated by a brass tablet in the north transept.

The church hall, at the east of the tower, was added in 1924 and the Lady Chapel and south transept (by H.L. Hicks, son of W.S. Hicks) in 1931. All this meant that the Vicar, Canon Robert Trotter, who had presided over the church for 30 years, was able to retire the following year with his dream realised. A powerful spiritual force in the locality, Trotter played a major part in design matters, successfully insisting, for example, on a higher chancel than had been originally intended. The church's polished granite font, with fine carved canopy, is in his memory.

Unlike the advanced, almost exotic character of nearby St George's, Jesmond (see p.190), where an effect of organic unity is achieved through the cumulative use of curvilinear, Art Nouveau-like motifs, the architectural personality of St Gabriel's is fairly plain, despite the presence of some fine details. Relying for effect on impressive massing and internal spaciousness, it seems to represent a clear restatement of the English parish church tradition.

Externally, mainly horizontal forms, of a slightly Arts and Crafts character, contrast with and build up to the rugged verticality of the strong, square tower at the south east, nearly 100 feet high and carved with the words of the Sanctus. Other features include a castellated porch and solid turrets at the west end that flank an excellent, Decorated-style window of six lights.

Inside the church, the fine hammer-beam roof in the nave, the carved ceilings of the transepts and the rood-beam (carved by the Ralph Hedley workshop in 1905) again show the influence of late English Gothic forms. So too do the column capitals, rich with leaf forms, and the figures of angels in the chancel arch.

At the entrance to the chancel is a low alabaster screen, near to which is a fine pulpit, by Ralph Hedley (1909). Also by Hedley are the lectern and screens and, above all, the elaborate, gilded reredos with panels depicting the Annunciation, Adoration and Ascension, with archangels, painted by James Eadie-Reid. This impressive ensemble was personally funded by Miss Easton in 1901. Above and behind it is an unusual wall-painting, depicting the Risen Christ (again by Eadie-Reid).

Notwithstanding these impressive individual elements, however, and with very little stained glass to dim the illumination, the overwhelming effect of this church interior is one of splendid simplicity and dignity, with large transepts, a light, spacious nave and wide arcades.

Left St Gabriel's Church, Heaton Road, Heaton, Newcastle upon Tyne, by F.W. Rich, 1898-1905: from the south west.

Above St Gabriel's Church, Heaton, interior: looking east.

BLANDFORD HOUSE

BLANDFORD SQUARE, NEWCASTLE, NE1 4JA

Blandford House was designed by Oliver & Leeson, and built in 1899 as a warehouse, offices and conference hall for the Co-operative Wholesale Society. The Society's willingness to fund such an expensive and elaborate structure is testimony to the wealth it accrued during the late Victorian period.

The building is of four main storeys, with two further attic storeys within the roof. It is constructed of red engineering brickwork with sandstone and terracotta dressings. Some of its details are classical, but the overall design, with its prominent gables, can perhaps be best described as institutional 'Queen Anne'.

The east facade on to St James's Boulevard, containing the main entrance, has thirteen regular bays articulated by shallow pilaster-like strips that meet, under the roof cornice, to form segmental arches. The windows are slightly recessed behind these strips. The largest windows are those on the second floor, which are double-height.

Attractive turrets with ogee domes in copper are located at each corner of this main, eastern block. Facades and roofs are clearly separated by a projecting cornice supported by substantial stone brackets. The cornice itself supports a maintenance gantry.

The roof, covered in graduated Lakeland slates, is one of the most impressive in the city, with large gables, finials and two more copper domes. The gables on the east facade have tall, arched windows lighting the attic floor and providing splendid views of the city. Large, semi-circular windows on the north and south facades are set within slightly plainer gables.

The original office accommodation was planned around a delivery-courtyard. This is now an atrium, used for exhibitions and displays as part of the building's present function as a museum; it now has modern staircases and balconies of glass and steel for access to higher levels.

In the 1930s the entrance hall of Blandford House was refurbished in 'Art Deco' style, by the C.W.S architect, W. Townsend Gray, featuring marble stairs and walnut panelling. The building also has attractive chrome and glass light fittings, in the same style, as well as much good stained glass and superb blue faience. The original conference hall on the top floor (see left, lower), which was also used as a ballroom for employees, survives largely intact. Blandford House is now Discovery Museum; it also contains Tyne and Wear Museums and Archives Headquarters.

THE BRIDGE HOTEL
CASTLE GARTH, NEWCASTLE, NE1 1RQ

Prominently located above the Close to the east of the High Level Bridge and on the south side of the castle, the Bridge Hotel stands on the site of the earlier 'New Bridge Inn' (which incorporated a brewery). This was purchased by Fitzgeralds in 1892 and the new public house was built to the designs of Cackett & Burns Dick in 1899. It is one of a number of fine, confident buildings of this period, such as Half Moon Chambers and Emerson Chambers (see p.217), that inventively and decoratively use combinations of Art Nouveau and Baroque elements to add exuberance to the city.

The hotel's principal (north) facade is typically late Victorian, both in its contrasting use of brick and stone and its touch of 'Free Style' asymmetry. Thus the side bays project slightly, with an open lantern tower above the right hand bay and a hipped gable to the left. The ground floor, in heavily moulded stone, has two large windows articulated by Tuscan columns and set between recessed doorways at each side. A deep fascia across the full width of the building carries the hotel's name in bold, flowing letters.

The first floor is of red brick, with stone details, such as the bold keystones of the sash windows on either side. Above a string course, the top floor is of stone and is asymmetrical, with two deeply recessed, paired sash windows placed in the centre, beneath a bold cornice. The characterful tower to the right rises above another cornice that ends in prow-like projections.

The building, on the south side of which is a terrace with fine views towards the quayside, contains both interesting stained glass and original furniture and fittings.

Above Left Blandford House, Blandford Square, Newcastle upon Tyne, by Oliver & Leeson, 1899 (detail): from the north east.

Below Left Blandford House, Blandford Square, Newcastle upon Tyne: the former conference hall.

Right The Bridge Hotel, Castle Garth, Newcastle upon Tyne, by Cackett & Burns Dick, 1899: from the north.

THE MALMAISON HOTEL

(FORMERLY THE CO-OPERATIVE WHOLESALE SOCIETY WAREHOUSE), EAST QUAYSIDE, NEWCASTLE, NE1 3DX

This building, before its renovation and conversion into a hotel, was one of the few remaining Victorian warehouses on the quayside. It is also important as one of the earliest examples of reinforced concrete technology in the locality, by the French firm of Hennebique. It was built in 1899-1900 as a warehouse for the C.W.S., to designs by the engineer L.G. Mouchel and the C.W.S. architect F.E.L. Harris. The attic storey was added in 1910.

Of functional, though still slightly classical character, this former warehouse has six storeys, including a double height ground floor, plus the aforementioned attic. There are six bays facing the river, and seven to the sides. A heavily bracketed cornice supports the attic floor; this has a curved roof, lit by a semi-circular window at each end, above the central bay. At the front, triple arches on the ground floor support the six bays, which are divided into pairs by a giant order of pilasters stretching through the five main floors to the cornice.

The entire structure is of reinforced concrete, now rendered to appear like Portland stone. Thus the floors are reinforced concrete slabs, on square columns, while the whole building is supported by a basement raft foundation to overcome the problem of poor ground conditions near the river's edge. The building now forms an important element in the overall redevelopment of the quayside (see p.303).

The Malmaison Hotel (formerly the Co-operative Wholesale Society Warehouse), East Quayside, Newcastle upon Tyne, by F.E.L. Harris and L.G. Mouchel, 1899-1900: from the south east.

THE REAL TENNIS COURT (JESMOND DENE)

MATTHEW BANK, NEWCASTLE, NE2 3RE

In 1894, F.W. Rich built this large indoor court for Sir Andrew Noble, for whom he worked at nearby Jesmond Dene House (see p.202). It is situated some distance from the main house, beside what is now the main road. It is an extraordinarily grand affair for what is really a large shed, laid out for the playing of real tennis – and still used for this purpose.

The court is in Tudor-Jacobean style with some Baroque features. Built of red brick with stone detailing, it has four octagonal corner turrets with conical roofs (slightly reminiscent of Rich's Ouseburn Board School, see p.199), and buttresses supporting the highly glazed side walls. The south wall has six large, circular, high-level windows; the north wall is similar but with arched ones. The playing area is also lit by continuous roof-lights.

The building has a single-storey, crenellated entrance to the east (away from the road) and incorporates an apartment for the professional to the west. It is one of the few purpose-designed real tennis courts in the country and provides yet another local example of the eclectic exuberance of late Victorian architecture.

The Real Tennis Court (Jesmond Dene), Matthew Bank, Newcastle upon Tyne, by F.W. Rich, 1894: the interior.

THE UNITED FREE METHODIST CHURCH

ST GEORGE'S TERRACE, JESMOND, NE2 2DL

The architect here, W.H. Knowles of Newcastle, was initially asked to design a large church together with a hall and meeting rooms. However, it was then decided to proceed with the hall and some of the rooms, but to postpone construction of the main church and remaining elements. The foundation stone was laid in 1900 and the building opened a year later, with the hall being used as a church.

The cost, however, was such that the original design was never completed. It must have become clear that the project to build a large church was too ambitious, because, in 1902, a schoolroom only was added to the north of the 'hall' on the St George's Terrace frontage. Jesmond Library (see p.285) now occupies the land originally intended for the larger church.

This change of plan explains the rather truncated and slightly unfinished appearance of the building, as well as its comparative plainness internally. The tower barely reaches above roof level and makes an uncomfortable-looking junction with the schoolroom. Yet the overall horizontality of the modified design ensures a measure of coherence. The church as it is now is a two-storey structure in a free, late Gothic style, with additional Arts and Crafts and even – in some of the decorative details – Art Nouveau influences.

After 1990 the United Free Methodist Church underwent a major refurbishment, carried out in order to accommodate the Wesleyan Methodists from Clayton Road when worship there ceased. Their own church – a fine neo-Gothic structure of 1881-83, designed by local architect J.J. Lish – had been demolished in 1981, but the congregation had continued to meet in the surviving church hall. This, incidentally, was now integrated in reduced form into a residential development built on the site of the former church.

The United Free Methodist Church, St George's Terrace, Jesmond, Newcastle upon Tyne, by W.H. Knowles, 1900-02: from the south east.

ST CHAD'S CHURCH

RAWLING ROAD, BENSHAM, GATESHEAD, NE8 4QL

During the 1890s houses began to be built on the fields of south Bensham and in 1895 Lord Northbourne donated land for the construction of a church. St Chad's, one of the most majestic churches in the North East, and probably the finest work by the eminent local architect W.S. Hicks, was the result. It still stands cathedral-like amid the terraced streets it was built to serve. Such splendour was of course realisable only through generous private patronage, in this case that of Miss Emily Matilda Easton of Felling (see p.207). Miss Easton, a member of a wealthy local coal-owning family and a noted charitable benefactor, made known her intention to erect a new parish church in 1900, when building work began. St Chad's was consecrated in 1903.

Perhaps appropriately, given its elaboration, St Chad's has always followed the Anglo-Catholic tradition as influenced by the 'High Church' Oxford Movement of the nineteenth century. Indeed, Neil Moat has memorably described the church as "the beau ideal of a triumphalist Anglo-Catholicism, at once highly wrought and emotionally charged". However, unlike, for example, St George's, Jesmond (see p.190), it was built to serve the working classes – even today Bensham remains one of the poorest wards in the Borough of Gateshead. All this means that to modern eyes an expensive church like St Chad's might seem deliberately indulgent, in an attempt to minister to, pacify, and even convert, its flock. Yet the Victorian age was an age of faith and surely the purpose behind the church's construction was not so much patronising as philanthropic. Indeed, at the time it was regarded as "a matter of sincere thankfulness and joy that such a building should have been placed in the midst of the vast working population of such a district", in order to animate and inspire "the monotony of hard-working lives".

The design of the church is in the late English Gothic style of the fourteenth century. Because of the restricted site, it was not possible to have fully projecting transepts, but the high transeptal roofs help to create a powerful cruciform effect. The church's most striking feature externally is the substantial octagonal tower; this is located over the well-lit central crossing and recalls the crossing tower of Ely Cathedral. It is crenellated, and crowned by slender pinnacles with crockets. On each face is a large, traceried window; a clock is fixed to every alternate face.

Both nave and chancel are aisled; the aisles of the chancel, which is almost as long as the nave, are much lower. The nave has four bays and is illuminated by a clerestory, as is the chancel. The window tracery is exceptionally fine throughout. In the detailing of the chancel arcades, with their chamfered mouldings, there seems to be a respectful reference to the late-medieval nave arcades of St Mary's Church, Gateshead.

The entrance to St Chad's is located in the north aisle of the nave. The porch has an elaborate door framed by deep archivolts and surmounted by a relief of the Annunciation. The doorway is further enriched by carved symbols of Christ and of the Evangelists within the mouldings of the arch and jambs. The symbolism of this arrangement is based on the text: "I am the Door, by Me if any man enter in he shall be saved." Above the entrance are sculpted figures in niches representing St Chad with his patrons St Aidan and St Theodore of Canterbury.

Internally, the transepts and the crossing are bathed in light, partly from the tower above. The church is highly decorated throughout and the interior is particularly rich. It would have been richer still had it been possible, as originally intended, to cover with paintings all those wall surfaces that were left finished in plain plaster, or if completed chancel murals and painted panels of the reredos, by James Eadie-Reid (see p.207), had not later been obliterated. The chancel contains carved choir and clergy stalls facing inwards, on the monastic pattern. Its marble floor resembles that of the choir in Durham Cathedral (designed by Sir George Gilbert Scott in 1870).

Even following substantial internal alterations, made in recent years and of questionable character (the church was re-ordered c.1990), it is still possible to appreciate at St Chad's the all-embracing unity of its architect's conception: "every detail, piece of furniture and altar silver was to his design". Of particular quality are the fine parclose screen, the font of Derbyshire alabaster, the lectern, the litany desk, the pulpit (which has carvings of famous sermons in the Bible, by James Taylor Ogleby), the richly embellished sanctuary, and the reredos, in the central panel of which is a representation of the Blessed Sacrament, again carved by Ogleby. Most of the other carving in the church, again of superb quality, was by Ralph Hedley of Newcastle. Noteworthy too are the three silver sanctuary lamps, the processional cross, the carved bishop's chair and sedilia, and the exquisite Paschal (Easter) Candle, usually placed near the font. Metalwork was supplied by The Newcastle Handicrafts Company (established in 1899).

There is also much exquisite silver, designed by Hicks in the manner of William Morris and executed by William Bainbridge Reynolds (1903, not normally displayed), as well as a wealth of outstanding stained glass, much of it fitted shortly after the completion of the church and again reflecting a strong Arts and Crafts influence. The great west window of c.1904 is a memorial to Hicks, who died in 1902, while the church was being constructed. The eastern chapel, dedicated to All Saints, has three small but distinctive sets of windows by Caroline Townsend of London (1904-09), the lateral ones providing an unusual depiction of English worthies such as William Blake, Izaak Walton, Sir Thomas More and Bernard Gilpin. The spectacular north transept window, inserted in memory of Miss Easton, who died at the age of 95 in 1913, is by Leonard Walker, also of London, and contains scenes of the Ascension, executed in glowing Arts and Crafts colours.

St Chad's Church, Rawling Road, Bensham, Gateshead, by Hicks & Charlewood, 1900-03: from the north west.

THE ROYAL VICTORIA INFIRMARY

QUEEN VICTORIA ROAD, NEWCASTLE, NE1 4LP

The Newcastle Infirmary had a long history before it moved to its present site in 1900-06 under the title the Royal Victoria Infirmary. In 1751 Richard Lambert, a prominent Newcastle surgeon, proposed the foundation of a voluntary hospital in the city, to be funded by public subscription. The idea was enthusiastically received and the hospital opened in a house in Gallowgate, procured for temporary use. The foundation stone for a new building on Forth Banks, on the west side of the town, was laid the same year. The new Infirmary (described in Chapter Two) opened in 1753. It received substantial extensions in 1801-03, and a further new wing (by John Dobson) in 1852-55.

By the later nineteenth century the Infirmary, now surrounded by urban development and railway works, had become inadequate for the city's needs. Following numerous calls for a replacement building, in 1896 the Mayor proposed the construction of a new hospital to celebrate Queen Victoria's forthcoming Diamond Jubilee. A public subscription was started immediately, with an enormous single gift of £100,000 coming from John Hall, a merchant and shipping magnate. Later, Lord Armstrong of Bamburgh provided another, similar donation in memory of his famous great-uncle, Lord Armstrong of Cragside. As a condition of Mr Hall's gift, the new hospital was now to be built, not on the original site, but on the Leazes, part of the Town Moor on the city's north-western edge. This new site was given to the city by the Freemen of Newcastle.

In 1900 the Prince of Wales laid the foundation stone for the new hospital and, as King Edward VII, returned with Queen Alexandra in 1906 to perform the opening ceremony. The total cost of the building was £326,577. The design was a collaborative effort by the hospital specialist Percy Adams and local architect W.L. Newcombe, a choice astutely adjudicated by the great Alfred Waterhouse from a competition of 1897-99. The Newcastle architects Dunn, Hansom & Fenwicke had been invited to submit a design for consideration, but did not do so. The original Infirmary on Forth Banks was now abandoned, although it was not finally demolished until 1954.

The Royal Victoria Infirmary was planned in the grand manner, in an eclectic Renaissance-Baroque style utilising red brick and ashlar, and laid out with a fine sweep to the central entrance and administration block. From this, long corridors link to a series of large, detached wards, eight for adults and two for children, at right-angles to the main block, as well as to a nurses' home at the extreme west end. The Infirmary was one of the last major hospitals in the country to adopt this 'pavilion', or 'Nightingale' ward system, designed to provide maximum light and ventilation.

Since the hospital's construction, there have been many extensions, some aesthetically unfortunate, and still ongoing. The latest changes have been major demolitions on Queen Victoria Road (the eastern wing of the original building was taken down in 2010) and the construction of a new entrance and accommodation including the Great North Children's Hospital. This structure strikes an especially discordant note. However, at the time of writing the southern block of the original hospital building, albeit extended to the west, remains largely intact (see photograph left).

The former main entrance is approached along Queen Victoria Road, where the original cast-iron railings still survive. By the entrance gates is a delightful single-storey lodge, in brick and stone, with a portico supported by Tuscan columns in front of the door. The main (south) facade of the hospital building is a magnificent composition, three main storeys high and topped by a stone parapet below attics set within a steeply pitched, hipped slate roof with tall brick chimneys. The ground floor of this very long facade is in ashlar, with brickwork above. Both end pavilions project slightly; they feature a canted bay window on the ground floor below two further windows set above one another between stone pilasters supporting a triangular pediment.

A powerful three-bay, three-storey central frontispiece also projects, behind a Roman-style round-arched porch with square piers. The spandrels of the porch have panels carved in relief (by the Arts and Crafts sculptor Conrad Dressler) depicting figures offering welcome. The whole frontispiece is in ashlar, surmounted by a segmental pediment and further emphasised by a central lantern tower on the ridge above.

The visitor enters through the porch into an impressive double-height vestibule. This is the Peacock Hall, so called because the pattern of its wallpaper (a sympathetic replacement for the original moulded leather) is based on a stylised peacock's feather motif. Most of the rest of the decoration is in Arts and Crafts style. There is fine teak woodwork with geometric ebony inlay, as well as a moulded plaster ceiling and frieze by G.P. Bankart. Round-headed doors are set within continuous glazing in arched openings, and a grand staircase with fine Art Nouveau balustrading rises to a balcony, lit at the upper level by stained-glass windows by G.G. Laidler representing the arms of local towns.

From the Peacock Hall, corridors give access not only to the ward pavilions, but also, on the right, to committee rooms and the former library, now the consultants' dining room. This is panelled in Arts and Crafts style and retains its original copper light fittings; the ceiling is again by Bankart. On the other side of the entrance hall is the tiny St Luke's Chapel, a little-known gem in neo-Byzantine style executed in Doulton's artificial 'Carrara' stone (see photograph above). It is Greek cross-shaped, with a dome in gold mosaic, also by Doulton, lit by a ring of small windows. Its four 'arms' have barrel vaults lined in blue mosaic; its main walls, arches and pendentives are in ashlar. The woodwork, again with ebony inlay (and fine, naturalistic carving), is of a similar style and quality to that of the entrance hall. Illuminated by fine stained-glass windows, this whole space glows with light.

The final surprise is in the children's ward, where 55 (of 61) surviving Doulton tile pictures line the walls with colourful scenes from nursery rhymes. Paid for through private benefaction, these delightful panels constitute probably the most complete set of its kind still in existence. They were designed and painted by J.H. McLennan, William Rowe and Margaret E. Thompson.

Far Left The Royal Victoria Infirmary, Queen Victoria Road, Newcastle upon Tyne, by Percy Adams and W.L. Newcombe, 1900-06: from the south. The statue of the young Queen Victoria is by Sir George Frampton (1906).

Left The Royal Victoria Infirmary, Queen Victoria Road, Newcastle upon Tyne: St Luke's Chapel.

CATHEDRAL BUILDINGS AND NOS 12-14, DEAN STREET

NEWCASTLE, NE1 1PG

These two large commercial buildings on either side of Dean Street contrast remarkably with the array of other late Victorian office buildings, eighteenth-century survivals and rather unfortunate late twentieth-century insertions found nearby.

Designed by Oliver, Leeson & Wood (W.H. Wood had joined the practice in 1900), they date from 1900-01 and are Jacobean in inspiration, with elements of the 'Queen Anne' and the neo-Baroque. Most unusually for the region, they have external coloured decoration. The building occupying Nos 12-14 is steel-framed and has a facade which is partly of red brick but with Jacobean-style woodwork on the upper storeys and blue and ochre tilework between the floors (see above, left). Originally a warehouse and offices for the leather and rubber manufacturers John Taylor & Co., it is now a hotel.

The structure known as Cathedral Buildings (see above, centre), on the western side of the street, is of the same date but is larger, more complex and even more exuberant; again its facades are partly of brick, cladding a steel frame. It has five storeys with an attic storey above and is seven bays wide. The main entrance to the offices, on Dean Street itself, is centrally placed and has Art Nouveau tilework within. Glass shop (or restaurant) fronts occupy the other ground-floor bays, separated by heavily ornamented, attached Ionic columns made of cast iron.

To the south of the entrance bay, the steep slope of Dean Street is cleverly accommodated by the insertion of a series of square windows, above the shop fronts between two entablatures. The upper entablature supports the windows on the first, second and third floors, which are oriels, with white painted Jacobean-style woodwork, very much in the manner of the then-fashionable London architect Norman Shaw. They are separated horizontally by decorative panels in relief, now painted in pink and cream, contrasting with both the painted woodwork and the expanses of red brick between the windows.

The oriel windows themselves, rising through three storeys, are capped by a projecting, railed balcony, supported on wooden corbels and placed in front of yet another floor. This in turn has square-headed, triple-light casements set in a rendered wall. Above that, a colourful, decorative frieze is surmounted by emphatic eaves and an attic storey complete with powerful, triangular gables above each bay. These were considered to harmonise well with the historic buildings in the vicinity.

A tall, brick gable to the south rises above Cathedral Stairs, leading up from Dean Street and again relating to the Gothic Cathedral of St Nicholas. Within the Cathedral Close, behind the street, is a second entrance, into the upper levels of the building. This is elaborately Baroque in style, with heavily rusticated jambs, decorative consoles and volutes, and a fanlight above the door. Higher still, a round window is surmounted by an architrave. On this sits a curious, almost grotesque, carving of a rabbit, or hare, popularly known as the 'vampire rabbit', the symbolism of which has never been satisfactorily explained (see above, right).

THE FORMER ELECTRIC TRAMWAYS BUILDING

MELBOURNE STREET, NEWCASTLE, NE1 2JS

This building of 1901, by B.F. (Benjamin) Simpson, perhaps befitting its more industrial character, is not quite as elaborate as his city-centre designs, Half Moon Chambers and Emerson Chambers (see p.220-221), but is nonetheless of considerable period interest. It is also noteworthy for its extensive use, internally, of iron and steel construction.

The main building, on the corner of Trafalgar Street and Melbourne Street, comprises four floors of offices and is in an eclectic and exuberant style, reminiscent of the architecture of Norman Shaw. The former turbine hall, or 'engine room', is seamlessly attached to the east along Melbourne Street. This is a lower, simpler and more classical structure, with a series of tall, round-headed windows as well as large entrance doors to the main space.

The office building, which very effectively adapts to its sloping, corner site, has a ground floor and basement in sandstone ashlar with heavy, square-headed windows. Three further floors in red brickwork lie above. The first floor has wide windows under depressed arches, while the windows above are casements with stone details. On either side of the central bay on the curve are oriel windows rising through two floors; above the cornice, each of these compositions is finished with a turret-like conical roof surmounted by a finial. In between, the central bay rises to a stone gable and steeply pointed roof. The entrance door, set back behind an arched opening and accessed by steps, provides a fashionably asymmetrical note, sitting just off centre in an otherwise symmetrical composition.

Behind the main building, approached through a fine Art Nouveau entrance arch, is the original boiler house (now known as the 'Generator Studios'), which provided the power for electricity generation. This became redundant and remained empty for many years before being imaginatively converted into offices (see p.323). Near the entrance stood a tall, well-proportioned chimney for the boiler house, now demolished.

Opposite, Left to Right
Nos 12-14, Dean Street, Newcastle upon Tyne, by Oliver, Leeson & Wood, 1900-01: from the south west.

Cathedral Buildings, Dean Street, Newcastle upon Tyne, by Oliver, Leeson & Wood, 1900-01: from the north.

Cathedral Buildings, Dean Street, Newcastle upon Tyne: detail of rear elevation with 'vampire rabbit'.

Right The former Electric Tramways Building, Melbourne Street, Newcastle upon Tyne, by B.F. Simpson, 1901: from the south west.

THE BEEHIVE HOTEL

THE CLOTH MARKET, NEWCASTLE, NE1 1EN

The Beehive Hotel was designed by Joseph Oswald for the Newcastle Breweries (see p.204) and opened in 1902. There had been several previous inns on this prime site where the Bigg Market meets the Cloth Market, the current Beehive being the second inn of this name.

The building is constructed out of brick and dressed stone, with the floors being defined externally by stone banding. The windows of the upper floors are of stone with chamfered mullions, while the ground-floor windows, beautifully carved with Composite capitals, are made of hardwood. On the roof a fine copper dome surmounts an octagonal tower, one of the faces of which defines the building's corner and emphasises its entrance.

The Beehive retains much of its original furniture and fittings, but is notable above all for its superb faience, a material often favoured by Oswald. Green and yellow tiles decorate both the interior and exterior. Especially impressive are the tile-clad columns framing the entrance and windows at ground-floor level. These columns culminate in somewhat unorthodox Corinthian capitals, each of which is surmounted by a frieze-like device in Art Nouveau style. These devices, so typical of the inventiveness and eclecticism of the period, support in turn another frieze, again in ceramic, placed below the brick and stone of the upper floors and attractively inscribed with the public house's name.

The Beehive Hotel, the Cloth Market, Newcastle upon Tyne, by Joseph Oswald, 1902: from the south.

THE FORMER SUN INSURANCE COMPANY OFFICES

COLLINGWOOD STREET, NEWCASTLE, NE1 1JE

The Sun Insurance Company Offices were designed by local architects Oliver, Leeson & Wood and built in 1902-04. They replaced the earlier, brick-built property of W.R. Pape, a famous Newcastle gunsmith, who moved into new premises in nearby Pink Lane. Designed in an eclectic French Renaissance style, with Baroque elements, these premises are built out of high-quality sandstone ashlar with a granite plinth.

The ground floor of the building is powerfully rusticated while the first floor is the most ornate. The second and third floors are comparatively plain; they are topped with a dentilled cornice, above which is an attic storey with a copper roof. On the south side, the attic storey is surmounted by a segmental pediment containing a large sunburst, emblematic of the company for which the premises were built. The sun motif also features on both the mosaic doorsteps and the first-floor wrought-iron balconies. Originally the building was further ornamented with urns and statuettes, long since lost.

The central entrance on the ground floor, facing west, is particularly striking. It has a large elliptical window above the door, as well as much fine relief carving and two large neo-Baroque atlantes, emblems of strength and vigour, supporting a balcony. This highly sculptural treatment may well reflect the influence of Beresford Pite, an Arts and Crafts architect and theorist noted for his advocacy of Michelangelesque motifs of this kind.

The former Sun Insurance Company Offices, Collingwood Street, Newcastle upon Tyne, by Oliver, Leeson & Wood, 1902-04 (detail of central entrance): from the west.

HALF MOON CHAMBERS

THE BIGG MARKET, NEWCASTLE, NE1 1UW

Left Half Moon Chambers, the Bigg Market, Newcastle upon Tyne, by Simpson, Lawson & Rayne, 1903-04: from the south.

Right Emerson Chambers, Blackett Street, Newcastle upon Tyne, by Simpson, Lawson & Rayne, 1903-04: from the south east.

This is one of a group of buildings in the centre of Newcastle designed by B.F. Simpson, now in partnership with S.H. Lawson (his nephew) and T.V. Rayne (a former pupil of F.W. Rich). Their combination of Art Nouveau and Baroque styles creates a wonderfully exuberant effect. Built partly as a public house for the brewer Archibald Arrol of Alloa, whose business was expanding at the time, Half Moon Chambers dates from 1903-04 and is the latest of a series of premises of this name that have occupied the site since 1550.

The present structure was first planned in 1897 as a rebuilding of an existing public house. Simpson's initial design was symmetrical and comparatively orthodox in its classicism. However, by the time the building contract was signed in 1903, Arrol had acquired the adjacent property and wanted a more complete reconstruction. Simpson and his colleagues therefore drastically modified their plans, not least to provide greatly increased office accommodation on the upper floors as well as front access to a ground-floor shop unit and service yard. As completed, the building has a complex and highly articulated facade. Above the ground floor is a prominent cornice. At first- and second-floor levels is an amazing variety of sills, Ionic columns, and curved balconies supported on curling ironwork brackets. Windows are flat, round-headed, circular and segmental. All these features typify these architects' enthusiastic mixing, and even distorting, of historical forms.

Similarly, on the top floor, above a further strongly projecting cornice, are blocked Ionic half-columns placed between the windows and supporting yet another heavy cornice. In the pitched roof is an attic floor featuring a highly decorated gable in the centre and strange, witches' hat-like dormers on either side. The facade is also enriched at first-floor level by carved lettering in Art Nouveau style above the doors.

EMERSON CHAMBERS

BLACKETT STREET, NEWCASTLE, NE1 7JF

The inventive and unusual work of Simpson, Lawson & Rayne reached a climax in Half Moon Chambers, discussed on the opposite page, and Emerson Chambers, another remarkable Baroque-cum-Art Nouveau commercial building in the city centre of the same date, 1903-04. B.F. Simpson, the firm's lead designer, has been seen as something of an outsider – thus, curiously, he never joined the Northern Architectural Association – and has even been likened to Charles Rennie Mackintosh in the strongly personal nature of his work. Be that as it may, he and his partners were never short of commissions.

Emerson Chambers was built for the developer R. Emerson jnr., and originally the building was to have been called 'Monument Chambers'. Its internal structure is iron-framed. It contained shops, offices, a wallpaper showroom and, in the basement, a restaurant (which soon gained a reputation as one of the best outside London). Probably designed to outdo its neighbours, Emerson Chambers succeeds in being one of Newcastle's most distinctive and popular buildings, prominently located on Blackett Street and visible from much of both Grey and Grainger Streets.

The main facade on to Blackett Street rises through five floors to an attic storey and provides "a frenzy of detail, splendid and arrogant against the serene classicism of Grey Street" (L. Gettings). This most exuberant of the facades, almost defying conventional architectural analysis, has two corner doorways framed by 'half-columns' of unorthodox design, and a central bay window, highlighted at ground-floor level by stumpy granite columns, of a Composite order, with bronze decoration that includes the capitals and the column bases; these bases feature shield-like emblems with lions' heads. Above all this is a variety of round turrets with balconies, attached blocked columns and cornices.

At attic level, the eastern corner turret culminates in a highly decorated, copper-clad clock placed above a dome, while its western counterpart rises to an unusual double dome articulated by columns. The facade's central, projecting bay is again supported by engaged, bulbous columns and rises through three floors. The top floor has comparatively plain windows, unlike its equivalent at Half Moon Chambers.

The whole facade rises to a cornice, lying above a richly decorated frieze with much fine carving in relief, incorporating the name of the building. Other, equally decorative friezes adorn parts of the facade at third-floor level. At attic level is a central, highly decorated gable, while in the hipped roof itself there are tall chimneys, and dormers with sharply peaked, witches' hat-like roofs (as at Half Moon Chambers), complementing the exquisitely decorated and detailed corner domes, mentioned above. The ensemble constitutes one of the most complex roofscapes in the entire city centre.

Little remains of the building's original interior, crafted by specialists from many areas of the country including A.R. Dean of Birmingham, responsible for much elaborate plasterwork. However, the surviving Art Nouveau main shop front has been well restored. The building is now a bookshop.

THE LAING ART GALLERY

NEW BRIDGE STREET AND HIGHAM PLACE, NEWCASTLE, NE1 8AG

Newcastle was late in establishing a municipal art gallery. After the Laing opened in October 1904, *The Studio* magazine commented, somewhat sarcastically, that "Newcastle has at last awakened from its long and peaceful sleep of indifference to all matters relating to art". Indeed, even then funds for the Gallery's construction came largely through the generosity of a local wine merchant, Alexander Laing, and it can be argued that a lack of wholehearted Corporation support is discernible in the building's design, detail and siting.

The Laing was conceived as an entity with the then-existing Public Library (see p.130) in New Bridge Street (itself at first planned to contain gallery and museum accommodation). Thus the impact of the building's main facade, facing east on to the narrow Higham Place rather than on to a main road, was much diminished. Nor did this entrance have the cathedral-like proportions of some other art galleries of the time. The fine tower, 111 feet high and containing the main staircase, was the only element originally visible to the pedestrian in central Newcastle.

The Gallery's 2005 extension, in 'post-modern' classical style, by the Newcastle City Architects Department (Project Architect: Jane Milner), has brought it more into line with New Bridge Street. However, a large area of rather unprepossessing brick wall, left exposed by the demolition of the former Public Library during the 1960s, still faces John Dobson Street. The extension provided a new entrance to the Gallery, and a new square was created in front, in an attempt to give the building greater civic presence. The design competition was won by Thomas Heatherwick, who proposed and executed a bold 'blue carpet' with tiles created from recycled blue glass. Unfortunately, however, the tiles have faded badly, and for many the square remains an unsatisfactory attempt to improve the area.

Notwithstanding the restrictions placed upon them, the original architects, Cackett & Burns Dick, showed great ingenuity in fitting the building into its awkward site and in making maximum use of the available space. Thus the building was planned as a 'hollow square' around a central court (now containing two exhibition galleries opened in 1976) and its principal entrance originally led into a vestibule, from which the visitor proceeded into a main exhibition hall.

To the left of the hall as one entered, was a sculpture court containing a fountain, placed directly below the still-surviving, top-lit, balustraded oculus on the first-floor landing. Beyond was the main staircase, as is still the case today. This in turn features a large, Arts and Crafts-style stained-glass window by J. Edgar Mitchell (1904) showing figures representing the various arts, all set within a classical temple surmounted by the Newcastle city coat of arms. To the right of the entrance hall was a 'museum' gallery (now the cafeteria), while the remainder of the ground floor was occupied by further gallery accommodation; all these rooms were originally lit by large windows facing the central court. The first floor featured top-lit picture galleries. The building makes effective use of the Edwardian neo-Baroque style, which suggested grandeur and prestige and locally seems to have reflected the widespread belief by some architects at this time that they were worthy successors to the heroic figures of 'Tyneside Classicism'.

More generally, the neo-Baroque style was also noted for its widespread incorporation of sculpture, a trend encouraged by the Arts and Crafts and 'New Sculpture' movements of the turn of the twentieth century. Thus at the Laing the main facade is enriched with relief sculpture, while a fine allegorical frieze depicting a procession of female figures is located high on the south and east sides of the tower. The tower has an arched and columned south-facing window at first-floor level (containing impressive stained glass, see above) and culminates in an octagonal lantern of complex design with coupled columns and pedimented arches, topped by an attractive dome.

The building's original main facade on to Higham Place, now in slightly neglected condition, has a rusticated ground floor, creating the effect of a plinth. Compositionally, the tower to the south balances the service wing to the north and the whole facade centres on the highly elaborate entrance. This has sculptured figures on either side, as well as detached columns supporting an ornate, broken pediment, within which is a niche, originally designed to receive additional sculpture. Below this, the former main doorway has elaborate wrought-iron gates with Art Nouveau detailing featuring sinuous curves.

Beyond, on either flank, detached Ionic columns project to carry entablatures with semi-circular pediments. Below these are the main first-floor windows and then empty niches, again presumably intended to contain sculpture, with bases adorned with ornamental heads. This effect of opulence is continued inside the building, which has heavy cornices, Ionic pilasters, Corinthian columns, tessellated marble and wood-block floors, and elaborate Art Nouveau door handles and other fittings. In addition, Cackett & Burns Dick, like many architects of this period, embraced progressive technical and constructional ideas. Thus the Laing, which was built by J. & W. Lowry of Newcastle, has reinforced concrete floors and was heated and ventilated by means of the innovative 'Plenum' system.

Recently the eminent architect Sir Terry Farrell, showing impressive commitment to his home city (see also, Chapter Eight), has produced a master plan for the replanning of the Laing, as yet unexecuted because of budget cuts. This plan, is, rightly or wrongly, highly critical of the present layout and facilities, describing the building as "not suitable for housing a major collection" and even condemning the new entrance of 2005 as "confused and constrained".

The Laing Art Gallery, New Bridge Street and Higham Place, Newcastle upon Tyne, by Cackett & Burns Dick, 1902-04: from the south east (the modern extension to the left dates from 2005).

MILBURN HOUSE
DEAN STREET, NEWCASTLE, NE1 1LE

Milburn House (1902-05) is a very large commercial building on the steep, triangular site where the Side meets Dean Street. This was previously occupied by Robinson's stationery warehouse, which burnt down in 1900. Oliver, Leeson & Wood designed Milburn House, as offices and shops, in collaboration with their local architect-colleagues Marshall & Tweedy. It was financed by the Milburn family, who made their fortune from shipping and coal and then reinvested in property. The shipping magnate William Milburn was the prime mover in this enterprise, the scale of which matches that of the huge and profitable ships he owned.

Built of brick with stone dressings, and with granite for the porches, Milburn House is a handsome composition, rising high above the pavement. The design is essentially classical and deals elegantly with the gradient of the site. It also turns the corner with admirable control. Here the building becomes curved, as with the same architects' Collingwood Buildings (see p.205), and an extra lower ground floor is cleverly inserted. The design has a Baroque flavour and also shows a strong Dutch influence, especially at attic level, where gigantic gables rise from a heavy cornice.

The floors are named rather like those of a luxury liner, perhaps because of the Milburns' association with shipping: each floor is assigned a letter, with 'A' at the top floor and 'G' on the lower ground floor. Constructionally, the building has a complex steel frame (with concrete walls faced in brick), on what was known at the time as 'the American plan'; this enabled it to be very large and so facilitated its capacity to house as many as 100 organisations at any one time.

Inside, Milburn House has a number of atria and open courtyards, providing light to its centre. The interior finishes are of exceptional quality, which is perhaps to be expected in view of the building's enormous cost, upwards of £120,000. These finishes combine stone, fine woodwork and stucco. There is also bevelled glass with heraldic emblems relating to Newcastle's history and identity (by the Newcastle-based J. Edgar Mitchell) and much superb Art Nouveau tilework, the latter supplied by Marsdens of Burslem, Stoke-on-Trent. Much of the tilework and other details had been painted over until revealed in a sympathetic restoration in the early 1990s by JDDK architects.

ST MARK'S WESLEYAN METHODIST CHURCH AND SCHOOLS

DURHAM ROAD, GATESHEAD, NE8 4AA

St Mark's Church is part of a large complex of buildings that once served a strong Methodist community in a typically working-class district of Gateshead. Designed in a bold neo-medieval style, almost certainly to match, or even rival, nearby St George's, just along the road (see p.201), it indicates that the Gothic Revival still remained a powerful force in architecture, persisting into the twentieth century.

As the population of Gateshead expanded, the area surrounding Durham Road and Shipcote Terrace developed into a residential quarter for the town's skilled workers. St Mark's Church was envisaged as the centre of a large Methodist community, with provision for future expansion. Accordingly, a large site was purchased from Lord Northbourne and plans for a church and school costing around £7,000 were drawn up by C.O. Ellison & Son in 1887. Christopher Obie Ellison was born in Liverpool c.1832 and commenced practice in 1855. He designed mainly for the Wesleyans, but was prominent enough to have become the first President of the Society of Architects in 1884. His initial design for the church was more conventional than that of the present building, with strong vertical emphasis in the nave and a full tower and spire.

A series of funding bids permitted the building of the Wesleyan schools at a cost of £2,430. Wealthy Methodists such as the Bainbridges of Newcastle contributed to the building fund. Opening on 14th March 1888, the schools were domestic in character and executed in rock-faced stone. The adjoining church was eventually built in 1905-06 to designs by William Stanley Ellison, who had joined the practice in 1886, taking over in 1901 when his father retired. Construction was carried out by the local building firm of Alexander Pringle. Completed on 6th June 1906, the structure accommodated 680 worshippers.

St Mark's Church was designed in a modernised Gothic style. The broad nave and plunging roof-scape create an effect of great solidity. Symmetry is broken by an octagonal tower, which culminates in an elongated belfry stage and eye-catching spire. The bulk of the church is built of rock-faced stone to convey strength, but the ashlar dressings have a contrasting, machine-like precision. Bold transepts project at the end of the nave and the school stands at the rear, along with a manse designed in complementary style.

Internally, the church takes the form of an uncomplicated but impressive preaching hall. The large open space of the nave is spanned by a wooden truss roof suggestive of stark engineering structures, rather than soaring Gothic vaults. This is surely a fitting image for a hardworking industrial parish. A relatively plain arch encloses the chancel, a space that was not always present in Methodist designs. However, in this case it deliberately lacks the ritualistic character of Catholic or High Anglican churches. The woodwork of the church is precise and austere throughout, particularly in the rather box-like pulpit.

In accordance with the building's modernised and simplified Gothic forms, the broad nave is illuminated by windows of predominantly clear glass that are sparingly embellished with abstract designs, resembling the curvilinear forms of Art Nouveau and contrasting with more conventional Victorian stained glass of the era. All this also reflects the tendency towards abstraction and linearity in art and design of the early twentieth century, as well no doubt as Methodist restraint.

The east window is illuminated by means of a light-well that was built between the church and the adjoining school-rooms. A number of pews have been removed in recent years. These originally ran right up to the edge of the altar, reflecting the former strength and numbers of the local Methodist community.

Left Milburn House, Dean Street, Newcastle upon Tyne, by Oliver, Leeson & Wood with Marshall & Tweedy, 1902-05: from the south west.

Above St Mark's Wesleyan Methodist Church and Schools, Durham Road, Gateshead, by W.S. Ellison, 1905-06: from the north west.

THE ROYAL GRAMMAR SCHOOL

ESKDALE TERRACE, JESMOND, NEWCASTLE, NE2 4DX

Newcastle's Royal Grammar School was founded in 1545 and was initially situated next to St Nicholas's Church. Since then it has moved five times, on the last occasion from its previous, neo-Gothic premises in Rye Hill, built to the designs of Johnson Hogg (see p.151) in 1866-70. For its new building the Grammar School turned not to a local architect but to the London-based Sir Edwin Cooper. Cooper obtained the commission, following a competition success in 1904, with a restrained neo-Georgian design, so different from most other architecture of the period. The building was then constructed in 1905-07, in red Leicestershire brick with local stone dressings.

It is a serene and symmetrical composition. The two-storey entrance block has five bays. The projecting ground floor is of brick, having tall, paired windows in stone surrounds with round windows in between. The entrance is marked by a semi-circular portico in ashlar, with Ionic columns. Above this, a stone bay contains a round-headed window set within a broken pediment; side bays are similarly arranged.

This essentially horizontal elevation is cleverly accented by a fine central clock turret on the ridge. Attached to the entrance block are two pavilions with hipped roofs and attic dormers, executed in brick with stone pilasters, which are linked to further brick buildings by glazed arcades.

Since the 1970s the Grammar School has seen a major development programme, with the addition of a music school in 1975. Further new buildings, by architects FaulknerBrowns, include an award-winning swimming pool and lecture theatre (1990), a sports centre (1996) and a science and technology centre (1997). The scale of these structures, around the sports field, matches that of the earlier portions of this traditional grammar school. Further expansion is currently under way, with internal remodelling and a major new swimming pool and sports hall, designed by the Howarth Litchfield Partnership.

Above The Royal Grammar School, Eskdale Terrace, Jesmond, Newcastle upon Tyne, by Sir Edwin Cooper, 1905-07: from the east.

Right Holy Trinity Church, Churchill Gardens, Jesmond, Newcastle upon Tyne, by Hicks & Charlewood and (later) Hoare & Wheeler, from 1905: from the south west.

HOLY TRINITY CHURCH

CHURCHILL GARDENS, JESMOND, NEWCASTLE, NE2 1HB

This fine neo-Gothic church, with its majestic, centrally placed western tower and spire, is a surprisingly recent addition to the Jesmond skyline. It is also a powerful demonstration of the continuing strength of the Gothic Revival tradition in the North East, even into the early twentieth century (see p.246). Perched dramatically on the edge of Jesmond Dene, the church occupies part of the site of the former Jesmond Park estate. It was built in stages during the period 1905-22, originally under the auspices of the Jesmond Church Extension Scheme of 1900.

Funds were donated in memory of Mr R.G. Hoare, a banker (of Hodgkin, Barnett, Pease, Spence & Co.) and local parishioner, and work commenced to the designs of Hicks & Charlewood in 1905, only to be halted following the completion of the chancel in October of the same year. This well-proportioned, aisleless structure, together with a 'nave' formed out of a temporary iron church transferred from nearby Springbank Road, served worshippers in this rapidly expanding part of Jesmond for at least fifteen years.

Ultimately the church was completed in 1920-22 by architects Hoare & Wheeler of London, as a memorial to the men of Tyneside who had died in the First World War. This was made possible through a donation by Jesmond parishioners Mr and Mrs R.S. Dalgliesh (Mr Dalgliesh was a ship-owner), given out of gratitude for the fact that their own family had been spared. The original design was considerably modified, although Hicks & Charlewood returned to supervise construction, which is immensely solid and craftsmanlike throughout.

In its present form the church is a long building, in snecked sandstone and ashlar. Both the nave and the chancel have buttressed aisles. Windows have Decorated-style tracery. The nave is surmounted by battlemented parapets, as is the tower, the corners of which have tall stone finials.

Internally, the effect is very spacious, thanks particularly to the width of the (six-bay) nave; the aisles are reduced almost to passageways. The nave arcades are round-headed, as is the impressive chancel arch (which is fitted with a fine rood-beam and screen, by Robert P. Appleby). Here perhaps the architects intended to suggest the effect of the combination of Norman and Gothic styles, or the transition from one to another, so often found in actual medieval buildings.

The carving and joinery in the church, some by Ralph Hedley & Co., is of uniformly high quality, but the chief glory of the interior is the unified scheme of stained glass by Nicholson Studios. Part of this, in the baptistery window, at the west end, is an unusual representation of King Solomon with the Temple under construction. The windows in the aisles have figures of saints and other sacred personages, as well as a diversity of more modern emblems and images, all poignantly commemorative of the First World War.

THE CENTRAL ARCADE

GREY, GRAINGER AND MARKET STREETS, NEWCASTLE, NE1 5BP

This is one of the finest Edwardian shopping arcades in the country. Designed by Joseph Oswald as a replacement interior after a fire in 1900 had ravaged the original (see p.116), it cost over £40,000 and opened in 1906 as a site of unashamed luxury shopping, rivalling similar arcades in Leeds and Manchester. A breathtaking cornucopia of yellow and brown decoration in Burmantofts faience, it is another example of this local architect's superb use of tilework (see p.218). Its style is perhaps best described as 'Art Nouveau Classical'.

Two new principal entrances were created for the arcade, one in Grey Street, and the other in Market Street, both having double-arches with a central column of the Composite order. Internally, above each entrance there is an impressive composition featuring a central niche placed between pilasters that support a segmental pediment; a sunburst radiates above. There is a third, subsidiary entrance into the arcade from Grainger Street.

The arcade is of two storeys and receives light from a curved glass roof, supported on cast-iron arches. It has a continuous balcony which services the shops at first-floor level, while the shop fronts themselves are delicately crafted; the full-height window frames are of teak, carved with residual classical detail. The floor is of mosaic, with a Greek fret design, originally supplied by Rust's Vitreous Mosaics of Battersea, although now carefully replaced with modern equivalents. This Greek-style motif was a favourite of Oswald's.

MILLMOUNT,
COWGATE, NEWCASTLE, NE5 3AL

Left The Central Arcade, Grey, Grainger and Market Streets, Newcastle upon Tyne, by Joseph Oswald, 1906.

Above Millmount, Cowgate, Newcastle upon Tyne, by Cackett & Burns Dick, 1908: from the north.

Robert Burns Dick, of the versatile local practice Cackett & Burns Dick, built this house for his own use in 1907-08. It stands near the Town Moor on the old Stamfordham Road at Cowgate, close to a motorway.

Although comparatively plain, its elevations show all the charm of a pleasant Arts and Crafts house, with rendering, steeply pitched tiled roofs, gables and tall, Tudor-style chimneys. The entrance lies within a projecting section, with a hipped roof and a first-floor oriel window tucked under overhanging eaves. Internally, the entrance hall, still with its original fireplace, leads into a series of attractive rooms.

After being vacated by Burns Dick following his retirement around the time of the Second World War, the building was for many years a nursing home. It is now the office of architects JDDK, who have renovated the building with care and sensitivity.

THE FORMER LADY STEPHENSON LIBRARY

WELBECK ROAD, WALKER, NEWCASTLE, NE6 2PA

Left The former Lady Stephenson Library, Welbeck Road, Walker, Newcastle upon Tyne, by J.W. Dyson, 1908: from the north west.

Right Houses in Kingsland, Jesmond, Newcastle upon Tyne, by J. Newton Fatkin, from 1909: from the south west.

The Lady Stephenson Library in Walker was designed by local architect J.W. Dyson. It was opened on 7th October 1908 by Sir Walter Runciman, President of the Board of Education, who declared in his address: “Here the most highly specialised clerk or artisan may widen his outlook or fertilise his mind.”

It is one of three very similar Stephenson libraries, all serving the new industrial suburbs and all designed by Dyson. The contractor in each case was Walter Scott of Newcastle. They were the gift of the philanthropic Alderman Sir William Haswell Stephenson, who felt that such libraries would be places where residents of densely populated areas “could assemble for the purpose of social intercourse, reading and refreshment, apart from the influence of the public house and strong drink” (see also, p.203). His other libraries are those at Elswick (1897) and Heaton (1898), which were the city’s first and second branch libraries.

The Walker Library was considered to be an improvement even upon the other two. Stephenson dedicated it to his wife, who had died in 1901 and whom he described as “one of the best women that ever lived upon the face of this earth”. Her name and coat of arms are displayed above the door (on the far left in the photograph).

The library described here is built of red engineering brick with sandstone dressings in an attractive, free Jacobean style with some Baroque details. Three large gables dominate the main facade, which is well balanced, although, typically for its period, just slightly asymmetrical. The central gable is faced with stone, enriched by carvings in high relief. The far left (entrance) bay is lower. At the centre of the roof ridge there is a small roof-light topped with an ogee dome – an endearing if slightly incongruous detail.

The entrance has a doorway and fanlight flanked by blocked piers supporting an open segmental pediment, all in stone. There is relief carving above. The carving throughout the facade is largely heraldic, embellished with floral and abstracted classical motifs reminiscent of Art Nouveau and Aesthetic Movement design. Inside, a marble entrance hall and staircase led to a large library hall on the first floor, with a reading room, newspaper room and ladies’ room below. A stained-glass window at the head of the stairs featured Stephenson’s family motto, ‘Fidus in Arcanum’ (‘Faithful in a Secret Matter’). The building was extended and attractively refurbished in 1991, but it closed in 2013, the library being transferred to the Walker Activity Dome (see p.287).

HOUSES IN HALDANE TERRACE, KINGSLAND, ESLINGTON TERRACE AND CLAYTON ROAD

JESMOND, NEWCASTLE, NE2 3AN

This delightful and unusual series of terraced houses was designed from 1909 onwards, mainly by local architect J. Newton Fatkin. His colleagues G. Bell and G. Ward were also responsible for some of the houses in Kingsland and Clayton Road respectively. The development reveals an interesting change in the design of terraced housing in the more affluent local suburbs such as Jesmond and Gosforth. During the great expansion of middle-class suburban housing in the late nineteenth and early twentieth centuries, the predominant terraced type in such areas had been characteristically Victorian, still demonstrating a strong influence from the classical terraces designed by John Dobson and others in the centres of both Newcastle and Gateshead. Indeed, such houses, with some minor changes in detail, were still being built after 1910.

The houses discussed here, the first of which were built on Haldane Terrace, are of two storeys with flat-roofed dormers to an attic floor. They are more informal and less grand than the conventional terraced type, although equally solid. Here, too, there is a greater emphasis, for visual effect, on the outward forms of construction and materials, as well as a different approach to the details. The contractors for the whole development were Elliott Brothers, of Jesmond, who commissioned the work from the architects and are said to have controlled the overall design style.

The houses have dark, red-brown brickwork, plain tiled roofs with deep overhangs at the eaves, and brick gables. Some of the bay windows are half-octagonal, with copper cladding or plain tiles between the ground and first floors; others are square-sided or canted, again in brick, sometimes with decorative stone inserts, and projecting above the eaves. Windows are frequently of casement type, with leading. The overall effect is Edwardian rather than Victorian, with influences from the Arts and Crafts Movement and the Art Nouveau style, and also from the domestic work of the eminent architect Sir Edwin Lutyens.

ST CHARLES'S CHURCH (R.C.)

ROTHWELL ROAD AND CHURCH ROAD, GOSFORTH, NEWCASTLE, NE3 1TX

Built early in the second decade of the twentieth century, St Charles's Church in Gosforth is another very late example of a design that still used the medieval Gothic style to inspire its parishioners. The parish of St Charles (Borromeo), in what was then still very much a mining area, was formed in 1861 and the needs of the congregation were initially met by a chapel-school and later by a very basic, temporary iron church. This was built on land donated by George Dunn jnr. in 1896, the site having been identified as early as 1884. Another major benefactor was Canon Joseph Watson, formerly Provost of the Cathedral Chapter of Hexham and Newcastle, who had retired to the locality.

The current church, built mostly of rock-faced sandstone with ashlar dressings, was begun in 1910 and the foundation stone was laid by the Right Rev. Richard Collins, Bishop of Hexham and Newcastle, on 14th August of that year. The church opened on 3rd December 1911. Its majestic neo-Gothic design is by Charles Jean Ménart (c.1876-c.1938). He was born in Belgium, but trained in Britain, and worked mainly in Glasgow, often in an Italianate idiom. The contractor was W.C. Fleck of Gosforth. Ménart may have been known to Canon Watson. Earlier plans drawn up by the Newcastle architect Stuart M. Mould in 1899 were abandoned.

The west end of the church is very striking, with twin towers framing a powerful west window. The spires, of coursed squared sandstone, are thought to have been loosely modelled on those of Cologne Cathedral. The whole effect of the composition is also more than a little reminiscent of that definitive Arts and Crafts-cum-Gothic church, Holy Trinity, Sloane Street, Chelsea (by J.D. Sedding and Henry Wilson, 1888-90).

Here at St Charles's, the four-bay nave is short, emphasising the church's pronounced verticality, but tall transepts and an apsidal chancel give the building dignity and scale. Rising above the aisles, the clerestory is pierced with large windows that flood the interior with light. Their tracery, basically Perpendicular, is also slightly reminiscent of the Art Nouveau style in some of its more sinuous details. The altar is enshrined within a polygonal apse, as was common in Roman Catholic churches. This splendid space is resplendent with polychrome marbling, as indeed is most of the rest interior; the apse is also flanked by side chapels.

Two large windows in the transepts, representing the Descent from the Cross and the Adoration of the Magi, and one in the south clerestory, depicting Christ before Pilate, are important examples of the work of Harry Clarke Studios of Dublin (1946). During the 1970s the church received a new, glazed west porch and in the 1980s some re-ordering, at which time an impressive Italianate baldachino by Ménart (1925) was partially dismantled.

CROSS HOUSE

WESTGATE ROAD, NEWCASTLE, NE1 4XX

Cross House was designed by Cackett & Burns Dick in 1911 as commercial premises replacing the previous Cross House, formerly the home of a wealthy banker that had been demolished in the widening of Westgate Road. The new Cross House accommodated mainly a substantial solicitors' practice and, on the ground floor, a banking hall.

The building is in the more monumental, classical style that these architects were later to simplify and develop so effectively between the wars (see Chapter Six). It efficiently fills the difficult, triangular, sloping site opening out from the junction of Westgate Road and Fenkle Street. At this eastern junction, the narrow end elevation is especially dramatic. There is a plinth of heavily rusticated stone to the ground floor (as on the other elevations), with an arched entrance set in a curved facade. This curved section rises through four more floors to a heavy cornice, above which is a gable storey set back behind a stone balustrade. The whole composition is given balance by a pair of chimneys either side of the gable, visually linked to the heavily rusticated quoins going down to the ground.

Although on a smaller scale, Cross House is reminiscent of Daniel Burnham's famous 'Flat Iron' Building in New York of 1902. Again like many American buildings of the time, it employs a reinforced concrete frame structure, in this instance based on the patented system developed by the French engineer François Hennebique and developed under licence on Tyneside by the civil engineer L.G. Mouchel (see also p.210). The frame is clad in Portland stone – with contrasting tooled and smooth profiles – giving the building a gleaming whiteness unusual in the city. The facades have four projecting windows at each of the corners of the main upper floors and are beautifully finished with a continuous dentil moulding, under a heavy cornice. In spite of its advanced structure, in 1919 Cross House was engulfed by a fire in which ten people died. In 1955 a substantial, but compatible extension was added to the building, also faced in Portland stone.

Left St Charles's Church, Rothwell Road and Church Road, Gosforth, Newcastle upon Tyne, by Charles Jean Ménart, 1910-11: from the south west.
Photograph newcastlephotos.blogspot.com

Right Cross House, Westgate Road, Newcastle upon Tyne, by Cackett & Burns Dick, 1911: from the east; the statue, 1906, by John Tweed, is of the local politician and journalist Joseph Cowen.

BUPA

CHAPTER 6

BETWEEN THE WARS, 1919-1939

The Tyne Bridge, by Mott, Hay & Anderson (consulting engineer: Ralph Freeman) with R. Burns Dick, 1924-28: from the south (detail).

INTRODUCTION

The period between the two world wars was one of economic decline for the North East, as the Victorian legacy of a strong industrial base of heavy engineering and shipbuilding was eroded. Newer industries, such as those of the automotive sector, chemicals, and processing, emerged nationally, but were less coal-dependent and generally found the South and Midlands more attractive and convenient locations than Tyneside. Firms amalgamated to become larger, establishing prestigious headquarters in London. Even companies that had been major contributors to the war effort, like Armstrong's, were forced to retrench and look for possible alliances: Armstrong's merged with Vickers of Sheffield in 1928, on rather unfavourable terms.

Between 1920 and 1930 nineteen shipyards closed. By 1931 about 80% of the workforce in Jarrow, on the south bank of the Tyne, was unemployed and in 1932 Palmers launched its last ship there. A further five shipyards on Tyneside closed by 1933, as the area's global share of ship production shrank from 80% before 1914 to little more than 20%. Unemployment was higher in the North East than in most of the rest of the country and by 1936 one in three workers in the region was out of a job.

The North East Coast Exhibition, held in Newcastle's Exhibition Park and opened on 14th May 1929 with a rousing speech by the Prince of Wales, was an attempt to revive the region's commerce and industry. Despite attracting nearly 4.5 million visitors, it failed in this aim. However, its essentially axial architectural layout, by local practitioners W. & T.R. Milburn, was considered a success. So too were its 'stripped classical' buildings, mostly by the same architects. One, the former Palace of Arts, still survives as Newcastle's Military Vehicle Museum.

As a response to the increasing problem of unemployment, the government introduced the Special Areas Act of 1934, allowing for the first time the use of Government money to support those areas in direst need, and to promote the diversification of industry. This led directly to the establishment of the Team Valley Trading Estate in Gateshead (see p.257) in 1936. It was only the second such industrial development in the country (after Slough in Berkshire). However, its early success, although by no means negligible, was limited, and its initial target of 15,000 peacetime workers was not achieved until the 1960s.

Newcastle ceased to be a centre of industry, becoming instead a regional service, administrative and retailing centre. Despite severe economic hardship, a significant number of people could still afford to buy the growing range of consumer goods available. In Newcastle, established department stores such as Bainbridges and Fenwicks expanded to meet this demand. Retail activity centered on (especially) Northumberland Street, and around Newgate Street, Westgate Road, Grey Street and Grainger Street. Commercial offices continued to be concentrated in the area between the Central Station and the junction of Mosley Street and Pilgrim Street.

At this time Newcastle was the administrative centre not only for the city itself but also for the County of Northumberland, and the number of local government employees increased significantly. There were proposals, not realised until the 1960s, for a new Newcastle Civic Centre on the northern fringes of the city (see below), while the Northumberland County Council Offices beside the castle were substantially enlarged by local architects Cackett, Burns Dick & Mackellar in 1929-34 (see p.250).

Because of the expansion of housing in the outer suburbs, there was a major increase in the demand for public transport. The late Victorian tram system could not cope and in 1935 was replaced in the central area by trolley buses (which had the advantage of using electricity derived from local fuel) rather than by motor buses. Although the new trolley buses proved very popular, motor buses were increasingly used to extend the service into the suburbs. Even so, this provision could not cater for the numbers moving in and out of the city centre and, as elsewhere, motor car use increased significantly during the period.

This increase in motor traffic led to demands for a second crossing to supplement the High Level Bridge, resulting in the opening of the Tyne Bridge in 1928. Built partly as an employment-creation scheme, the Tyne Bridge further encouraged businesses to move away from the quayside to higher locations on both sides of the river, although the line of its access

Left *Newcastle upon Tyne: Suggested Plan for Future Development*, 1924, by Robert Burns Dick (detail) (© Newcastle Libraries).

Right Drawing of proposed site for new Civic Centre in Exhibition Park, Newcastle upon Tyne, by Robert Burns Dick (from *Report* of the Northumberland and Newcastle Society, 1934).

road on the south side actually served to reduce the importance of the old centre of Gateshead by causing it to become partially bypassed from the main crossing. In Newcastle, the bridge consolidated Pilgrim Street and Northumberland Street as the main north-south route and it further accelerated the drift northwards whereby Northumberland Street, rather than Grainger Street, became the city's main shopping street.

Residential housing, both public and private, provided a major focus of building activity in Newcastle and Gateshead during the period. The end of the First World War saw thousands of servicemen returning to conditions of housing shortage and unemployment. Spurred on by fear of unrest in the wake of the Russian Revolution, the Government's 'Homes fit for Heroes' campaign led in 1919 to two new Housing Acts. For the first

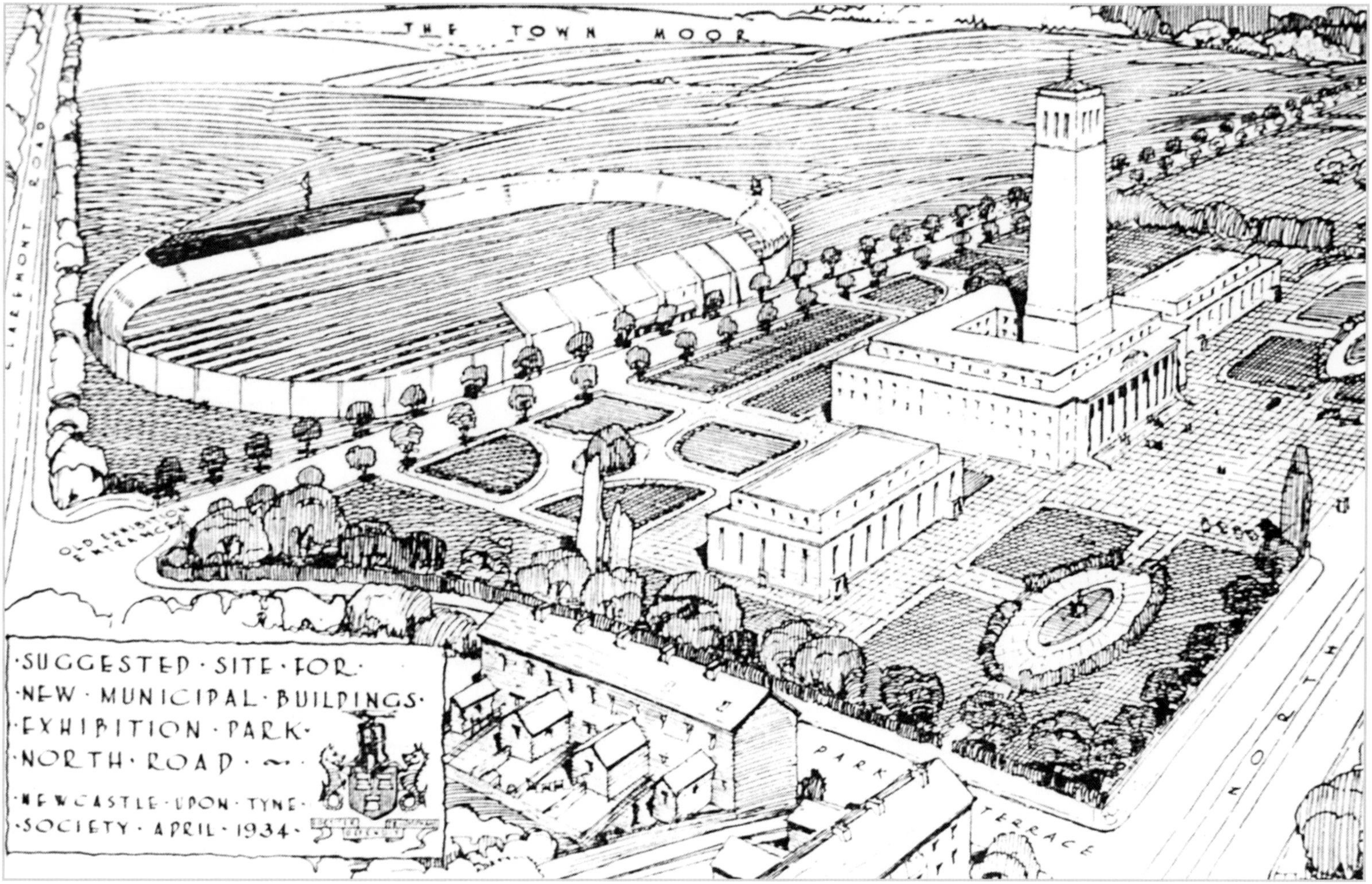

time, local authorities were required to assess housing need and provide housing for rent, leading to the first council houses.

In Newcastle the Council immediately purchased five areas of land for housing schemes, circling the city centre. These were at Fenham, North Elswick, Heaton, West Road (the former Pendower Estate) and Kenton Road, with additional land at Cowgate being bought in 1924, thus establishing the locations of the city's main inter-war municipal housing estates. Furthermore, in 1919 the highly capable R.G. Roberts (see p.261) was appointed City Housing Architect. By 1935 11,000 houses had been erected under his charge (in some cases the actual design was delegated to private architects) and a year later Roberts was appointed Newcastle's first official City Architect.

These new municipal developments, inspired by the early twentieth-century Garden City Movement, were to be low-rise and of low density, with extensive and thoughtful landscaping. Estates such as the Pendower, built from 1922 to 1929 between the West Road and Benwell Lane in Newcastle, and the Carr Hill in Gateshead, designed by Richard Wylie and begun in 1921, are typical. Given their limited budget these estates were also remarkably well built, utilising friendly red brick and tile, with sensitive and careful detailing. For the most part they were made up of conventional semi-detached houses, but also included a considerable variety of other dwelling types such as semi-detached cottages, 'double semis' (a form of 'Tyneside flat'), and horizontal, terrace-like blocks of six or even eight flats.

The overall planning of these municipal estates was sometimes rigid and unimaginative, blandly flanking the new suburban and arterial roads. However, at their best they successfully broke away from the grid-like arrangements of earlier, speculatively built working-class housing through the use of diagonals, crescents and cul-de-sacs, sometimes with enclaves of dwellings radiating from small, communal greens. For example, the large Deckham Hall Estate in Gateshead (1936-39) was laid out as a series of concentric rings. Such arrangements seemed pleasantly informal in comparison to earlier terraced grids, while also offering a reassuring sense of organisation derived from the underlying geometric patterns on which these layouts are based.

Private housing also increased substantially during the period. Tyneside, like other conurbations, saw much low-density ribbon development of detached and semi-detached houses – often accompanied by new, more family-friendly public houses of the 'road house' type – along its main roads, giving rise to concern over 'urban sprawl'. This led ultimately to the post-Second World War Planning Acts (see Chapter Seven), which encouraged the high-density developments of the 1960s.

Despite the recession, there were areas of growth. Newcastle's Armstrong College (then still part of Durham University) expanded considerably and in 1937 was re-organised under the name of King's College. Many of its developments during the inter-war period, including the Students' Union Building on King's Walk (see p.240), continued the Jacobean-inspired styles of earlier University buildings. The King George VI Building (see p.262), which mixes classical external details with modern steel construction, came slightly later.

Mass entertainment also flourished. The popularity of the 'talkies' led to the construction during the 1930s of fifteen new cinemas in Newcastle and four in Gateshead. Newcastle supported between 30 and 40 cinemas during the inter-war period. Many were splendid Art Deco creations, but few survive. In Newcastle the Tyneside Cinema on Pilgrim Street (see p.260) retains its 1930s auditorium and is still in use, but at the present time the Odeon opposite, which once had a grand Art Deco interior (see p.248), is still awaiting a decision about redevelopment. In Felling, Gateshead, the former Palace Cinema, dating from as early as 1909 and capable of housing 1,450 people, survived until very recently, albeit as a warehouse and in poor condition; it has now been demolished.

The constraints of economic recession resulted in a comparative paucity of 'Modern Movement' buildings in Newcastle and Gateshead. The clean, white structures built in continental Europe and to a lesser extent the south of England during the 1920s and 30s are rare in the North East. A few modernist houses were designed, although in Newcastle the archetypal 'Wedge' house on Moorside North, by Cackett, Burns Dick & Mackellar, was demolished in the 1960s to make way for a motorway. However, the 'Shilling House' (see p.244) still remains on the West Road.

Although Modern Movement structures were considered appropriate for specific industrial uses, as once could be seen in the crisp lines of a number of local collieries' pit-head baths, the movement inspired few major structures in Newcastle and Gateshead before 1939. Large commercial and public buildings were generally built with steel or concrete frames, but with stone or brick cladding. Many were in the then-fashionable 'stripped classical' style characteristic of much public and commercial architecture in London at the time. Others, such as the aforementioned University buildings, and the Newcastle City Hall and Baths (see p.245), drew inspiration from even more obviously historical styles. A few, like the Newcastle Co-operative Society Building in Newgate Street and the former GEC Building in Gallowgate (see pp.249 and 253), display an Art Deco or 'Moderne' character.

Many clients still employed local architects, with such practices as Cackett, Burns Dick & Mackellar exerting a major influence. The principal designer from this practice, Robert Burns Dick (1868-1954), was probably the most talented local exponent of the 'stripped classical' style, mentioned above, which also served to develop the earlier, nineteenth-century tradition of monumental architecture in Newcastle and Gateshead.

Like John Dobson before him, Burns Dick also had considerable, if largely unused, abilities as a planner. For example, in 1924 he put forward a Plan for Newcastle (see p.236). This proposed an intersection from the Tyne Bridge, south of the present Pilgrim Street roundabout, and feeding a new road to the quayside. A major new axial route would have led from the Tyne Bridge to Barras Bridge, running east of Northumberland Street (its northward section anticipating the present John Dobson Street); this element of the plan was derived from an even earlier scheme of 1905, by Burns Dick's partner J.T. Cackett (1860-1828). Another new north-south route parallel to this was planned to lie to the west of Pilgrim Street. The most impressive feature of the plan would have been a Parisian-style boulevard leading from Barras Bridge to a monumental new Civic Centre in Exhibition Park (see p.237). Although Burns Dick's plan was not realised, the redevelopment of Pilgrim Street – occasioned by the construction of the Tyne Bridge – gave some indication of his grand vision. Here were built such monumental structures as the Central Police Station, Magistrates' Court and Fire Station (1931-33, see p.251) and Carliol House (1924-28, see p.241).

However, notwithstanding the local talent that was on offer, organisations in Newcastle and Gateshead now increasingly employed London-based and other southern architectural practices. Admittedly, these normally worked in co-operation with local firms, but before long Newcastle and Gateshead architects were completely sidelined when an open competition for the design of a new Newcastle Civic Centre, approximately on the site of the present building, was organised in 1939 following the rejection of several earlier proposals by Burns Dick. The competition was won by a little-known firm of Bournemouth architects, Collins & Geens, although their rather conservative design was quickly abandoned with the onset of war. Ultimately, further architectural activity, and certainly significant innovation, in the North East had to wait until after 1945.

THE SHIPLEY ART GALLERY AND GATESHEAD PUBLIC LIBRARY

PRINCE CONSORT ROAD, GATESHEAD, NE8 4JB

The Shipley Art Gallery (see right, top) resulted from a bequest by Joseph Shipley (1822-1909), a wealthy local solicitor, who at one time resided at nearby Saltwell Towers (see p.152). The bequest offered his substantial and eclectic art collection, together with the sum of £30,000 for the construction of a gallery, to the city of Newcastle. However, the Corporation promptly refused the gift, as many of Shipley's paintings were thought to be copies. The same offer was then made to the less affluent borough of Gateshead, which was most unlikely to have been in a position to afford such a gallery from the public purse. After much deliberation, the offer was accepted. The Shipley has since proved to be a significant asset to the town.

The gallery was designed by Arthur Stockwell and built during the First World War, in 1915, in a restrained and simplified version of the slightly earlier Edwardian Baroque style. It is constructed of high-quality sandstone ashlar, with Welsh slate for the roof. The front facade is dominated by a rather grand, single-storey porch that features a central balustrade, as well as life-size sculptures (by W. Birnie Rhind, representing the Arts and Sciences), Corinthian columns and rusticated piers. Behind the porch are unusual, bow-ended wings, containing offices. To the rear is the gallery block itself, containing a large central space and four smaller rooms, two on each side.

Stockwell also initially designed the adjacent Gateshead Public Library, as a companion to the Shipley. He used the same architectural palette, but his later composition, in its original form, was somewhat heavy in comparison. The building of the library was made possible by a grant of £15,000 from the Carnegie Trust in 1916, but Stockwell's design proved to be beyond budget and the project was delayed until after the First World War. When it was resumed, yet further funding was required. Stockwell died whilst this money was being sought and eventually a scaled-down library was realised in 1926, under the direction of architect David Ditchburn (see right, lower). The building was later extended to the designs of Gateshead Borough Architect Leslie Berry in 1976. It still serves as the town's main library and received further major extensions and alterations, completed in 2010 and funded by the Big Lottery Community Libraries Fund. This work involved a complete refurbishment of the building, the reopening of a disused entrance, and the creation of a new children's library, gallery, café and community facilities. The work was done by Gateshead Council Planning and Design Services, with Oksana Holgate as the job architect and Stephen Easten Ltd the contractor.

Top The Shipley Art Gallery, Prince Consort Road, Gateshead, by Arthur Stockwell, 1915: from the east.

Above Gateshead Public Library, Prince Consort Road, Gateshead, by David Ditchburn, 1926: from the east.

THE STUDENTS' UNION

NEWCASTLE UNIVERSITY, NE1 7RU

The Students' Union is one of the first University buildings to be encountered on the way from the Haymarket to the Arches and the main quadrangle. It dates from 1923-25 and was commissioned by an anonymous donor.

With its use of brickwork with stone details, it continues the neo-Jacobean and English Renaissance theme of the first phase of University buildings (see Chapter Five), although in a more overtly revivalist way. Moreover, its orange brickwork and white Portland stone contrast with the darker brick and sandstone of the earlier structures. Given the conservative nature of the design, it is perhaps surprising to find that it was the work of the normally progressive architects Cackett & Burns Dick.

The building has three storeys above a basement and a U-shaped plan with two projecting wings. The central entrance bay is topped by a tower and an open stone belfry, while the doorway is entered through a round arch flanked by paired Tuscan pilasters. Portland stone is used for the window surrounds, quoins and balustrading, and the brickwork contains a diaper pattern.

The Students' Union was extensively remodelled behind its facade during the 1960s, and in 2011 a further refurbishment of the whole enlarged structure was completed by architects FaulknerBrowns (see p.283).

CARLIOL HOUSE

MARKET STREET AND PILGRIM STREET, NEWCASTLE, NE1 6NE

Left The Students' Union, Newcastle University, by Cackett & Burns Dick, 1923-25: from the north east.

Right Carliol House, Market Street and Pilgrim Street, Newcastle upon Tyne, by Burnet, Tait & Lorne, 1924-28: from the south west.

Carliol House, one of Newcastle's finest inter-war buildings, was designed by Burnet, Tait & Lorne of London in collaboration with local architect L.J. Couves (1878-1951), a specialist in modern constructional techniques.

Built in 1924-28 as prestigious new headquarters for the North East Electricity Supply Company, Carliol House was intended not only to promote a modern image of efficiency and progress but also to celebrate the importance of electricity to society – at a time when the number of consumers in the North East was rising dramatically. Named after the Carliol family, who were rich Newcastle merchants, the building also commemorated the work of the local inventor Sir Joseph Swan.

Constructed from Portland stone on an internal steel frame, Carliol House is a synthesis of the 'stripped classical' and Art Deco styles, its monumentality according well with the earlier 'Grainger-Dobson' architecture in the vicinity. Like many other buildings in central Newcastle, it turns the corner gracefully, in this case by means of three curved bays that form an impressive rotunda-like accent topped by a lead-clad dome. These three bays sweep the view round the street corner from the two bays of the building on Pilgrim Street to the 24 bays on Market Street. They also emphasise the building's entrance and vertical circulation route.

A heavy cornice accents the facade, as well as defining an attic storey above – a feature seen in much nineteenth-century architecture throughout Newcastle, although here rationalised into a more modern style. The interior of the building has been greatly altered; much of the original effect is now concealed by modern retail and office conversion work.

THE TYNE BRIDGE
GATESHEAD AND NEWCASTLE, NE1 6BG

This magnificent river crossing (see also chapter frontispiece) was built in 1925-28, with government assistance, to improve road and tram access at high level between Gateshead and Newcastle. It augmented Stephenson's High Level Bridge of 80 years earlier, which had now become congested. In addition to its status as a Tyneside icon, not least as a symbol of the region's engineering skills, the Tyne Bridge has had a major influence on Newcastle and Gateshead in many ways. In particular, it redefined the major routes through both urban areas.

Various schemes for a new high-level bridge in approximately this location had been put forward during the late nineteenth and early twentieth centuries, but it was not until 1923 that serious planning was initiated, reflecting the growth of motor traffic in particular. It soon became an official joint venture between Newcastle and Gateshead Councils, receiving formal approval in April 1924. Government approval was given four months later and the contract was awarded in December 1924. Previously unemployed labour was used in the construction of the bridge as much as possible.

The bridge was designed by Mott, Hay & Anderson (consulting engineer: Ralph Freeman) and the contractors were Dorman Long & Co. of Middlesbrough. It is a reduced version of the Sydney Harbour Bridge that the same team of engineers had already designed, but not then built. The construction of the Sydney bridge began slightly earlier, but because of its much greater size it was not completed until 1932. Dorman, Long & Co. provided the steelwork for both. To make way for the Tyne Bridge

some earlier quayside buildings had to be demolished, including offices, a bank, a lodging house, a powder mill, a pickle factory, and such long-forgotten riverside hostelries as 'The Goat Inn', 'The Earl of Durham', 'The Ridley Arms' and 'The Steamboat Inn'.

The Tyne Improvement Commissioners insisted that the river be kept open during the bridge's construction, necessitating the ingenious use of cranes on both sides. They also stipulated that the height of the completed traffic deck should allow full navigational use. The engineers addressed this requirement by spanning the river with a single, two-hinged steel arch and by suspending the road deck below it at 84 feet above high water. King George V and Queen Mary opened the Tyne Bridge on 10th October 1928. At the time it was the largest single-span bridge in Britain.

The visual impact of the bridge is stirring, thanks to its span of 531 feet, its height and the powerful simplicity of its arched form. And at quayside level, the huge, visible hinges that are supported on massive concrete foundations add further drama to the steep slope from the river frontage.

Local architect Robert Burns Dick was responsible for the monumental architectural treatment of the bridge. Particularly impressive are the paired, granite-faced 'pylons' at each end. These are modelled on ancient Egyptian temple entrances and add enormously to its visual impact (if minimally to its structure). The pylons contain warehouses, which were never used, and lifts.

Splendid though the ensemble is, Burns Dick's unexecuted original scheme for the bridge, involving yet larger pylons and a gigantic arch, would have provided Newcastle with an even more magnificent approach. As it is, the bridge still forms a dramatic entrance to the city from the south, although its impact has been reduced by the construction during the 1960s and 70s of the All Saints' Centre office development and of the Cale Cross House tower block to the west.

On the south-east approach to the bridge, and originally associated with it, is an interesting small building of 1928: the former Public Conveniences and Reading Room, by Arthur Bashford, Architect to Gateshead Borough Engineers (see left, lower). Carefully respecting the design of Burns Dick's bridge pylons and of concrete block construction, which succeeds in resembling the granite used in the bridge approach, the structure also cleverly exploits its position to provide an upper-level entrance to a square reading room with set back chamfered corners; there was also access at lower level to public toilets. On each projecting face of the upper level is a round-headed opening, while the alternate, recessed faces have smaller, rectangular windows. The reading room, lit by a shallow glass dome, was sadly never used until in the 1990s it was imaginatively converted into an architects' office by Nigel and Cathy Jenkins. This features a suspended meeting room, accessed by a cantilevered wooden staircase. The room is now occupied by a design consultancy.

Above Left The Tyne Bridge, by Mott, Hay & Anderson (consulting engineer: Ralph Freeman) with R. Burns Dick, 1924-28: from the west.

Left The former Public Conveniences and Reading Room, Tyne Bridge (Gateshead), by Arthur Bashford, 1928: from the south west.

THE 'SHILLING HOUSE'

WEST ROAD, NEWCASTLE, NE4 9RL

The 'Shilling House' was designed as a demonstration house in 1925, the architects being Bunney & Makins of London, well-respected figures who had earlier been involved in the celebrated Hampstead Garden Suburb development. The house was built on behalf of the *Newcastle Chronicle*, who donated it to a relief fund set up for the families of the 38 men and boys who died in the local Montagu Pit disaster of March 1925. Its name derives from a money-raising competition organised by the fund, whereby entrants paid a shilling to guess how many people travelled on Newcastle tramcars on one day, the prize being the house itself.

The building is designed in a stark modernist style and is constructed out of reinforced concrete, cast *in situ* and with a render finish. The severity is slightly relieved by means of a discreetly crenellated parapet and a protruding central bay that contains the entrance. The house has a plain, introverted quality, not unlike early twentieth-century dwellings designed by the Viennese architect Adolf Loos, who was noted as an arch-opponent of decoration.

The 'Shilling House' is not without charm, but it does now appear somewhat anomalous, contrasting markedly with its more conventional, pitched-roofed neighbours, built of brick and tile during the 1930s. In recent years the building suffered from lack of maintenance, but has now been carefully restored for its present owner by architect Lin Hopper.

Above The 'Shilling House', West Road, Newcastle upon Tyne, by Bunney & Makins, 1925: from the south.

Right The City Hall and Baths, Northumberland Road, Newcastle upon Tyne, by Nicolas & Dixon-Spain, 1928: from the south west.

THE CITY HALL AND BATHS

NORTHUMBERLAND ROAD, NEWCASTLE, NE1 8SF

This group of buildings, opened in 1928 and designed by Nicolas & Dixon-Spain, was the first major public complex in Newcastle to be constructed after the First World War. It covers a block near the centre of the city and the hall itself can house up to 2,000 people; until recently it was the only sizeable concert venue in the region.

Although failing to achieve the grandeur demanded by local architects and planners such as Robert Burns Dick (see p.238), the facade is nonetheless a reasonably imposing classical composition. Constructed of brown brick with stone details, it has a central entrance section of ashlar (with recessed joints), with three arches supported by plain square pillars and leading through arched doors into an open entrance lobby.

The upper floor has banded quoins, and stone surrounds to the windows; classical details include a pediment containing an oculus, and a heavy parapet above. To the left and right are Tuscan colonnades with steps up to round-headed entrance doors, with a powerful entablature above. The symmetry of the facade conceals the structure's internal organisation: the central entrance bay gives access to the swimming baths, and the right-hand colonnade to the concert hall.

The City Hall is now somewhat isolated by its position on what is in effect a large traffic island within the city's modern road management scheme. Access is poor for both concert-goers and performers' support vehicles, and the complex faces an uncertain future following the opening near the riverside of the large Metro Radio (formerly Telewest) Arena in 1995 and of Sage Gateshead in 2004 (see p.320). The swimming pool section closed in 2013, and at the time of writing the building's future is uncertain, with the City Council seeking a buyer.

THE CHURCH OF ST JAMES AND ST BASIL

FENHAM HALL DRIVE, NEWCASTLE, NE4 9UT

This church, in suburban Fenham, was paid for by the wealthy industrialist and shipping magnate Sir James Knott (1855-1934). Dating from 1928-31, it commemorates the lives of his two sons, James and Basil, who were killed during the First World War. Reflecting this is the church's unusual plan: a stark and austere rectangle divided by a four-and-a-half bay arcade into a nave and a virtually identical aisle, each serving as a memorial to one of the greatly mourned army officers.

Like many patrons of his era, Sir James retained personal control of the project; it is said that the inspiration for the design (which combines Gothic and Arts and Crafts elements) came from a church in northern France that he had seen and admired. Nominally, at least, the Fenham church was designed by E.E. Lofting of London. The contractor was Alexander Pringle of Gateshead. A massively buttressed church hall, a vicarage and a memorial garden, were all completed in 1932.

Lofting was a little-known Gothic Revival architect who had become Assistant Surveyor to Westminster Abbey, working under W.R. Lethaby, a noted Arts and Crafts figure. It is now known that Lethaby himself may well have been involved in the design of the church and that the mastermind behind the whole scheme was his friend and colleague George Jack, a former pupil and assistant of the distinguished Arts and Crafts architect Philip Webb.

Collaboration between several architects (and craftsmen) was of course very much an Arts and Crafts ideal. However, it remains unclear how Sir James came to recruit his team. It is possible that the architect Temple Moore, who designed the nave of Hexham Abbey (1907-09) and to whom Lofting had been articled, may have acted as an intermediary.

The church, entered via the garden to the west, is built mainly of local Kenton stone; recycled masonry from the old Newcastle Gaol of 1822-28, then being demolished, was also used, with, by contrast, concrete for the foundations. The building's external appearance is robust and powerfully articulated. A massive, battlemented tower, over the memorial chapel on the south-eastern corner, dominates the elevation to Fenham Hall Drive. It has three stages, its east face having a traceried window with hood mouldings, above which is a 'Lombard frieze' and belfry windows. The top of the tower has crenellation. A turret is attached to the south face of the tower, along with a clock, positioned on the south-east corner.

The interior, a generous, well-lit space, is equally well handled. Octagonal piers support king-post trusses and blind arcades frame the tall windows on either side. The interior surfaces are comparatively plain, finished for the most part in stucco and ashlar dressings, but character is provided by a corbelled, arcaded frieze beneath the sill level. There is also much fine carved timberwork, by Lawrence Turner. Of particular note are the 'Moorish' lattice-work screens to the organ and organ gallery and the finely carved altar table, framed in oak against the wall. Turner was also responsible for all the furniture. The metalwork is by J.P. Cooper.

The stained glass glitters with colour and is of exceptional quality. Eight of the thirteen windows are by George Jack himself, while the remainder are by Edward Woore, who introduced some Art Deco motifs into the windows' general Arts and Crafts vocabulary. Jack was also responsible for the church's crystal chandeliers and its Jacobean-style altar table. Lofting himself described the church of St James and St Basil as "a frankly modern building", which makes sense up to a point, in view of the structure's comparatively plain exterior. However, a more accurate assessment is that it "remains largely as its architects intended it – one of the last great Arts and Crafts churches in England" (Neil Moat).

ST JOSEPH'S CHURCH (R.C.)

ARMSTRONG ROAD, BENWELL, NEWCASTLE, NE15 6JL

Left The Church of St James and St Basil, Fenham Hall Drive, Newcastle upon Tyne, by E.E. Lofting and others, 1928-31: from the south east.

Right St Joseph's Church (R.C.), Armstrong Road, Benwell, Newcastle upon Tyne, by Stienlet & Maxwell, 1929-31: from the south east.

Local architects Stienlet & Maxwell designed this church in 1929. It was completed in 1931 and opened by Bishop Joseph Thorman, replacing a temporary iron structure that had been built in 1903. A new church was required due to the population explosion in this area, particularly in the years 1850-1910.

St Joseph's is one of several large churches perched on the northern banks of the Tyne (see, for example, page 198). Unlike the others, however, this example is inspired by the architecture of the eastern Mediterranean. Perhaps because of the high praise accorded to J.F. Bentley's monumental, neo-Byzantine Westminster Cathedral following its completion in 1903, the Roman Catholic Church commissioned a number of provincial churches in a similar style.

This church, which was partly paid for by an anonymous benefactor, is constructed of dark brick with a pantile roof. The nave is long and wide, in order to accommodate a large congregation (now very much diminished). There are two domes, the larger of which is placed over the crossing and is surmounted by a cross; the other is placed over the entrance. The transepts, which have pitched roofs, are large, each having an apse-like projection built into the west face, topped with a half-dome. Perhaps the most interesting feature of the whole ensemble is the large chancel with apse, reminiscent of the Byzantine Church of the Holy Apostles in Salonika, Greece.

The interior of the church is a pure volume finished in white stucco, except for the sanctuary, which is constructed from Italian marble. It is entered through an arch. However, substantial changes have taken place since the church was first built, principally those resulting from a re-ordering of the interior of 1982, designed to bring it into line with modern liturgical practices.

As part of this phase of work, by local architects Dietz-Lyons, a stained-glass screen was erected within the sanctuary arch, separating the nave from the day chapel (formerly the sanctuary apse). Designed by L.C. Evetts and built by Elders Walker Millican of Gateshead, this screen contains no fewer than 1,116 pieces of glass and is perhaps the finest example of modern stained glass in the region. Unfortunately, this impressive work can be seen only during services, because of the threat of vandalism.

THE FORMER ODEON CINEMA

PILGRIM STREET, NEWCASTLE, NE1 6QE

This major cinema was designed by Frank Verity and Samuel Beverley in 1929-30. It opened on 7th September 1931 as the Paramount, becoming the Odeon in 1940. In 1954, it became the first cinema in Newcastle to be equipped with Cinemascope.

The building is said to be a simplified version of Verity's Italianate Carlton Theatre, London (1927), although its interior, by American designer Charles M. Fox, was in the "French Watteau style". Its lavishness reflected the need for fantasy, entertainment and escapism during difficult economic times.

The foyer originally had light fittings finished in nine-carat gold and an ornamental balustrade in aluminium alloy crafted by Mark Aynsley & Sons of Newcastle. The 2,600-seat auditorium featured large silk panels, hand painted by Turner Lorder & Co. of London, while a contemporary description also noted "a ceiling fancifully resembling a night sky upon which gilded designs are seen on a dark ground, and in its centre a modern light fitting of opal glass". The account continued: "the walls are divided into panels by pilasters which 'flower' into glass illumination fittings behind which, as in the ceiling fixture, coloured lamps in amber, blue and red create a very dainty result. Above them graceful figures in metal enhance the general effect." Following the building's conversion to a multi-screen complex during the 1970s, this vast space was divided horizontally from the front of the balcony.

The Odeon's exterior is fairly austere, large areas of plain brick being relieved only by tall pilasters, a stone cornice and more elaborate first-floor windows. The building is no longer in use as a cinema and remains empty. Until recently some of the original decor survived above the partitioning, but almost all of the original fittings have now been somewhat crudely taken out, evidently prior to the building's Grade II listing being removed in 2010.

An authoritative report of the same year by the Northumberland and Newcastle Society, which had tried to save the Odeon, partly as a functioning cinema and partly as a film and entertainment museum, noted glumly that "the elegant and elaborately worked ornamental balustrades have been ripped out leaving gaping holes in the concrete stairs … shadows on the walls are all that remain of the decorative lighting sconces and other original fittings."

At the time of writing, therefore, this important former cinema is likely to be demolished as part of the forthcoming East Pilgrim Street redevelopment.

Far Left Above The former Odeon Cinema, Pilgrim Street, Newcastle upon Tyne, by Frank Verity and Samuel Beverley, 1929-31: from the north west.

Far Left The Paramount (later Odeon) Cinema, 1938: from the north.
Photograph Newcastle Libraries.

Left The Paramount (later Odeon) Cinema, interior, 1940: from the west.
Photograph Newcastle Libraries.

THE FORMER CO-OPERATIVE DEPARTMENT STORE

NEWGATE STREET, NEWCASTLE, NE1 5RZ

The former Co-operative Department Store, Newgate Street, Newcastle upon Tyne, by L.G. Ekins, 1929-32: from the south east.

This stylish former department store was built in 1929-32 in the Art Deco manner. One of the city's most impressive structures of its age and type, it is Grade II listed. The design was by L.G. Ekins, Chief Architect to the London C.W.S. However, Ekins also had local connections, having earlier held a similar position with the Newcastle C.W.S. (1905-16) before taking up his appointment in London.

The building has stone facades, but also a continuous, glazed shop frontage on the ground floor, made possible by the whole structure's internal steel frame. On the main Newgate Street elevation two dominating circulation towers give the building its monumental character. These are topped with mosaics and stone fluting, and have tall vertical windows, several storeys high. On the fourth floor the facade steps back to create a full-length balcony, protected by railings that feature an Art Deco wave motif. In 1959 three extra bays were added to the left-hand side of the store; although marring the intended symmetry, they have weathered so well that they appear original. Inside, much of the 1930s decor is now concealed behind studwork and suspended ceilings. However, the circulation towers still retain the original marble cladding and metal window sets, while the staircases feature delicate steel handrails, supported on metal figurines of walking men. The top floor is perhaps the most impressive, with Egyptian-style columns supporting the roof and suggesting something of the exuberance the building must have displayed when first opened.

The department store closed in 2007, with the food hall remaining open until the end of 2011. With the building empty, it began to deteriorate through water damage and also became prone to vandalism and theft (copper faces from the exterior clocks were stolen in 2012). However, in 2014 the building was bought by DTZ Investment Management, and in April that year work began on converting it into a Premier Inn hotel.

THE VERMONT HOTEL (FORMERLY THE NORTHUMBERLAND COUNTY COUNCIL OFFICES)

CASTLE GARTH, NEWCASTLE, NE1 1RQ

Left The Vermont Hotel (formerly the Northumberland County Council Offices), Castle Garth, Newcastle upon Tyne, by J.A. Bain, 1910, enlarged by Cackett, Burns Dick & Mackellar, 1929-34: from the south west.

Right The Central Police Station, Magistrates' Court and Fire Station, Pilgrim Street, Newcastle upon Tyne, by Cackett, Burns Dick & Mackellar, 1931-33: from the north west.

John Tomlinson stayed here 14/02/19 we had a pint in the hotel bar Ground floor. £80 per night.

This important building is in close proximity to two major Newcastle monuments, the castle and the Moot Hall. It is a massive, stepped block resulting from a comprehensive enlargement (1929-34) by Cackett, Burns Dick & Mackellar of an earlier structure of 1910. The style is a 'stripped classical', with some influence also from American commercial architecture of the period. The offices opened in October 1934, having cost more than £128,000. The contractor was Henry Kelly Ltd.

The building has a difficult and dramatic site, with the north and east sides of the structure extending a further four storeys (55 feet) down to the Side. This presented considerable technical problems, which the architects overcame by producing a steel-framed building, clad in stone, and also making early use of hollow-block floor construction and a specialised excavation technique called sheet piling.

The earlier building of 1910 (by J.A. Bain) was in a restrained classical style, responding to the Moot Hall opposite, having a rusticated ground floor, with pilasters and half-columns rising through two floors and above that to a cornice. Cackett, Burns Dick & Mackellar (J.T. Cackett had in fact died in 1928) designed major extensions and alterations in keeping with the original scheme, adding extra floors, stepping them back from the main facade and substantially extending the building, not only to the north and east, but also, as we have seen, down to the Side below. The service yard at this lower level is enclosed by fine railings and the facade rises through eleven storeys, next to the magnificent arch of the railway viaduct over Dean Street, designed by Robert Stephenson (1849, widened 1894).

Internally, the entrance hall, tiled stairwells with coats of arms, and grand council chamber, were highly appropriate for a County Hall. However, after the County of Northumberland moved its offices to Morpeth, the building remained empty for many years, before being converted into a hotel for the 'Vermont' chain. Some remodelling has taken place but the main public spaces retain their original features.

THE CENTRAL POLICE STATION, MAGISTRATES' COURT AND FIRE STATION

PILGRIM STREET, NEWCASTLE, NE1 6XA

This excellent complex was built in 1931-33 (replacing a structure of 1874 by John Lamb), though the design, by Cackett, Burns Dick & Mackellar, seems to date back to 1928. The building consolidated several police and fire stations within the city, as well as providing a central magistrates' court.

Robert Burns Dick's inclination towards monumentality, as revealed in his slightly earlier architectural treatment of the Tyne Bridge (see p.242), is again seen to good effect in this important, 'stripped classical' structure. However, in this instance, a few more overtly historical details are used, including some decorative sculpture.

The building is constructed from fashionable Portland stone and conveys a sense of great authority and solidity: this is architecture of law and order. With its comparatively small, unadorned windows, the complex has the appearance of being carved out of solid stone. The public entrance, on the corner, is appropriately well defined and is surmounted by an imposing balcony accessed through a grand doorway; one could almost expect a papal address from this platform. Internally, meanwhile, much of the original decor survives.

At the time of the opening of the complex in June 1933, the *Evening Chronicle* commented: "Could Mr Burns Dick have the opportunity of replanning Newcastle as he planned this building, the city might become a modern Athens or Rome." Currently, however, the future of the building is uncertain: the fire station component has closed and while the police station is still open, this facility will shortly be relocated to the new police headquarters at Forth Banks, Newcastle.

THE FORMER ALFRED WILSON HOUSE (NOW CENTRALOFTS)

WATERLOO STREET, NEWCASTLE, NE1 4DE

In 1933 the Newcastle Co-operative Wholesale Society built Alfred Wilson House as a seven-floor warehouse, located to the west of the city centre and south of Westgate Road, close to the Society's main offices and distribution centre at Blandford House (see p.208). In 1970 the building was converted into offices, bar, nightclub and cinema, but the area became increasingly run down and Alfred Wilson House stood empty from 2002. Demolition was considered, until the building was purchased by a property developer; it became an integral part of the rejuvenation of this area, which was being redeveloped around the new Waterloo Square in proximity to Dance City (see p.330), car parking, offices and a hotel.

Napper Architects, who were responsible for the master plan for the area, proposed the refurbishment and adaptation of the original structure into residential and commercial accommodation, rather than demolition, because of its importance as one of the few remaining examples of Art Deco architecture in the city.

The original rear facade of Alfred Wilson House, facing the new square, had suffered from a number of unattractive alterations and additions over the years, and was therefore removed and replaced with a new lightweight facade. The change in level between front and rear was used to provide separate entrances for the residential and commercial sections, with the entrance to the apartments from Waterloo Street to the east, and that to the offices from the new square. The generous floor-to-ceiling heights and tall windows were used to good effect with the insertion of mezzanines in the apartments, while a new lightweight storey was added on the roof to accommodate luxury penthouses. The original Art Deco facade has been sensitively repaired and restored, using where necessary specially manufactured matching bricks.

Overall, the Centralofts project has proved to be an important and successful example of restoration work, which makes a valuable contribution to the rejuvenation of this area of the city. Napper Architects themselves moved into the ground floor of the development when it opened in 2007.

MAGNET AND ANDREWS HOUSES (GEC BUILDING)

GALLOWGATE, NEWCASTLE, NE1 4SN

Left The former Alfred Wilson House (now Centralofts), Waterloo Street, Newcastle upon Tyne, built by Newcastle Co-operative Wholesale Society, 1933: from the south.

Right Magnet and Andrews Houses (GEC Building), Gallowgate, Newcastle upon Tyne, by Cackett, Burns Dick & Mackellar, 1933-36: detail of facade, from the south east.

The General Electric Company Building was designed in the Art Deco style by Cackett, Burns Dick & Mackellar, as company offices, with shops on the ground floor. Dating from 1933-36, it is a substantial structure, built of light brown brickwork and Portland stone on a steel frame.

The building was originally six storeys high. It curves slightly to follow the line of the road. The central three bays (of 21) are picked out in Portland stone, with the principal entrance on the ground floor. There are also two further entrances to the building on either side.

The front facade is particularly distinctive thanks to its series of coloured relief panels depicting 'heroic' scenes of men at work symbolising the power of electricity, a figurative detail borrowed from Sir Giles Gilbert Scott's Battersea Power Station in London. The top of the facade is effectively accented with a stone band and shallow cornice.

The building was threatened with demolition during the 1990s but has now been converted into flats. The conversion includes the addition of an attic-storey extension of loft apartments.

THE NEWCASTLE CREMATORIUM

WEST ROAD, BENWELL, NEWCASTLE, NE5 2JL

The Newcastle Crematorium and Cemetery, designed by local architect J.J.Hill, was opened in 1934. The Newcastle Corporation recognised that a substantial facility was now needed to cope with the large number of people who had moved out to new suburban residences in the 1930s, not least in the west end of Newcastle. At the time, the crematorium was believed to be the only one between Edinburgh and Darlington, and ranked as one of the finest in Europe.

The history of cremation in Britain dates back to the Bronze Age, but the practice was virtually eradicated by the arrival of Christianity and its doctrine of resurrection. In the nineteenth century, however, factors such as urban expansion, soaring population and the inadequacy of existing burial grounds meant that cremation was revived as a hygienic and efficient means of disposing of the dead. The passing of the Cremation Act of 1902 further encouraged its use and many crematoria were built across Britain in the early decades of the twentieth century.

This facility is both a crematorium and a traditional cemetery. The initial work to prepare the site was carried out in 1931, with designs completed, but building work was not started until 1934 due to issues with finance; the complex cost nearly £54,000. Somewhat surprisingly, Hill used the Gothic style for his design. By this date, architects were generally much more interested in the pared-down language of Art Deco and Modernism, with Gothic being regarded as old-fashioned, even for religious buildings.

Hill did, however, in the spirit of the age, use some constraint: his Gothic is somewhat simplified and there is very little adornment or detail throughout the composition, except for some tastefully understated window tracery. The crematorium has two chapels, one for burials and the other for cremation. These are some distance apart and connected by a low cloister. In this respect the architect broke with the earlier Victorian convention of having such chapels positioned close together and joined by an arch with a spire.

The chapels are at the end of a wide carriage drive, and the route continues through an impressive double-height archway to the gardens of remembrance; above this archway is a handsome clock-tower. Internally the chapels are laid out as 'preaching-boxes', each having a focus towards a free-standing, curtained catafalque. Consistent with the rest of the architecture, these interiors are modestly detailed. They feature timber panelling and solid wood flooring below dado level, while above is stucco, which helps distribute light evenly within the spaces.

To the left of the crematorium is a two-storey columbarium, which is approachable either from the cremation chapel or from outside, while also noteworthy is a robustly detailed, three-storey tower that is used as an exhaust for the furnaces.

OSBORNE COURT AND GRANVILLE COURT

OSBORNE AVENUE AND GRANVILLE ROAD, BOTH JESMOND, NEWCASTLE, NE2 1TQ

These two blocks of flats are among the few good Art Deco buildings to be seen anywhere in Newcastle and are similar in concept and execution to the slightly later Moor Court, Westfield (see p.261).

Osborne Court (see right, top) is a four-storey block of 40 flats grouped around a central courtyard, designed in 1935 for Messrs Alec Woolf (Builders and Contractors) by J. Newton Fatkin, who was also responsible for an earlier and very different Edwardian development of terraced houses just off Osborne Road (see p.231). It is of red brick on a concrete frame with several subtly decorative courses of brickwork on the upper levels. The main (north) facade, which faces on to Osborne Road, has a projecting central section with entrance lobbies set into the angles. The principal living rooms of the flats have curved bay windows. These windows rise elegantly through all four floors, with metal glazing and white rendered panels.

Granville Court (see right, lower) is a larger block of 80 flats, designed a year later. It again features a central courtyard and is faced in red brick. The majority of the building is five stories high, with the main entrance section rising to six. This section is of dressed stone at ground-floor entrance level and is dominated by a tall narrow window, with elaborate original metalwork, which lights the main stairwell. Rising through five storeys, this window is capped by a decorative, truncated tower.

There are projecting white rendered balconies in the angles where the facade is set back. The brickwork is relieved by white horizontal bands at window head level. The architect of the structure is not definitely known, but as it was designed for the building firm of Cussins, which was also responsible for the slightly later Moor Court (see p.261), and has similar details, Granville Court is very probably the work of the same architect, C. Solomon.

Left The Newcastle Crematorium, West Road, Benwell, Newcastle upon Tyne, by J.J. Hill, 1931-34: from the east.

Above Right Osborne Court, Osborne Avenue, Jesmond, Newcastle upon Tyne, by J. Newton Fatkin, 1935: from the north east.

Below Right Granville Court, Granville Road, Jesmond, Newcastle upon Tyne, 1936: from the north east.

THE CHURCH OF THE HOLY CROSS

OVINGTON GROVE, FENHAM, NEWCASTLE, NE5 2QP

Left The Church of the Holy Cross, Ovington Grove, Fenham, Newcastle upon Tyne, by H.L. Hicks (Hicks & Charlewood), 1935-36: from the south west.

Right The Team Valley Trading Estate, Gateshead, by William Holford with L.J. Couves, from 1935: the central headquarters, from the east.

J.R. Blackett Ord of Whitfield Hall, near Hexham, was one of the major landowners in Northumberland and in the 1930s he began to sell off his extensive estates in Fenham for suburban housing. He then financed the building of Holy Cross Church, in memory of family members who had lived at nearby Fenham Hall (see p.56).

Blackett Ord also selected and donated a prominent site for the church, as well as personally appointing the architect, H.L. (Harry) Hicks, of Hicks & Charlewood (see also p.207). Hicks (1883-1947) had been trained in the Gothic tradition by his distinguished father W.S. Hicks (see Chapters Four and Five). However, in this instance the younger Hicks broke with tradition and worked in an uncharacteristic modern style, almost totally devoid of decoration.

Holy Cross Church was built in 1935-36, constructed largely of plain, recycled bricks from a demolished nineteenth-century building. The design is uncompromising in its simplicity, based on a careful balance of regular, geometric shapes. Its starkness is, however, softened by the mellowness of the old bricks – although this texture was not matched when a west porch was added in 1965.

Perched at the top of a hill, the church has an impressive 82-feet-high bell tower, with long belfry openings, visible across the west side of Newcastle. The building is without transepts and the aisles, which are little more than passageways, have flat roofs. The nave and chancel form a continuous space, twice as long as it is wide; this has low, round arches that spring directly from the floor and lead the eye towards a plain altar, framed by a round arch with a crucifix above. There is no east window.

Above, a barrel vault of reinforced concrete reflects light from the high-level clerestory windows and emphasises the powerful forms of the church's simple, white interior. The severe, unadorned modernity of the design did not altogether please the Church authorities of the time. Among very few decorative details is the later stained-glass window in the Lady Chapel, designed by L.C. Evetts, of the Fine Art Department of Newcastle University, c.1957.

THE TEAM VALLEY TRADING ESTATE

GATESHEAD, NE11 OBQ

Although it did not reach its target employment figures until the 1960s, and many of its individual buildings are post-1945, the Team Valley Trading Estate was a product of the inter-war years. It was part of an effort to relieve unemployment, whereby public funding was provided to encourage new, diversified and mainly light industries into the region.

This pleasant, accessible industrial estate, separated from housing, was planned in 1935 by William (later Lord) Holford, in collaboration with local architect L.J. Couves. Holford went on to become Chief Technical Officer to the Ministry of Town and Country Planning, where he is credited with laying the foundations for post-war British town planning legislation.

Construction of the Team Valley Estate began in 1936. Three years later, it provided over 2,500 jobs. It covers just over a square mile and has three tree-lined avenues with roundabouts and cross-streets. This essentially formal layout centres on Kingsway, at the time one of the widest roads in the country. The estate's central headquarters was built as a crescent-shaped block embracing a roundabout. Factories were provided in a range of sizes, including modest but innovative 'nursery' units intended to encourage new businesses. All the earliest factories, designed by Holford and Couves themselves, are low buildings of brick, one and two storeys high, with metal-framed strip windows.

The estate has the feel of a garden suburb, laid out with good services and leisure facilities, plenty of open space, and attractive landscaping, all rather like an industrial version of the garden cities envisaged nearly half a century earlier by Ebenezer Howard. At the same time, the design reflects the classical principle of axiality, resulting from Holford's architectural training at Liverpool University under Professor Sir Charles Reilly. There is also the presence of a certain Arts and Crafts legacy in the unfailingly sensitive use of materials.

After the war some larger bespoke factories were built at the Team Valley; the plant for Sigmund Pumps, designed in 1948, is of particular significance (see p.273). Subsequently, the estate continued to expand and it now boasts a wide range of commercial and industrial enterprises, which still include some of the original occupiers. It has the highest concentration of employment in Gateshead.

THE CHURCH OF THE VENERABLE BEDE

BENWELL GROVE, NEWCASTLE, NE4 9PR

Built in 1936-37 to serve Newcastle's expanding industrial western suburbs, and replacing an earlier wooden structure, this church was designed by Professor W.B. Edwards (1898-1964), Head of Architecture at King's College (later Newcastle University). A renowned teacher, and an important architect in Newcastle, Edwards was responsible for several of the University's major buildings after the Second World War (see Chapter Seven).

Edwards was an admirer of classicism, and especially of Lutyens. Like William Holford (see p.257), he had been trained at the celebrated Liverpool University School of Architecture. His work was invariably sensitively crafted, while also showing an awareness of Modernism. These qualities are much in evidence in the scholarly and inventive design of the Church of the Venerable Bede, which reflects an Arts and Crafts inheritance while also effectively alluding to trends in modern architecture; Early Christian architecture provides yet another influence.

The plan of the church is essentially traditional, with a longitudinal nave, aisles, transepts and a small chancel. An unusual broad tower, placed at right angles to the nave, has a double-pitched roof with exposed rafters internally, a detail also used for the other roofs.

By contrast, the window treatment is unequivocally modern, with simple forms, such as rectangles and narrow, round-arched shapes regularly disposed in groups. The arrangement of windows on the western face of the tower is especially pleasing.

A concern for detail and texture within the building is revealed not only in the judicious selection of materials (mainly sand-faced bricks, tiles and fine York stone) but also in the craftsmanlike use of these materials. For example, tiles are used to create arches, while bricks on end form the upper windows of the tower. There are also tympana above the two western portals, with modernist relief carvings illustrating scenes from the life of Bede (see left, lower).

Internally, the design is equally effective and features a four-bay nave; the altar is framed by two round arches. The church, although fairly modest in scale, is probably the finest in Newcastle from the period between the wars and represents an extremely effective combination of modern and traditional forms.

THE FORMER WHICKHAM VIEW SCHOOL

BENWELL, NEWCASTLE, NE15 6TT

Above Left The Church of the Venerable Bede, Benwell Grove, Newcastle upon Tyne, by W.B. Edwards, 1936-37: from the north east.

Below Left The Church of the Venerable Bede, Benwell Grove, Newcastle upon Tyne: scene from the life of Bede (detail of relief carving in tympanum).

Right The former Whickham View School, Newcastle upon Tyne, by F.W. Harvey, 1936-38: from the north east.

Whickham View School was built in 1936-38 to the designs of the talented F.W. Harvey, Newcastle's first Education Architect (1927-56), and reflects the comparatively generous expenditure on school-building at this time. It contained a gymnasium, craft rooms and indoor lavatories, and was one of the first schools in the country to have a swimming pool. Harvey also designed the original furniture and fittings, not only here, but also for his other schools within the city. Before it was closed in the early 1990s, this one became known as the John Marley Comprehensive School, named after a prominent Newcastle Royalist who – as mayor – had led the defence of the town against the besieging Scots during the Civil War. Rather surprisingly, the school was then threatened with demolition.

One of the finest Art Deco buildings in Newcastle, the school is constructed from brick with concrete dressings and granite bands. Windows are metal-framed. The structure's composition, with its interlocking blocks, recalls the work of the post-First World War 'Amsterdam School' of architects. Two low wings, with rounded ends, spread from a stepped, central block incorporating an octagonal tower; this is supported on concrete piers with inlaid granite bands. The symmetry of the design reflects the original provision of separate boys' and girls' facilities.

The main entrance, at the foot of the tower, is surmounted by a balcony with a stone coping. A tall, slender vertical window, flanked by two horizontal ones, is centrally located below a continuous clerestory that sits high on the tower; this in turn is elegantly crowned with a lead pitched roof. Two lower blocks sit either side of the entrance tower and look outwards, north and south.

Currently, this former school is Grade II listed and is a Newcastle College facility. Much of its interior has been modernised, in a contemporary version of the Art Deco style.

THE TYNESIDE CINEMA

PILGRIM STREET, NEWCASTLE, NE1 6QG

The Tyneside Cinema, Pilgrim Street, Newcastle upon Tyne, by George Bell (Dixon & Bell), 1937: from the east.

This cinema opened in February 1937 as a news theatre. Designed by George Bell of Dixon & Bell, it was, belatedly, one of the first news theatres in Newcastle – Birmingham, for example, had possessed one since 1932. It is also one of the few news theatres in the country to survive in anything like its original condition. The cinema ceased to show newsreels in 1968, and later that year it reopened as the Tyneside Cinema. Although situated opposite the much larger Odeon (see p.248), it remained popular by screening art-house films.

The cinema originally had two auditoria, the larger with a capacity of 270, and a coffee room, in operation since the 1930s and with authentic Art Deco detailing. A recent major refurbishment by Fletcher Priest Architects, with Cyril Winskell as conservation architect, had Heritage Lottery Funding and support from the Tyne and Wear Partnership, the European Regional Development Fund and a number of local donors. Much of the original ornate interior has been revealed as well as a 'lost' mural executed in 1976 by Peter Yates (of Ryder and Yates, later RyderHKS and now Ryder Architecture) when he re-designed the club cinema.

The original cinema has been restored with new seating for 200 in the stalls and with 60 luxurious armchairs and sofas in the circle. A multi-purpose 'Digital Lounge' has been provided to show local digital and experimental work, and for other events, while a new roof-top extension houses two cinemas with capacities of 114 and 100 seats. These are linked by a foyer bar, with the whole complex enclosed in a translucent envelope which appears to glow at night.

This major extension does not detract from the original building frontage, which is in a more restrained Art Deco style, harmonising well with its largely classical neighbours. This frontage, of sandstone ashlar, has incised pilasters below a cornice; under each window is a carved panel. A modern canopy with neon lighting illuminates the facade at night. When it re-opened in 2009, *The Guardian* newspaper rated the Tyneside as one of the ten best independent cinemas in the UK.

More recently, the central section on the building's ground floor, occupied for many years by a bank, have been converted into a café-bar, with the remaining original Art Deco features restored.

FENHAM LIBRARY

FENHAM HALL DRIVE, NEWCASTLE, NE4 9XD

Fenham Branch Library was built in 1938 and is a fine example of the highly competent municipal architecture characteristic of that time. Designed by City Architect R.G. Roberts (see p.237), it adopts a restrained classical style, with overtones of Art Deco – especially in the treatment of the interior.

The building's principal facade is a symmetrical, single-storey composition, constructed of brick with a base and entrance surround in ashlar. Square-headed windows are set within slightly recessed panels. The double door has an attractive 'fish-scale' fanlight and is surmounted by fine bronze lettering, while the library's interior is light, spacious and well organised. High-quality woodwork is present throughout; the vestibule, where the entrance is flanked by square Tuscan columns in light oak, is particularly well designed.

Above Fenham Library, Fenham Hall Drive, Newcastle upon Tyne, by R.G. Roberts, 1938: from the north.

Left Fenham Library, Fenham Hall Drive, Newcastle upon Tyne: vestibule interior.

MOOR COURT, WESTFIELD

OFF KENTON ROAD, GOSFORTH, NEWCASTLE, NE3 4YD

This seven-storey block of high-quality flats in Gosforth, overlooking the Town Moor, is one of the best Art Deco buildings in either Newcastle or Gateshead. It stands near the site of the Victorian racecourse grandstand, which was demolished when racing moved to Gosforth Park in 1881 (see p.58).

Moor Court was designed by C. Solomon for the building firm of Cussins (see p.255) in 1938, and was restored in the first few years of the present century. It is built of brick on an internal concrete frame, with white horizontal banding at the window heads and sills. There is more banding on the top floor beneath a flat roof. The whole composition has a strongly horizontal emphasis, which avoids monotony through clever variations of massing.

The main entrance, on the north side, lies beneath a concrete canopy supported by square, fluted columns. The lobby and main staircase are within a projecting bay, faced in Portland stone and lit by a dramatic vertical strip of glass blocks. The name of the building is inscribed above the entrance in appropriate Art Deco-style lettering; two similar, but smaller entrances are placed symmetrically on either side.

On the south side are further areas of vertical glass blocks, as well as another, central entrance. This side also features round corner bays with eye-catching curved horizontal windows. Some of the flats have balconies, either projecting or recessed, with those to the south enjoying excellent views across the Town Moor.

Moor Court, Westfield, off Kenton Road, Gosforth, Newcastle upon Tyne, by C. Solomon, 1938: from the north east.

THE KING GEORGE VI BUILDING (NEWCASTLE UNIVERSITY)

QUEEN VICTORIA ROAD, NEWCASTLE, NE1 7RU

Left The King George VI Building (Newcastle University), Queen Victoria Road, Newcastle upon Tyne, by P. Clive Newcombe, 1938: from the west.

Right The Church of the Divine Unity, Ellison Place, Newcastle upon Tyne, by Cackett, Burns Dick & Mackellar, 1938-40: from the north west.

This building, for the then King's College Medical School, was designed in 1938 by P. Clive Newcombe. It is a steel-framed structure, clad in brick with some stone details. Although more overtly historical in style, it has affinities with the monumental 'stripped classical' architecture of this period. Overall, in fact, the building offers a blend of traditional and modern elements not untypical of much 1930s official architecture.

The King George VI Building has metal-framed windows placed within plain, recessed brick setbacks running vertically through the three original floors, with a remaining reference to classicism in the stone detailing. The building, originally of three storeys but now with an extra floor added during the 1950s in compatible style, has a complicated plan. This can be described as being like two large 'E's placed back-to-back, thus creating four, three-sided courtyards.

Within this symmetrical plan, the principal elevation faces west, on to Queen Victoria Road, and includes the main entrance, placed within the south-west courtyard. This has a two-storey stone entrance porch with two inset Doric columns (see photograph above). The north and east elevations are more utilitarian in character, although the south elevation, facing on to St Thomas's Street, forms a monumental, essentially symmetrical composition in its own right.

Meanwhile, in the central projection on to Queen Victoria Road, the three original floors are expressed through an almost neo-classical arrangement that features triple windows, again in stone and with the whole ensemble being framed in brickwork. On the ground floor, these windows are separated by inset Roman Doric half-columns, while giant Corinthian half-columns, again inset, rise through the two upper floors, above a weighty entablature.

Such classical details perhaps fit slightly uncomfortably within the brickwork cladding and vertical emphasis of those parts of the design that express the building's obviously framed structure. Once into the entrance hall, the building again steps back in time, with panelled oak wainscoting, plaster friezes and a highly decorated, Jacobean-style ceiling.

THE CHURCH OF THE DIVINE UNITY

ELLISON PLACE, NEWCASTLE, NE1 7RU

The church of the Divine Unity was designed for the Unitarians by Cackett, Burns Dick & Mackellar (project architect: W. McAndrew) in 1938 and opened in January 1940. Built by J. & W. Lowry of Newcastle at a cost of £38,000, the complex includes a very large meeting hall (the Durant), as well as a smaller hall, a caretaker's apartment and numerous utility rooms.

It replaced the former St Peter's Church (Anglican, by John Dobson, 1840-43). Before moving to Ellison Place the Unitarians, named for their understanding of God as one person and rejection of the idea of the Trinity, had previously worshipped at their own church on New Bridge Street (also by Dobson, 1853-54). This was subsequently demolished.

The present church shows Burns Dick's earlier monumental classicism being abstracted and simplified in the direction of 'Modern Movement' design, perhaps influenced by his younger partner, R.N. Mackellar. Its style is particularly reminiscent of certain examples of modern Dutch architecture, such as W.M. Dudok's Hilversum Town Hall (1924-31).

The building is an essentially rectangular composition of simple interlocking blocks with flat roofs, based on reinforced concrete construction with cladding of very plain brick. The strong verticals of the tower, main entrance and windows balance its overall horizontality. The choice of colour for the brick is in keeping with the neighbouring Georgian town houses. However, the church tower does abut rather clumsily on to what survives of the southern terrace – as did, incidentally, the east end of the previous Dobson church.

The main entrance to the present building is through a noble tripartite stone screen, into a small open forecourt. The impressive and exceptionally well-lit interior is a large, plain space (60 by 52 feet) in the preaching-box tradition, with aisles but without transepts. A contemporary account of the building noted that "the severely rectangular forms and rhythmic decoration upon pulpit, communion table, reading desk and choir stalls proclaim the 'Modern' school." The nave of the church has six bays, lit by tall windows with concrete reveals; the clerestory has 'landscape' windows with similar surrounds. There is also a spacious gallery at the western end.

The oak furniture, also designed in the modern tradition, complements the simplicity of the space. The bold pattern of joists in the flat ceiling provides a textural contrast to the purity of the rendered walls and helps to create a most effective arrangement of intersecting planes that recalls the work of the great American architect Frank Lloyd Wright. His 'Unity Temple', at Oak Park, Chicago (1904-07), also of course for the Unitarians, appears to have been a specific influence.

THE QUEEN ELIZABETH HOSPITAL

QUEEN ELIZABETH AVENUE, GATESHEAD, NE9 6SX

The original Queen Elizabeth Hospital was built in 1938-40 to the designs of F.H. Patterson, under the supervision of Gateshead Borough Architect H.J. Cook. Initially a hospital for infectious diseases, it is now part of a much larger modern facility.

The building illustrated here is a symmetrical, three-storey, flat-roofed block, designed in the Art Deco or 'Moderne' style. Although completed in 1940 and opened by the Mayoress of Gateshead, Mrs P.S. Hancock, it was not fully used until after the war, in 1948. It has since served as an operating suite, an X-ray department and as general wards. More recently it became the administrative headquarters of the hospital.

There are semi-circular stairwells, with large vertical windows, at both ends of the block; these stairwells also provide access, via two single-storey lobbies. The building's main entrance is centrally located and set within a sandstone surround with attached planters, which are likewise of sandstone.

Above the entrance is a canopy, supported by two columns faced in fluted ceramic tiles. Further articulation is provided by the use of sandstone dressings, contrasting with the predominant expanses of plain brick. Unattractive modern extensions have been added to the rear of the building, which is much less impressive.

THE LITTLE THEATRE

SALTWELL VIEW, GATESHEAD, NE8 4JS

Left The Queen Elizabeth Hospital, Queen Elizabeth Avenue, Gateshead, by F.H. Patterson with H.J. Cook, 1938-40: from the south.

Right The Little Theatre, Saltwell View, Gateshead, by H.L. Honeyman, 1939-43: from the south east.

The Little Theatre is one of Gateshead's very few modern-style buildings from the inter-war period, and was actually completed and opened during the Second World War, a rare if not unique occurrence for a theatre in this country. It was designed in 1939 to house the Progressive Players, a theatrical group established in Gateshead in 1920. The Players performed in the Westfield Hall until the outbreak of war. Faced with the loss of this venue, the group was saved by the financial generosity of three founder members, the Misses Hope, Ruth and Sylvia Dodds, through which it acquired a vacant site for a new building, looking across to Saltwell Park. Who designed the Little Theatre? Archival research appears to indicate that, however surprisingly, H.L. Honeyman was responsible. A noted antiquarian and author, as an architect Honeyman concentrated mainly on church restoration work and country house alterations.

Despite the commencement of war, and enforced interruption to building work, the theatre opened in the autumn of 1943. It incorporated the adjoining house (No. 3 Saltwell View) and originally had a simple rendered front elevation on to Saltwell View, with a curved corner and double-height, semi-circular bay window overlooking Avenue Road. A dominant red cornice follows the curves, producing a 'streamlined' effect, typical of many buildings of this style during the 1930s. This part of the building houses the bar and foyer. Unfortunately the auditorium, on Avenue Road, does not continue in the same manner, being merely a simple box with a pitched roof.

The Little Theatre has been modified and extended over the years, for example with the purchase of No. 4 Saltwell View and the construction in 2013 of a double-height bay window in order to increase the foyer area. Despite these changes, this unusual building still appears as a dramatic modern insertion into an area of Victorian terrace houses.

CHAPTER 7

POST-WAR ARCHITECTURE, c.1945-1980

Extension to Newcastle University Students' Union, King's Walk, Newcastle upon Tyne, by Sir William Whitfield, 1961-63: from the south west (detail).

INTRODUCTION

The end of the Second World War saw the central areas of Newcastle and Gateshead largely undamaged by bombing, despite being important targets for the enemy. However, not surprisingly, many areas of the industrial riverside had been destroyed, and the region also suffered drastically in the post-war slump. The nationalisation of the mines in 1947 offered little help, for the National Coal Board soon initiated a programme of mine closures which began to transform for ever the North East's traditional reliance on mining and heavy industry.

Of great importance at this time for the economy of Newcastle – if not for its architecture – was the establishment of the Department of Health and Social Security Records Centre in the northern suburb of Longbenton. This immediately became one of the largest employers in the area, creating an increased demand for clerical workers which, with the continuing decline in heavy industry, began to change Tyneside to an essentially service-sector economy. By 1971 this sector accounted for 53 per cent of the total number of people employed.

In Gateshead a response to the earlier depression of the 1930s had been the founding of the Team Valley Trading Estate (see Chapter Six). Although this had a swift take-up, the war brought other priorities. However, after 1945, the estate continued to expand (see p.257). Some of the region's other industrial buildings from the start of this period, such as the Wills Factory on the Coast Road, Newcastle (see p.272), and the Baltic Flour Mill on the Gateshead Quayside (see Chapter Eight), were also not really post-war in character, having been designed in the late 1930s, with their construction delayed by the war.

At the start of the 1950s the centre of Newcastle still represented a coherent expression of Georgian and Victorian classicism, while Gateshead possessed a significant legacy of Victorian and earlier housing. However, the whole conurbation was very run-down and also faced problems of severe traffic congestion. Through traffic converged on the Tyne Bridge, with its bottle neck to the north, while the main route from London to Edinburgh still passed along not only Gateshead High Street but also Northumberland Street in Newcastle, the city's principal shopping street.

The first radical attempt to solve Newcastle's traffic problems was made as early as 1945. Percy Parr, the City Engineer, who was also a qualified planner, proposed a ring road around the heart of the city, running from the Tyne Bridge to the south of Brandling Place on its eastern side, and on its western side from the High Level Bridge to Queen Victoria Road via the Bigg Market and Newgate Street. This unexecuted plan also envisaged moving the hub of the city northwards, from near the old quayside to the area of Barras Bridge, where a new Civic Centre, a substantial educational precinct, and a major new shopping centre (around Northumberland Street) were to be developed. If these proposals had been implemented, they would have destroyed a significant part of the city's heritage.

The Town and Country Planning Act of 1947 required development proposals to take account of their possible effect on listed buildings of special or historic interest. It also promoted the ideas of 'zoning', whereby housing would be separated from industry and commercial development, and of the 'green belt', to prevent continued ribbon development. In response, Newcastle Council produced a second development plan in 1951.

This plan was broadly similar to that of 1945, although now the western bypass was to be realigned westward to link with the Redheugh Bridge and the Team Valley to the south. The proposed loss of two significant historic buildings, the Royal Arcade (by John Dobson) and the Holy Jesus Hospital, was accepted as necessary for the construction of the eastern bypass, but the proposals for the shopping area around Northumberland Street were ultimately rejected by the Council because of their impact on Eldon Square.

In the event, little was done in Newcastle until the 1960s, by which time Wilfred Burns, a specialist planner, had become the city's Chief Planning Officer, and T. Dan Smith was the Leader of the Council. This inactivity reflected post-war economic stringency and also, perhaps, Newcastle's geographical remoteness, although the new Civic Centre (see p.278) was started in 1958, and King's College (part of Durham University until 1963) continued to expand.

Model of proposed city centre redevelopment, Newcastle upon Tyne, 1961-63. The Civic Centre and St Thomas's Church are visible to the top left of this photograph, while the new Central Library and proposed cultural plaza adjacent to John Dobson Street can be seen to the middle left (© Newcastle City Council).

There was now a perception that Newcastle was falling behind the times. T. Dan Smith called for a comprehensively modernised city, with new buildings that could spearhead economic renewal. His slogan, 'the Brasilia of the North', however ludicrous it might seem today, captured both public and political imagination at the time. The city's leaders were now prepared to sacrifice much of its essentially classical heritage in their search for a new image based on International Modernism.

Not surprisingly, therefore, the city's 1963 Development Plan – the main proposals of which were first put before the Council in April 1961 and described in a lecture by Burns to the Northern Architectural Association in November of that year – was radical in conception (see above). Initially, it was well received, the *Evening Chronicle* describing it as being of "sweeping grandeur and magnificent vision". Its main concerns were traffic congestion, continuing economic decline and the perceived need for modernisation.

The scheme retained many elements from earlier plans, including a new street aligned east of Northumberland Street (the present John Dobson Street) while, similarly, its idea for an enlarged central motorway was based on the earlier scheme for an inner eastern ring road. Also proposed was a new central motorway from the Redheugh Bridge to the Great North Road via the Haymarket, to be linked to the proposed eastern motorway by two major, east-west routes, one actually passing underground. Pedestrian and traffic routes were to be segregated wherever possible, as advocated by the Swiss-born modernist architect and theorist Le Corbusier.

One important element of the 1945 plan, deriving from schemes proposed as early as the 1930s and now finally realised, was the development of a major education precinct near the new Civic Centre. This involved the construction, to the east, of Rutherford College (see p.275). This fine building, by George Kenyon, City Architect and also the designer of the Civic Centre, formed the nucleus of what later became Newcastle Polytechnic and ultimately Northumbria University. Importantly, too, the 1963 Plan contained proposals for the regeneration of the quayside and the 'comprehensive' redevelopment of both Eldon Square and the area around New Bridge Street and John Dobson Street. Eldon Square was envisaged as a prestigious shopping complex, with a new hotel on its western side (see p.295), whilst the New Bridge Street area was to involve a new Central Library and Museum overlooked by a residential tower spanning the road.

Furthermore, the city was now keen to utilise the services of the most eminent modern architects. Sir Robert Matthew received the commission for a major new office block (see p.284) that would occupy the Pilgrim Street intersection of the central motorway (east), while Sir Basil Spence was brought in to design the new Central Library (see p.268). Meanwhile, T. Dan Smith personally recruited Arne Jacobsen, the famous Danish modernist, to design the ultimately abortive new Eldon Square hotel.

These sweeping proposals obviously had a highly significant impact on the city's historic fabric. The plan's more worthy (and little-known) proposals to conserve and improve the 'Grainger-Dobson' central area, to create conservation areas, and to revitalise certain older areas of housing elsewhere, are now largely forgotten in the wake of the misguided decisions to demolish Eldon Square and the Royal Arcade, and to align the central motorway (east) too close to the city centre. This motorway, linking to the Tyne Bridge via the Pilgrim Street roundabout (see p.284), also contributed to the decline of the lower Pilgrim Street area.

The situation was made worse by the over-eager demolition of 'outworn' Georgian and Victorian buildings and by excessively harsh juxtapositions of old and new architecture. Examples of this include the inappropriate scale and character of buildings such as Westgate House, Westgate Road (completed in 1975, now demolished), and the block opposite St Nicholas's Cathedral (No. 1 Cathedral Square, also 1975), which replaced the old Town Hall and which was originally designed to be part of an even larger scheme.

The various failings of the 1963 plan were exacerbated by the non-completion of many important developments, partly arising from the fact that T. Dan Smith's career ended in 1974 when he was jailed for corruption. These failings included the proposed cultural centre near New Bridge Street. Here, those new buildings that were constructed were complemented only by a windswept and little-used concrete walkway spanning the street. This has now been largely demolished (along with the more worthy Central Library, see p.335), perhaps symbolising the at least partial failure of these schemes. Similarly, as mentioned above, Westgate House, the office building that blocked the view along Westgate Road, has now been removed, while the Pilgrim Street roundabout has recently undergone a drastic remodelling, with the flagship 'Swan House' office block (see p.284) being converted into flats. But perhaps the saddest legacy of this period is the Northumberland Street relief road, which required the destruction of the Victorian former Public Library next to the Laing Art Gallery (see p.130). With supreme inappropriateness, this bleak thoroughfare was named by the City Council 'John Dobson Street'.

During this period a number of important, if unexecuted redevelopment proposals were also submitted by architects working in the private sector. Examples included Ryder & Yates's innovative Tyne Deck scheme, of May 1969, which, remarkably, foreshadowed many of the ideas about linkage that ultimately led to the construction of the Gateshead Millennium Bridge, discussed in Chapter Eight. Presupposing the removal of the political boundary between Newcastle and Gateshead and the formation of a new, unitary city of Tyneside, the scheme had as its main feature a vast platform to be built across the Tyne. Lying between the Tyne Bridge and a point approximately half way towards the site of the present Millennium Bridge, this would have contained major public buildings relating to the administration of this new city.

Some elements of this visionary project had actually been anticipated four years before by a leader article in *Northern Architect* (probably by local architect Edward Nicklin), which had also called for the unification of Tyneside into a single city. For this, a centre actually spanning the Tyne was proposed. Science fiction-style drawings (by Derek Lawson) showed a monumental bridge, sited between the Tyne Bridge and the Swing Bridge and housing a superstructure containing shops, restaurants, offices and nightclubs, as well as a hotel, theatre, dance hall and bowling alley.

Meanwhile, even Newcastle's unique and hitherto inalienable Town Moor could not escape the attention of the planners and architects at this time. Thus a Council Report of 1961 judged that the Moor was in poor condition and not used to the city's best advantage, and went on to suggest that it should now contain playing fields and car parks, and be "harmonised" by tree planting. A further report of 1965, commissioned from the designer Professor Misha Black, proposed the holding of a major Industrial Exhibition on the Moor and the subsequent permanent construction of roads, a sports stadium and multi-sports centre. Based on this, the Council quickly organised a competition for a 'Landscape Master Plan for the Town Moor'. Of nineteen schemes submitted, the winner was that of Derek Lovejoy & Associates of Croydon, who, in a manner typical of the time, proposed that new roads across the Moor should be placed in cuttings, augmented by numerous bridges over the projected new motorway system. However, nothing came of this ambitious scheme.

During the period under review Gateshead followed Newcastle's example in sponsoring massive redevelopment. The Great North Road was realigned in the early 1960s to provide a dual carriageway bypassing the centre of Gateshead (thus causing further decline) and linking directly to the Tyne Bridge; the western bypass followed ten years later. The fact that link roads to the Team Valley Trading Estate and the Redheugh Bridge, together with the existing railway network, formed a barrier between the town centre and the quayside was not then seen as a problem, although currently it represents a major obstacle to the borough's attempts to develop the south bank of the river.

Like its neighbour, only more so, Gateshead was also tearing out most of its old centre – including several fine Georgian terraces – to provide new shopping facilities. This resulted, for example, in the construction of the controversial, albeit undeniably monumental, 'Brutalist' shopping centre and multi-storey car park designed by the Owen Luder Partnership (see above). This eye-catching structure of 1964-69, made famous by its use as a location in the gangster film *Get Carter* (1971), has now been demolished as part of yet another wholesale redevelopment of the centre of Gateshead.

The aspiration to improve people's lives was not confined to the redevelopment of town and city centres. The need to tackle the acute housing problem, caused by wartime damage and also by the poor condition of many tightly packed streets close to the factories and shipyards along the Tyne, led immediately after the war to the construction of much prefabricated temporary housing. Some 'prefabs' still survive in Gosforth and Longbenton.

A period of widespread 'slum clearance' followed, with older dwellings replaced in the fashion of the time by Le Corbusier-inspired medium- and high-rise, system-built housing. Many such blocks have now been demolished and others are undergoing renovation. Better examples include the Vale House flats in Jesmond, Newcastle, by Douglass Wise & Partners (see p.293), although Gateshead's dramatic Dunston 'Rocket'

(1967-69), again by the Owen Luder Partnership, has recently been demolished. Montagu Court, Gosforth (see p.288), was a more middle-class, private-sector example (unusual during the earlier post-war years) and illustrates the fact that, if money and care are invested in the design, then high-rise can be a successful solution.

One entirely different type of housing development did emerge during this period, with Newcastle Council's appointment of the Swedish-based but English-born architect Ralph Erskine to design the Byker Wall estate (see p.296). The approach here, not unlike that also adopted by Erskine several times in Sweden, involved a more informal style of architecture and was based on consultation, using a system of progressive re-housing to retain community cohesion.

Large-scale relocation also took place, from the urban centres to lower-rise perimeter redevelopments, such as the estate at Kenton Bar, Newcastle (see p.291). Similarly, in the early 1960s, the construction of the nearby Cramlington, Killingworth and Washington New Towns led to further outward moves. Such major developments fuelled the steady decline in population of both Newcastle and Gateshead, while also increasing reliance on the car. This in turn led to traffic congestion. Major road improvements of the period included the re-routing of the A1 to bypass the centres of Gateshead and Newcastle, thanks to the building of the Tyne Tunnel (1961-67).

By the 1970s, both Newcastle and Gateshead Councils were pressing on with unfinished business. Newcastle, for example, was yet to complete a number of large projects that had been planned in the 1960s but had taken many years to finance. Of these, the Eldon Square Shopping Centre, finally completed in 1975 after numerous changes of plan (see p.295), was probably the most significant. Delays had been caused not only by budgetary concerns but also by the trial and subsequent imprisonment of the former Newcastle Council Leader T. Dan Smith.

The new council leaders maintained their resolve and, outwardly at least, were self-congratulatory. However, in seemingly contradictory fashion, they now abruptly changed policy in order to conserve some of the city's remaining historic buildings, such as the Castle Keep, the Black Gate and Black Friars, as well as embarking on a major stone-cleaning programme in the city centre.

But the final years of the 1970s were for the most part characterised by timid inactivity, partly as a result of a deep economic recession. A notable exception was the construction of the Tyne and Wear Metro system, started in 1974, which re-used much of the route of the Victorian suburban line but also went underground to link the centres of Gateshead and Newcastle. Although this network revolutionised public transport across the region, it also proved to be more costly than originally predicted. Moreover, planned modern replacements for some outstanding historic buildings demolished in haste over the preceding fifteen to twenty years never materialised, as the recession caused budgets to be frozen. With their reliance on traditional industries, Newcastle and Gateshead suffered more than most towns and cities during this period.

Overall, the major characteristic of architecture in Newcastle and Gateshead during the post-war period was its commitment, in one form or another, to Modernism. Much is tainted by the ill effects of the over-rapid development of low-cost, high-rise housing and office building, although Newcastle University, which continued to expand its student numbers, was one institution that maintained the overall quality of its developments.

In recent years, however, commercial pressures, and the high cost of maintaining the many concrete structures of this period have led, rather regrettably, to the loss of several significant modernist buildings in the area. As mentioned above, two major developments by Owen Luder, the Gateshead car park and shopping centre and the Dunston 'Rocket', have been demolished. So too have the Felling Pool by Napper Architects (1961-63) and the imposing Bank of England building at the lower end of Pilgrim Street, Newcastle (by Fitzroy, Robinson & Partners, 1968-71). Similarly, the Newcastle Central Library by Basil Spence and Partners (1968-70) has been replaced by a new library (see p.335), and the Newcastle Playhouse has been significantly altered as a result of new developments at Newcastle University.

In terms of architects responsible for the work discussed in this chapter, we find that the major local buildings of the period were now designed by national names – although local talent still existed. Newcastle and Gateshead Councils retained major architecture departments and a number of able practitioners taught at the Newcastle University School of Architecture. These included Professor W.B. Edwards (see also Chapter Six); Professor J.H. Napper, who founded Napper, Errington & Collerton (now Napper Architects and still a major Newcastle practice); Professor Douglass Wise; and others, such as Brian Robson (see p.286), Richard Turley, noted for his commercial architecture, and Harry Wood (see p.69).

In addition, two local practices emerged which have since become international names (see Chapter Eight). One (now FaulknerBrowns) was founded by Harry Faulkner Brown and developed a particular reputation in library design, with many major commissions to its credit (see p.285 and 308). The other was Ryder & Yates (now Ryder Architecture), founded in the early 1950s by Gordon Ryder and Peter Yates, two uncompromising modernists who met when they joined the Peterlee (New Town) Development Corporation in 1948. Ryder & Yates designed not only MEA House in Newcastle (see p.299), but also major buildings for the Gas Board at Killingworth, North Tyneside.

Left Trinity Square shopping centre and multi-storey car park, Gateshead, by the Owen Luder Partnership, 1964-69: seen prior to demolition in 2010.

THE FORMER W.D. & H.O. WILLS TOBACCO FACTORY

THE COAST ROAD, NEWCASTLE, NE7 7FR

Left The former W.D. & H.O. Wills Tobacco Factory, the Coast Road, Newcastle upon Tyne, by Cecil Hockin, designed c.1939, constructed 1946-50: detail of Coast Road facade: from the south west.

Right The former Sigmund Pumps Factory, the Team Valley Trading Estate, Gateshead, by Yorke, Rosenberg & Mardall, 1948 (refurbished by RyderHKS): from the north west.

This former factory and office complex was designed by Cecil Hockin, then Architect to the Imperial Tobacco Co., and occupies a prominent position on the Coast Road, just east of Red Hall Drive. American factory design of the 1930s provided the inspiration. In fact the design does date back to just before the war, although construction did not take place until 1946-50, and its architectural language is very similar to that of, for example, the Moor Court flats in Gosforth of 1938 (see p.261). However, it still seems to have succeeded in conveying an appropriate image of modernity, combined with authority.

The building has a steel frame and is clad in red brick (in continuous bands) and Portland stone. Its metal-framed windows are typically industrial. It is in sympathy with its surroundings, its horizontal banding and ribbon windows perhaps reflecting the movement of vehicles travelling on the adjacent dual carriageway of the Coast Road, also designed in the 1930s.

This horizontal emphasis is, however, effectively balanced by a massive central entrance tower, faced in stone that conveys a sense of monumentality, while the robust entrance section, raised on a half-storey stone plinth, adds further character. Here, two stout piers support a moulded architrave and frame the entrance. The tower, which features a large clock, is stepped back at the top and is fluted in Art Deco style – as are the stone caps of the flanking staircase towers.

The former factory itself – located to the rear of the office block element – was originally integrated with offices, administrative headquarters, a staff restaurant and other facilities, an arrangement which reflected the company's egalitarian policies and the general ethos of the new, 'clean', suburban industries. A contemporary description noted the building's "remarkable layout and planning" and the internal effect "of light, space and airiness".

The complex closed in 1986 and stood empty and dilapidated for a number of years. Ultimately, listing did not prevent the factory element being demolished in 1995 under a redevelopment scheme by architects Wildblood Macdonald of Wetherby, for George Wimpey plc. The surviving office block, facing the road, was converted into 114 one-, two-, and three-bedroomed apartments, arranged on either side of a central access corridor; the building's original facade has been substantially retained.

THE FORMER SIGMUND PUMPS FACTORY

THE TEAM VALLEY TRADING ESTATE, GATESHEAD, NE11 0QD

This factory, on Queensway in the Team Valley Trading Estate (see p.257), was designed in 1948 by architects Yorke, Rosenberg & Mardall for the firm of Sigmund Pumps. It is significant for being one of the first, and best, early post-war modernist buildings on Tyneside.

It originally consisted of a large, steel-framed, open-plan factory, fronted to the west by a two-storey administration block and a separate canteen, complete with cinema and garden for the workers. The factory was lit by north-facing 'monitor' lights set within a flat roof. The administration block was designed to take a third floor, which was added a few years later. This portion of the complex is of particular interest, having steel columns set behind the facade to allow the steel-framed windows to form continuous, horizontal strips, separated by brick panels at each floor. The end walls of the block were also originally of brickwork.

The building, unoccupied for some time until the beginning of the present century, was refurbished by Ryder HKS (now Ryder Architecture) for UK Land Estates. Parts of the main factory building have been demolished and the reminder re-clad. The original brickwork of the administration block has been rendered and painted in bold colours, typical of these architects' work, with the central entrance section modernised. Gone are the curved glass roof porches on the north side, a notable feature of the original building and often illustrated in earlier photographs. Nevertheless, in spite of these changes, the new facade retains much of the quality of the original.

The old canteen block has been imaginatively modernised for use as offices, with a mezzanine floor inserted into the original double-height main space. Re-named the Picture House, in reference to one of its original uses, the building won a regional award (the 'Hadrian') in 2005, for excellence in architectural design.

THE FORMER DRYDEN ROAD GRAMMAR SCHOOL FOR GIRLS

GATESHEAD, NE9 5UR

Gateshead Corporation embarked on a programme of school and college building after the war, utilising the services of its own Architect's Department, to effect a much-needed improvement in the standards of education and skills within the town. In fact, a number of these facilities were planned before the war but not realised until the 1950s. The monumental, residually classical Technical College (later Gateshead College), on Durham Road, was completed in 1955, but at the time of writing has recently been demolished for housing development.

The former Grammar School for Girls in Dryden Road opened in 1956. Its modernist design is far more progressive than that of the Technical College and more typical of the period in that it is devoid of decoration. Even so, it is directly reminiscent of a famous pre-war design, Gropius and Fry's seminal Impington Village College, near Cambridge, of 1939.

The school, mainly in brick, is symmetrically composed, although at the same time its forms derive largely from the function of the internal spaces. The classrooms are light and spacious, with a considerable connection to the outside thanks to the large windows, which occupy most of the wall space. The building's modernist aesthetic was subsequently much copied within the borough, and elsewhere, although for the design of schools Gateshead Architect's Department soon adopted the 'CLASP' method of construction. This was a prefabricated system that was quick to build and was especially suitable for use in areas with mining subsidence. The building illustrated here now serves as the Dryden Professional Development Centre.

THE ELLISON BUILDING (NORTHUMBRIA UNIVERSITY)

ELLISON PLACE, NEWCASTLE, NE1 8YW

Left The former Dryden Road Grammar School for Girls, Dryden Road, Gateshead, by the Gateshead Borough Architect's Department, 1956: from the east.

Right The Ellison Building (Northumbria University), Ellison Place, Newcastle upon Tyne, by George Kenyon, from 1949: the Ellison Place elevation, from the south west.

George Kenyon, in his capacity as Newcastle City Architect, designed the Ellison Building as a College of Technology for the then Rutherford College. It was built in five stages between 1949 and 1965. Originally, the structure was meant to be connected to other college buildings, and also to the Civic Centre, by means of overhead walkways; perhaps fortunately, this aspect of the design was never carried out.

For the later stages of the building Kenyon borrowed a number of architectural elements and details that he also used in his design for the Newcastle Civic Centre (see p.278). The plan typology is the same, with four ranges around a square lawn, and so too is the choice of (comparatively expensive) materials for the building, albeit of a lesser specification. The courtyard, incidentally, has now been opened up to provide a route through to the new City Campus East at the Manors (see p.333). The six-storey teaching and laboratory block, to the west, is unashamedly functional and its architectural language is comparable to that of the office-block component of the Civic Centre. It has a similar concrete frame, clad in Portland stone and slate, embracing a regular disposition of windows with panels beneath.

The southern block (see photograph above) contains non-teaching rooms such as administrative offices, an assembly hall and a refectory, as well as a main lecture theatre. It too is faced in Portland stone. The projecting upper floors, supported by exposed concrete columns, give the facade an effect of depth, especially in sunlight. The columns also help to define the main entrance. Internally, the public spaces – especially the entrance foyer, which is double-height, with walls and floors clad in a variety of stones and timbers – echo the work of the Finnish modern architect Alvar Aalto. The building is now part of Northumbria University. The original high quality of the interior is slowly being eroded by modern refurbishment.

THE STEPHENSON BUILDING (NEWCASTLE UNIVERSITY)
CLAREMONT ROAD, NEWCASTLE, NE1 7RU

The Stephenson Building, housing mainly engineering departments, was one of the first structures to be built in accordance with the University's post-war master plan, drawn up by Professor W.B. Edwards (see p.195) and Sir Howard Robertson. Designed by Edwards's own practice of Edwards & Manby in 1951-52, the building is in a plain modern style, characterised by block-like forms and faced in buff brick with a long, four-storey principal facade. The overall design illustrates Edwards's propensity for axially arranged elements, which, together with his craftsmanlike use of materials, shows European 'Modern Movement' architecture being modified to accord with Britain's still slightly conservative tastes. This restraint was not untypical of the early post-war years.

The ground floor of the building has a continuous sill to the vertical windows, which are separated by broad, brickwork panels. The recessed main entrance is centrally placed and flanked by two dark, grey, cylindrical columns, a reminder of classical design principles (see left). Victor Pasmore, Master of Painting in the University Department of Fine Art from 1953 to 1961, was responsible for two abstract sculptural reliefs (now in storage) that used to hang inside this entrance. The metal windows of the three upper floors, separated by slate cladding between head and sill and with stone mullions, have a horizontal emphasis. The building amply fills its site, with central service courtyards accessed through the curving west facade on to Park Terrace.

Situated opposite the Stephenson Building's main facade and in a similar style is the University's Fisher Cassie Building (1955), another Edwards design. Both buildings bear some resemblance to the later portions of the Ellison Building, designed for the then Rutherford College (see p.275), although here the frame structure is more overtly expressed.

The Stephenson Building (Newcastle University), Claremont Road, Newcastle upon Tyne, by Edwards & Manby, 1951-52: from the east.

THE HERSCHEL BUILDING (NEWCASTLE UNIVERSITY)

THE HAYMARKET, NEWCASTLE, NE1 7RU

This eight-storey slab block again formed part of the post-war development of the University. It was built in stages between 1957 and 1962, to accommodate the Physics Department, and was designed by Sir Basil Spence & Partners. Spence had earlier designed Coventry Cathedral and was typical of the 'big name' architects now being commissioned by universities.

The Herschel occupies the site of a former Corporation tram depot. Originally, it was largely obscured by a miscellaneous group of buildings (including a much-loved Victorian public house) on the west side of the Haymarket. However, following the demolition of these buildings and their replacement by modern structures aligned more to the north, the Herschel became for a time much more visible from the street. Recently a new building ('INTO'), designed by FaulknerBrowns to provide facilities for overseas students (see p.342), has been built on part of the open space that had been created adjacent the Haymarket, positioned to leave a clear view of the older structure.

The main block of the Herschel has a strongly horizontal emphasis, with panels of dark grey slate placed between metal windows. A parapet, supported by exposed concrete columns, is raised above roof level, where the curved forms of the projecting, upper-level facilities make a dramatic impact. There is an open gallery on the fourth floor, again with the structural columns visible.

The east end of the building, facing the Haymarket, has a plain but powerful facade, clad in slate with the University shield attached (see right). By contrast, the west end has a striking, fully glazed staircase tower. The building's ground floor is recessed, and at the east end the shape of the cantilevered, fan-shaped Curtis Auditorium (a fine lecture theatre, with excellent acoustics) creates an impressive effect.

The Herschel Building (Newcastle University), the Haymarket, Newcastle upon Tyne, by Sir Basil Spence & Partners, 1957-62: the east end, showing part of the Curtis Auditorium.

NEWCASTLE CIVIC CENTRE

BARRAS BRIDGE, NEWCASTLE, NE1 8QH

After war forced the abandonment of plans for a new civic centre on the site adjacent to Barras Bridge (see Chapter Six), it was not until 1950 that design work for the present structure began. The design, by the then City Architect, George Kenyon, was approved by the City Council in December 1950. Further delays followed while funds for the building were sought, with central government only authorising work in August 1956. Construction (utilising reinforced concrete frame techniques) started in 1958 and continued in stages until 1968. Although the building is of high quality, by the time it was finally complete it was not surprisingly regarded as decidedly old-fashioned.

The Civic Centre was conceived as a departure from the form and idea of a traditional town hall, being intended to embody a less hierarchical structure. There is no dominating facade or grand entrance. Instead, the building's accessibility is highlighted by entrances from a number of approaches. The Centre was planned to encourage and symbolise democracy, embracing the people of Newcastle, and was also designed to include facilities that the general public could hire for non-Council functions. Overall, therefore, the emphasis is on the expressive articulation of distinct elements (linked internally by an impressive grand staircase hall), in contrast to the greater unity of the superseded 1930s designs.

Yet the building is as lavish as any traditional civic hall. It was seen as a marriage of art and architecture, and Council Leader T. Dan Smith installed a considerable quantity of contemporary art to form a kind of 'democratic' art gallery. Nor can the Centre be accused of failing to make a grand statement. Its unusually expensive facing materials – marble and rich, even exotic, wood veneers internally; Portland stone and Norwegian Otta slate externally – combine to give distinctly Scandinavian overtones. Indeed, the building, which has no real parallel in Britain, bears a clear resemblance to Stockholm City Hall (by R. Ostberg, 1911-23) and even more so to the slightly later Oslo City Hall (by A. Arneberg and M. Poulsson); the latter was begun in 1931 but not completed until 1950, the same year the Civic Centre was planned.

The design of the Centre also makes reference to Newcastle's medieval, and especially its ecclesiastical, past, something which, together with the presence of numerous decorative elements, goes against the usual tenets of modernist architecture current at that time. The building's plan, with four main blocks grouped around a central lawn, recalls the typical monastic disposition of cloister ranges around a garth, and the carillon tower similarly echoes the bell tower of St Nicholas's Cathedral (see p.24). The ensemble is completed by the chapter house-like Council Chamber and the almost baronial Banqueting Hall, which were the last elements to be finished (both date from 1965-68).

The building's ceremonial entrance, placed discreetly underneath the Council Chamber, is at the end of a promenade that flanks the west range, with the trees of St Thomas's Green on the other side (see opposite page). Nine tall gas flambeaux, designed by Charles Sansbury, line the promenade, and at the end, adjacent to the Council Chamber, is the huge bronze 'River God' fountain by David Wynne. The three-storey western range, containing committee rooms, has an open ground storey with stout, block-like piers supporting a brick-clad vaulted roof (see p.280, bottom). Between the piers are delicately sculptured metal screens, again designed by Sansbury, that slide up and down like a portcullis.

Left Newcastle Civic Centre, Barras Bridge, Newcastle upon Tyne, by George Kenyon, 1958-68: from the west. Photograph Bethany Jane Robertson.

Right Newcastle Civic Centre, Barras Bridge, Newcastle upon Tyne: west range looking up to the tower. Photograph Bethany Jane Robertson.

The south and east blocks, which are of three storeys inside the garth and four from the outside, are simpler in form. Their elevations to the garth, which contains fountains with another Wynne sculpture, 'Swans in Flight', are in warm, hand-made brick with recessed joints, and have regularly spaced vertical windows.

The Rates Hall (the east block) was the first to be built, in 1958-59, and includes fine murals by Victor Pasmore, who was then teaching in the Fine Art Department of what is now Newcastle University. To the north, the large twelve-storey range of administrative offices, dating from 1960-63, has windows (with slate-faced panels beneath) set within granite frames, defined by an overall concrete grid clad in Portland stone. This block has an underground car park for 225 cars. The carillon tower at its west end, completed in 1963, is topped with a series of copper fins supporting sea horses (an allusion to Newcastle's coat of arms) sculpted by J.R.M. McCheyne. The tower was strategically positioned to align with the major route into the city from the north.

One of the most striking elements in the Centre's overall composition is the Council Chamber (see top left). This concrete-clad, cylindrical volume, 66 feet in diameter, is supported on slender iron 'pilotis' and partly circled by a moat lined with granite setts. The water in the moat reflects light on to the underside of the chamber, looking towards the ceremonial entrance.

North of the Council Chamber is a block that includes the Banqueting Hall and the Lord Mayor's and Sheriff's suites. The Banqueting Hall, which can accommodate some 600 people, is faced with pitted roach-bed Portland stone; inside, its walls are incised with the names of mayors and sheriffs dating back to 1216. There is also a handsome tapestry by John Piper. Other artists whose work can be seen in the Centre include Geoffrey Clarke (cast aluminium leaves and reveals within the ceremonial entrance), John Hutton (engraved glass screens at ground level), A.B. Reid (seahorses decorating the chandelier in the grand staircase hall) and Elizabeth Wise (murals in the marriage suite).

Unusually, but appropriately, in view of its Scandinavian character and Newcastle's historic trading links with the Baltic, the Civic Centre was officially opened by His Majesty King Olav V of Norway – rather than the British monarch – on 14th November 1968. The building cost £4,855,000.

Top Left Newcastle Civic Centre: council chamber from the south.

Centre Left Newcastle Civic Centre: ceremonial entrance under council chamber.

Bottom Left Newcastle Civic Centre: arcade under west range looking north. Photograph Bethany Jane Robertson.

Right Extension to former Library, Newcastle University, by Easton, Robinson, Cusdin, Preston & Smith, 1959 (detail): from the north west.

Photographs Bethany Jane Robertson.

EXTENSION TO THE FORMER LIBRARY

NEWCASTLE UNIVERSITY, NE1 7RU

The extension to A. Dunbar Smith's original University Library of 1923-26 (see p.195) was designed in 1959 by architects Easton, Robinson, Cusdin, Preston & Smith, in a rather decorative modern style derived from the 1951 Festival of Britain exhibition.

The rectangular main block, looking out across a pleasant, grassed area towards Claremont Road, has a semi-circular projection, originally with bookshelves radiating outward like spokes in a wheel to provide good visibility for the librarian at the central desk. This arrangement can also be seen in some of the slightly later Newcastle branch libraries by Williamson, Faulkner Brown & Partners (see, for example, page 285).

Externally, the library extension is built of pale brown brickwork with double-height window bays, in the semi-circular portion, lighting the main reading room. Above the windows is a continuous concrete balcony, with areas of brickwork set vertically as cladding. The balcony level features unusual decorative panels of human figures in a subdued Cubist style.

The building ceased to be used as a library following the construction of the new Robinson Library in 1982 (see p.308). Subsequently it was employed mainly as a cafeteria. This still occupies the ground floor of what is now a multi-purpose facility currently also housing the Department of Modern Languages.

The building's original purity of form has been badly compromised by the addition of glazed fire escapes around the perimeter.

HENDERSON HALL (NEWCASTLE UNIVERSITY)
ETHERSTONE AVENUE, NEWCASTLE, NE7 7UY

As part of the inter-war expansion of Newcastle University (then King's College, Durham), student residences were built on an open site three miles from the main city-centre college buildings. These residences were designed by Smith & Brewer of London in 1929, on collegiate lines, and form three sides of a large quadrangle. The buildings, of warm, red-brown brick and tile, are in a conservative, modified 'Queen Anne' style, with an additional Arts and Crafts influence. They comprise three floors of study-bedrooms, arranged around a series of staircases with access from the quadrangle.

Later university expansion led to a major development of the complex in 1961. The architects responsible were Napper, Errington & Collerton (Professor J.H. Napper had now become Head of the Newcastle University School of Architecture in succession to Professor W.B. Edwards; this practice is now known as Napper Architects). Their work is illustrated here.

The newer residences, although much more modern and block-like, are nevertheless quite compatible with the older buildings, being simple, rectangular units in red brick, three and five storeys high. Large glass panels light the communal spaces on the ground floor; roofs are clad in green copper and are set behind brick parapets with stone coping. The development also features a central building, again with a green copper roof, with walls clad in slate above a highly glazed lower section, housing a double-height dining hall, communal spaces and administration rooms. Additional blocks, more recently inserted within the 1960s layout, have significantly increased the density of the site.

Henderson Hall (Newcastle University), Etherstone Avenue, Newcastle upon Tyne, by Napper, Errington & Collerton, 1961: from the south west.

EXTENSIONS TO NEWCASTLE UNIVERSITY STUDENTS' UNION

KING'S WALK, NEWCASTLE, NE1 8QB

The neo-Jacobean Students' Union of 1923-25 (see p.240) became largely a facade when it was extended in 1961-63 by Sir William Whitfield as part of the University's expansion plans. It was "designed to avoid mutilation of the earlier students' union building, which meant limiting the height so that the old building could be seen properly from the north east" (B. Allsopp). Even so, the extension is unashamedly modern, built out to the south from the back of the original building, with a series of large blocks containing student facilities. These include a dance hall, debating chamber and refectory, all finished internally with wood veneers.

The extensions have large windows, protected by a complex solar shade of pre-cast concrete columns and beams that create a highly articulated facade (see right, top and also chapter frontispiece). The restaurant and ballroom form a separate building, fronting King's Walk and linked to the Union through the basement; its volume is disguised by the slope of the ground towards the Haymarket.

Probably the most impressive of the blocks is a narrow, three-storey structure along King's Walk, supported on concrete 'pilotis' (see right, lower). It is over 160 feet long and has an impressive, 39-foot cantilever at the southern end, finished with concrete panels. The street facade is clad in bronze, with narrow strips of vertical glazing set back from the face, while the longer rear facade, facing the Herschel Building (see p.277), is an especially effective rectilinear composition.

This block was originally linked with the debating chamber (a short extension bridging King's Walk, decorated with distinctive bronze lions, emblematic of the University). However, the chamber was removed to open up the street, under the terms of the 2002 master plan by Sir Terry Farrell (see Chapter Eight).

In 2011 a further refurbishment of the whole of the Students' Union was completed by architects FaulknerBrowns. All six floors were reorganised and upgraded, and new facilities added, based on surveys of students that generated a 'most wanted' list of improvements. The work won a prestigious Interior Design Award in the same year.

Above Right Extension to Newcastle University Students' Union, King's Walk, Newcastle upon Tyne, by Sir William Whitfield, 1961-63: from the south west (detail).

Below Right Extension to Newcastle University Students' Union, King's Walk, Newcastle upon Tyne: the three-storey structure along King's Walk, from the west.

SWAN HOUSE

PILGRIM STREET ROUNDABOUT, NEWCASTLE, NE1 6BG

The Swan House complex, occupying a roundabout forming the Pilgrim Street motorway intersection, was designed by Sir Robert Matthew & Partners in 1961 and built in 1963-69. A northern version of the London Post Office Tower had originally been proposed for the site, but the city was unable to attract the necessary funding and instead this office block, named after the famous local scientist Sir Joseph Swan, was constructed. It became the headquarters of GPO Telecommunications (later British Telecom).

Swan House was an integral part of the redevelopment plan for Newcastle and was seen as one of the major gateways to what T. Dan Smith called the "modern city wall", formed by the new central motorway (east). However, the building had the detrimental effect of severing the northern exit of the Tyne Bridge from its original outlet, Pilgrim Street. Furthermore, its scale and architectural treatment are incongruous in the context of the surrounding historic structures.

Controversially, too, Swan House was built on the site of Grainger and Dobson's much-admired Royal Arcade (1831-32), which, after many changes of plan, was demolished in stages between 1963 and 1969. Initially, the re-design of the Pilgrim Street roundabout by Wilfred Burns (Chief Planner) and Derek Bradshaw (the new City Engineer) included an ingenious scheme to conserve the Arcade's interior as a pedestrian thoroughfare, while rebuilding the western part of the exterior in a different position; both elements would have been integrated into the design of Swan House. However, in 1966 the Council resolved to completely demolish the Arcade and in the end a seven-bay facsimile of the Arcade's original eight-bay, glass-domed interior was incorporated into the new office premises. This absurd replica was constructed, like a film set, out of studwork and moulded fibreglass. Although hailed by T. Dan Smith as a victory for conservation, it is no more than a rather forlorn folly.

Not surprisingly, therefore, many saw Swan House, standing defiant above the motorway, as a monument to the destruction of Newcastle's heritage. Nevertheless, the building itself is far from a bleak and oppressive block. It is structurally elegant, with clean modernist lines, and it successfully integrates an ingenious variety of contrasting textures, levels and forms. Moreover, as we have seen, the design had to be adapted to a difficult and rather isolated site and was subject to many enforced modifications.

The plaza level beneath the office block was the least successful element of the complex: a confused composition of once-fashionable pedestrian walkways and staircases, strangled by roads on three sides. These structures were always little used and for many years the Swan House plaza was an urban 'non-place', connected to the rest of the city only by a maze of forbidding subways and decks.

During the 1990s the complex remained empty for a number of years, as did many of its modern neighbours. Architects RyderHKS (now Ryder Architecture) converted the main block into luxury apartments, known as '55 Degrees North'. This involved partial demolition, thus reducing the impact of the building's once-heroic forms, and the addition of a penthouse floor set back from the main facade, with a projecting roof. One improvement is that the plaza level is now more animated due to the improvement of access at street level and the recent opening of a café-bar which spills out on to the external space.

Left Swan House (now '55 Degrees North'), Pilgrim Street Roundabout, Newcastle upon Tyne, by Sir Robert Matthew & Partners, 1961-69 (conversion by RyderHKS): from the south west.

Right Jesmond Library, St George's Terrace, Newcastle upon Tyne, by Williamson, Faulkner Brown & Partners, 1962-63: from the north east. Photograph Bethany Jane Robertson.

JESMOND LIBRARY

ST GEORGE'S TERRACE, NEWCASTLE, NE2 2DL

This small modern library, consisting principally of a steel-framed, open drum, is set amid Victorian terraces on a busy suburban street in Jesmond. An early work (1962-63) by Harry Faulkner Brown, of architects Williamson, Faulkner Brown & Partners (now FaulknerBrowns), it is the most notable of a number of fine branch libraries he built in the city during this period. It can house up to 18,000 books.

At the time, the Jesmond Library represented a departure from the typical form, and was developed from a rigorous analysis of use, resulting in a circular, rather than a rectilinear form. Thus there is a central desk with book shelves radiating outwards for complete supervision, while a saw-tooth arrangement of the perimeter windows gives good daylight across the spines.

Ancillary accommodation, including staff rooms, services and a reading room, is set back discreetly within an angular brick block, with the drum of the library (56 feet in diameter) inset. The relationship between the drum and the block is perhaps the least satisfactory part of the scheme. Even so, the library's unusual shape "is popular both with staff and public, and creates a dramatic focus – outwardly a book supermarket, inwardly a well lit and attractive place to browse" (M. Webb).

The building occupies a small corner site, and continues the Newcastle tradition of using a curve to 'turn the corner'. The architect solved the problem of locating an entrance on a curve by setting it back within the structural grid. The construction matches the layout. A simple, black steel frame supports a flat roof and is augmented by a delicate steel sub-frame, containing glazing, and aggregate panels that are carefully related to the surroundings. The detailing is carefully considered, even through to the hard landscaping on the site.

The library closed in 2012 as a result of local authority cutbacks, but was taken over by a community partnership and re-opened a year later under the management of volunteers.

FENWICK CLOSE

OFF BUSTON TERRACE, JESMOND, NEWCASTLE, NE2 2LE

This small development was built in 1962-65 in the former garden of the end house of Fenwick Terrace. It forms one side of a suburban square and is a delightful modern insertion within this largely Victorian area. Its architect, Brian Robson, then a lecturer at the Newcastle University School of Architecture, was also a talented landscape designer.

The development consists of a terrace of five two-storey, and two single-storey houses in light buff brick, with their main entrances on the garden side (see left, top) and with small enclosed courtyards on the street side. From the garden side, the houses are entered through brick porches. Above, a continuous black concrete lintel acts as a string-course, while a similar black lintel runs the length of the wall above the upper windows. The roofs, of timber on steel trusses, take the form of paired, curved shapes, clad in copper and meeting at the ridge.

Internally, the ground floors of the houses are open-plan, with a judicious treatment of levels and a Scandinavian feeling of lightness, attributable to the use of exposed brickwork and plain timber finishes (see left, lower). Large windows at the rear open on to the private courts.

Above Left Fenwick Close housing, off Buston Terrace, Jesmond, Newcastle upon Tyne, by Brian Robson, 1962-65: the garden side, from the north east.

Below Left Fenwick Close housing, off Buston Terrace, Jesmond, Newcastle upon Tyne: an interior.

THE WALKER ACTIVITY DOME

WHARRIER STREET, NEWCASTLE, NE6 3BR

This eye-catching sports hall, originally called the Lightfoot Sports Centre, was designed by Williamson, Faulkner Brown & Partners (now FaulknerBrowns) and built in 1963-65. Ingeniously and efficiently, the architects utilised a dome to cover the space. This creates an elegant structure that appears almost to hover above the ground. The building alludes to the work of such modernists as the Italian Pier Luigi Nervi and the Finnish-born American Eero Saarinen.

Constructed from laminated pine ribs, fixed to a ring-beam at the apex of the dome, which creates an oculus, the hall gives a clear span of 192 feet and covers a floor area of 25,000 square feet – enough for two tennis or eight badminton courts. Known for their pioneering approach to new technologies and materials, the architects here used polyester panels, fixed to the structural ribs, to create a pleasantly airy interior.

After a major refurbishment the centre reopened in 2012, renamed the Walker Activity Dome. The following year the Lady Stephenson Library (see p.230) closed and the facility was transferred to a purpose-built area within the dome complex.

The Walker Activity Dome, Wharrier Street, Newcastle upon Tyne, by Williamson, Faulkner Brown & Partners, 1963-65: from the east.

MONTAGU COURT FLATS

MONTAGU AVENUE, GOSFORTH, NEWCASTLE, NE3 4JL

Like the nearby Moor Court flats of 1938 (see p.261), this high- and medium-rise structure on the edge of the Town Moor was built (in 1964) to provide high-quality private apartments. Designed by local architects Waring & Netts, it consists of a single, long block of seven floors, raised on 'pilotis', giving open views of the moor even from the lower levels, and an attached tower, rising seventeen floors above the entrance lobby.

The tower, finished in buff brick and white concrete, has three wings projecting from a central core, providing panoramic views for all the apartments within. The sides have projecting concrete balconies with inset glazing behind. The lower, horizontal block has white concrete panels between the areas of glazing. With its bold contrast between horizontal wing and vertical tower, and the powerful accents of its balconies, this is one of the most visually satisfying apartment blocks in Newcastle.

Montagu Court Flats, Montagu Avenue, Gosforth, Newcastle upon Tyne, by Waring & Netts, 1964: from the south.

KENTON BAR HOUSING ESTATE
NEWCASTLE, NE3 3YF

Kenton Bar Housing Estate is a low-rise development designed for Newcastle City Council by the local practice of Ryder & Yates (now Ryder Architecture). Built on the north-western outskirts of the city, it dates from 1964-68 and is in marked contrast to the ubiquitous high-rise and tenement housing that was the favoured type in and around Newcastle and Gateshead at that time. Even so, the houses at Kenton Bar are uncompromisingly modern and block-like, with white-rendered external finishes.

Ryder & Yates intended the development to respond to the open, sloping site, with the individual dwellings having fine views to the distant Cheviots, to the north west. The site covers 81 acres, and although this is fully used, not only for housing but also for shops and external play areas, the architects were keen to create an essentially compact development, prioritising efficiency of movement between units and across the estate. For variation, the architects designed three house types. Internally, the spaces are well lit and were designed to official standards, ensuring reasonably generous room sizes.

Kenton Bar Housing Estate, Newcastle upon Tyne, by Ryder & Yates, 1964-68: detail of three-storey housing, from the east.

THE CLAREMONT ROAD DEVELOPMENT

NEWCASTLE UNIVERSITY CAMPUS, NE1 7RU

This important group of buildings was constructed in 1964-68, for the most part from reinforced concrete faced with brick. Designed by Sheppard, Robson & Partners, it formed the centrepiece of Newcastle University's major expansion programme after it ceased to be King's College, Durham, and achieved independent status in 1963.

Bounded by King's Walk, Claremont Road and Queen Victoria Road, the group occupies most of the area to the north of the late Victorian and Edwardian University quadrangle (see p.194) and bridges Claremont Road to link with earlier developments to the north. There is a large, grassed pedestrian area between the main blocks, in front of the extension to the former Library (see p.281) – the only earlier building that faces Claremont Road. Indeed, one of the features of the layout of the newer structures is the way in which they relate to one another, and to earlier buildings, to create a series of attractive public spaces and access routes.

It was intended that future expansion would continue eastwards on the other side of a projected bridge over the dual carriageway of the Great North Road. Some of this development has taken place, notably in the case of the Robinson Library (see p.308). However, another major building, planned to sit on the bridge itself, never materialised. It would have been incorporated within a monumental arch linking the Civic Centre and the University, thereby forming a new 'motorists' gateway' to the city centre on the northern side.

The buildings of 1964-68 form distinct entities. Those along Claremont Road – principally, the six-storey Daysh Building (for Geography) and the twelve-storey Claremont Tower – are simple blocks, with dark brown brickwork separating horizontal bands of glazing. This banding, relieved by open walkways at ground level and at a number of upper levels, provides a strongly horizontal emphasis that contrasts with the verticality of the blocks themselves (although their height was constrained by the planners of the day so as not to overshadow the Civic Centre, then under construction). Similarly, the squareness of the Claremont Tower balances the rectangularity of the adjacent five-storey bridging block across Claremont Road. The Tower itself has five upper floors rising above a recessed open gallery and is connected to the School of Architecture via a horizontal block, originally housing the Building Science section but now used as studios and staff offices.

Beyond the landscaped area in front of the former library is Merz Court, built to house the Department of Chemical and Electrical Engineering and the Department of Mathematics. The first part of the development to be completed (in 1965), it consists of a six-storey, semi-enclosed block with an open, trapezium-shaped courtyard in the centre, and continues the horizontal rhythm of the other buildings, although this is varied by taller windows lighting the laboratories.

The Claremont Road Development (Newcastle University), Claremont Road, Newcastle upon Tyne, by Sheppard, Robson & Partners, 1964-68: from the north east.

THE KING'S WALK DEVELOPMENT

NEWCASTLE UNIVERSITY CAMPUS, NE1 7RU

At the other (eastern) end of the Claremont Road development, the Daysh Building, which continues the use of dark brown brickwork and horizontal strip windows, occupies the corner with King's Walk. It also links to a major extension to the Department of Fine Art; this is of a very different architectural character (see photograph above). Again designed by Sheppard, Robson & Partners, who were responsible for the Claremont Road development (see opposite), this structure is raised on rectangular columns that not only provide service access to the buildings at the back of the Claremont quadrangle but also create a pedestrian route behind the Daysh Building and the Claremont Tower to the quadrangle and the other University buildings beyond. This route also links with King's Walk, now pedestrianised as part of Sir Terry Farrell's master plan for the University (see p.305).

The building is of powerful horizontal form, having a top floor containing a series of generous roof-lit studios, with a projecting upper section (somewhat marred by the recent addition of an oriel) above low-level glazing with prominent mullions. The extension is linked to the Hatton Gallery and the late Victorian Arches (see p.195) by a long, linear exhibition space for student work. Built almost entirely of concrete, which shows the pattern of the original rough timber shuttering, the building is unashamedly influenced by the later work of Le Corbusier, especially the Monastery of La Tourette, near Lyon, France (1953-60).

Forming a dramatic yet effective link between the red brick of the late Victorian work and the dark brown brick of the Daysh building, the King's Walk extension is also the only overtly Brutalist structure on the University campus. Indeed, now that the Gateshead car park and shopping centre, the Dunston 'Rocket', the Felling Pool, the Newcastle Bank of England branch office, and Sir Basil Spence's former Newcastle Central Library (for these buildings see p.271) have all been demolished, it is one of the few remaining examples in the entire region of this once-prevalent architectural style.

The Kings Walk Development (Newcastle University), Newcastle upon Tyne: extension to the Department of Fine Art from the south east.

SALTWELL CREMATORIUM
SALTWELL ROAD, GATESHEAD, NE9 6DT

Saltwell Crematorium, Saltwell Road, Gateshead, by Leslie Berry, with assistance from K. Hare, W. Heads and C. Winskell, 1966: from the north west.

Saltwell Crematorium is a notable example of post-war architecture on Tyneside. Located on the edge of the Victorian Saltwell Park, and built on the site of South Dene Tower (see p.152), it is an impressive structure that draws fully on the language of modernist architecture.

Victorian crematoria were often designed to resemble chapels. Since the twentieth century, however, the majority of such buildings have been designed without reference to specific religious doctrines, allowing them to accommodate all faith groups. At the same time, the design of crematoria presents architects with a complex challenge. Such buildings must be solemn and dignified, respecting the grief of mourners, but they must also be efficient, coping with a steady stream of funerals.

Designed in 1966 by the Gateshead Borough Architect Leslie Berry, with assistance from K. Hare, W. Heads and C. Winskell, Saltwell Crematorium reveals the influence of the celebrated German modernist Mies van der Rohe. There is also more than an echo of the classically inspired Forest Crematorium, on the outskirts of Stockholm (mainly 1935-40), by the eminent Swedish architects Gunnar Asplund and Sigurd Lewerentz.

At Saltwell the ground floor is of dark blue brick and the upper storey is clad in pre-cast white concrete panels. A simple canopy spans the full width of the building, supported on five slender steel beams. This functions as a porte-cochère, allowing hearses to enter the glazed entrance and remain sheltered from the elements. Inside, a simple vestibule leads directly into a central chapel, lit from above by a barrel-vaulted skylight. Its walls are lined with the same concrete panels as the exterior. A steel catafalque stands within an alcove that can be concealed behind a curtain at the end of services. The pews and lectern are of afrormosia. With the exception of a large crucifix displayed on the wall, the building is devoid of any overt religious symbolism.

The austere design of this crematorium could easily have been insensitively utilitarian. Instead, its impact is softened by careful landscaping and by references to the ancient tradition of classical architecture. A solemn processional approach leads, via an imposing archway, through mature trees, before climbing a slope clustered with lush cypress trees. Perched on the crest of this slope, the crematorium building itself has the serenity of a classical pavilion and its stark canopy is in essence a modernised version of a temple portico. By evoking the classical past, the design recalls the pre-Christian origins of cremation and achieves a timelessness that poignantly counterpoints the sense of mortality inevitably present here.

VALE HOUSE

LANSDOWNE GARDENS, JESMOND VALE, NE2 1PH

This is one of the best of the post-war blocks of flats built for the City Council, designed in this case by the private practice architects Douglass Wise & Partners (although with the assistance of D. Cunningham, then City Housing Architect). Vale House was built in 1966-68, using 'MWM', a structural system involving load-bearing, cross-wall construction and pre-cast concrete blocks, developed in collaboration with the architects by the engineers Mouchel & Partners and the developer Stanley Miller Ltd.

The 28-storey tower, at 80 metres (262 feet) the tallest building in Newcastle, stands dramatically on the edge of Jesmond Vale, enjoying magnificent views across the city. It is rectangular in plan, the long sides having a horizontal emphasis with steel windows separated by dark cladding panels, capped at the top by a deep, white fascia.

The shorter sides are divided into three vertical areas; the central one is recessed, with glazing and dark infill panels, while the two outer areas are formed from pre-cast, profiled concrete panels. On the Jesmond Vale side these panels are given additional texture by the use of standard profiles designed by the sculptor Derwent Wise, brother of the architect and then a tutor at the Department of Fine Art, Newcastle University. The building has unusual elegance, enhanced by its wooded surroundings.

Vale House, Lansdowne Gardens, Jesmond Vale, Newcastle upon Tyne, by Douglass Wise & Partners with D. Cunningham, 1966-68: from the west.

ST GEORGES CLOSE

OSBORNE ROAD, JESMOND, NEWCASTLE, NE2 2TB

This attractive development, consisting of a terrace of four houses and a detached vicarage, was completed in 1969 to replace the original, now dilapidated St George's Vicarage. The architects for St George's Close were Cyril Winskell, then working for J.H. Napper and Partners (now Napper Architects) and later noted for his conservation work, Winston Barnett, with whom he afterwards created the practice of Barnett Winskell, and Keith Banyard, who became a developer of high-quality housing (see p.300). Each bought one of the terraced houses for himself.

The terrace block, in buff facing brick, presents a simple pitched-roofed elevation to the main road. All the units share the same generic layout, as does the new vicarage, with the main entrance to the centre dwellings in the terrace being via the gardens at the rear, and from the side in the case of the end units. In each case the main entrance accesses a single-storey studio-cum-living space, lit by a dramatic saw-tooth roof-light that faces west, with additional windows on to both the garden and a central courtyard; a corridor overlooking the courtyard gives access to the house, with an open-plan ground floor and bedrooms above.

Internally the finishes are Scandinavian-inspired exposed brickwork and timber and, despite their deep plan, the houses are filled with light.

St George's Close, Osborne Road, Jesmond, Newcastle upon Tyne, by Cyril Winskell, Winston Barnett and Keith Banyard, 1969.

NORTHERN STAGE (FORMERLY NEWCASTLE PLAYHOUSE)

BARRAS BRIDGE, NEWCASTLE, NE1 7RH

Northern Stage, formerly Newcastle Playhouse and originally known as the University Theatre, was built in 1969-70 (although it is now much remodelled, see below) as a joint venture between the University and a local repertory company. It replaced the Flora Robson Playhouse, demolished during the 1960s for motorway development. The architect was Sir William Whitfield, who created a robust, introspective, almost windowless box, with curved end staircase towers and a dramatic, angular, copper-clad roof. Most of the external surfaces of the theatre are faced in dark brown Sussex brick, intended to contrast with the copper of the roof.

The interior, now reconstructed, was originally well-planned, with generous circulation spaces, a wide auditorium and a very deep stage, although the foyer-bar, while spacious, was very stark. A much smaller studio theatre, the Gulbenkian, with its own separate entrance, dressing rooms and wardrobe facilities, completed the ensemble. With its excellent performing spaces and flexible stage arrangements, the Playhouse became one of the principal Newcastle homes of the Royal Shakespeare Company.

However, the building always had a somewhat unfinished appearance, with a particularly unsatisfactory entrance, approached through a car park at street level. This was intended to be temporary, before being moved to the upper level when the grand plan of Wilfred Burns and T. Dan Smith for the city centre was completed. The intention had been to locate a motorway along Barras Bridge, with a high concrete wall along the eastern edge of the Playhouse car park, the area behind being developed at the same level as the entrance to the Students' Union.

Instead the theatre remained unchanged for 35 years, until it underwent a major reconstruction for its present occupants, the Northern Stage Company. This has seen the creation of a new main performance space in the centre; an accommodation block on the north side; and a new foyer (see photograph above), opening, at long last, on to King's Walk in front of the Students' Union, with which the theatre was always intended to be grouped.

Julian Middleton, of architects Renton Howard Wood Levin, has described the reconstruction work as "an abstract and cultural composition", expanding the theatre through the addition of two glazed "book-ends" on either side. However, much of the impact of the original Whitfield building has been lost, especially as a large new administration building for the University now stands between the theatre and Barras Bridge, and the entrance to the theatre itself, now at first-floor level and from the side, works even less effectively than did the old entrance for the flow of people at well-attended performances. This led through the foyer bar and thence up via the two semi-circular staircase towers to the auditorium. The old foyer remains as a bar, however, and is still a dramatic space, with the sloping concrete beams that support the auditorium articulating the ceiling, and with wall surfaces finished in the same dark brick as the exterior.

ELDON SQUARE SHOPPING CENTRE

NEWCASTLE, NE1 7JB

Left Northern Stage (formerly Newcastle Playhouse), Barras Bridge, Newcastle upon Tyne, by Sir William Whitfield, 1969-70: from the south west.

Right Eldon Square Shopping Centre, Newcastle upon Tyne, by Chapman Taylor & Partners, 1969-75: from the south east.

In the 1960s, not wishing to be left behind other English cities, Newcastle City Council proposed the construction of a major city-centre shopping complex as part of their overall redevelopment scheme (see p.269). Controversially, Georgian Eldon Square (see p.94) was chosen as the site.

The initial plans incorporated a prestigious, high-rise hotel on the western side, designed by the Danish architect Arne Jacobsen, but these were abandoned. After much indecision the present Eldon Square Shopping Centre was built in 1969-75, to the designs of Chapman Taylor & Partners in conjunction with Wilfred Burns, then the City Planning Officer. The Centre, although much less spectacular than the original concept, still represented Newcastle's most significant building project since Richard Grainger's central redevelopment of the 1830s (see Chapter Three).

At the time of its construction the design of the shopping complex was seen as progressive, or at worst inoffensive. Now, however, the structure is generally regarded as rather faceless, with little or no detail, its brown brickwork contrasting incongruously with neighbouring buildings constructed from local stone. Moreover, some fine historic buildings had to be demolished to make way for it, including two ranges of the old Eldon Square (the third surviving only by default); the complex also obliterated a number of attractive vistas. In addition, the development seemed to turn its back on the city. It was an introverted, almost fortress-like centre, featuring wide malls with indoor shop units, mostly artificially lit. Its major entrances were few, and far apart. A number of surrounding streets, once animated by shoppers, were also compromised.

The complex has been added to on a number of occasions, not always with great distinction, as, for example, with Eldon Garden, dating from 1987-89. The block that bridges Blackett Street is perhaps the most unsightly. Built out of mirrored glass, in the 'Post-Modern' style, it looked dated almost before it was complete. Unfortunately, it now forms the main gateway into the city centre from the west.

Recently, there have been further alterations to address the problem of the introverted nature of the development. These have included a new landscaping scheme, and the provision of surrounding restaurant-cum-retail units on the north and west sides of the old Eldon Square that open outwards, animating the space, and providing a new entrance to the shopping centre. The malodorous and unfriendly subterranean bus station has been replaced by a glass pavilion to the north for waiting passengers, and a new through route has been created with shop units, between Percy Street and old Eldon Square. On the other hand, another major extension, demolishing the southern wing of the complex, and providing more shop units between Newgate Street and Clayton Street, is considerably less successful.

Internally, throughout the complex, there have been significant attempts to open up the spaces and to provide more natural light. However, recent work on the main mall in the northern range of the complex, with a new and more prominent entrance from Northumberland Street, has done nothing to improve the introspective nature of this part of the development.

THE BYKER WALL HOUSING DEVELOPMENT

BYKER, NEWCASTLE, NE6 2DJ

During the 1960s, Newcastle City Council decided upon a policy of wholesale replacement of its unmodernised Victorian terraced housing, much of it consisting of 'Tyneside flats', which covered large areas of Byker and Walker to the east, and of Scotswood, Benwell and Elswick to the west. Replacement housing was usually provided in the form of groups of tower blocks. At the same time, families were also being relocated to satellite New Towns or to new estates on the perimeter of the city, thus splitting up established communities.

In 1968 the Council began to clear old housing in Byker, initially to make way for a proposed urban motorway (ultimately, a major link road was built instead) that was to connect with the central motorway (east). Within a year, however, realising that the area was unusually socially cohesive, the authorities adopted a completely different approach, unexpectedly appointing the architect Ralph Erskine (see p.271) to mastermind the redevelopment. Erskine had attracted notice through the success of housing he had designed at nearby Killingworth Township, North Tyneside (1967-69). A supporter of community consultation and of a sympathetic, human-scale approach to landscape and housing, and noted for his 'organic' approach, he believed that an architect had to be a builder, a technician, a social engineer and also "a bit of a poet".

Vernon Gracie, the project architect from the practice, set up a 'drop-in' office in a former undertaker's shop in the heart of the redevelopment area, and the residents were consulted at all stages of the process. Key features of the architects' approach were to keep the community (even including specific groups of residents) together, constructing new buildings in stages, and demolishing at a similar rate to minimise disruption. Also unusual for the time were the decisions to retain within the development a number of existing buildings, including a Victorian church, and to place families with children only in apartments on the ground floor, with gardens.

Initially, a successful pilot development of low-rise, courtyard-style houses was built at Janet Square, in the south-east corner of the site. This was followed by the Byker Wall itself, occupying land that was already cleared. The estate as a whole was largely complete by 1981. Its site is large, covering an area of approximately a third of a square mile, to the east of the Ouseburn, and slopes down towards the river from Shields Road; it affords wonderful views south and west over both the city and the Tyne.

The 'wall' element is a long building, with minimal openings on its northern side, which is conceived as a barrier to protect the main site from both motorway noise and cold, northerly winds. Curving, rather than with right-angles, it contains flats, ingeniously organised as overlapping maisonettes, and rises in height from three storeys at the east, to eight-storey portions, and then to the wedge-shaped, thirteen-storey block at the west end, added slightly later ('Tom Collins House'). It also incorporates the retained Shipley Street Baths (now converted for use as a climbing-centre). The symbolism of a protective wall is powerful in Newcastle, given the historic legacy of both Hadrian's Wall and the medieval town wall. Hadrian's Wall passed close to the site and a short section of its foundations – unearthed by archaeologists in 2000 – can be seen in nearby Hadrian Square.

Facing north across to the main road, the only openings from the flats are small, sound-proofed kitchen and bathroom windows, and ventilation ducts. The flats' living rooms and bedrooms face south and have seating, walkways, planting boxes and balconies looking out towards the Tyne. The 'wall', or perimeter block, is inherently varied in profile because of the differences in height. Furthermore, its fortress-like north face is decorated with patterned brick (see left, top) in a design that further breaks down the scale of the building while at the same time highlighting pedestrian and vehicular entry points. By contrast, the large-windowed south side (see right), facing away from the road, has pale grey cladding panels, brightly coloured timber for the balconies, and blue, corrugated metal for the shallow pitched roofs.

To the south of the 'wall' is an informal layout of one- and two-storey terraced houses (see left, lower), and three- and four-storey blocks, grouped in 'zones'; Raby Street, an original street running north-south, has been retained as a centrepiece. These structures to the south are of brick and timber, again with shallow corrugated metal roofs. They are surrounded by imaginative planting and reduce in scale as they descend down the slope. There is play space for children, with cars and pedestrians carefully segregated. The overall development was totally unlike the traditional grid-like arrangement it replaced, but was of a similar density, and, because residents were given choice as to the type of house they wanted, was initially both popular and successful.

However, problems have emerged over the years. The original mix of residents changed, with many of the older ones having either died or moved out. The estate started to contain a much higher proportion of young people and children, as well as many problem families, transferred from elsewhere. The landscaping became overgrown and was reduced in scale as a cost-saving measure. Inadequate maintenance and vandalism led to some of the lower blocks becoming uninhabitable. Concern grew that parts of the estate would have to be demolished, and the land sold off to developers – an ironic turn of events in view of the current popularity of inner-city apartments.

Yet the Byker Wall remains an outstanding example of a more humane attempt to solve the problem of social housing, offering scope for both privacy and neighbourliness. It has been described as "the foremost act of concentration and courage in British housing after Roehampton" (Andrew Saint) and has also been hailed as a major, and early, example of 'Post-Modernist' architecture – even though Erskine would probably have disapproved of this epithet. Its status is such that it has been visited by professionals from all over the world.

Fortunately, the City Council reconsidered initial demolition proposals and the development is now listed as being of architectural importance. Ryder Architecture was appointed to bring the vandalised and damaged blocks up to current standards whilst maintaining the architectural philosophy of Erskine's original proposals. In 2012 Bolam Coyne, which had been derelict for ten years, was re-opened as the first phase of the redevelopment. There have also been changes in the tenant mix, and improvements to landscaping, with the result that the Byker Wall estate is once again becoming a good place to live.

Opposite above The Byker Wall Housing Development, Byker, Newcastle upon Tyne, by Ralph Erskine and others, c.1969-81: the north face of the 'wall'.

Opposite below The Byker Wall Housing Development, Byker, Newcastle upon Tyne: low-rise terraced houses.

Above The Byker Wall Housing Development, Byker, Newcastle upon Tyne: the south face of the 'wall'.

ST TERESA'S CHURCH (R.C.)

HEATON ROAD, NEWCASTLE, NE6 5HN

The second half of the twentieth century was not a prolific period for church building in Newcastle and Gateshead, or, indeed, elsewhere. Instead, a significant number of churches and chapels were now being demolished, or deconsecrated and put to other uses. Those that were built were usually unpretentious preaching-boxes, often of brick and designed to fit in with the suburban housing estates that they served.

The church of St Teresa, built in 1972 to the designs of local architect David Brown, is noticeably different. It was a response to the discussions of the time about the liturgy and the greater involvement of the congregation in worship, and moves away from the normal rectangle to a more centralised plan. It shares this feature, albeit on a much smaller scale, with Liverpool's Roman Catholic Cathedral, consecrated in 1967.

The church's form develops from its plan. The building is octagonal, with a series of steeply gabled roofs radiating from a central flèche and large areas of glazing above brick walls, creating a very striking effect. The internal space, shaped by the folded roof, has six of its segments occupied by pews and the remaining two by the Blessed Sacrament Chapel. The altar and font are simple granite forms.

Above St Teresa's Church (R.C.), Heaton Road, Newcastle upon Tyne, by David Brown, 1972: from the south east.

Right MEA House, Ellison Place, Newcastle upon Tyne, by Ryder & Yates, 1974: from the east.

MEA HOUSE

ELLISON PLACE, NEWCASTLE, NE1 8XS

MEA House, designed by Ryder & Yates (now Ryder Architecture), with David Lonsdale as project architect, was completed in 1974. It was the first purpose-built centre for voluntary charitable organisations in the country. Placed across the roadway of Ellison Place, it houses charity shops, offices and a public hall and takes its name from the forenames of three major benefactors to the trust which funded it: Mungo Campbell, Esther McCracken and Alastair Fife.

Ryder & Yates often referenced the work of Le Corbusier in their designs. This scheme is no exception, although here the language deviates from their usual 'distilled modernist' aesthetic because of the need to accommodate pedestrian decks and ramps within the structure and to bridge a road. The influence of the then-fashionable Brutalist style of architecture may also have played its part.

In response to the constraints of the site, the building's floors and pedestrian decks are suspended, by means of square section ties connected to four main girders at roof level. Overall, the building is impressive in massing and the partially exposed structure adds character.

The rectilinear main block is clad with a mirror glass curtain wall, contrasting with the curvilinear auditorium (not visible in the photograph above), faced in brown brickwork. Other curves occur within the building, which somewhat soften its slab-like angularity. Even so, the meeting between this uncompromisingly modern structure and the remaining early nineteenth-century town houses on Ellison Place (earmarked for demolition but saved) is incongruous. Moreover, the pedestrian ramp to the first floor cuts across what was once a pleasant square.

Harsh juxtapositions of old and new architecture of this kind, based on the principle of 'dynamic contrast', were not untypical of the period. In this instance the reflection of the late Georgian terrace in the new building's mirror glass curtain wall was not only intentional but even considered desirable. Yet, despite the pleas of conservationists, then beginning to grow in influence, such was the popularity of modernist design within the British architectural establishment at this time that in 1974 *The Architectural Review* had no hesitation in stating that MEA House was "much too good for its site".

BLYTHSWOOD

OSBORNE ROAD, JESMOND, NE2 2AZ

Blythswood is a block of luxury apartments, built in 1976 on a prominent site in the heart of this Victorian suburb. A product of the co-operation between architects Barnett Winskell and the architect-developer Keith Banyard, the design is significant for what at the time was its confident, modern approach, very different from the tentative pastiche that characterises many other developments of this kind. Here the development consists essentially of two four-storey blocks set high above basement car parking. It is approached from the main road by a bridge leading into an entrance hall, situated between the two blocks. Blythswood is built of smooth, hard red brick with matching mortar, topped by copper-clad roofs and with concrete balconies looking south over gardens. Curved and rectilinear surfaces are effectively contrasted throughout.

Blythswood, corner of Osborne Road and Clayton Road, Jesmond, Newcastle upon Tyne, by Barnett Winskell and Keith Banyard, 1976: from the west.

THE SALVATION ARMY HOSTEL

CITY ROAD, NEWCASTLE, NE1 2BR

This distinctive modern men's hostel was built in 1976, on a site formerly occupied by John Dobson's neo-classical Royal Jubilee School (1810). Designed by Ryder & Yates (now Ryder Architecture) it consists of a long, gently curving block constructed from purple, engineering brick. Aluminium-framed windows are irregularly placed on the facade and a fully glazed section protrudes at first-floor level (see photograph above), giving the front elevation character, while a sweeping canopy leads to the main entrance. Typically for these architects, the building is well landscaped. Also, the height and relative proportions of the neighbouring Keelmen's Hospital (see p.48) have been carefully respected. At the time of writing, the hostel, now called a social services centre, is scheduled to close.

The Salvation Army Hostel, City Road, Newcastle upon Tyne, by Ryder & Yates, 1976: detail of City Road elevation, from the south.

ELSWICK SWIMMING POOL

OFF ELSWICK ROAD, NEWCASTLE, NE4 6SQ

Elswick Pool was built in 1979-81 to the designs of the Napper Collerton Partnership (now Napper Architects). Within a general improvement scheme for Elswick Park, it was a major new facility for the deprived community around it. Its construction was assisted by a Government grant.

Built at the top of a sloping site, on the site of the former Elswick Hall (demolished in 1978, see p.47), this is a 'High-Tech' complex, constructed largely from steel and glass; corrugated metal cladding is also used at the rear and to the east, where the services are located. The south and west sides of the building overlook the park and have full-height mirrored glazing. At the same time, the use, in parts, of more traditional materials give this swimming pool an additional 'Post-Modern' quality.

The roof is an interesting structure of triangular trusses (doubling-up as roof-lights), projecting out to form a canopy running the full length of the pool on the south side; this also acts as a solar shade. The roof is supported on tree-like steel structures, which stand within the pool area. One row of these structures is exposed externally, giving additional interest to the south elevation.

The large amount of glazing connects the interior of the building with the park, and also presents users with a fine view of St Michael's Church (see p.198). However, the interior effect is generally functional, with surfaces clad with ceramic tiles and exposed corrugated panels. The swimming pool itself is an amorphous shape that contrasts effectively with the geometric, rectilinear structure of the building as a whole.

Elswick Swimming Pool, off Elswick Road,
Newcastle upon Tyne, by the Napper Collerton Partnership,
1979-81: from the south west.

CHAPTER 8 RECENT AND CONTEMPORARY ARCHITECTURE, FROM c.1980

Sage Gateshead, St Mary's Square, Gateshead Quays, Gateshead, by Foster & Partners, 1997-2004: from the north west (detail).

INTRODUCTION

The architecture produced during the period from c.1980 cannot be categorised by a style, type, or approach, unlike most of that discussed in earlier chapters of this book. Some of it can be described as 'Post-Modern'; much has been designed with an industrial aesthetic, or has displayed a tendency towards pastiche. This lack of uniformity is typical of the period under review generally and is perhaps linked to the fact that there has been a quick-fire series of economic recessions and recoveries during this time. However, despite economic uncertainty, in both Newcastle and Gateshead the period saw major programmes of urban renewal, especially along the riverside.

The first half of the 1980s was a depressing time for the region, as it struggled to come to terms with industrial decline and to find solutions to the problem of high unemployment. The clean, optimistic architecture of the modern dream was starting to turn grey under northern skies. There was also unrest within the suburbs. The high-rise housing experiment of the 1960s seemed to have failed and there emerged a plethora of new social problems linked with this kind of modern living. Many occupants of high-rise flats, feeling the loss of the communities that traditional housing had fostered, were calling for the return of the terraced house.

In the mid-1980s there were signs of a national economic recovery, although little significant architecture was built in Newcastle and Gateshead. The few projects that were undertaken tended to be public buildings; their designs, often lacking in confidence and direction, were at best derivative. A similar general lack of confidence even prevailed during a short-term economic boom, and, although consumerism noticeably increased, new wealth was directed away from the older commercial centres to newly built, out-of-town trading estates and superstores. The largest of these was the Gateshead Metro Centre, completed in 1986. For a while, its popularity threatened the vitality of inner Newcastle and Gateshead's retail economy: at this time there was over one million square feet of vacant space available within the central business district of Newcastle alone.

Many fine buildings were vacant and falling into disrepair. Some, like Wenger's Store and the former Union Club (see Chapter Five), were threatened with demolition. The *Newcastle Journal* later commented: "the problem is that while we are quite good at looking after historic castles, cathedrals and palaces, we are not so careful with the legacy of commercial buildings which make up the urban landscape." Even so, some parts of Newcastle did enjoy new investment. The city's bar culture was expanding, especially around the Bigg Market and quayside areas. Although this growth added little to the architectural heritage, at least new uses were now being found for some of the vacant buildings previously under threat.

By the beginning of the 1990s the national economy was experiencing another recession. High interest rates raised the cost of borrowing, and there was no significant building work for half a decade. Nevertheless, the recession did not stop council leaders and officers from formulating plans to re-shape the urban landscape, especially along the Tyne. The quayside, where much existing industry had failed, was in desperate need of new attention and investment, particularly on the Gateshead side. Various redevelopment schemes were proposed, before Gateshead Council took the initiative by planning – as part of a co-ordinated public arts policy – major new riverside art and music centres, with a new pedestrian bridge connecting these facilities to the Newcastle side.

The advent of National Lottery funding helped Gateshead Council to realise its ambitions, although additional funding still had to be found. What the Council managed to achieve is little short of remarkable. For the first time, its capital works programme overshadowed developments planned by its larger neighbour to the north. The Baltic Centre for Contemporary Art (by architects Ellis Williams) and the Millennium Bridge (by architects Wilkinson Eyre) gained national and even international recognition (see p.319), although Sage Gateshead, by Foster & Partners (see p.320), has not been received with the same enthusiasm, despite gaining an R.I.B.A. award. However, its popularity with both music-lovers and tourists cannot be denied.

In partnership with the Tyne and Wear Development Corporation, Newcastle Council also became active in redeveloping the quayside, around the new Law Courts (see p.310). In 1991 the Council employed Sir Terry Farrell to produce a master plan for the area east of the Law Courts, and much of this was implemented during the following decade. Although Farrell is London-based, he spent much of his childhood in Newcastle and was a graduate of Newcastle University's School of Architecture. Later, he was also engaged in substantially remodelling the campus of his old university (see below). The employment of Farrell exemplifies the fact that high-profile architects from outside the region were now frequently chosen for its more important work, although the two most significant local practices, FaulknerBrowns and RyderHKS (now Ryder Architecture), have made a substantial contribution.

Meanwhile, Newcastle Council now belatedly concentrated much of its effort on further conservation work, partly in the hope of attracting tourism. The Grainger Town Project was established in 1997 as a collaborative venture by the Council, English Partnerships and English Heritage, its aim being to breathe new life into the area designated as 'Grainger Town'. This included not only the central zone redeveloped by Richard Grainger in the early to mid-nineteenth century (see Chapter Three) but also much more besides.

However historically inauthentic it might be, the concept of 'Grainger Town' did succeed in attracting sufficient funds to renovate and restore many dilapidated historic buildings. New paving, lighting and street furniture were also provided. In total, £160 million was invested: £40 million from the public purse and a further £120 million from the private sector. Before long, there were also various 'millennium' developments under construction nearby. These included the International Centre for Life (see p.318), given extra prominence by the overdue completion of the central motorway (west).

Yet even in this considerably more conservation-conscious period a number of decidedly inappropriate developments still managed to gain planning permission. For example the Gate Leisure Complex, in Newgate Street, Newcastle, not only compromises the adjacent former Co-operative Department Store, but also heavily overshadows the nearby Black Friars precinct and its associated medieval streets and fragments of the old town wall. Yet the Odeon Cinema on Pilgrim Street (see p.248), one of the city's finest buildings from the period between the wars, is threatened with demolition, and, outside the area defined by 'Grainger Town', many other important historic buildings have been left to decay. Thus the fine nineteenth-century warehouses between the Close and Hanover Street (see p.125) lay derelict for many years, with a series of major fires compromising their possible restoration to new uses. Eventually a significant proportion of the complex was demolished and replaced by flats, with the remaining sections also converted for residential use.

In the period leading up to the end of the century the region saw a progressive movement of population back to the urban centres, with new apartment blocks being built in both Newcastle and Gateshead. The finest, however, tended to be renovations and conversions of existing structures by gifted local practitioners such as Hopper Howe Sadler Architects (now Sadler Brown), who found opportunities to work successfully, as for example with the apartments created within the former Turnbull's Warehouse (see p.196).

The massive investment in urban renewal by Newcastle and Gateshead in the early years of the new millennium helped to rebuild the area's confidence, both within and beyond its boundaries. Both urban areas have experienced an architectural renaissance and there was, for a while, a renewed optimism and energy, founded on the substantial improvements made to the built environment. Both councils have continued to address developments on the quayside. Gateshead continues to investigate the important connection between its older town centre and the prestigious new developments on the quayside, still somewhat impeded by the existing road and rail network.

Since 2000, the region's architectural heritage has been compromised by the construction of many poor-quality buildings. Once the flagship projects associated with the new millennium, such as Sage Gateshead (see chapter frontispiece and p.320) and the Millennium Bridge (see p.319), were completed, a period of low ambition in terms of design quality followed. At least to begin with, this low ambition was not always associated with a lack of finance; indeed, the region was enjoying a boom period. Developers continued to build apartment blocks for the new 'young professional' class, especially on the Gateshead side of the quayside. A significant number of office blocks were also constructed, partly to house the blue-chip companies that were moving to the region, attracted by the availability of cheap land and development grants. New commercial buildings were also required to accommodate the growth of established local companies that arose from the region's increasing economic prosperity, but many tended to be derivative and out-of-scale.

A massive public-sector building programme was also needed. For decades there had been little or no investment in public buildings. Schools and hospitals had been particularly neglected; some were so dilapidated they were beyond repair. The public purse could not provide the funding for such a capital programme, so finance was sought from the private sector through the 'Private Finance Initiative' (P.F.I.) scheme. Private developers, who had access to cheap finance, funded these projects with a view to renting the facilities back to public tenants. At first, this initiative was universally welcomed. Councils received new facilities at little initial cost to the tax-payer and the developers were paid handsome rents, guaranteed for decades to come. The tenants however were less convinced, quickly realising the design-and-build quality was very poor in many cases, as some developers saw opportunities to maximise their returns by reducing the budgets for such work.

New schools in the region were particularly uninspiring, with a few notable exceptions (see p.332). Again, the majority were procured by private finance and designed as introverted compositions with sequences of artificially lit classrooms and little or no communal or storage space. Such, though, was the initial enthusiasm for this new procurement method that a number of architecturally impressive schools from the Victorian, inter-war and even post-war periods, which could have been repaired or refurbished, were unfortunately demolished, only to be replaced with formulaic substitutes with little of the design quality inherent in their predecessors.

The universities and colleges did, however, at least in part, carry on their tradition of contributing positively to the region's architectural heritage and also managed to undertake their work without resorting to P.F.I. methods. Instead, new buildings were financed partly from the considerable extra income generated from the expansion of higher education in the U.K. Thus, for example, in the early years of the millennium, Newcastle University constructed the Devonshire Building (see p.326), thereby showing at the same time its commitment to more energy-conscious architecture.

In addition, Sir Terry Farrell's recent master plan for Newcastle University sought to connect the university more closely to the city, with more emphasis on pedestrian routes and new quadrangles within the campus, and with car parks re-located to the fringes (see p.342). Farrell also proposed additional walkways from the university, one to the quayside and the Millennium Bridge via the city centre, and another to St James's Park and the new Science Central on the cleared Newcastle Breweries site and thence to the area around the International Centre for Life, via Queen Victoria Street. Science Central already contains the Newcastle University Business School and will further extend the campus into the city. More recently Newcastle University has also constructed a number of buildings along Percy Street, including the 'INTO' Building for International Students by architects FaulknerBrowns (see p.342). This new architecture has helped to define the street and give a better frontage to the University, missing for many years due to the prominence of a number of empty sites. A further idea of Farrell's is to link the Town Moor, via the University and Barras Bridge, to the quayside along a so-called 'Geordie Ramblas' promenade via Pilgrim Street.

Innovative college architecture of the period includes two important buildings for Newcastle College, the Mandela Building (for Art and Design) and the Performance Academy (see p.308 and p.328), while Northumbria University, based in Newcastle, has also been responsible for some major new projects. Its new campus at Coach Lane, Longbenton, begun before the millennium, was completed before the construction in 2006 of its new 'City Campus East', for the Schools of Design, Management, and Law on the former Warner Brothers Cinema site east of the central motorway (see p.333). Two years later the University built 'Sports Central' on a car park site at the end of Northumberland Road.

In addition, access routes around the University have been improved, particularly thanks to the creation of a new northern entry point for vehicles on Sandyford Road. This has had the additional benefit of allowing the section of Northumberland Road that lies within the university to be pedestrianised. Similarly, by opening up and landscaping the Ellison Building quadrangle and building a new pedestrian bridge across the motorway at the east end of Ellison Place, Northumbria University has provided access to and from its new campus developments east of the central motorway. This development has also created, at least partially, a much-needed public route to the city centre from the inner-city suburbs of Shieldfield, Byker and the Ouseburn area, where a large number of student flats have been built. The University has also sensitively renovated some of the older buildings in its possession, such as surviving houses in Ellison Place, the Sutherland Building (see p.192), Burt Hall and the former Riding School (see p.140).

The recession caused by the recent financial crisis and accompanying government austerity measures brought about a very sudden end to public spending within the region, whether funded by the P.F.I. programme or not. The confidence associated with the early 2000s evaporated, with a number of sites that had been earmarked for development being 'mothballed'. Thus planned major redevelopment in such areas as the former Newcastle Breweries site, Pilgrim Street East, Scotswood (for housing), the Spillers' Tyne Mill site on the east quayside and the 'Stephenson Quarter' (see p.142) is proceeding much more slowly than anticipated.

In Gateshead there has been some development of the east quayside in the 'knowledge quarter' around the Baltic Centre for Contemporary Art, with Gateshead College having relocated from its suburban home on Durham Road. The former Gateshead College building, on a site that is being redeveloped for housing, has been demolished. Gateshead is also seeing a major redevelopment of the town centre, funded by supermarket giant Tesco and involving the demolition of architect Owen Luder's multi-storey car park and market area (see p.271), mentioned in Chapter Seven. The new development (which retains the name Trinity Square) has shopping and leisure facilities, as well as a large amount of student accommodation.

Across the river, in Newcastle's historic Ouseburn valley, slums were cleared in the more immediate post-war period. Now, because of low rents, numerous small businesses from the 'creative industries', as well as bars and cafés, have been attracted to the area, which has developed a reputation as a cultural hub. Both council leaders and developers have recognised its potential, and the lower part of the valley was made a conservation area in 2000. Even so, a number of unlisted historic buildings have been demolished and there are also plans for a speculative housing scheme, close to surviving historic mills and warehouses, which would be incongruous in terms of scale and materials.

However, much more appropriate to the area's unique architectural character have been a number of residential conversions of small-scale historic industrial units, along with the construction of a number of new-build facilities that have an environmental and educational focus. Similarly, several of the larger former warehouses have been successfully transformed into cultural and art venues. Once again, Sir Terry Farrell has ambitious plans to further link the Ouseburn valley with the city centre via the Northumbria University campus (see above), as yet in abeyance.

Overall, therefore, despite recent reduced activity, it can be seen that a considerable number of highly worthwhile buildings and developments have been completed in both Newcastle and Gateshead during the period since c.1980, the most noteworthy of which, in the opinion of the authors of this book, are described in the following pages.

JESMOND METRO STATION

ESLINGTON TERRACE, NEWCASTLE, NE2 1DB

This station is part of the Tyne and Wear Metro system, which is based on an integrated transport approach that has influenced later, larger systems across the world. The Metro system relied on the re-organising and updating of an existing suburban railway that already covered much of Tyneside, including the coastal towns north and south of the river. It was eventually extended to Newcastle Airport at Woolsington and later to Sunderland.

The system's overall architectural design, including signage, was by Faulkner Brown, Watson, Hendy & Stonor (now FaulknerBrowns), who devised for the station interiors a limited but effective palette of white vitreous enamelled panels and high-quality, light coloured terrazzo flooring. In addition, dark brown and red brick, ribbed concrete, and tubular steel canopy supports were used for the station entrances.

At the same time a number of local architects, working within the overall design parameters, were involved in the design of specific groups of stations. L.J. Couves & Partners were responsible for the central area group, including Jesmond Metro Station, opened in 1980. One of many successful designs, this unassuming, flat-roofed structure is extensively glazed. Simple, almost minimalist in character, it resembles a modernist pavilion in a small park. Public sculpture outside the north facade enhances the effect.

In 2012 a programme of refurbishment of the Metro was started; this includes significant updating of the major stations, including those in the city centre.

THE FORMER ARMSTRONG WORKS (FORMERLY ALSO VICKERS DEFENCE SYSTEMS)

SCOTSWOOD ROAD, NEWCASTLE, NE99 1BX

This slender building, over 200 metres long, stretches out like a streamlined train along the banks of the Tyne. Designed by Ryder & Yates (now Ryder Architecture) in 1981-82, and constructed to a tight budget and timescale, it possesses an industrial beauty that derives from prefabrication.

Around this time, 'large shed' constructions of this kind had become a popular architectural typology. In this case there is no break between the wall and the roof, as the continuous silver-grey cladding wraps around the steel structure. The prefabricated vertical window apertures give rhythm to the design, while on the Scotswood Road side (not illustrated here) a horizontal band runs the entire length of the building.

Meanwhile, Vickers defence systems became a casualty of the late twentieth-century recession and the building was taken over by BAE systems, who in turn sold the building to the local defence and offshore engineering giant the Reece Group, in 2013. It is to be hoped this move will see a positive future for the building, which lies on the site of W.G. Armstrong's original Elswick Works, established in 1847.

Left Jesmond Metro Station, Eslington Terrace, Newcastle upon Tyne, by L.J Couves & Partners (consulting architects: Faulkner Brown, Watson, Hendy & Stonor), 1980: from the north.

Above The Armstrong Works (Vickers Defence Systems), Scotswood Road, Newcastle upon Tyne, by Ryder & Yates, 1981-82: from the south.

THE ROBINSON LIBRARY (NEWCASTLE UNIVERSITY)

JESMOND ROAD, NEWCASTLE, NE2 4HQ

By the late 1970s Newcastle University had outgrown its original library and extension (see p.281). It therefore commissioned architects Faulkner Brown, Watson, Hendy & Stonor (now FaulknerBrowns) to provide a new building, completed in 1982.

The compact site, on Jesmond Road, was linked to the main campus by a concrete bridge over the Great North Road and presented considerable difficulties. It lay among the grand Georgian and Victorian terraces of the area, yet was adjacent to a noisy main road. Also, the new building had to compete visually with the splendid Hancock Museum (now the Great North Museum, see p.184) across the road.

The library was conceived on a cruciform plan, with the west corner cut at an angle parallel to the road and providing the main entrance, facing the link bridge, at that point. Three storeys high, above a basement, with a service block on the flat roof, the building is concrete-framed and clad in dark brown brick. Natural light is provided by tall, narrow windows recessed within the walls, with brick piers set at an angle to protect the interior from both traffic noise and direct sunlight.

This arrangement gives character to an otherwise slab-like structure, while the brickwork provides a link with both the adjacent terraces and the 1960s University developments to the west. However, the exterior of the building is still slightly unprepossessing. By contrast, the interior is not only functionally successful, but also attractive, with a sympathetic treatment of textures and materials, good lighting and generous spaces. The library was extended in 1995, without compromising the original design.

The Robinson Library (Newcastle University), Jesmond Road, Newcastle upon Tyne, by Faulkner Brown, Watson, Hendy & Stonor, 1982: from the south west.

ST OSWALD'S HOSPICE

REGENT AVENUE, GOSFORTH, NEWCASTLE, NE3 1EE

The competition brief (1982) for this building stressed that a hospice's job is "not to cure but to relieve pain … and to provide peace and security while the patients' relatives gain confidence and support". Thus the objective was to create a building with a domestic, rather than an institutional, atmosphere, housing around thirty people and with a day centre for a further fifteen. Accordingly, a site was purchased in a quiet suburban setting north of the city centre, although the hospice was completed only in 1987, partly because of the time needed to raise sufficient funds.

The competition assessors had been unanimous in their choice of a design by the young architectural practice of Jane and David Darbyshire (now operating as the separate practices of JDDK – formerly Jane Darbyshire Architects – and Darbyshire Architects) that satisfied both the functional and the spiritual requirements of the brief. It provided a building that evokes the image of the medieval almshouse, as well as effectively referencing the architecture of the Arts and Crafts Movement.

The structure is largely single-storey, and is informally grouped around two courtyards. It has pitched roofs with large overhangs. There is an emphasis on homely materials such as brick, tile and especially timber. The quality of construction is high, as is that of the landscaping, which includes timber decking and sheltered sitting areas (see photograph above). The building received the accolade of the R.I.B.A. 'Building of the Year' and has become a national model for hospice design. It has since been sympathetically extended.

St Oswald's Hospice, Regent Avenue, Gosforth, Newcastle upon Tyne, by Jane and David Darbyshire, 1987: enclosed garden area.

MANDELA BUILDING, NEWCASTLE COLLEGE

RYE HILL CAMPUS, SCOTSWOOD ROAD, NE4 7SA

The Art and Design Building of Newcastle College (the Mandela Building) was constructed in 1987 to the designs of the then City Architect, George Oldham. It adopted the 'High Tech' idiom popular at the time and is constructed from grey and blue steel sections that allow generous glazing, protected by deep eaves. Patterned coloured glass, designed by Susan Bradbury, is used at the gables.

The building is organised around a top-lit atrium (see photograph above), which provides a venue for reviews and exhibitions and helps to promote a sense of community. The design studios that surround the atrium benefit from the resultant natural light. Prominent ductwork runs throughout the interior, contributing to an overall industrial aesthetic.

The Mandela Building, Newcastle College, Rye Hill Campus, Scotswood Road, Newcastle upon Tyne, by George Oldham, 1987: interior of atrium.

THE LAW COURTS
THE QUAYSIDE, NEWCASTLE, NE1 3LU

The Law Courts were built in 1984-90, in order to consolidate a number of regional courts. Funded by Central Government, the building was designed by the Napper Collerton Partnership (now Napper Architects). It takes up a substantial site between Broad Chare and the line of the Pandon Burn, formerly one of the most densely populated parts of town, and dwarfs its small-scale neighbours. The eye-catching red sandstone that clads its steel frame was deliberately chosen to contrast with other buildings in the vicinity.

The front facade facing the river is in an eclectic, 'Post-Modern' version of the neo-classical style, with a kind of gigantic Tuscan order supporting a public gallery that gives fine views of the quayside (see photograph above). The porthole windows elsewhere on the facade (see photograph right) allude to Newcastle's maritime heritage. The entrance to the building is raised above the pavement and is accessed via a wide staircase. A glazed, vertical circulation block on the front facade allows further views that can be enjoyed as people move between floors. The glazing to the south is tinted to reduce glare.

The building's oak-panelled interior is pleasant and light. The public spaces are generous, while a number of the law courts themselves are circular, an unexpected feature in a building with a basically rectilinear form.

Above The Law Courts, the Quayside, Newcastle upon Tyne, by the Napper Collerton Partnership, 1984-90: from the south.

Right The Law Courts, Newcastle upon Tyne: from the west.

THE NEWCASTLE AND GATESHEAD QUAYSIDE REDEVELOPMENT

Newcastle's once-populous riverside, for centuries the commercial and industrial centre of the city, began to fall into decline during the nineteenth century. The High Level Bridge (see p.136) bypassed the quayside, and later Victorian developments tended to be sited well away from this steeply sloping area. Even more rapid decline occurred from the mid-twentieth century onwards, made worse by the move of local government administration to the new Civic Centre (see p.278) and by the construction of motorway links to the Tyne Bridge, which had itself earlier bypassed the quayside. The closing of many quayside industries led to widespread dereliction and decay. With the focus of both commercial and recreational activities in the Bigg Market and northwards, the city had in effect turned its back on the original source of its prosperity.

Yet the potential for redevelopment had been recognised as early as 1963, when Newcastle's Development Plan (see Chapter Seven) proposed the regeneration of the quayside. However, nothing was done until the early 1980s, when the Lord Chancellor's Department was persuaded to build new Law Courts (see opposite) on a derelict riverside site near Trinity House. This initiated the redevelopment process, and in 1987 the newly formed Tyne and Wear Development Corporation identified the regeneration of the east quayside as a potential flagship scheme.

In 1991, following widespread public consultation and a competition, a master plan for the redevelopment of the area was commissioned from architects Terry Farrell & Partners (now Farrells), providing design guidelines and a framework for development. Extensive stabilising of the quayside and its retaining walls was then carried out under the direction of engineers Arup & Partners.

Sir Terry Farrell's approach to urban planning prioritises the pedestrian, who, he feels, has tended to be neglected in more orthodox, 'reactive' planning schemes. Thus Farrell is just as interested in the spaces between buildings as in the buildings themselves. The aim of his master plan was, in his own words, "the rediscovery of the quayside as a place", utilising an innovative layout that is "like the beads of a necklace" to achieve "a seamless integration between the existing context and new interventions". Buildings "are arranged to resemble the urban blocks of warehouse architecture, and the spaces between them reflect the narrow routes between old warehouses".

Top The Newcastle and Gateshead Quayside Redevelopment: nineteenth-century brick warehouses on the Newcastle East Quayside, now converted into apartments: from the south.

Above The Newcastle and Gateshead Quayside Redevelopment: The Pitcher & Piano public house: from the south west.

Opposite The Newcastle and Gateshead Quayside Redevelopment: the 'Gateshead Quays' development (seen to the right in this photograph).

Accordingly, the quayside now possesses an exciting mix of buildings, mainly for commercial, residential and leisure purposes and organised around a south-facing quayside promenade that is the hub of the development (see p.311). These buildings all face the river, as is traditional in this locality; this was something insisted upon by Farrell, thinking perhaps of Venetian palazzi. Moreover, with the addition of public squares, high-quality hard landscaping, and interesting public works of art, the quayside has once again become populated, by day and by night.

Within the development, the quality of the new buildings varies, although many, such as The Pitcher & Piano public house (by architects Panter Hudspith, 1995-97, see left, lower), undoubtedly have merit; this building certainly conforms to the original idea of an elegant quayside pavilion, as envisaged by the Tyne and Wear Development Corporation.

To the east of the historic area around the Tyne Bridge and Trinity House few earlier buildings survive. However, the ingenious conversions of nineteenth-century brick warehouses into apartments (see left, top), and of the former Co-operative Wholesale Society Warehouse into the Malmaison Hotel (see p.210), help to sustain the quayside's original character. So too does the scale and form of the major new commercial and residential blocks further along the riverside, which follow the guidelines of the master plan. At the rear of the commercial development, the multi-storey car park by Terry Farrell & Partners (now Farrells), backing on to the north retaining wall and providing a link to the road and pedestrian network above, successfully handles a very difficult building type.

As the site narrows to the east, the development is predominantly residential, including a terrace of highly desirable apartments on the quayside itself that extends to the recently restored Victorian Sailors' Bethel (see p.170). Similarly, the narrow tongue of land where the Ouseburn – once one of the cradles of Newcastle industry – joins the Tyne is also scheduled for major residential redevelopment. A scheme for a tall, wedge-shaped apartment block (Crescent Housing), designed by the firm of Terry Farrell & Partners (now Farrells) itself, has been abandoned, even though such a building would have effectively completed the 'sweep' of the quayside. However, other proposals of this kind remain under discussion.

The east quayside development has been an outstanding success, transforming a greatly neglected area of the city. Much still remains to be done, especially in linking the quayside to the main centres of Newcastle and Gateshead, but some of these issues are now beginning to be addressed, as for example by proposals in Sir Terry Farrell's master plan for Newcastle University (see p.305).

Despite this success, the newly created views of the Tyne from Newcastle's quayside were initially marred by scenes of decay across the river in Gateshead. However, Gateshead Borough Council's ambitious plans for the redevelopment of its own side of the river bank (see photograph above), including the regeneration of 'Gateshead Quays', a formerly derelict stretch downstream of the Tyne Bridge, have now led to the construction of two major buildings for the arts, the Baltic Centre for Contemporary Art and Sage Gateshead (see pp.316 and 320).

An equally important factor has been the linking of the two quays by the stunning Millennium Bridge (see p.319). In combination with the Victorian Swing Bridge, to the west, this has also created an attractive pedestrian circuit embracing both sides of the river. On the Newcastle side, this circuit links to Sandgate Steps, connecting to City Road. Here the new retaining wall has carvings in relief, emphasising its position as a riverside landmark.

An additional part of the ongoing regeneration of 'Gateshead Quays' is Baltic Quay, a major housing development by Taylor Woodrow plc that lies behind the Baltic Centre for Contemporary Art itself. It consists of 241 private apartments contained within seven high-rise blocks. A second phase will be situated next to the Sage and will include hotels, restaurants and leisure facilities. Another important initiative within the area will be the £250 million Baltic Business Park, a third of which will be given over to a so-called 'Knowledge Campus'. There will be a continued emphasis on public spaces and routes within and between all these developments, which, crucially, will link to a redeveloped Gateshead town centre, the Gateshead Transport Interchange, Newcastle Central Station and the Newcastle quayside, by means of a new rapid transit system. Ultimately, more than a billion pounds of public and private funding will have been committed to the regeneration of Gateshead and its riverside alone.

The redevelopment of the quaysides on both sides of the river, with their spectacular buildings, public spaces and walks, all now for the first time inextricably linked, has brilliantly exploited the natural advantages of the site and introduced a European dimension into the urban experience of Newcastle and Gateshead. Importantly, too, it also reflects the movement of the conurbation into a 'post-industrial' era, with a new, leisure-based economy becoming predominant.

JACOBINS CHARE

STOWELL STREET, NEWCASTLE, NE1 4YB

This small mixed-use development of 1991-92, by Jane Darbyshire Associates (now JDDK), addresses two different situations. On the Stowell Street frontage is the bustle and gaudy decoration of Newcastle's China Town, but an archway leads through it to the quiet, contemplative Black Friars cloister (see p.19). The range of housing in the photograph above forms the fourth side of the cloister, on Dispensary Lane. Jacobins Chare attempts to maintain a consistent design approach, while providing frontages to suit the two contrasting settings.

In fact, the historic Black Friars drives much of the building's form and detail, so that, for example, the archway from Stowell Street is of Gothic form. This street frontage also has bright red and white timber framing set amid the straw-coloured brickwork. Similarly, the housing facing Black Friars is of a suitable scale for the cloister, and recalls the character of both medieval and Arts and Crafts buildings. This range is symmetrical, with two wings, and tall chimneys punctuating the steeply pitched roof. Small courtyards are enclosed by an arcade of pointed arches, another reference to nearby Black Friars.

Like much of its architects' other work, Jacobins Chare is a well-crafted and thoughtful development. It responds effectively to a difficult location, and, although its detailing may now seem dated, its scale and choice of materials make it a worthy companion to its historic neighbour. The contrast with a major new leisure complex situated immediately to the north ('The Gate') could hardly be more marked.

Jacobins Chare, Stowell Street, Newcastle upon Tyne,
by Jane Darbyshire Associates, 1991-92: from the south west.

THE COPTHORNE HOTEL
THE QUAYSIDE, NEWCASTLE, NE1 3RT

The Copthorne Hotel, designed by Arup Associates, dates from 1992 and was the first project to be built as part of the Tyne and Wear Development Corporation's quayside regeneration scheme. It occupies a historic riverside site, across the road from that of Newcastle's now-demolished Mansion House (see Chapter Two) and at the point where the medieval town wall met the river. Also across the road, tall Victorian warehouses, (see p.125), enclose the site to the rear.

The building is organised in response to these conditions. The public rooms on the ground floor, and the four floors of bedrooms above, look out across the river. A multi-storey car park faces the street and the entrance foyer is set within a tall, glass-roofed atrium. This atrium forms a delightful space. Also, it is deliberately located above remains of the town wall and one of its towers, so that these fragments could be uncovered if it is ever deemed archaeologically necessary. However, the car park is a disappointment; here a blank, rather featureless facade fails to properly signal the entrance to the hotel.

The river frontage (see photograph above) is the most successful element of the scheme, setting a standard sadly unmatched by some of its later neighbours immediately to the east. Long wings flank the atrium, and the ground-floor rooms are set behind a rusticated, reconstituted sandstone colonnade. Above, slender, gunmetal columns support a regular arrangement of oriel windows, while the attic-storey bedrooms have balconies beneath a projecting canopy; this is supported by delicate spars from the columns. The extensive use of stone and metal in the design makes clear reference to the building's industrial context and in particular to the bridges over the Tyne nearby.

The Copthorne Hotel, the Quayside, Newcastle upon Tyne, by Arup Associates, 1992: from the south east.

BALTIC CENTRE FOR CONTEMPORARY ART

SOUTH SHORE ROAD, GATESHEAD, NE8 2BE

In 1992 Gateshead Council conceived the idea of converting the disused former Baltic Flour Mill, one of Tyneside's last remaining major industrial structures, into a national and international centre for contemporary art. Two years later the Council organised a competition for the conversion, which was now a crucial element in its overall quayside redevelopment scheme (see p.311). The competition was won by architects Ellis Williams of London, with Dominic Williams being responsible for the successful design. However, the Council had still to find £46 million from both public and private funds before the project could be undertaken, and work on site did not begin until 1998.

The converted building is the silo element of the former Baltic Flour Mill, which opened in 1950 for the production of flour and animal feed. Its owners were Joseph Rank Ltd (who invariably named their mills after seas of the world). Built to the designs of architects Gelder & Kitchen of Hull and civil engineers Mouchel & Partners, on a site formerly occupied by Gateshead Iron Works, the mill appeared dated from the start, for construction work had begun in the late 1930s, only to be halted by the Second World War. At one time the mill employed 300 people, but production ceased in 1981 and its warehouse element was demolished. However, it was deemed cheaper to leave the enormous brick and concrete silo building in place; it remained empty for over twenty years.

Baltic Centre for Contemporary Art is a new type of highly flexible public art venue, an 'art factory' rather than a gallery. It comprises two buildings. The principal one is the redeveloped mill structure itself, of which only the longer north and south facades have been retained and into which six main floors and three mezzanines have been inserted. Now surmounted by a lightweight, steel and glass structure, containing a fully glazed rooftop restaurant, this building accommodates 3,000 square metres of multi-purpose exhibition space as well as artists' studios, a cinema, lecture spaces, a media laboratory, a library and an archive for the study of contemporary art. The other major element of Baltic is the new 'riverside' building, a low, two-storey structure to the west. This contains a bookshop and another restaurant; it also provides the main entrance to the Centre.

One of the main intentions of Dominic Williams's design was to connect the new complex to its riverside context. This was achieved by removing the original building's east and west facades and replacing the walls with glass, thus opening up the building to views of the cityscape along the Tyne. Similarly, glass lifts carry visitors up and down, offering further dramatic views. The architect was also keen to preserve the building's industrial aesthetic and simple, functional forms. The new structures are fabricated from aluminium, steel and glass, and this restricted palette of industrial materials creates a successful marriage of old and new architecture.

The conversion and refurbishment of this major riverside building was a difficult assignment. Before other work could proceed, the massive concrete silos had to be demolished and the remaining external walls supported with a complex, counter-balanced scaffolding structure. Only when the silos were removed could the internal floors be constructed to help brace the external walls. However, even before this work was completed, Baltic signalled its intentions to attract leading contemporary artists: in 1999, a 50-metre long installation in red PVC, *Taratantara*, by the sculptor Anish Kapoor was displayed within the unfinished shell. The building officially opened in July 2002.

Baltic Centre for Contemporary Art, South Shore Road, Gateshead: conversion by Dominic Williams (Ellis Williams), 1994-2002: from the north.

THE INTERNATIONAL CENTRE FOR LIFE

FORTH BANKS, NEWCASTLE, NE1 4EP

Left The International Centre for Life, Forth Banks, Newcastle upon Tyne, by Terry Farrell & Partners, from 1996: 'Life Interactive World', from the south.

Right Gateshead Millennium Bridge, Gateshead and Newcastle Quaysides, by Wilkinson Eyre with Gifford & Partners, 1996-2001: from the south east.

Terry Farrell & Partners (now Farrells) designed this £60 million project (half of the funding came from the National Lottery) in 1996. The Centre provides a 'biotechnology village', a national facility for exploring genetic science. At the same time it was intended to be a new landmark, helping to secure the regeneration of the dislocated – and still diffuse – west central area of Newcastle and providing a key gateway into the city for both road and rail travellers.

The architecture of the Centre is complicated. It combines organic and rectilinear forms and reflects Farrell's fascination with the twin themes of ambiguity and context. In his own words, it is "the product of a collection of diverse narratives … reflecting Newcastle and its local history as well as elements of bioscience". Its curved layout was based on the image of an embryo, and also merges with the area's curving cityscape of streets and railway lines.

The Centre is made up of three main buildings: 'Life Interactive World', a visitor attraction featuring an exhibition space, an educational facility and conference suite (see photograph above); Biomedicine East, housing Newcastle University's Institute of Human Genetics; and Biomedicine West, containing commercial laboratories and office space. Each building has a distinct typology and is constructed from different materials.

'Life Interactive World' is a 'black box' structure of metal, lower in height than its counterparts and with glazed screen walls at either end. The vertical metal eastern screen around the conference centre links to the five-storey, curved Biomedicine East block, which is rendered both externally and internally, though the internal elevation has a large area of curtain walling. Biomedicine West, which is independent of the other wings, is also of five storeys and is faced in sandstone, render and glass blocks.

The entrance to the visitor attraction, virtually a building in its own right, is particularly striking. It has an amorphous shape deriving from that of a folded leaf and incorporates a highly engineered, geometrically complex, copper-clad roof constructed of steel and timber.

The buildings that make up the Centre hug the perimeter of the site. Within their confines is Times Square, a newly created, pedestrianised external space and the first major square to be built in Newcastle for more than a century. Its main entrance is marked by a 23-metre steel screen, placed between the Institute of Human Genetics and the Bioscience Centre and symbolically located on the axis of Scotswood Road, a street redolent of Geordie culture.

The square contains not only Charles Jencks's large sculpture of a double-helix, but also John Dobson's (former) Market Keeper's House of 1839-40, worthily preserved as part of the scheme. However, this historic structure is somewhat dwarfed by the scale and proximity of the surrounding buildings and looks isolated, even a little forlorn. Moreover, the overall space lacks a defined focus.

GATESHEAD MILLENNIUM BRIDGE

GATESHEAD AND NEWCASTLE QUAYSIDES, NE1 3DX

As part of its quayside redevelopment strategy, begun in the early 1990s, Gateshead Borough Council determined that a pedestrian link between the north and south sides of the Tyne was essential to the success of the major new cultural quarter proposed for the south bank. This link, at quayside level, would convert two parallel walks into a mile-long promenade, crossing at the Swing Bridge (see p.160) to the west, and at the proposed new bridge itself to the east.

In 1996, in line with its policy of commissioning architecture of the highest quality, the Council launched an open competition for the design of the bridge. The brief was demanding, requiring a scheme that would not detract from the famous view of the existing bridges, while at the same time being fully accessible at quayside level to pedestrians, wheelchair users and cyclists. In addition, it could not be allowed to impede any shipping that could already pass beneath the Tyne Bridge.

The winning scheme constituted the world's first tilting bridge. The design, by architects Wilkinson Eyre with engineers Gifford & Partners, combines sophistication with simplicity. It consists of a curved steel arch, reflecting the shape of the Tyne Bridge, with a laterally curved walkway suspended from it by cables. Because of the extra length resulting from its curve, the walkway can be raised smoothly to allow a 50-metre clearance in the centre for ships to pass through, while comfortably reaching quayside level at both ends when flat.

The bridge opens by means of turning the walkway on hydraulically powered pivots within its concrete bases on each side of the river. This apparently simple operation, recalling the rotation of the nearby nineteenth-century Swing Bridge, takes four and a half minutes and requires the hydraulic rams in the bases at either end to move exactly together. The movement of the new bridge's two matching curves while opening has been likened to the opening of a human eye.

In November 2000, tens of thousands of people watched the delivery of the bridge's structure (by floating crane) and the bridge opened on 17th September 2001 (a dedication ceromony by the Queen followed on 7th May 2002). Funded largely by the Lottery Commission, the bridge has been acknowledged as one of the most successful of the country's millennium projects, and, with its landmark status enhanced by spectacular night-time lighting, it won the prestigious R.I.B.A. Stirling Prize in 2003. Even more importantly, it is in constant use and has succeeded in linking both sides of the river as never before.

SAGE GATESHEAD

ST MARY'S SQUARE, GATESHEAD QUAYS, GATESHEAD, NE8 2JR

Sage is a £70-million music education and performance centre on the south bank of the Tyne, opened in the autumn of 2004 (see also, chapter frontispiece). Built on the site of a former rope and wire factory, it is carefully located, at a suitable distance from Baltic Centre for Contemporary Art (see p.316) and approximately half way between the Tyne Bridge and the Millennium Bridge (see p.319). The complex was designed by architects Foster & Partners, who were appointed after winning an international competition in 1997. The acoustic engineers were Arup & Partners.

As a music venue, Sage is world-class, employing the most up-to-date acoustic technology. As a building, it is an amorphous, shell-like form of glistening stainless steel and glass, enclosing three separate auditoria – carefully designed for different music conditions – as well as a series of public spaces including cafés, restaurants and bars. The complex also contains 26 practice rooms and workshops.

The largest auditorium is a 'shoebox'-shaped concert hall, holding up to 1,700 people. With its proportions based on those of Vienna's celebrated Grosser Musikvereinssaal, it acoustically favours the symphony orchestra, although reflectors in the ceiling and walls can be adjusted to accommodate other musical types. The second auditorium provides a more intimate, 'nightclub' space, seating 450 people on three levels. It is acoustically designed for all music genres, from classical to electronic. The third auditorium is smaller still, intended for an audience of 300; it is used mainly as a rehearsal space for the local Royal Northern Sinfonia Orchestra. A glazed walkway in front of the auditoria forms part of an open-access, east-west route along the Tyne.

The complex's eye-catching roof was designed as an independent structure by engineers Buro Happold. Four enormous steel arches span 80 metres, supporting a secondary structure which in turn supports 300 stainless-steel and 280 glass cladding panels. Internally, the design team concentrated on ensuring the high quality of the building's acoustics, and the public spaces are functional and unpretentious. In keeping with Gateshead's traditions, the materials used are industrial, with exposed steelwork, cladding panels and painted block-work. Even so, Sage is out of scale with other architecture on both banks of the Tyne, and, as an important civic building, has received criticism for its unconventional form and its failure to relate visually to the riverside. However, its external appearance is partly redeemed by its kinetic nature, reflecting the movement of the river and sky.

'SEVEN STORIES'

30 LIME STREET, OUSEBURN, NEWCASTLE, NE1 2PQ

'Seven Stories' is a conversion project of a Grade II listed Victorian flour warehouse, built in the Ouseburn valley in 1872 by W. Proctor & Sons. After 1916 the building was leased to a number of small businesses, including a farmers' co-operative and a brewery.

After decades of continuous use this former warehouse slowly lost its tenants and by the 1970s had become dilapidated. It was bought by the Workers Revolutionary Party, which undertook basic repairs before selling the premises to the Trade Union Printing Service. This organisation – established by re-trained miners – further restored the structure and occupied it until the late 1990s, when the 'Centre for Children's Books' bought it and converted it into 'Seven Stories'. This conversion project, by GWK Architects (now ADP), was completed in 2000 at a cost of £3.2 million.

The building now includes a spacious entrance foyer, galleries, activity areas, a café, and a large bookshop. The new-build component of the scheme includes the entrance block, lift and stairwell. The curve of the entrance block represents half of an open book, with curtain-wall glazing and textures of white concrete and green enamelling.

It has to be admitted that the exterior additions, especially with their graffiti-like 'embellishments', created presumably for the enjoyment of children, jar with the simplicity of the original structure. However, the subtle interior work is more successful. Both the client and the architect were keen to conserve as much as possible of the original listed building, retaining important features such as the exposed cast-iron pillars, the original flooring (where possible), and the impressive roof timbers in the attic, which still support the historic winch gear.

Since its opening the facility has been very successful in attracting children from across the region and is a welcome addition to the cultural amenities of the Ouseburn valley.

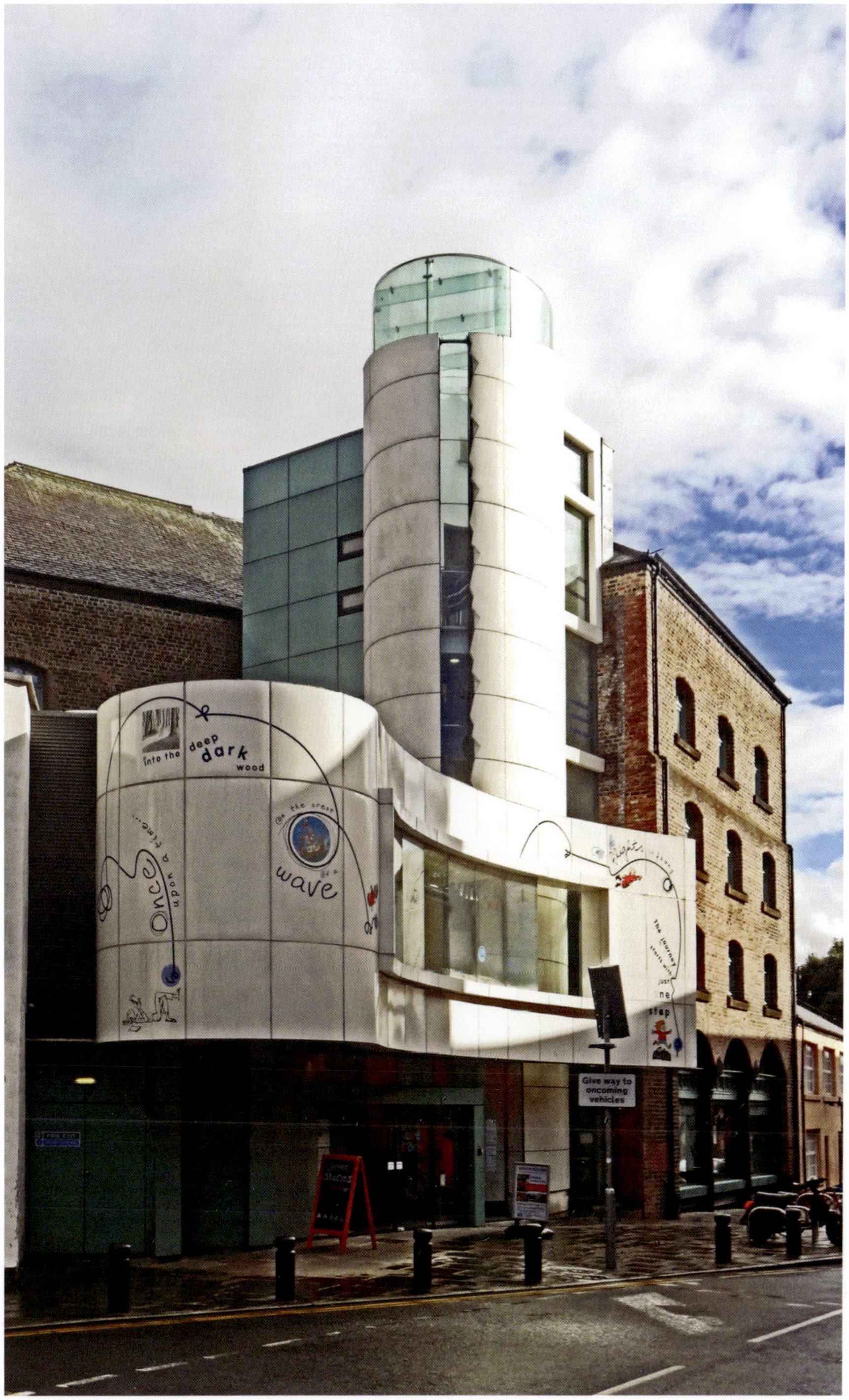

Far Left Sage Gateshead, St Mary's Square, Gateshead Quays, by Foster & Partners, 1997-2004: from the north west.

Left Sage Gateshead: glass façade and interior, looking west. Photograph Bethany Jane Robertson

Right Seven Stories, 30 Lime Street, Ouseburn, Newcastle upon Tyne, converted by GWK Architects (now ADP), 2000: from the north west.

CENTRAL SQUARE

FORTH STREET, NEWCASTLE, NE1 3PJ

This speculatively converted office block, completed in 2000 to the designs of architects Carey Jones (now CJCT), is located behind Newcastle Central Station. It began life as a Royal Mail sorting office, constructed in 1935, with four floors and a basement connected to the station by a tunnel. The intention was to use the conversion of this sound but neglected building as a catalyst to help regenerate a centrally located yet run-down part of the city. The area contains not only a significant stretch of the medieval town wall but also George and Robert Stephenson's first locomotive works (see p.142), while the quayside is only a short walk away.

The original U-shaped block was refurbished, with the addition of an extra, highly glazed attic floor. The south-facing courtyard was closed in to make an atrium, which is now the heart of the building. It contains a café, sculptures and a water feature, with a dramatic staircase giving access to the upper floors, and is covered by a curved membrane roof that has become a major feature of the Newcastle skyline. Externally, the building was transformed by large areas of coloured render, forming a ground-floor 'plinth', and by the addition of a glass entrance tower. Similarly, its surroundings were carefully landscaped, and initially included *Vulcan*, an impressive sculpture by Sir Eduardo Paolozzi, part of a five-year rolling programme of public art works on the site. *Vulcan* was followed by Abigail Fallis's *DNA DL90*, and in June 2014 by the bronze *Advocate* by American sculptor Bruce Beasley.

Through the careful re-use of a redundant structure, incorporating innovative, energy-saving features, the architects, and the consulting engineers, Arup & Partners, created with Central Square a model 'green' building that is providing a powerful stimulus for regeneration. Sadly, however, the success of the development led to the construction of a much less successful office block immediately to the south. This is too tall, blocking much of the light to the first building's atrium.

Central Square, Forth Street, Newcastle upon Tyne, by Carey Jones, 2000: view from the north east showing sculpture *Advocate* by Bruce Beasley.

GENERATOR STUDIOS

MELBOURNE STREET AND TRAFALGAR STREET, NEWCASTLE, NE1 2LA

Behind the main block of the former Electric Tramways Building of 1902 (see p.217) is this former boiler house. It had been empty for many years when, in 2000, architects RyderHKS (now Ryder Architects), seeking to move from Killingworth, began to convert it into offices and studios for their own use.

They created loft-style studios within the shell of the building, while retaining its original character and carefully keeping old and new work clearly distinct. Thus the original brickwork and steel beams are clearly visible. In addition, services are left exposed and a huge window has been inserted at the west end of the structure to provide light for the new, double-height drawing office.

The converted building was first occupied in 2002. It is entered via a sloping ramp that leads past the original Tramways Building into a lively and robustly detailed reception and café area; this has glazed links to the individual studios and also to bookable meeting rooms.

This bold, colourful and imaginative conversion of a redundant and unpromising building houses not only the architects themselves but also a number of other creative consultancies. It provided a catalyst for the further redevelopment of what was a run-down area of the city. Ryder Architects have since moved to new converted offices in the city centre (see p.336).

Generator Studios, corner of Melbourne Street and Trafalgar Street, Newcastle upon Tyne (conversion by RyderHKS, 2000-02): from the west.

ST JAMES'S PARK STADIUM

GALLOWGATE, NEWCASTLE, NE1 4ST

Left St James's Park Stadium, Gallowgate, Newcastle upon Tyne: new stadium by Taylor, Tulip & Hunter and WSP, completed 2000: from the south west.

Right St James's Park Stadium, Gallowgate, Newcastle: from the south.

Football has been played on Gallowgate since 1880, next to the early nineteenth-century Leazes Terrace development (see p.99) and not far from the historic site of the town's gallows. The football ground has had a turbulent history. There have been many disagreements between Newcastle United F.C., the city and local residents, and the stadium has been rebuilt many times.

As early as 1905 the ground could accommodate almost 60,000 spectators, but proposals made in the 1950s to increase the capacity to 80,000 never bore fruit and relationships between the club and the City Council became very poor. This situation culminated in Newcastle United unexpectedly missing out on the opportunity to host World Cup matches in 1966 because its ground was considered unsuitable. Eventually the club proposed a move to a new ground in Gosforth Park. Opposition to this idea provoked the Council to agree to a development of the existing stadium, which saw the construction of a new concrete stand on the Leazes Terrace side. This stand, designed by architects Williamson, Faulkner Brown & Partners (now FaulknerBrowns) in a Brutalist style in 1973, still overshadows Leazes Terrace. It too attracted much local opposition.

Following a tragic fire at Bradford City's football ground in 1985, in which 56 people died, safety at football stadia became an important issue and all major clubs were required to re-assess their provision for spectators. This led Newcastle United to propose further redevelopment, which was only partially completed. Then, in the early 1990s, an injection of capital by the property developer and new Club Chairman Sir John Hall led to yet more redevelopment proposals, including the idea of building a completely new stand on part of the adjacent Leazes Park. This scheme was vigorously opposed by local residents and conservationists. Finally, after the club threatened once again to move to another location on Tyneside, permission was granted for the most recent rebuilding of the stadium.

However, there were serious technical and planning problems, largely because of the restricted nature of the site, which has its west side next to the main road on Gallowgate and its east side close to buildings of major architectural importance. In the event, the new stadium, designed by architects Taylor, Tulip & Hunter (now TTH architects) and structural engineers WSP, was completed in 2000. With the redeveloped Milburn Stand to the west and the Sir John Hall 'Millennium' Stand to the north, it can accommodate nearly 53,000 people (seated) and is one of the country's major football venues.

The two main stands are of structural steel with pre-cast concrete floors and a huge cantilevered roof. This is one of the longest roofs in any football ground and projects 64.5 metres unsupported by columns, giving an unobstructed, if distant, view of the pitch from the topmost seats. The weight of the roof is transferred to ground level by means of a steel frame that is visible to the rear of the stand, a structural solution that allows part of the frame to project over Gallowgate itself. Only three sides of the ground have been redeveloped, the fourth side remaining limited to the height of the earlier stand because of its close proximity to the much-loved Leazes Terrace.

The new stadium has received a mixed reaction. Technically innovative, it is a dominant feature of the Newcastle skyline, dwarfing many of the city's historic landmarks. Yet it still seems unfinished. Only half of the ground is surrounded by huge stands; the third side is somewhat lower, and the fourth (Leazes Terrace) side lower still.

THE PAUL O'GORMAN BUILDING: NORTHERN INSTITUTE OF CANCER RESEARCH

FRAMLINGTON PLACE, NEWCASTLE, NE2 4HH

This £11 million research institute was built to promote integrated, multi-disciplinary research. It opened in 2005 and accommodates over 200 clinical and laboratory staff. Designed by architects FaulknerBrowns, it has open-plan workspaces, encouraging the exchange of information.

Noted for their ongoing research into the design of academic institutions, the architects conducted a rigorous assessment of their clients' needs and the building has been well received by its users. L-shaped, it is clad in a 'rain screen' of buff tile and its interior is exceptionally light, thanks to continuous glazing on the south and west facades; this also connects with a pleasant, open courtyard space. The glazing incorporates solar shades.

The Paul O'Gorman Building: Northern Institute of Cancer Research (Newcastle University), Framlington Place, Newcastle upon Tyne, by FaulknerBrowns, 2005: the south and west facades.

THE DEVONSHIRE BUILDING

OFF CLAREMONT ROAD, NEWCASTLE, NE1 7RU

Newcastle University's Devonshire Building was designed as an environmental research facility by architects the Dewjoc Partnership (later Devereux Architects, now PM Devereux), in collaboration with engineers White Young Green and Battle McCarthy. It cost £11 million and opened in 2004. Standing behind the historic former Hancock Museum (see p.184), the building contains six storeys of laboratories and open-plan office spaces, and was the first university laboratory in the country to achieve an 'excellent' 'BREEAM' rating ('BREEAM' – the Building Research Establishment Environmental Assessment Method – is a nationally recognised indicator of environmental performance).

The Devonshire's energy-efficient features include photovoltaic panels to generate electricity; natural ventilation, so as to minimise the use of air conditioning; and a 'grey water' recycling system. The southern elevation of the building has a glazed facade set behind a climate-responsive, louvred solar shade that is also sculptural in effect. The building's large areas of glazing are fixed to a structural steel frame; this is left exposed to provide further visual accent. However, the strident blue colouring of other parts of the exterior is perhaps less attractive. Internally, an impressive, top-lit atrium admits large amounts of natural light.

The Devonshire Building (Newcastle University), off Claremont Road, Newcastle upon Tyne, by the Dewjoc Partnership, with White Young Green and Battle McCarthy, 2004: from the east.

i6 CHARLOTTE SQUARE
NEWCASTLE, NE1 4XF

i6 Charlotte Square is based on two adjoining properties in this historic square (see p.61): a three-storey eighteenth-century house, and a four-storey 1930s warehouse. They were combined and renovated by architects Bill Hopper Design (now Sadler Brown) and the newly refurbished building opened in April 2004. The project, costing £1.6 million, was funded by Newcastle City Council, the Tyne Wear Partnership's Single Programme and the European Regional Development Fund, as part of an initiative to encourage the formation of new businesses within the multimedia industry.

The development provides state-of-the-art office and meeting accommodation, as well as the latest telecommunication infrastructure. The choice of materials is uncompromisingly modern, based on steel, glass and concrete. Hopper has produced an elegant, well-crafted scheme that contrasts with, yet respects, the historic fabric, which is cleverly utilised as part of the design. Rarely, in Newcastle, has contemporary architecture been so well integrated into a historic context.

The principal feature of the scheme is a glazed atrium, linking the two original buildings and providing a circulation hub as well as a meeting area. Its sharp lines contrast dramatically with the brick of the original structures as well as with the weathered and eroded surfaces of the adjacent medieval town wall. The atrium also floods the heart of the building with daylight and facilitates natural ventilation.

i6 Charlotte Square, Newcastle upon Tyne (conversion by Bill Hopper Design, 2004): from the south west.

THE PERFORMANCE ACADEMY, NEWCASTLE COLLEGE

RYE HILL CAMPUS, SCOTSWOOD ROAD, NEWCASTLE, NE4 7SA

This is one of the country's largest single educational facilities for music, performance, arts and media, and is the first building of a planned development on the Rye Hill Campus that is intended to relocate Newcastle College departments from elsewhere in the city. The architects were the international firm RMJM, which has offices in Edinburgh, Glasgow and around the world.

The building's specialist spaces, including a 250-seat cinema as well as recording and rehearsal studios, are contained within a 'black box', designed for good acoustic and environmental control. This in turn is set behind a contrasting 'light box', housing the entrance and offices, clad on the first and second floors with tinted, polycarbonate panels. These panels light up at night and can also be used as projection screens.

The ground floor is fully glazed, with the entrance highlighted by bold concrete panels, cast *in situ*. The entrance also serves as a dramatic foyer to the theatre and becomes the hub of the whole building, thanks to the insertion of a full-height slot separating the 'light box' from the 'black box'. The Academy, which opened in September 2004, won an R.I.B.A. award for excellence.

The Performance Academy, Newcastle College, Rye Hill Campus, Scotswood Road, Newcastle upon Tyne, by RMJM, 2004: from the north.

OUSEBURN FARM
OUSEBURN, NEWCASTLE, NE1 2PA

Ouseburn Farm began life in 1976 as Byker City Farm – a community project aimed at giving city children a chance to learn about animals and the environment. It had to close in 2002 when its land was found to have been contaminated by a Victorian lead mine that once occupied the site. After the land had been cleaned, the facility reopened in 2007 as Ouseburn Farm, centred on this building by Malcolm Newton Architects, completed in 2005. Newcastle City Council was the client for the project and their brief to the architects included new facilities for the farm as well as educational space for the local community. They were also asked to design a structure that was demonstrably environmentally friendly in terms of both material and form. The ground floor of the building houses the organisation and service spaces, as well as a number of activity rooms used as part of the farm facilities. The first floor is used for educational purposes.

The facility, built almost entirely of timber, has an informal quality, and among its numerous environmentally sensitive features are facades with solar shading that allows daylight into the rooms but eliminates overheating in summer. The external walls are 'breathable' and the building utilises natural ventilation, through opening windows and roof lights.

In addition, the timber external cladding is highly insulated, using non-toxic cellulose. At the base of this cladding is a slatted timber retaining structure that also doubles as a growing wall for herbs, while a sedum green roof minimises overheating in the summer by adding thermal mass to the building. The additional load of this roof type is supported by an engineered timber frame. The building also employs renewable energy generation systems, in the form of solar thermal hot water and photovoltaic panels.

Ouseburn Farm, Ouseburn, Newcastle upon Tyne,
by Malcolm Newton Architects, 2005: from the south west.

DANCE CITY

ST JAMES'S BOULEVARD, NEWCASTLE, NE1 4BR

Dance City was designed by Malcolm Fraser and completed in 2005. The facility was purpose-built for the organisation from which the building takes its name, which is described on its website as 'the National Dance Agency for the North East of England'. The aim of this organisation is to engage with dance in all its guises and at all levels of ability.

Prior to this building's construction, Dance City was obliged to use inappropriate facilities in a dilapidated warehouse adjacent to the new premises, yet still established a national profile for its outreach work within the community. As a result, it gained funding to construct what must be regarded as one of Newcastle's architectural highlights from the early years of the millennium.

The building has a commanding position, located on St James's Boulevard, one the busiest routes in and out of the city. The brief for its design included a 250-seat performance space, four large naturally ventilated dance studios, a café and an open-plan office. Its architecture is one of contrast between heavy and light elements. The dance studios and theatre are located within a substantial block built of grey engineering brick; this faces on to the busy road and is punctuated with small window openings. The thermal mass of the building absorbs heat generated from the activities taking place within it, thus stabilising internal temperatures.

By contrast, with extensive use of brick being considered less appropriate for the public and social spaces, lighter-framed elements were created to house the administration and café areas. Attached to this frame is a double-height glazed curtain walling system that wraps around the east and south elevations, with a random pattern of ceramic colour-coated panels. As well as being aesthetically pleasing, this device is very effective in giving these facades a human scale.

The entrance is positioned off the square at the rear and opens directly into an impressive, triple-height atrium that also doubles as an informal performance space featuring raked seating, in wood. The other spaces within the building open off the atrium, which also serves as the main circulation space. Here the material palette inside, predominantly of brick, concrete and wood for low maintenance, has an enduring civic quality that should stand the test of time.

Dance City, St James's Boulevard, Newcastle upon Tyne, by Malcolm Fraser, 2005: from the south.

THE LIFESTYLE ACADEMY, NEWCASTLE COLLEGE, RYE HILL CAMPUS

SCOTSWOOD ROAD, NEWCASTLE, NE4 7SA

Lifestyle Academy, Newcastle College, Rye Hill Campus, Scotswood Road, Newcastle upon Tyne, by RMJM, 2006: from the south.

The Lifestyle Academy, completed in 2006 at a cost of £16 million, was the third building designed for Newcastle College by RMJM, the others being the Performance Academy (see p.328) and Rye Hill House. The brief for the Lifestyle Academy was particularly challenging: to create a world class educational facility bringing together the College's departments of Beauty, Sport and Tourism. Thus the architects had to accommodate a wide variety of educational and leisure spaces within the building. These included classrooms, studios and workshops, as well as a commercial gym, a spa, and a 60-seat restaurant.

In addition, the College wanted a landmark building to give more definition to the south-eastern edge of its campus. RMJM achieved this by conceiving a robust and uncompromising four-storey structure that is built on a plinth, thereby increasing its impact on to Scotswood Road, a major road leading into Newcastle. Indeed, with this design, the architects used their tight budget very effectively, delivering one of the better recent educational buildings in Newcastle.

The architectural form and language of the Academy recall that of the Utrecht University Library (1997-2004) in Holland, designed by Wiel Arets. Its plinth supports an introverted 'black box', which is surmounted in turn by a 'silver box'. The black box houses the educational spaces and has slit windows irregularly placed across all four facades. The silver box is accessible to the public and houses the leisure activities. Here large windows are strategically placed to give excellent views over the city and the Tyne valley to the south. There is one entrance, leading users into the heart of the building. Here we find a student 'hub', where the vertical circulation is also located. The teaching spaces wrap around this area. Internally, RMJM have created a sense of uniformity by carefully limiting the choice of materials, while also endeavouring to add some spatial drama into what is a densely planned structure via the use of double- and triple-height spaces.

The Academy is exemplary in terms of its sustainability, with a number of innovative constructional techniques being used to reduce the amount of material and energy in the building. For example, hollow plastic balls are cast into the concrete base slab, thus reducing the amount of concrete used and thereby halving the associated carbon emissions generated during the building's construction. All this has been done without compromising the building's performance. The structure's skin is also highly insulated to reduce heat loss.

CARDINAL HUME CATHOLIC SCHOOL
OLD DURHAM ROAD, GATESHEAD, NE9 6RZ

At a time when there was a significant school building programme under the Schools for the Future programme, partly funded by the Private Finance Initiative, the new Cardinal Hume Catholic School in Gateshead was procured by a traditional tendering process, at a cost considered by the Department of Education to be very economical. There was extensive consultation between the design and production team, staff, governors and pupils throughout the design process. The building, designed by GWK Architects (now ADP) was opened in 2007 and has received both R.I.B.A. and Hadrian awards for its design quality.

The school was planned to accommodate 1,200 pupils on a site considered small for its occupancy level, with a difficult legacy left by mineshafts, quarrying and landfill. As a result, rather than having the usual two-storey school design, there is a six-storey teaching block, with the noisier and communal activities housed separately. Externally, there is a clear separation between perimeter vehicular access and pedestrian movement in the centre of the site, while all the excavated material from the building work was used to provide soft mounded landscaping, concealing the necessary areas of tarmac from the view of students, visitors and staff.

The tall block provides a landmark for the school in the community. The remaining accommodation is arranged around a central atrium, which is not only the welcoming arrival point, with a café and learning resource centre, but also a multi-use space for teaching, performing, assemblies and exhibitions. It is the 'hub' of the school, minimising the walking times and long corridors normally associated with schools of this size, as well as being an invaluable space for use by pupils during bad weather. Other elements include a chapel, a four-court sports hall, a dance studio, a music recording studio, a film and AV studio, and a purpose-built Sixth Form Centre. In addition, spaces are organised to allow use by the community outside school hours; IT facilities are also accessible by means of a 'wireless cloud'.

A great deal of attention has been paid to minimising the building's running costs and reducing its carbon footprint, with a number of passive sustainable measures being incorporated. Thus the school has been designed to allow as much use of daylight as possible, with solar shading to prevent overheating. All general teaching spaces are naturally ventilated, with materials being specified to minimise their environmental impact through recycling or local sourcing.

This is a school for the twenty-first century, providing a mature and 'collegiate' feel. The 2008 'OFSTED' report stated that "Cardinal Hume is an outstanding school, providing a stimulating and challenging environment for all its students."

CITY CAMPUS EAST, NORTHUMBRIA UNIVERSITY

THE MANORS, NEWCASTLE, NE1 8ST

City Campus East, a £50-million development designed by Atkins, an international architectural practice and also a leading engineering consultancy, was constructed to house Northumbria University's Schools of Design and of Law, as well as the Newcastle Business School. Built opposite Manors Metro station, it was completed in 2007. Its prominent site, formerly that of the Warner Brothers Cinema, presented the architects with an opportunity to make a powerful architectural statement and indeed the University was keen to create a new landmark. By developing this site the University also helped define the eastern edge of the city centre.

This new complex is split into two blocks, basically an eastern and a western, by a public route that connects it with the University's original city campus. The western block houses the School of Law and the Business School. As well as containing cellular learning spaces and lecture theatres, this block also houses a café and a mock law court. The eastern block, specifically built for the School of Design, contains specialist workshops, studios and teaching spaces for a wide range of design activities including fashion, graphic, industrial and web design.

Despite there being two separate blocks, unity is achieved with a coherent and consistent approach to the selection of materials that maximises the building's performance and financial value for the university. Externally, both buildings are wrapped with a 'solar veil' of stainless steel mesh, attached to bow-string trusses that run across the east and west facades. This device reduces solar radiation by 50%, thus alleviating the need for air conditioning. Both blocks also use inexpensive translucent panelling on the elevations facing the public route, providing soft natural lighting to the internal spaces through the day. At night, coloured light emitted from the internal spaces makes the whole building glow.

Internally, within each of the blocks, the architects have endeavoured to avoid the monotonous stacking of floor 'plates' with the use of multi-height spaces that add spatial drama. Particularly impressive is the entrance foyer of the School of Design, which is light and spacious and also doubles as a flexible exhibition space. Within the other, western block is an ovular-shaped atrium that penetrates all four floors, bringing in daylight to the centre of the building.

City Campus East also incorporates a number of sustainable features, including rainwater collection to flush toilets and a heat recovery system to reduce fuel consumption. These have led to the building gaining, among other environmental accolades, a CIBSE Low Carbon Performance award and a RICS award for Sustainability, Design and Innovation.

Left Cardinal Hume Catholic School, Old Durham Road, Gateshead, by GWK Architects (now ADP), 2007: from the south west.

Above City Campus East, Northumbria University, the Manors, Newcastle upon Tyne, by Atkins, 2007: from the west.

101 OUSEBURN ROAD
JESMOND, NEWCASTLE, NE6 5AF

Situated on the eastern edge of Jesmond Vale, this house was designed by architects Steve and Jane Miller in 2008 for themselves and their family. At this time Steve Miller was working for Hopper Howe Sadler Architects and was a major part of the design talent responsible for such excellent modern projects in Newcastle as i6 Charlotte Square and the former Turnbull's Warehouse apartment building (see p.61 and p.196). For the building described here, the architects utilised a steep hillside site that had access problems. They also had to battle with adverse conditions created by excessive ground water and the presence of a medieval drift mine that the house had to span. Yet the resulting two-storey building is perhaps the best contemporary house in the city. This is in no small measure thanks to its making excellent use of such a difficult site.

Thus both the design language and materials used here are appropriately constrained. The ground floor of the house, built principally of brick, contains the garage and office space and anchors the building into the hill. The living spaces, meanwhile, are at first-floor level and are set back from the road, looking on to an attractive landscaped courtyard on the same level. These spaces are in marked contrast to those on the ground floor; constructed of glass and steel, they are much lighter and very transparent.

Left Above 101 Ouseburn Road, Jesmond, Newcastle upon Tyne, by Steve and Jane Miller, 2008: from the north west.

Left Middle 101 Ouseburn Road, glass façade and interior.

Left Below 101 Ouseburn Road, interior.

NEWCASTLE CITY LIBRARY (CHARLES AVISON BUILDING)

NEW BRIDGE STREET, NEWCASTLE, NE1 8AX

Newcastle City Council took the bold step of responding to the challenge posed by the reduction in the public use of libraries by replacing its existing city centre library with a new, model twenty-first century facility designed by Ryder Architecture, one that would "delight and inspire" and be a welcoming civic landmark and meeting-place. The building was procured through the Private Finance Initiative (P.F.I.), with developer Kajima Partnerships Ltd, and opened in June 2009 (with an official opening by the Queen following on 6th November that year).

The refurbishing of Sir Basil Spence's noteworthy 1960s library was not deemed to be feasible. For some, at least, the resultant demolition of this earlier structure was a considerable architectural loss, but the opportunity was now taken to reorganise access to the site and increase the new building's prominence. This was done by creating a highly transparent envelope, with a new main entrance from New Bridge Street (see right, top), visible from Grey's Monument in the heart of the city. The main entrance to the former library, originally from the previously uninspired Princess Square, now serves as an alternative entrance at café level, and in summer opens on to a new landscaped area.

The design team saw the new building as a 'bookshelf' for the city, with its glazed steel frame and four-storey entrance atrium giving on to the six floor 'plates' ('shelves') of the main library space (see right, lower). This gives a feeling of openness, while similarly the main staircase on the east side of the building visibly ascends through all six floors. There are also twin glazed lifts, arguably appropriate to their context if somewhat reminiscent of contemporary commercial and retail locations.

The library's public areas are kept as open and accessible as possible, with the reserve book store positioned out of the way on the fifth floor. The sixth floor houses the archive, local studies and reference sections and also has a viewing deck giving spectacular views over the city.

Whilst this new library is light, transparent, colourful and welcoming, overall it remains solidly 'grounded', and so appropriate to its civic status. Its success is also shown by the significant increase in visitors, borrowers and café users. This flagship new building has been described by the chief executive of the Museums, Libraries and Archives Council as "an inspiration to the other 148 library authorities in England … a building that speaks of style, learning, confidence and a warm welcome".

Above Newcastle City Library (Charles Avison Building), New Bridge Street, Newcastle upon Tyne, by Ryder Architecture, 2009: from the south east. Photograph Bethany Jane Robertson.

Left Newcastle City Library, (Charles Avison Building), New Bridge Street: interior. Photograph Bethany Jane Robertson.

COOPER'S STUDIOS

WESTGATE ROAD, NEWCASTLE, NE1 3NN

Cooper's Studios, Westgate Road, Newcastle upon Tyne, by Ryder Architecture, 2009: from the south.

Cooper's Studios is another imaginative re-use of a redundant building by Ryder Architecture (see also, p.323) and dates in its present form from 2009. There were many challenges: the building lies within Newcastle's central conservation area; it is Grade II listed; it had received a number of unfortunate alterations; it had lain derelict for a number of years; and it also lies on the line of Hadrian's Wall, which meant that the existing ground floor had to be excavated to record any remains before work could start.

The original building was constructed in 1897 as a horse, carriage and cycle auction room and parking place, with internal ramps to give access for horses to first- and second-floor stalls. It also incorporated a glazed atrium which provided daylight to a ground-floor auction ring, with a ladies' viewing gallery on the first floor.

With the advent of the motor age, and the consequent lack of demand for city-centre stabling, the building began to lose its function and proved to be one of the last of its kind in the country; it is also one of the few to survive. There have been a variety of newer uses for the building, and modifications to its fabric; these modifications included the insertion of shop frontages to the ground floor in the 1930s, thereby breaking up the strong rhythm of brick bays on the main facade.

The challenge faced by the designers was to restore the building and convert it into flexible, lettable, commercial space, while remaining sympathetic to the original fabric and protecting the site's archaeology. The key to all this was the provision of extra natural light, which was achieved by replacing four of the brick bays with full-height glazing, and using the saved material to restore the remaining panels to their full height from ground level.

Internally, alterations to the structure were kept to a minimum, and insertions – such as the first-floor bridge across the atrium, which improves circulation – are modern but sympathetic in nature. Most importantly, the building's original robust character has been maintained, with the existing internal brick walls having been repaired and painted, and services largely exposed. Meanwhile, the need to provide a new roof provided an opportunity to increase the thermal performance of the building as a whole. Thus, despite the difficulties the architects had in working within the imposed constraints, the building has achieved an environmental performance rated as 'very good' by the internationally recognised 'BREEAM' assessment method.

Ryder Architecture themselves moved from Generator Studios (see p.323) to Cooper's Studios in 2011. The building has won a number of awards and has been described by English Heritage as "a bold scheme that acknowledged the building's most historically significant features and protected the site's archaeology".

VISITOR CENTRE, MILLFIELD HOUSE
JESMOND DENE, NEWCASTLE, NE7 7BQ

Set within the historic park of Jesmond Dene, this visitor centre and café, designed by Mosedale Gillatt Architects, is integrated with a Victorian building called Millfield House. The work was completed in 2011 as the centrepiece of a £6-million capital programme funded by the Heritage Lottery Fund to enhance the facilities at the Dene. Other new facilities included a bridge over the Ouseburn, a children's area and an additional animal enclosure at 'Pets' Corner'. The picturesque setting of the Dene is a perfect backdrop to this sensitively designed addition, nestling as it does within the courtyard of a Victorian building.

The centre also uses materials chosen to be at one with its context. Thus it is clad in larch, has a sedum roof and cleverly uses an existing stone boundary wall as part of its western elevation to help anchor the building to the site. At the same time, the glass frontage on to the courtyard creates a contemporary feel.

The architects were keen that the design of the facility was as environmentally friendly as possible. Thus the construction utilises a super-insulated building skin, an efficient heating system and rainwater collection tanks for the flushing of the toilets. Mosedale Gillatt won a number of awards for this project, including the R.I.B.A. Hadrian Medal for design excellence in 2011.

Visitor Centre, Millfield House, Jesmond Dene, Newcastle upon Tyne, by Mosedale Gillatt Architects, 2011: from the west.

THE TOFFEE FACTORY

LOWER STEENBERG'S YARD, OUSEBURN, NEWCASTLE, NE1 2DF

The former Maynard's toffee factory has been converted by Xsite Architecture into a £6-million facility providing managed work space for creative industries. The project was completed in 2011. The original building, dating from the mid-Victorian period, was an important structure within the Byker area, employing many people over the last 150 years. However, decades of neglect had left the building in a state of dereliction, with vegetation growing out of the walls and what remained of the roof.

The architects have sensitively retained as much as possible of the original fabric, while rebuilding parts that were beyond repair. Conceptually, the project is an exercise in insertion and intervention. New internal floors and walls are sensitively placed so as to heighten the qualities of the original structure, while new exterior walls are constructed out of boldly coloured cladding panels that contrast markedly with the old brickwork. To the existing three-storey structure an extra storey has been added. For clarity this has been picked out with lime green panels and set back from the face of the brickwork. The whole building now makes a considerable impact on to City Road.

Its interiors are well-lit and crisp; the detailing is simple and appropriate, with exposed steelwork and brickwork used to retain the industrial quality of the original structure. Another visually effective aspect of the project is the external courtyard space. Here the architects have retained the distinctive 30-metre high chimney that has for so long dominated the skyline of the valley. Once a purely functional structure, the chimney has been elevated to being the centrepiece of the composition, beautifully re-pointed and now a monument to the building's regeneration.

Maximising as it does the natural lighting and ventilation of the internal spaces, and utilising a Biomass boiler, the scheme as a whole achieved a 'BREEAM' 'very good' rating. In addition, it has already received numerous awards for its design quality including the R.I.B.A. North East Sustainable Building of the Year and the R.I.B.A. North East Building of the Year.

The Toffee Factory, Lower Steenberg's Yard, Ouseburn, Newcastle upon Tyne, by Xsite Architecture, 2011: from the east.

SLEEPERZ HOTEL

WESTGATE ROAD, NEWCASTLE, NE1 1SE

Sleeperz is a budget hotel built adjacent to a Grade II listed viaduct on Westgate Road. Designed by Clash Architects, a London-based practice, and completed in 2011, it replaced a large but discreet timber-clad Victorian parcel store that served Newcastle Central Station.

The 'Sleeperz' chain features small and medium-sized hotels located in major cities throughout the U.K. Their bespoke design represents a departure from the typical generic budget examples that offer little to the urban architectural scene. Here the architects have made excellent use of the difficult site, squeezing the accommodation into a very long, thin plot. Indeed, the hotel has no fewer than 98 bedrooms, and also contains 1,000 square metres of lettable retail and office space on the ground floor; this extends into the railway arches at the rear of the site.

For the building's north facade on to Westgate Road, the architects have used glass and steel, rising through six storeys. However, this eye-catching modern structure still succeeds in complementing its Victorian neighbours, thanks to its scale, and also to the effective use of Blaxter sandstone on its lateral, east and west facades; these also act as 'bookends' to the composition. The south facade, facing the railway, is clad in zinc and stucco and is, appropriately, if perhaps less attractively, more 'closed-down'. In 2012 the building received an R.I.B.A. Hadrian prize for its architectural excellence.

Sleeperz Hotel, Westgate Road,
Newcastle upon Tyne, by Clash Architects,
2011: from the south east.
Photograph Sally Ann Norman.

THE INSTITUTE OF TRANSPLANTATION, THE FREEMAN HOSPITAL

FREEMAN ROAD, HEATON, NEWCASTLE, NE7 7DN

The Institute of Transplantation at Newcastle's Freeman Hospital, designed by Ryder Architecture and opened in 2011, provides the first dedicated organ transplant facility in the country. Bringing together and improving the existing facilities at the hospital (originally built in the 1970s), with a single access point for patients, it forms one of a new group of buildings on the southern boundary of the hospital grounds, adjoining a housing estate. It provides a three-storey facility with four dedicated transplant theatres and high-dependency and in-patient wards.

The building's main external materials are dark blue-grey engineering brick, blue-green copper cladding panels and glass. The dramatic atrium entrance forms a contrasting element to the essentially horizontal main block. With its careful detailing – and thoughtful external planting – the Institute provides a distinct yet unobtrusive addition to the older, mainly red-brick hospital buildings.

Institute of Transplantation, Freeman Hospital, Freeman Road, Heaton, Newcastle upon Tyne, by Ryder Architecture, 2011: from the south.

MAGGIE'S NEWCASTLE CANCER CARE CENTRE, THE FREEMAN HOSPITAL

FREEMAN ROAD, HEATON, NEWCASTLE, NE7 7DN

Maggie's Newcastle Cancer Care Centre, Freeman Hospital, Freeman Road, Heaton, Newcastle upon Tyne, by Ted Cullinan, 2013: from the north west.

The Maggie's Newcastle Cancer Care Centre is the latest in a series of such drop-in centres – all funded by public donations – run by a charity initiated by garden designer Maggie Keswick Jencks (1941-95). Diagnosed with advanced breast cancer in 1993, she campaigned for buildings where those suffering from the disease could find 'practical, emotional and social support' in attractive surroundings. Her first centre opened in Edinburgh in 1996; the Newcastle one, completed in 2013, is the eleventh. Many of these buildings have been designed by well-known architects.

The R.I.B.A. Royal Gold Medallist Ted Cullinan designed this centre, located beside the Freeman Hospital, with the aim of providing a positive environment based on a sound environmentally conscious approach. The building has two wings, one for counselling and the other a large living room space with kitchen, linked by a double-height circular library block.

This overall L-shaped form shelters a south-facing courtyard, which is further protected by sloping earth banks; these will be covered with meadow flowers, changing character and colour with the seasons. The open southerly access, shelter, and high levels of insulation make the building very energy efficient, and this quality is enhanced by the solar panels, well integrated into the sloping roof of the library. The flat roof above the wings is accessible, and allows those attending the centre to use the exercise equipment and to become involved in developing the rooftop garden.

This building continues the high standards set by previous Maggie's Centres, and will become a significant part of the support provided within the region for cancer patients.

THE 'INTO' BUILDING (NEWCASTLE UNIVERSITY)

HAYMARKET, PERCY STREET, NEWCASTLE, NE1 7RU

The 'INTO' Building (Newcastle University), Haymarket, Percy Street, Newcastle upon Tyne, by FaulknerBrowns, 2012: from the east.

The 'INTO' development of 2012 is a group of buildings dedicated to the needs of international students who are studying on a range of programmes provided by the 'INTO' University Partnerships company in conjunction with Newcastle University. It contains administrative offices and teaching and student facilities, including residential accommodation.

This important development includes the main building on Percy Street; part of the former car park that lay between the Herschel Building (see p.277) and the Students' Union (see p.240); and new construction on a significant frontage on to St Thomas's Street. This has involved the redevelopment of a particularly important open space on the Percy Street frontage that gives an open view to the Herschel Building; this delicate issue has been sensitively handled by the architects, FaulknerBrowns.

Their work is in line with Sir Terry Farrell's master plan for the University (see p.305). This proposed new pedestrian routes and quadrangles within the campus, generating good links between the city and the University, while providing outdoor private space for the student accommodation and public space along the main pedestrian link from Percy Street into the campus.

By leaving a gap between the reception block (see below) and the former Newcastle Breweries Offices on Percy Street (see p.204), rather than fully redeveloping all the available space, the architects have created both a small public square and a 'framed view' of the Herschel Building, which is a considerable improvement on the screening by trees of the previous open space. In addition, the development's two residential blocks, Bernicia Halls (which can be glimpsed on the far right of the photograph) and Joseph Cowen Halls, respect the scale and materials of the surrounding buildings and are only five to seven storeys high, although they provide living accommodation for over 500 students.

The main building of the development is the reception, administration, teaching and social hub on Percy Street (see photograph above). Entered from the reception square to the south, this four-storey building is organised with a full-height atrium to the entrance-cum-reception area, and communal social areas on the ground floor. This gives a lively, active frontage and provides a welcome addition to the streetscape of Percy Street and the Haymarket.

Administration and teaching spaces are stacked behind the communal ones, with views to the rear. The entrance area is glazed on the east, and partly to the south – to the full height of the building – and is protected from solar gain by a dramatic perforated metal screen, which dominates the building's south-eastern corner.

There is a clear visual distinction between the highly glazed public areas and the teaching and administration accommodation to the rear. To the north of the entrance area, along the street, polished grey granite is used to form a solid base to the front facade, while a two-storey projection in polished red sandstone, with offset vertical windows, sits above; there is rusticated grey stone for the administration block at the rear. The substantial use of stone in the 'INTO' building fits well with the material quality of the adjacent former Newcastle Breweries Offices.

BIBLIOGRAPHY AND REFERENCES

F. Aalen (ed.), *England's Landscape: The North East* (London: Collins, for English Heritage, 2006)

J. Addyman, B. Fawcett et al., *The High Level Bridge and Newcastle Central Station: 150 Years Across the Tyne* (Newcastle upon Tyne: the North Eastern Railway Association for the High Level Bridge and Central Station 150 Committee, 1999)

C.J. Allen, *The North Eastern Railway* (London: Ian Allan, 1964)

B. Allsopp, *Historic Architecture of Newcastle upon Tyne* (Newcastle upon Tyne: Oriel Press, 1967)

B. Allsopp, *Modern Architecture of Northern England* (Newcastle upon Tyne: Oriel Press, 1969)

B. Allsopp & U. Clark, *Historic Architecture of Northumberland and Newcastle* (Stocksfield: Oriel Press, 1977)

C. Amery, "Byker by Erskine", in *The Architectural Review* (Dec., 1974)

B. & W. Armstrong, *The Arts and Crafts Movement in the North East of England: A Handbook* (Wetherby, Yorks: Oblong Creative Ltd, 2013)

C. Armstrong, *Tyneside in the Second World War* (Chichester: Phillimore, 2007)

E.M. Atkins, "The Genesis of the Laing Art Gallery, Newcastle upon Tyne", in T.E. Faulkner (ed.), *Northumbrian Panorama: Studies in the History and Culture of North East England* (London: Octavian Press, 1996)

I. Ayris, *A City of Palaces: Richard Grainger and the Making of Newcastle upon Tyne* (Newcastle upon Tyne: Newcastle Libraries and Information Service, 1997)

I. Ayris & S. Linsley, *A Guide to the Industrial Archaeology of Tyne and Wear* (Newcastle upon Tyne: Tyne and Wear Specialist Conservation Team, 1994)

I. Ayris & P. Sheldon, *On the Waterfront: An Historical Tour of Newcastle's Quayside* (Newcastle upon Tyne: Newcastle upon Tyne City Libraries and Arts, 1995)

C. Baglee, *The Holy Jesus Hospital: A Short History* (Newcastle upon Tyne: Frank Graham, 1971)

C. Baglee, *The North-East Coast Exhibition, Newcastle upon Tyne* (Newcastle upon Tyne: Frank Graham, 1979)

M. Barke, *Discovering Cities: Newcastle upon Tyne* (Sheffield: Geographical Association, 2002)

M. Barke & R. Buswell (eds), *Newcastle's Changing Map* (Newcastle upon Tyne: Newcastle upon Tyne City Libraries and Arts, 1992)

E. Bateson et al. (eds), *A History of Northumberland,* 15 vols (Newcastle upon Tyne: Andrew Reid, Sons & Co. for the Northumberland County History Committee, 1893-1940)

R.C. Bell & M.A.V. Gill, *The Potteries of Tyneside* (Newcastle upon Tyne: Frank Graham, 1973)

B. Bennison, *Brewers and Bottlers of Newcastle upon Tyne from 1850 to the Present Day* (Newcastle upon Tyne: Newcastle upon Tyne City Libraries and Arts, 1995)

H. Berry, "Creating Polite Space: The Organisation and Social Function of the Newcastle Assembly Rooms", in H. Berry & J. Gregory (eds), *Creating and Consuming Culture in North-East England* (Aldershot: Ashgate Publishing, 2004)

H. Berry, "Promoting Taste in the Provincial Press: National and Local Culture in Eighteenth-Century Newcastle upon Tyne", in *British Journal for Eighteenth-Century Studies,* 25 (2002)

R.W. Billings, *Illustrations of the Architectural Antiquities of the County of Durham* (1846; facsimile edition, Newcastle upon Tyne: Frank Graham, 1974)

I.S. Black, "National Provincial Bank Buildings in North-East England in the Later Nineteenth Century" in *The Durham Archaeological Journal,* vol. 17 (2003)

H. Bourne, *The History of Newcastle upon Tyne, or, the Ancient and Present State of that Town* (Newcastle upon Tyne: John White, 1736)

J.R. Boyle, *Vestiges of Old Newcastle and Gateshead* (with illustrations by W.H. Knowles, Newcastle upon Tyne: Andrew Reid & Co., London: E. Stock, 1890)

J. Brand, *The History and Antiquities of Newcastle upon Tyne* (London: B. White & Son and T. & I. Egerton, 1789)

A. Brazendale, *Gateshead, History and Guide* (Stroud: Tempus Publishing, 2004)

A. Brazendale, *Images of England: Old Gateshead* (Stroud: Tempus Publishing, 2000)

J.R. Breihan, "Army Barracks in the North East in the Era of the French Revolution", in *Archaeologia Aeliana,* 5, vol. xviii (1990)

G.W.D. Briggs, *Medieval Churches of Northumberland* (Jesmond, Newcastle upon Tyne: Keepdale Publishing, 2002)

G.W.D. Briggs, "William Newton and Long Benton Church", in *Archaeologia Aeliana,* 5, vol. xiii (1985)

J. Collingwood Bruce, *A Hand-Book to Newcastle-on-Tyne, etc.* (Newcastle upon Tyne: A. Reid, 1863)

J. Collingwood Bruce, *Lectures on Old Newcastle* (Newcastle upon Tyne: Andrew Reid & Co., 1904)

C. Buckley & L. Walker, *Between the Wars: Architecture and Design on Tyneside, 1919-39* (exh. cat., Newcastle upon Tyne: Newcastle Polytechnic, 1982)

W. Burns, *Newcastle: A Study in Replanning at Newcastle upon Tyne* (London: Leonard Hill, 1967)

A. Burton, *Cityscapes: A Tour around the Great British Cities* (London: André Deutsch, 1990)

R.J. Buswell, "Reconciling the Past with the Present: Conservation Policy in Newcastle upon Tyne", in *Cities* (Aug. 1984)

[Byker Priority Area Team], *From Roman Wall to Byker Wall: A Centenary History Presented under the Auspices of Byker Priority Area Team* (Newcastle upon Tyne: Rev. I. Falconer and St Silas's Parochial Church Council, 1986)

W. Camden, *Britannia, or, a Chorographical Description of England, Scotland and Ireland* (1586, first English edition 1610, revised and republished by Edmund Gibson, 1695; facsimile edition, Newton Abbot: David & Charles, 1971)

J. [John] & J. [Joyce] Carlson, *Newcastle Through Time* (Stroud: Amberley Publishing, 2009)

I.C. Carlton, *A Short History of Gateshead* (Gateshead: Gateshead Corporation, 1974)

R. Carroll, *Ryder and Yates* (London: R.I.B.A. Publishing, 2009)

R.J. Charleton, *A History of Newcastle-on-Tyne* (1885; edition of 1950, Newcastle upon Tyne: Harold Hill)

L.G. Charlton, *The First Locomotive Engineers* (Newcastle upon Tyne: Frank Graham, 1974)

W. Collard & M. Ross, *Architectural and Picturesque Views in Newcastle* (1841; edition with an Introduction by S. Middlebrook, Wakefield: S.R. Publishers, 1971)

R. Colls & B. Lancaster (eds), *Newcastle upon Tyne: A Modern History* (Chichester: Phillimore, 2001)

P. Collymore, *The Architecture of Ralph Erskine* (London: Academy Editions, 1994)

D. Cressy, "Social Status and Literacy in North East England", in *Local Population Studies,* 21 (1978)

F. Cullen & D. Lovie, *Newcastle's Grainger Town, An Urban Renaissance* (London: English Heritage, 2003)

J.S. Curl, "Northern Cemetery under Threat", in *Country Life* (2 July 1981)

I. Curry, "The Newcastle upon Tyne Architectural Practice of Hicks & Charlewood and their Successors, 1882-1936", in *Archaeologia Aeliana,* 5, vol. xxxviii (2009)

D. Defoe, *A Tour through the Whole Island of Great Britain* (1724-26; edition with an Introduction by G.D.H. Cole, London: Peter Davies, 1927)

F.W. Dendy, *An Account of Jesmond* (Newcastle upon Tyne: Robinson & Co., 1904)

F.W. Dendy, *Three Lectures on Old Newcastle, its Suburbs and Gilds, etc.* (Newcastle upon Tyne: the Northumberland Press, for the Literary and Philosophical Society of Newcastle upon Tyne, 1921)

H. Dixon, "Thomas Bewick and the North-Eastern Landscape", in T.E. Faulkner, H. Berry & J. Gregory (eds), *Northern Landscapes: Representations and Realities of North-East England* (Woodbridge, Suffolk: Boydell Press, 2010)

J. Donald, *Not Just Bricks and Mortar* (Newcastle upon Tyne: Newcastle upon Tyne Community and Leisure Services Department, Libraries and Arts, 1994)

D. Dougan, *The Great Gun-Maker: The Story of Lord Armstrong* (Newcastle upon Tyne: Frank Graham, 1971)

D. Dougan, *The History of North East Shipbuilding* (London: George Allen and Unwin, 1968)

D. Dougan, *Newcastle and Present* (Newcastle upon Tyne: Frank Graham, 1971)

W.G Elliott, *The Parish and Church of St Bartholomew, Long Benton: A Social History* (Benton, Newcastle upon Tyne: W.G. Elliott, 2002)

J. Ellis, "A Dynamic Society: Social Relations in

Newcastle upon Tyne 1660-1760", in P. Clark (ed.), *The Transformation of English Provincial Towns 1600-1800* (London: Hutchinson & Co., 1984)

T. Farrell, H. Pearman & J. Tobin, *Ten Years, Ten Cities: The Work of Terry Farrell and Partners, 1991-2001* (London: Laurence King Publishing, 2002)

T.E. Faulkner, "Aspects of Late 19th Century Church Architecture", in T.E. Faulkner (ed.), *Northumbrian Heritage* (special issue of *Northern Architect,* 5th ser. no. 1, 1994-95)

T.E. Faulkner, "The Early Nineteenth Century Planning of Newcastle upon Tyne", in *Planning Perspectives,* 5 (1990)

T.E. Faulkner, "The Laing Art Gallery: The Building", in *Friends News: Newsletter of the Friends of the Laing Art Gallery,* no. 39 (Dec. 2001)

T.E. Faulkner (ed.), *Northumbrian Panorama: Studies in the History and Culture of North East England* (London: Octavian Press, 1996)

T.E. Faulkner, "Robert James Johnson, Architect and Antiquary", in *The Durham University Journal,* n.s., vol. lxi, no. 1 (Jan. 1995)

T.E. Faulkner, "Urban Landscapes of Newcastle upon Tyne", in T.E. Faulkner, H. Berry & J. Gregory (eds), *Northern Landscapes: Representations and Realities of North-East England* (Woodbridge, Suffolk: Boydell Press, 2010)

T.E. Faulkner & A. Greg, *John Dobson: Architect of the North East* (Newcastle upon Tyne: Tyne Bridge Publishing with Tyne and Wear Museums, 2001)

[T.E. Faulkner & A. Greg], *Twelve Newcastle Churches: An Architectural Journey* (exh. cat., Newcastle upon Tyne: Tyne and Wear County Council Museums, 1982)

T.E. Faulkner & P.A.S. Lowery, *Lost Houses of Newcastle and Northumberland* (York: Jill Raines, 1996)

B. Fawcett, *A History of North Eastern Railway Architecture* (Newcastle upon Tyne: the North Eastern Railway Association, 2001)

R. Finch, *Coals from Newcastle: The Story of the North East Coal Trade in the Days of Sail* (Lavenham, Suffolk: Terence Dalton, 1973)

A. Flowers & V. Histon (eds), *Water Under the Bridges: Newcastle's Twentieth Century* (Newcastle upon Tyne: Tyne Bridge Publishing, 1999)

C. Foote Wood, *T. Dan Smith, "Voice of the North", Downfall of a Visionary: The Life of the North East's Most Charismatic Champion* (Co. Durham: Northern Writers, 2010)

W. Fordyce, *The History and Antiquities of the County Palatine of Durham,* 2 vols (Newcastle, London and Edinburgh: A. Fullarton & Co., 1855-57)

W.R. Foster, *Some Notes on House Building in Newcastle upon Tyne, 1820-1860* (1981: typescript deposited in Newcastle Central Library)

C.M. Fraser & K. Emsley, *Tyneside* (Newton Abbot: David & Charles, 1973)

T. Friedman, *The Georgian Parish Church 'Monuments to Posterity':* (Reading: Spire Books Ltd, 2004) (esp. chapter vii)

T. Friedman, "Gibbs's Library at St Nicholas, Newcastle upon Tyne", in *Architectural History,* 41 (1998)

K. Galley, "Newcastle upon Tyne", in J. Holliday (ed.), *City Centre Redevelopment: A Study of British City Centre Planning* (London: Charles Knight & Co., 1973)

L. Gettings, "Benjamin Simpson, F.R.I.B.A.: Parts 1 and 2", in *Northern Architect,* n. s., 12 (April, and July/Oct., 1977)

R.D. Giddings, "Thomas Oliver, 1791-1857" (unpublished B.Arch. dissertation, University of Newcastle upon Tyne, 1981)

D. Godfrey, *"The Unknown Architect": Robert Burns Dick (1868-1954), Cackett, Burns Dick & MacKellar* (exhibition booklet, R.I.B.A., Northern Region, Northumbria Branch, Newcastle upon Tyne, 1984)

F. Graham, *The Castle and Walls of Newcastle* (Newcastle upon Tyne: Frank Graham, 1976)

F. Graham, *Historic Newcastle* (Newcastle upon Tyne: Frank Graham, 1970)

F. Graham, *Maps of Newcastle* (Newcastle upon Tyne: Frank Graham, 1984)

F. Graham, *Newcastle Quayside, The Sandhill, The Side and The Close* (Newcastle upon Tyne: Frank Graham, 1991)

F. Graham, *The Old Halls, Houses and Inns of Northumberland* (Newcastle upon Tyne: Frank Graham, 1977)

H.J. Grainger, *Death Redesigned: British Crematoria, History, Architecture and Landscape* (Reading: Spire Books, 2005)

W. Gray, *Chorographia, or A Survey of Newcastle upon Tyne* (1649; facsimile of the 1883 edition, Newcastle upon Tyne: Frank Graham, 1970)

M. Greatbatch et al., *Benwell's Big Houses: A Social History* (Newcastle upon Tyne: Newcastle Community Heritage Project and Tyne Bridge Publishing, 2012)

F. Green, "Impolite Landscapes: Making Private Parks Public", in T.E. Faulkner, H. Berry & J. Gregory (eds), *Northern Landscapes: Representations and Realities of North-East England* (Woodbridge, Suffolk: Boydell Press, 2010)

F. Green et al., *A Guide to the Historic Parks and Gardens of Tyne & Wear* (Newcastle upon Tyne: Tyne and Wear Development Department et al., 1995)

J. Green (ed.), *Richard Grainger and the West End of Newcastle* (Newcastle upon Tyne: St James's Heritage and Environment Group, 2013)

A. Greg, "The Architects of the Laing Art Gallery", in *Friends News: Newsletter of the Friends of the Laing Art Gallery,* no. 38 (Oct. 2001)

A. Greg, "The Building and its Architect", in *The Literary and Philosophical Society of Newcastle upon Tyne Bicentenary Lectures* (Newcastle upon Tyne: Literary and Philosophical Society, 1994)

A. Greg, 'Newcastle's Victorian Architecture: Patronage, Prestige and the Public Good"' in T.E. Faulkner (ed.), *Northumbrian Heritage* (special issue of *Northern Architect,* 5th ser., no. 1, 1994-95)

A. Greg, "Robert Spence Watson and William Morris in Gateshead", in *The Victorian Society North East Group Newsletter,* no. 11 (Jan. 1989)

A. Greg, "The Royal Victoria Infirmary for the Counties of Newcastle upon Tyne, Durham and Northumberland", in *The Victorian Society North East Group Newsletter,* no. 13 (July 1989)

[A. Greg], *The Tyneside Classical Tradition: Classical Architecture in the North East, c.1700-1850* (exh. cat., Newcastle upon Tyne: Tyne and Wear County Council Museums, 1980)

[A. Greg et al.], *Victorian and Edwardian Architecture in the North-East* (exh. cat., Newcastle upon Tyne: Tyne and Wear County Council Museums, 1981)

A. Guy, *Steam and Speed: Railways of Tyne and Wear from the Earliest Days* (Newcastle upon Tyne: Tyne Bridge Publishing, 2003)

M. Hall, *The Artists of Northumbria: An Illustrated Dictionary* (1973; third edition, Bristol: Art Dictionaries Ltd, 2005)

M. Hall, *Newcastle between the Wars: Byron Dawson's Tyneside* (Newcastle upon Tyne: Tyne Bridge Publishing, 2011)

G. Harbottle, *Gosforth and its Parish Church: A Thousand Years of History* (Newcastle upon Tyne: G. Harbottle, n.d.)

G. Harbottle, *Gosforth Parish Church: A Historical Account of the Life of the Church* (Newcastle upon Tyne: G. Harbottle, 1968)

S. Harbottle, *The Reverend William Turner: Dissent and Reform in Georgian Newcastle upon Tyne* (Leeds: Northern Universities Press, for the Literary and Philosophical Society of Newcastle upon Tyne, 1997)

E. Harwood, *A Canny Weekend in Newcastle and the North East* (Twentieth Century Society, London: 1995)

V. Haworth, *Robert Stephenson, Engineer and Scientist: The Making of a Prodigy, 1803-1859* (Newcastle upon Tyne: The Robert Stephenson Trust, 2005)

H. Heald, *William Armstrong, Magician of the North* (Newcastle upon Tyne: Northumbria Press, 2010)

F.J.C. Hearnshaw, *Newcastle upon Tyne* (1924; edition with an Introduction by S. Middlebrook, Wakefield: S.R. Publishers, 1971)

P. Hepplewhite, *Images of England: Newcastle upon Tyne* (Stroud: Tempus Publishing, 1999)

D. Heslop, B. Jobling & G. McCombie, *Alderman Fenwick's House* (Newcastle upon Tyne: Society of Antiquaries of Newcastle upon Tyne, Buildings of Newcastle series no. 3, 2001)

D. Heslop, G. McCombie & C. Thomson, *Bessie Surtees House: Two Merchant Houses in Sandhill, Newcastle upon Tyne* (Newcastle upon Tyne: Society of Antiquaries of Newcastle upon Tyne, Buildings of Newcastle series, no. 2, 1995)

P. Hetherington, *Newcastle/Gateshead: Shaping the City* (London: R.I.B.A. Publications, 2010)

V. Histon, *Unlocking the Quayside: Newcastle and Gateshead's Historic Waterfront Explored* (Newcastle upon Tyne: Tyne Bridge Publishing, 2006)

J. Hodgson, *The Picture of Newcastle upon Tyne, being a Brief Historical & Descriptive Guide to the Principal Buildings, Streets, Public Institutions, Manufacturers, Curiosities, &c. Within That Town, etc.* (Newcastle upon Tyne: D. Akenhead & Sons, 1812)

J. Hodgson, *A Topographical and Historical Description*

of the County of Northumberland (London: Sherwood, Neely and Jones, 1817)

J. Hodgson et al., *A History of Northumberland,* 7 vols (Newcastle upon Tyne: E. Walker, 1820-58)

T. Hopkins, *A Portrait of Newcastle* (Tiverton, Devon: Halsgrove, 2004)

P.M. Horsley, *Eighteenth-Century Newcastle* (Newcastle upon Tyne: Oriel Press, 1971)

R. Howell jr., *Newcastle upon Tyne and the Puritan Revolution: A Study of the Civil War in North England* (Oxford: Clarendon Press, 1967)

E. Hughes, *North Country Life in the Eighteenth Century: The North-East, 1700-1750* (London: Oxford University Press, 1952)

W. Hutchinson, *A View of Northumberland, etc.,* 2 vols (Newcastle: W. Charnley and Vesey & Whitfield, 1778)

M.A. Johnson, "Architectural Taste and Patronage in Newcastle upon Tyne, 1870-1914" (unpublished Ph.D. thesis, University of Northumbria at Newcastle, 2008)

M.A. Johnson, "The Architecture of Dunn and Hansom of Newcastle" (unpublished M.A. dissertation, University of Northumbria at Newcastle, 2003)

D. Keys & K. Smith, *Armstrong's River Empire: Tyne Shipyards that Supplied the World* (Newcastle upon Tyne: Tyne Bridge Publishing, 2010)

R. Kirkup, *Newcastle Then and Now* (Stroud: History Press, 2013)

J. Knott, "A History of the Libraries of Newcastle upon Tyne to 1900" (unpublished M.Litt. thesis, University of Newcastle upon Tyne, 1975)

W.H. Knowles, "Architecture of Old and Modern Newcastle", in G.B. Richardson & W.W. Tomlinson, *The Official Handbook to Newcastle and District* (London: The British Association, 1916)

W.H. Knowles, "The Castle, Newcastle upon Tyne", in *Archaeologia Aeliana,* 4, vol. ii (1926)

B. Lancaster (ed.), *Working Class Housing on Tyneside 1850-1939* (Whitley Bay: Bewick Press, 1994)

P. Leach, *James Paine* (London: A. Zwemmer, 1988)

P. Lockley, "Jesmond Churches: Architecture and Denomination in a Late Nineteenth Century Suburb" (unpublished B.A. dissertation, University of Newcastle upon Tyne, 2002)

W.H.D. Longstaffe, "The New Castle upon Tyne", in *Archaeologia Aeliana,* n. s., vol. iv. (1860)

D. Lovie, *The Buildings of Grainger Town: Four Townscape Walks around Newcastle* (Newcastle upon Tyne: North East Environmental Education Forum, 1997)

P.A.S. Lowery, "William Newton: An Eminent Architect?", in T.E. Faulkner (ed.), *Northumbrian Heritage* (special issue of *Northern Architect,* 5th ser., no. 1, 1994-95)

D. Lumley, *The Story of Gateshead Town: The Earliest Age to Mid-Victorian* (Newcastle upon Tyne: Northumberland Press, 1932)

F. McCombie & M. Cullen, *A Parish in its Time: A History of St Charles' Parish Gosforth, 1896-1996* (Newcastle upon Tyne: St Charles' Parish, Gosforth, 1996)

G. McCombie, "The Buildings of Trinity House, Newcastle upon Tyne", in *Archaeologia Aeliana,* 5, vol. xiii (1985)

G. McCombie, "A House in Town: Newcastle Houses to 1824", in T.E. Faulkner (ed.), *Northumbrian Heritage* (special issue of *Northern Architect,* 5th ser., no. 1, 1994-95)

G. McCombie et al., *Newcastle and Gateshead* (Pevsner Architectural Guide) (New Haven and London: Yale University Press, 2009)

N. McCord, *North East England, An Economic and Social History* (London: Batsford, 1979)

N. McCord, *North-East History from the Air* (Chichester: Phillimore, 1991)

N. McCord, *Northumberland History from the Air* (Newcastle upon Tyne: Frank Graham, 1972)

D.F. McGuire, *Charles Mitchell 1820-1895, Victorian Shipbuilder* (Newcastle upon Tyne: Newcastle upon Tyne City Libraries and Arts, 1988)

N. MacKellar, "The Story of the N.A.A." [Northern Architectural Association] in *Northern Architect,* no. 40 (May 1968)

E. Mackenzie, *A Descriptive and Historical Account of the Town and County of Newcastle upon Tyne,* 2 vols (Newcastle upon Tyne: Mackenzie & Dent, 1827)

R. Mains & A. Tuck (eds), *Royal Grammar School, Newcastle upon Tyne: A History of the School in its Community* (Stocksfield: Oriel Press, 1986)

F.W.D. Manders, *Cinemas of Gateshead* (Gateshead: Gateshead M.B.C. Libraries and Arts, 1995)

F.W.D. Manders, *Cinemas of Newcastle: A Comprehensive History of the Cinemas of Newcastle upon Tyne* (Newcastle upon Tyne: Newcastle City Libraries and Arts, 1991)

F.W.D. Manders, *A History of Gateshead* (Gateshead: Gateshead Corporation, 1973)

F.W.D. Manders & R. Potts, *Crossing the Tyne* (Newcastle upon Tyne: Tyne Bridge Publishing, 2001)

P. Meadows & E. Waterson, *Lost Houses of County Durham* (York: Jill Raines, 1993)

S. Middlebrook, *Newcastle upon Tyne, its Growth and Achievement* (1950; new edition, Wakefield: S.R. Publishers, 1968)

G.J. Milne, *North East England, 1850-1914: The Dynamics of a Maritime Region* (Woodbridge, Suffolk: Boydell Press, 2006)

N. Moat, "An Appreciation of William Wailes", in *The Victorian Society North East Group Newsletter,* no. 6 (Nov. 1987)

N. Moat, "'A Frankly Modern Building': The Church of St James and St Basil, Fenham, Newcastle upon Tyne", in *The Victorian Society North East Group Newsletter,* no. 29 (April 1996)

N. Moat, "A Theatre for the Soul: St George's Church, Jesmond: The Building and Cultural Reception of a Late-Victorian Church" (unpublished Ph.D. thesis, University of Newcastle upon Tyne, 2011)

A. Moffat & G. Rosie, *Tyneside: A History of Newcastle and Gateshead from Earliest Times* (Edinburgh and London: Mainstream Publishing, 2005)

D.R. Moir, *The Birth and History of Trinity House, Newcastle upon Tyne* (Glasgow: McKenzie Vincent & Co., 1958)

A. Morgan, *Beyond the Grave: Exploring Newcastle's Burial Grounds* (Newcastle upon Tyne: Tyne Bridge Publishing, 2004)

A. Morgan, *A Fine and Private Place: Jesmond Old Cemetery* (Newcastle upon Tyne: Tyne Bridge Publishing, 2000)

A. Morgan, *Heaton: From Farms to Foundries* (Newcastle upon Tyne: Tyne Bridge Publishing, 2012)

A. Morgan, *Jesmond: From Mines to Mansions* (Newcastle upon Tyne: Tyne Bridge Publishing, 2010)

A. Morgan, *Victorian Panorama* (Newcastle upon Tyne: Tyne Bridge Publishing, 2007)

C. Morris (ed.), *The Journeys of Celia Fiennes* (London: Cresset Press, 1949)

A.F. Munden, *Jesmond Parish Church, Newcastle upon Tyne* (Newcastle upon Tyne: Clayton Publications, 1981)

A.F. Munden, *A Light in a Dark Place: Jesmond Parish Church, Newcastle upon Tyne* (Newcastle upon Tyne: Clayton Publications, 2006)

F. Musgrove, *The North of England: A History from Roman Times to the Present* (Oxford: Blackwell, 1990)

S. Newman & G. Peacock, *Newcastle upon Tyne* (Cramlington, Northumberland: 2005)

D. Newton & A.J. Pollard (eds), *Newcastle and Gateshead Before 1700* (Chichester: Phillimore, 2009)

C. O'Brien et al., *The Origins of the Quayside* (Newcastle upon Tyne: Society of Antiquaries of Newcastle upon Tyne, Monograph Series no. 3, 1988)

T. Oliver, *A New Picture of Newcastle upon Tyne* (1831; facsimile edition, Newcastle upon Tyne: Frank Graham, 1970)

H. Oswald, *The Theatres Royal in Newcastle upon Tyne* (Newcastle upon Tyne: Northumberland Press, 1936)

J. Oswald, "Ecclesiastical Architecture in Newcastle and Gateshead", in G.B. Richardson & W.W. Tomlinson, *The Official Handbook to Newcastle and District* (London: The British Association, 1916)

W. Page (ed.), *The Victoria History of the County of Durham,* 3 vols (London: Archibald Constable and Co., 1905-28)

K. Pearce, "Newcastle's Tyneside Flats 1850-1900: By-Law Housing or Cultural Phenomenon?", in B. Lancaster (ed.), *Working Class Housing on Tyneside 1850-1939* (Whitley Bay: Bewick Press, 1994)

R. Pears, "William Newton (1730-1798) and the Development of the Architectural Profession in North-East England" (unpublished Ph.D. thesis, University of Newcastle upon Tyne, 2012)

L.F. Pearson, *Northern City: An Architectural History of Newcastle upon Tyne* (Newcastle upon Tyne: Tyne Bridge Publishing, 1996)

L.F. Pearson, *The Northumbrian Pub: An Architectural History* (Warkworth: Sandhill Press ,1989)

J. Pendlebury, "Alas Smith and Burns? Conservation in Newcastle upon Tyne City Centre, 1959-68", in *Planning Perspectives,* 16 (2001)

J. Penn, "The Enigmatic Architect: Frank West Rich

(1840-1929)", in *Archaeologia Aeliana,* 5, vol. xxxviii (2009)

N. Pevsner & E. Williamson, *The Buildings of England: County Durham* (1953; revised edition, Harmondsworth: Penguin Books, 1983)

N. Pevsner et al., *The Buildings of England: Northumberland* (1957; revised edition, London: Penguin Books, 1992)

W.S.F. Pickering (ed.), *A Social History of the Diocese of Newcastle* (Stocksfield: Oriel Press, 1981)

Plan Newcastle upon Tyne 1945: Report of the Town Planning Sub-Committee (Newcastle upon Tyne: 1945)

D. Potter, "Bensham Grove, Gateshead, and Robert Spence Watson", in *The Victorian Society North East Group Newsletter,* no. 27 (Oct. 1993)

S. Prins & R. Massingberd-Mundy (eds), *A Guide to the Anglican Churches in Newcastle and Northumberland* (Newcastle upon Tyne: Newcastle Diocesan Bishop's Editorial Committee of the Link, 1982)

A.W. Purdue, *Newcastle: The Biography* (Stroud: Amberley Publishing, 2011)

G. Purves (et al.), *Churches of Newcastle and Northumberland: A Sense of Place* (Stroud: Tempus Publishing Ltd, 2006)

L. Redhead, *Newcastle Revisited: Hospitals* (Newcastle upon Tyne: Newcastle Libraries and Information Service, 1996)

R.W. Rennison, "The High Level Bridge, Newcastle: Its Evolution, Design and Construction" (typescript of paper presented to the Newcomen Society, *Transactions,* vol. 52, 1980-81, deposited in Newcastle Central Library)

A.E. Richardson, *Monumental Classic Architecture in Great Britain and Ireland in the Nineteenth Century* (1914; edition with an Introduction by H. Stafford Bryant, New York and London: Norton & Co., 1982)

M.A. Richardson, *Descriptive Companion through Newcastle upon Tyne and Gateshead* (Newcastle upon Tyne: M.A. Richardson, 1838)

M.A. Richardson, *The Local Historian's Table Book, etc.,* 8 vols (Newcastle upon Tyne: M.A. Richardson, 1841-46)

D.W. Ritson, *Newcastle East Through Time* (Stroud: Amberley Publishing, 2012)

F. Robinson (ed.), *Post-Industrial Tyneside: An Economic and Social Survey of Tyneside in the 1980s* (Newcastle upon Tyne: Newcastle upon Tyne City Libraries and Arts, 1988)

K. Robinson, *Newcastle upon Tyne's Theatre Royal, 1788-1870* (Newcastle upon Tyne: Society of Antiquaries, 1988)

F. Rogers, *Gateshead: An Early Victorian Boom Town* (Newcastle upon Tyne: Priory Press, 1974)

[The Royal Archaeological Institute], *Report of the Summer Meeting at Newcastle upon Tyne, 1976* (reprinted from *The Archaeological Journal*, vol. 133, 1976)

J.E. Ruscoe (ed.), *Churches of the Diocese of Durham* (Durham: Millennium Committee of the Diocese of Durham, 1994)

P. Russell et al., *England Displayed, Being a New, Complete, and Accurate Survey of the Kingdom of England, etc.* (London: Adlard & Browne, 1769)

R. Rutherford, "Frank West Rich, F.R.I.B.A.: Newcastle Architect" (unpublished B.A. dissertation, University of Newcastle upon Tyne, 1996)

A. Saint, *Richard Norman Shaw* (London and New Haven: Yale University Press, 1976, revised edition 2010)

[St George's Church, Jesmond, Newcastle upon Tyne], *Architectural Drawings of St George's Church, Jesmond (from the Northumberland Collections Service)* (CD-ROM, n.d., available at the church)

A.E. Smailes, *North England* (London and Edinburgh: Thomas Nelson, 1960)

K. Smith, *Emperor of Industry: Lord Armstrong of Cragside* (Newcastle upon Tyne: Tyne Bridge Publishing, 2005)

K. Smith & T. Yellowley, *The Great Walls of Newcastle* (Newcastle upon Tyne: Tyne Bridge Publishing, 2012)

T.D. Smith, *Dan Smith: An Autobiography* (Newcastle upon Tyne: Oriel Press, 1970)

[The Society of the Sacred Heart], *St Mary's College Fenham 1905-1985* (London: Society of the Sacred Heart, 1985)

T. Sopwith, *A Historical and Descriptive Account of All Saints' Church in Newcastle upon Tyne* (Newcastle upon Tyne: Edward Walker, 1826)

[J. Speed], *An Atlas of Tudor England and Wales: Forty Plates from John Speed's Pocket Atlas of 1627, Introduced and Described by E.G.R. Taylor* (London: Penguin Books, 1951)

J. Strachan, *Northumbrian Masonry and the Development of the Craft in England* (London: Bro. George Kenning, 1898)

J. Straker, "Robert Burns Dick" and "James Thoburn Cackett", in *Friends News: Newsletter of the Friends of the Laing Art Gallery,* no. 38 (Oct. 2001)

R. Surtees, *The History and Antiquities of the County Palatine of Durham,* 4 vols (1816-40; facsimile edition with an Introduction by E. Birley, Wakefield: EP Publishing, 1972)

J. Sykes, *Local Records, or, Historical Register of Remarkable Events, which have Occurred Exclusively in the Counties of Durham and Northumberland, Town and County of Newcastle upon Tyne, and Berwick upon Tweed, etc.* (first published by the author, Newcastle upon Tyne, 1824 and later editions; reprinted 1857-76, London: British Library, Historical Print Editions, 2011)

S. Taylor & D. Lovie, *Gateshead: Architecture in a Changing Urban Landscape* (London: English Heritage, 2004)

W.W. Tomlinson, *The North Eastern Railway, Its Rise and Development* (Newcastle upon Tyne: Andrew Reid & Co., 1915)

P. Usherwood, J. Beach & C. Morris, *Public Sculpture of North-East England* (Liverpool: Liverpool University Press, 2000)

T. Wake et al., *The Cathedral Church of Saint Nicholas, Newcastle upon Tyne* (Newcastle upon Tyne: Society of Antiquaries of Newcastle upon Tyne, 1932)

R.F. Walker, *The Institutions and History of the Freemen of Newcastle upon Tyne* (Newcastle upon Tyne: The Stewards' Committee of the Freemen of Newcastle upon Tyne, n.d.)

R.F. Walker, *The Origins of Newcastle upon Tyne* (Newcastle upon Tyne: Thorne's Students' Bookshop, 1976)

A. Warren & D. Sasitorn, *North-East England from Above* (London: Myriad Books, 2004)

R.S. Watson, *The History of the Literary and Philosophical Society of Newcastle-upon-Tyne* (London: Walter Scott, 1897)

J. Weaver, *Exploring England's Heritage: Cumbria to Northumberland* (London: HMSO, 1992)

M. Webb, *Architecture in Britain Today* (Feltham, Middlesex: Hamlyn, for Country Life Books, 1969)

R. Welford, *History of Newcastle and Gateshead; vol. 1: Fourteenth and Fifteenth Centuries; vol. 2: Sixteenth Century; vol. 3: Sixteenth and Seventeenth Centuries* (London: Walter Scott, 1884-87)

R. Welford, *A History of the Parish of Gosforth* (1879; facsimile edition, Newcastle upon Tyne: Frank Graham, 1975)

N. Whitaker & U. Clark, *Historic Architecture of County Durham* (Newcastle upon Tyne: Oriel Press, 1971)

L. Wilkes, *Tyneside Portraits: Studies in Art and Life* (Newcastle upon Tyne: Frank Graham, 1971)

L. Wilkes & G. Dodds, *Tyneside Classical: The Newcastle of Grainger, Dobson and Clayton* (London: John Murray, 1964)

P. Willis, *Capability Brown in Northumberland* (Newcastle upon Tyne: Northumberland and Newcastle Society, reprinted from *Garden History*, 1983)

M. Wills, "One of Its Kind: The Newcastle Infirmary", in *Country Life* (10 Oct 1991)

M. Wills, "William Newton – An Elusive Practitioner", in *Archaeologia Aeliana,* 5, vol. xxxvi (2007)

R. Woodhouse, *Gateshead: A Pictorial History* (Chichester: Phillimore, 1992)

T. Wooldridge, "Gateshead Town Hall" (unpublished M.T.P. project, University of Newcastle upon Tyne, 2003)

Sir C. Wren, "Letter on Building Churches" (1711), reprinted with annotations in L.M. Soo, *Wren's "Tracts" on Architecture and Other Writings* (Cambridge: Cambridge University Press, 1998)

Interior of the Laing Art Gallery, Newcastle upon Tyne.

GLOSSARY OF ARCHITECTURAL TERMS

aedicule. An ornamental architectural frame, generally consisting of a pair of columns or pilasters flanking an opening, niche or decorative panel, with a pediment above.

aisle. A subsidiary space along the side of a building, particularly a part of a church flanking the nave, chancel or transept (on either or both sides) and usually separated from the main space by arches or columns. More informally, the term is applied to a passageway between rows of seats.

antae (singular anta). Pilasters at the ends of a colonnade, portico or other feature. Columns in between these pilasters are described as 'in antis', so a portico in antis typically has two columns flanked by pilasters.

apse. A semi-circular or polygonal projection in a building, often referring to the east end of a church.

arcade. A row of arches supported on columns or piers. See also blind arch.

arch. An upwardly curved or pointed construction – typically of brick or stone – used to span an opening and usually carrying a structure above it. The term is also applied to similar forms used decoratively (see blind arch) rather than structurally.

architrave. A beam or lintel supported across the top of columns, specifically the lowest part of the entablature in classical architecture. More loosely, the term is applied to the moulded frame of a door or window.

archivolt. A term applied to both the underside of an arch and to a moulding around an arch.

ashlar. Stonework laid in regular courses, with flat, even surfaces and right-angle joints, as opposed to rubble masonry of roughly cut stones of differing shapes and sizes.

Art Deco. A style fashionable in the visual arts in the 1920s and 1930s characterised by sleek forms, often in stylised patterns.

Art Nouveau. A style in the visual arts (including architectural decoration) flourishing from about 1890 until the First World War; it is characterised by sinuous, asymmetrical lines, often evoking plant forms.

Arts and Crafts. A movement in architecture and the applied arts in the late nineteenth and early twentieth centuries that championed craftsmanship in the face of increasing mechanisation.

atlas (plural atlantes). A sculpted figure of a muscular male used as a supporting column-like feature in architecture.

atrium. A term originally applied to an open central courtyard in an ancient Roman house and later to a forecourt (usually colonnaded) in front of a basilican church. In modern architecture it refers to a central, covered, skylighted space rising through several storeys of a large building, providing light and ventilation.

attic. In architectural terminology, a storey above the main entablature of a building, or more loosely a top storey that is squatter than the storeys below it. In everyday usage, the word refers to a room or space within the sloping roof of a house.

balustrade. A low decorative railing supported on bulbous posts (balusters).

baptistery. The part of a church used for baptism.

barbican. A tower or other structure forming an outer defence guarding the approach to a castle or fortified town.

Baroque. An exuberant style of architecture characteristic of seventeenth-century Europe and sometimes revived in later times (neo-Baroque).

barrel vault. A vault with an uninterrupted semicircular section, like that of a tunnel (tunnel vault is an alternative name).

battlement (usually used in the plural: battlements). In medieval military architecture, a defensive parapet at the top of a wall, with an indented outline formed by raised sections (merlons) alternating with spaces (embrasures or crenels); in later buildings, battlements were often used decoratively.

bay. A vertical division or compartment of a building or part of a building, usually one marked by some regularly repeated constructional feature or unit of design such as a row of arches, columns or windows. The term is not to be confused with a bay (projecting) window.

belfry. A tower or steeple (or a part of a tower or steeple) in which bells are hung.

blind arch. An arched shape applied to a wall or other surface as a decorative motif rather than used structurally. A row of such arches is called a blind arcade.

boss. An ornamental projection, roughly circular in shape and often richly carved, at a point where two or more ribs intersect in a vault. The term is also applied to similar knob-like projections used elsewhere, for example at the end of mouldings.

bow window. A curved bay window.

broach spire. See spire.

broken pediment. See pediment.

Brutalism. A massive, chunky architectural style characteristic of the 1950s and 1960s, usually featuring rough concrete ('béton brut' in French).

buttress. A solid, upright mass of stone or brick built against a wall to strengthen and support it.

capital. The topmost part of a column, pilaster or pier, often carved in various distinctive forms.

casement. A window hinged at the side, so that it opens outwards and/or inwards, like a door.

chamfer. A narrow flat surface created by cutting obliquely across the corner of a block or post of wood or stone, a treatment often found in the surrounds of doorways and windows, for example. More loosely, the term has been applied to decorative grooves or furrows.

chancel. The eastern part of a church containing the altar (or the main altar). In a cross-shaped church the term generally refers to the whole of the building east of the central crossing.

chancel arch. The main arch at the east end of the nave of a church, forming an entrance to the chancel.

chantry. A small chapel, in or attached to a church, endowed for saying masses for the soul of the founder of the chapel or for the souls of other specified people.

chevron. A V-shaped pattern. In architecture the term usually refers to series of Vs arranged in zigzag decoration, a form of ornament used particularly in Romanesque buildings.

choir. The part of a church occupied by the singers who perform or lead the musical parts of services. It is usually in the eastern limb of a cross-shaped church and in architectural contexts 'choir' is often loosely used as a synonym for 'chancel'; however, in large churches the choir sometimes includes part of the nave.

CLASP. An acronym for 'Consortium of Local Authorities Special Programme', a body formed in 1957 to develop a scheme of prefabricated school building in England during a time of post-war reconstruction. It devised a system of construction – using light steel frames – that became known as the CLASP method.

classical. A very broad term referring to ancient Greek and Roman architecture and all later architecture that is derived from it. The term embraces more specific styles and movements such as Renaissance and Greek Revival.

clerestory. The upper part of the main longitudinal walls of a church, above the aisle roofs, pierced with a row of windows. By extension, the term is also applied to elevated rows of windows in other types of building.

cloister. A covered passageway around an open, usually square space (known as the cloister garth); cloisters are found particularly in monasteries, connecting the church with various other buildings.

colonnade. A row of regularly spaced columns supporting arches or an entablature.

columbarium. A building or room lined with recesses for storing urns of cremation ashes. The word comes from the Latin *columba* (dove or pigeon) and originally referred to a pigeon house or dovecot; it acquired its additional meaning because the rows of recesses for urns resemble those of compartments for birds.

column. An upright, fairly slender supporting member, usually consisting of a base, a cylindrical shaft (often tapering slightly towards the top) and a spreading capital at the top.

Composite. See order.

console. In classical architecture, a boldly curved ornamental bracket.

corbel. A bracket projecting from the face of a wall to support a parapet, beam or other horizontal member.

Corinthian. See order.

cornice. A projecting band of ornament at or near the top of a wall or other feature; more specifically, in classical architecture the term refers to the topmost part of the entablature.

crenellation. The indented top of battlements.

crocket. In Gothic architecture, a leaf-like projection used at regular intervals to embellish sloping surfaces, such as those of gables and pinnacles.

crossing. In a cross-shaped church, the central area formed by the intersection of the nave, chancel and transepts.

crucks. Pairs of heavy timbers (individually called blades), rising usually from ground level and inclining inwards, which together with other pairs form the framework of certain vernacular buildings.

cupola. A dome, particularly a small one.

curtain wall. In a castle or other fortification, a perimeter wall, usually linking various towers. In modern architecture, a non-load-bearing cladding wall fixed to a framed structure.

dado. The lower part of the wall of a room (from about waist-height downwards) when it is decorated differently from the upper part.

Decorated. See Gothic.

dentil. A small projecting block used as a repeated, closely spaced decorative motif in classical cornices, producing an effect somewhat like a row of gappy teeth.

depressed arch. An arch with a flattened top, like the handle of a basket.

diaper. A grid-like pattern of repeated motifs used as architectural enrichment (carved, moulded, painted or – in brickwork – achieved through the use of contrasting colours).

dogtooth. A small pyramidal ornament, used as architectural enrichment, particularly in closely spaced sequence along Gothic mouldings.

dome. A vaulted roof with a circular, polygonal, or elliptical base and generally a more or less hemispherical shape.

Doric. See order.

dormer. A window projecting vertically from the slope of a roof and with a roof of its own.

drawbridge. A short wooden bridge, hinged at one end, that can be raised or lowered (usually by means of chains) to prevent or allow access to a place. Such bridges were often used over a moat or ditch at the entrance to a castle.

dressings. Stonework or brickwork used to give a decorative accent around a window, wall angle or other feature.

drip moulding. See hood moulding.

drum. A wall (usually circular or polygonal in plan) forming the supporting structure for a dome.

Dutch gable (or Flemish gable). A gable having curved sides and a crowning pediment. It was characteristic of seventeenth-century Dutch architecture and was later imitated in England.

Early English. See Gothic.

eaves. The lower edge of a roof, overhanging the wall of a building.

elevation. A facade or side of a building.

Elizabethan. Architecture of the reign of Elizabeth I (1558-1603) or in a style imitating it.

encaustic tiles. Decorative glazed earthenware tiles, used in architecture mainly for flooring.

engaged column. A column attached to or embedded into a wall so that only about half its diameter projects from the flat surface; half-column is a virtually synonymous term.

engineering brick. A type of very dense brick, impervious to water and with high compressive strength, used mostly for industrial buildings and in civil engineering.

English bond. Brickwork in which courses are alternatively of headers and stretchers (that is, bricks laid respectively with the short side and the long side showing on the surface of the wall). In Flemish bond each course consists of alternate headers and stretchers. These are two of the most common types of bond, but there are many others, including English garden wall bond, which has one course of headers for every three (or four or five) courses of stretchers.

entablature. In classical architecture, the broad horizontal band of ornament that surmounts a row of columns; it consists of three parts: (from bottom to top) architrave, frieze and cornice.

facade. The front face of a building, particularly when it is treated as a prominent architectural feature.

faience. A type of glazed pottery, sometimes used in architectural decoration.

fanlight. A window above a door, specifically a semi-circular one with glazing bars arranged like the ribs of a fan.

fascia. A flat, horizontal band. The term is used in various ways in architectural contexts, for example to describe part of an entablature and a wooden board used to cover the ends of rafters at the edge of a roof.

fenestration. A collective term for the design and general arrangement of windows in a building.

finial. An ornament at the top or upper corner of a building or decorative object.

flambeau. A flaming torch, especially – in architectural contexts – a large ceremonial one.

flèche (also called spirelet). A slender spire that rises from the roof ridge of a building (typically over the crossing of a church) rather than from a tower. The word is French for 'arrow'.

Flemish bond. See English bond.

Flemish gable. See Dutch gable.

fluting. A series of shallow vertical grooves (flutes) decorating a column or pilaster.

flying buttress. A type of external reinforcement used to help support the vaults of a large Gothic church. It consists of a stone arch (or section of an arch) connecting the upper part of a wall to a buttress that stands apart from this wall rather than up against it like a conventional buttress. By extension, the term has been applied to similar arch-like supports used in other contexts.

frieze. A horizontal band of ornament, more specifically the middle section of an entablature.

frontispiece. An elaborate entrance bay or pavilion on the main facade of a building.

gable. The triangular section of wall at the end of a pitched roof.

gallery. A term describing a balcony or elevated passage and used with various more specific meanings in architecture, for example to denote an upper storey over an aisle in a large medieval church, looking onto the nave.

gargoyle. A projecting waterspout on the roofline of a building (particularly a church) carved in the shape of a grotesque human or a monstrous beast, the rainwater emerging through the mouth. The term is also loosely applied to similar grotesque sculptures used purely decoratively.

Georgian. A period label embracing the reigns of George I, II, III and IV, who ruled Britain successively from 1714 to 1830. Various styles were current in this period, but the term Georgian has come to be associated chiefly with elegant, restrained classicism.

giant order. See order.

gin gang. A farm building, usually circular or octagonal, containing equipment for threshing grain, powered by a horse walking round and round. Such buildings were very common on farms in the late eighteenth and early nineteenth centuries.

Gothic. The style of architecture prevalent in Europe in the late Middle Ages, characterised most obviously by the use of pointed arches. English Gothic architecture is conventionally divided into three phases (all of which were imitated during the Gothic Revival): Early English (c.1175-c.1275), Decorated (c.1250-c.1350) and Perpendicular (c.1330-c.1530).

Gothick. A term sometimes used to describe the style of buildings erected in the early days of the Gothic Revival; these buildings tend to be rather playful in spirit, with medieval forms used superficially, whereas nineteenth-century Gothic Revival architects were generally much more serious in approach.

Gothic Revival. A fashion for the imitation of the Gothic style of the Middle Ages; it began in the eighteenth century and became a major strand in nineteenth-century architecture.

Greek fret. A band of geometric ornament arranged in a rectilinear pattern, used in classical architecture.

Greek Revival. A fashion for the scholarly imitation of the style of ancient Greek buildings, at its peak in the 1820s and 1830s; it is an aspect of neo-classicism.

ha-ha. A trench or sunken fence forming a boundary to a garden or estate; it created a barrier for livestock without interrupting the view from the house.

half-column. A column integrated with a wall, so that only half of it projects above the surface.

hammer-beam roof. A type of wooden roof characterized by a series of short horizontal beams (hammer-beams) that project from opposite interior walls and support an arching superstructure.

header. A brick laid so that the short end is exposed on the surface of the wall. A brick laid with the long end exposed (as is more normal) is called a stretcher. See also English bond.

High Tech. A movement in modern architecture, beginning in the 1970s, in which various constructional and operational aspects of a building are emphasised for expressive effect; elements that are normally hidden, such as heating pipes, for example, might be deliberately exposed to view and sometimes brightly coloured.

hipped roof. A roof in which the end faces, as well as the sides, slope inwards.

hood moulding. A projecting moulding over a window, door or arch, serving to divert the flow of rainwater; also called a drip moulding or dripstone.

International Style (or International Modern Style). The dominant style among progressive architects in Europe (and later the USA) in the 1920s and 1930s, marked by clarity and rationality of design, with clean lines prevailing and traditional detailing renounced.

Ionic. See order.

Jacobean. Architecture of the reign of James I (1603-25) or in a style imitating it.

jamb. The vertical side of a doorway, window or other opening.

Jesse window. A church window depicting the ancestry of Jesus traced back to Jesse (the father of King David). Usually a tree is shown rising from Jesse at the bottom of the window, with various descendants on the branches and Jesus at the top.

joists. Beams of timber (or more recently steel or reinforced concrete) laid horizontally between the walls of a building to support a floor.

keep. The largest and strongest tower of a castle, usually centrally situated and more or less independent of the other defences, so it could be used as a final refuge in times of siege.

keystone. The central wedge-shaped block at the top of a stone arch, often given prominence through decorative carving.

king post. In a wooden roof, a vertical post standing centrally on a transverse beam (tie beam) and connecting it to the apex. Pairs of similar vertical posts placed symmetrically on a tie beam are called queen posts.

Lady Chapel. A chapel dedicated to the Virgin Mary (Our Lady), usually found at the eastern end of a church, as an extension to the chancel or an aisle.

lancet. A tall narrow window with a plain pointed head without any tracery, one of the most characteristic features of the Early English style.

lintel. A horizontal beam of stone or other material lying across the top of an opening, such as a doorway, and usually supporting the wall above.

Lombard frieze. A frieze resting on a row of corbels.

mansard roof. A roof with two slopes, the lower slope steeper and usually longer than the upper.

mausoleum. A large and imposing tomb or such a building housing a tomb or tombs.

mezzanine. An intermediate storey, particularly a low storey between two main ones.

Modernism (also Modern Movement). A movement or ideology in the arts involving a repudiation of traditional styles and attitudes in favour of consciously progressive values; in architecture, Modernism is characterised most obviously by the elimination of decoration and the rational use of new materials and technologies.

motte-and-bailey castle. A type of fortification much used by the Normans after their conquest of England in 1066, featuring a stockade or tower on a natural or artificial mound (motte) linked by an inclined bridge to a courtyard (bailey) defended by a palisade and ditch; such castles were essentially temporary wooden structures that could be built quickly and cheaply, but many of the mottes remain, some of them supporting later stone structures.

moulding. A band of ornament used in various architectural contexts, for example to accentuate or enrich the outline of a door or window. There are many distinctive types of moulding characteristic of different styles and periods.

mullion. A vertical strip (of stone or other material) dividing a window into upright panels called lights (a window with four mullions has five lights). A similar horizontal strip, at right angles to a mullion, is called a transom.

nave. A term applied to the western limb (usually the largest section) of a cross-shaped church, as opposed to the eastern limb (the chancel), and more specifically to the central division of the western limb, as opposed to the aisles that generally flank it. In non-cross-shaped churches, the term can be loosely applied to the main body of the building.

needle spire. See spire.

neo-Baroque. See Baroque.

neo-classicism. A broad movement in European art and architecture in the late eighteenth and early nineteenth centuries characterised by a revival of the forms and spirit of the art of ancient Greece and Rome.

neo-Gothic. An alternative term for Gothic Revival.

neo-Norman (or Norman Revival). A style imitating the rugged architecture of the Norman period in England (eleventh-twelfth centuries). It had a vogue in the eighteenth and nineteenth centuries, particularly in country houses.

neo-Renaissance. A style consciously evoking the look of Renaissance buildings, specifically the opulence of Italian palaces of the sixteenth century; it was popular in England in the mid-nineteenth century for certain types of buildings, including banks, country houses and gentlemen's clubs.

niche. A shallow, vertical recess in a wall, typically used to display a statue or other ornamental object.

Norman. See Romanesque.

obelisk. A tall, four-sided stone shaft that tapers to a pointed pyramidal top. Obelisks were much used in ancient Egypt, and from the Renaissance onwards have been adapted in various ornamental contexts.

oculus. A term for a round or eyelike opening (*oculus* is Latin for 'eye'), in particular a circular window or the aperture at the apex of a dome.

ogee. A double curve in which one part is convex and the other concave, like a letter 'S'. An ogee arch has two such curves, meeting in a point at the apex. An ogee dome has a slightly bulbous outline.

order. In classical architecture, a unit of design described mainly in terms of the type of column used. The ancient Greeks used three types of column – Doric, Ionic and Corinthian, getting progressively slimmer and more ornate. The Romans added two more – Tuscan (a starker form of Doric) and Composite (the most elaborate of all, combining features of Ionic and Corinthian). In a giant order, the column (or pilaster) runs through two or more storeys.

oriel. A bay window projecting from an upper storey and overhanging the wall below.

palace front. A type of architectural composition in which a row of houses or other buildings is treated as a unified design, with projecting centre and 'wings', giving something of the effect of a single palatial facade.

palazzo. The Italian word for 'palace', but typically used in a different sense from the normal English meaning of an official residence of a monarch or other high-ranking person; rather, it is applied to large town houses and to certain public buildings.

Palladian. A term applied to architecture influenced by the style and ideas of the Italian architect Andrea Palladio (1508-80), whose dignified and graceful buildings were regarded by many admirers as setting unsurpassable models for civilised living.

pantile. A roofing tile with an S-shaped cross section, laid so the convex side of one tile overlaps the concave sides of adjoining ones.

parapet. A low protective wall or balustrade built where there is a sudden drop, for example along the edge of a roof.

parclose screen. A screen partitioning off a chapel from the main body of a church or enclosing an object such as a tomb.

pavilion. A term used with various meanings in architecture, notably to describe an ornamental building for occasional use, such as a summerhouse, and to describe a projecting subdivision of a large building.

pediment. A triangular area over a portico or a similar feature (sometimes curved – or segmental – rather than straight-sided) above a window or door. A broken (or open) pediment is one in which there is a gap at the apex or (less usually) along the base.

pendentives. The curved triangular areas between the arches that support a dome and the rim of the dome.

Perpendicular. See Gothic.

piano nobile. A term (Italian for 'noble floor') that refers to the principal storey of a palace or large house (usually the first floor) containing the main reception rooms.

Picturesque. A term used in the eighteenth and nineteenth centuries to describe buildings or landscapes that were considered attractive in a rough, irregular or quaint way. The word was originally applied to natural forms that were thought to be suitable for including in a painting, and Picturesque views became a mainstay of many landscape artists.

pier. A substantial vertical supporting member of stone or brick, thicker than a column.

pilaster. In classical architecture, a kind of flattened column, attached to a wall and projecting slightly from it.

pilotis. In modern architecture, a term for stilt-like columns, usually of concrete or steel, that support a building above an open ground floor.

pinnacle. A pointed decorative termination common in Gothic architecture, for example at the top of buttresses.

pitched roof. The commonest type of roof, with two sloping sides meeting at the top. More loosely the term is applied to any sloping roof.

portal. A doorway or other entrance, especially one that is large and imposing.

portcullis. A heavy grating (of wood and/or iron) used as part of the defences of a fortified medieval gateway. It was mounted in vertical grooves at the sides of the passage through the gateway and was raised or lowered by a winch to allow or block access.

porte-cochère. A portico that is big enough for a wheeled vehicle to be driven through it.

portico. A large, formal entrance porch, usually with a roof supported by columns.

Portland stone. A white limestone quarried on the Isle of Portland (a peninsula rather than a true island) in Dorset. From the seventeenth century it has been much used for public buildings in Britain because of its attractive texture and colour. It varies somewhat in appearance and characteristics. Whitbed (from 'white bed') is regarded as the best-quality Portland stone on account of its fine grain and durability. Roach or roach-bed stone has a distinctive pitted appearance caused by the presence of large amounts of shell fragments.

Post-Modernism. In architectural contexts, a term describing a reaction against the sleekness of much modern architecture in favour of a more flamboyant and eclectic approach to design, often involving references to historical or vernacular buildings.

pulpit. A raised platform in a church or chapel, usually constructed of stone or timber, used in religious services, notably for preaching.

quatrefoil. An ornamental motif consisting of a stylised flower head with four rounded leaves radiating from a common centre (rather like a four-leaved clover). It was much used in Gothic decoration, particularly in tracery. A trefoil is a similar motif with three leaves.

Queen Anne style. A style of architecture that flourished in England from about 1660 to about 1720, mainly in domestic buildings, which are characteristically unpretentious designs in red brick. The style was revived – often in more elaborate contexts – in the late nineteenth century.

queen post. See king post.

quoins. The stones or bricks forming an external corner of a building, particularly when they are emphasised in some way to give visual reinforcement to the corner (for example by using stone quoins on a brick building)

rafter. One of a series of parallel, sloping beams (usually of wood) that support a pitched roof.

random rubble. See rubble.

Regency. A term applied to British art of the period when the future George IV was Prince Regent (1811-20) or more loosely of the period from about 1800 to 1830. Styles popular at this time included neo-classicism and the Gothic Revival (earlier phases).

Renaissance. See neo-Renaissance.

rendering. A coating of plaster or similar material applied to an external wall.

reredos. An altarpiece occupying the wall behind an altar; it may take any of various forms, such as a screen or mural.

rib. A projecting band (typically of stone or brick) on the surface of a vault, dividing the vault into various compartments (or 'cells'). Ribs may be either structural (particularly in the form of intersecting arches crossing from side to side) or ornamental.

ribbon window. A series of windows grouped side by side to form a virtually continuous band of glass across a facade.

rock-faced masonry. Stonework laid in regular courses but given a rough-textured surface, as though it had come straight from the quarry – a type of rustication.

Rococo. A light and graceful style of art and architecture characteristic of the early eighteenth century.

Romanesque. The style of architecture prevalent in Europe in the eleventh and twelfth centuries, characterised by massiveness of construction and the use of round-headed arches. Romanesque architecture in Britain is often described as Norman, as it was introduced largely as a consequence of the Norman Conquest of England in 1066.

rood beam. An elevated beam spanning the entrance to the chancel of a church and supporting a crucifix. A screen separating chancel from nave is called a rood screen.

rose window. A large circular window filled with petal-like tracery. A similar type is the wheel window, in which the tracery has more definite spokes radiating from a centre. Both types are used most commonly in the end walls of large churches, particularly the nave and transepts.

rotunda. A round building or room, particularly one surmounted by a dome.

rubble masonry. Stonework made up of rough stones of varied shapes and sizes (as opposed to smooth, regular ashlar). In coursed rubble the stones are arranged in fairly regular horizontal bands, but in random rubble the stones are laid in unsystematic fashion. In snecked rubble the stones are squared but of various sizes and not laid in regular courses.

rustication. Stonework that is given a rough-textured effect or cut with deep grooves between the blocks to produce a feeling of rugged strength.

sacristy. A room in or attached to a church in which are kept the vessels and vestments used by priests during services.

sandstone. A type of stone, much used in building, consisting essentially of grains of rock or mineral compressed together. Sandstone is typically reddish brown, but it is found in many other colours.

sash window. A window featuring two frames (sashes), one or both of which can be slid over the other in vertical grooves to open the window.

segmental arch. An arch with a fairly shallow curve – one that is part of a segment of a circle.

sett. A small rectangular block of stone used for paving.

snecked rubble. See rubble.

soffit. The visible underside of any architectural member, such as an arch, balcony or cornice.

spandrel. A triangular area with one or more curved sides, e.g. the surface between two adjacent arches.

spire. A tall structure, tapering upwards to a point, surmounting a tower or roof, particularly of a church. A needle spire is a comparatively slender one, with a base that starts well inside the parapet of the tower. A broach spire is one that starts square in plan but becomes octagonal, the transition being effected by sloping triangular faces (broaches) at the base.

spirelet (see flèche).

strapwork. A type of ornament using forms resembling elaborately pierced and interlaced strips of leather or parchment.

stretcher. See header.

string-course. A moulding or band of masonry running horizontally along a wall. A string-sill is such a moulding that runs at the level of the window sills.

stripped classicism. A style of architecture, popular particularly in the inter-war period for large public buildings, in which the forms and proportions characteristic of classical architecture are used but most of the decorative detail is omitted.

stucco. A type of light plaster used for sculpture and architectural decoration.

studwork. Light partitioning walling.

swag. An ornamental carving in the shape of a graceful sweep of drapery suspended between two points.

tie beam. In a wooden roof, a transverse beam connecting the two side walls and preventing them being pushed outwards.

tracery. An openwork pattern of stone (or less commonly brick) embellishing a window (usually only the upper part of the window), one of the most characteristic features of Gothic architecture. In the earliest type, called 'plate tracery', solid areas of flat stone are pierced with simple decorative shapes. This developed into the more sophisticated 'bar tracery', in which thin strips of stone are arranged into a meshwork or other pattern. Various names, such as 'reticulated' (netlike), are applied to particular types of pattern. By extension, the term 'tracery' is applied also to similar ornament used in other contexts, for example to decorate a wall ('blind tracery') or furniture.

transepts. In a cross-shaped church, the pair of wings projecting at right angles to the main body of the building that form the 'arms' of the cross.

transitional style. A term used to characterise medieval (or neo-medieval) buildings that have features typical of both the Romanesque style and the Gothic style into which it evolved.

transom. See mullion.

trefoil. See quatrefoil.

triglyph. In classical architecture, an ornamental tablet with vertical grooves used at regular intervals in the frieze of the Doric order.

truss. In a wooden roof, a number of timbers grouped together to form a rigid frame spanning the building from side to side.

Tudor. Architecture of the Tudor period or in a style imitating it; in this context the word usually refers to the early Tudor period (1485-1558), when the final phase of the Gothic style (Perpendicular) was still prevalent in England (hence the term 'Tudor-Gothic'), as later Tudor architecture, which was more classical in style, is generally distinguished as Elizabethan.

Tuscan. See order.

tympanum A term applied to the area enclosed by the cornice of a triangular pediment and also to the space (usually semi-circular) between the lintel of a door and an arch over it.

Tyneside flats. A type of two-storey terraced housing in which flats are arranged in pairs (one above the other) and each flat has its own front (and back) door, the upstairs flats having a staircase directly behind this door. Such flats were built in large numbers in Newcastle, Gateshead and other parts of Tyneside from about 1870 to 1914, but they are found virtually nowhere else in the country.

Venetian window. A large window divided into three vertical parts, the central one being fairly broad, with a round top that rises higher than the two flanking parts, which are narrower and have flat tops. This type is also called a Palladian window (as it was much used by Andrea Palladio – see Palladian) or Serliana (as it was first illustrated in a treatise by the sixteenth-century Italian architect Sebastiano Serlio.

vernacular. A term describing buildings that are constructed using local materials and traditional methods, rather than being designed by architects.

volute. A decorative spiral form, used in various ways in architecture.

waterleaf capital. A type of capital characteristic of late twelfth-century English architecture, featuring broad, curving, stylised leaf forms.

wheel window. See rose window.

Wyatt window. A distinctive type of window named after the English architect James Wyatt (1746-1813), who invented it in about 1780; it consists of three sections (the middle one wider than the other two) beneath a segmental arch.

INDEX

Page numbers in **bold** type indicate the principal references to the buildings specified, accompanying the colour photographs; page numbers in *italic* indicate other illustrations (mainly in black-and-white) in the chapter introductions. In determining alphabetical order, names beginning with Mc and St are treated as if they were spelled Mac and Saint respectively.

A

B

C

D

E

F

G

H

CUMBERLAND HOUSE